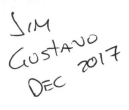

"*Transformative Imagery* is essential reading for serious students of the imaginal world… Read this book. You will benefit. So will all those whose lives you touch."

—*Michael Lerner, Ph.D., President and Co-founder, Commonweal*

"At the heart of dance is the transformation of images into a physical language… Transformative Imagery is the truth of how we create our life's dance in a similar way, expanding our own individual human potential from the inside out. It embodies the past while pointing to the future, making the present vibrant and full of possibilities."

—*Ann Marie DeAngelo, Artistic Director, DeAngelo Productions*

"Leslie Davenport and her expert co-contributors have created a comprehensive resource which opens multiple pathways to the seen and unseen realms of our existence."

—*William B. Stewart, M.D., Medical Director and Co-founder, Sutter Health*

"A must-read for change agents in integrative health and healing, these chapters will convince the reader that the most important tool in medicine remains one's own imaginative power."

—*Professor Meg Jordan, Ph.D., RN, CWP, California Institute of Integral Studies*

"Leslie Davenport's *Transformative Imagery* provides a unique and valuable historical and contemporary review of imagery's clinical and popular applications, and will be extremely valuable to academics, clinicians and the general public."

—*John A. Patterson, M.D., MSPH, FAAFP, Center for Mind Body Medicine*

"Thanks so much for your beautiful offering to bring healing into the world."

—*Bob Stahl, Ph.D., Author of* A Mindfulness-Based Stress Reduction Workbook

"Leslie Davenport has assembled a broad array of excellent contributors to...reinforce the vitally important message that our inner worlds contain a richness of personal resources...to improve well-being on many levels. What a gift from Davenport to give readers the chance to be able learn and use these experiential approaches in so many beneficial ways!"

—*Michael D. Yapko, Ph.D., Clinical Psychologist and*
Author of Mindfulness

"This book is a must-read for anyone who wants to know about or use imagery for implementing change. *Transformative Imagery* will contribute to your soul's growth and evolution at many levels. I highly recommend it!"

—*Kay Porter, Ph.D., CC-AAS, Author of* The Mental Athlete

"Imagery may be our most profound resource for change and transformation… [This book] covers it all; from science to spiritual traditions. [It] is a must-read for us in clinical practice as well as all who want to learn more about the power of imagery."

—*Susan Ezra, RN, HN-BC and Terry Reed, M.S., RN, HN-BC,*
Co-founders of Beyond Ordinary Nursing

"This book brings together the writings of highly skilled clinicians, coaches, and researchers with extensive experience utilizing imagery. *Transformative Imagery* is a real gift for anyone interested in learning more about the healing power of imagery and how to apply it both personally and professionally."

—*Robin Casarjian, Author and Executive Director,*
The Lionheart Foundation

"*Transformative Imagery* is a rich collection of authors and topics addressing imagery… The perspectives [Davenport] taps range from Sufism to Taoism, to Jungian depth psychology, to psychoneuroimmunology and clinical guided imagery… I recommend this book for practitioners and academics alike."

—*Donald Moss, Ph.D., Dean, College of Integrative Medicine*
and Health Sciences, Saybrook University

"Within this compilation is a compelling depth and breadth of essays, including evidence-based research, on the curative and creative powers of an age-old spiritual practice—using our inner minds to support physical, mental, and emotional health… *Transformative Imagery* sets a high standard and establishes guided imagery in its rightful place."

—*Julie Clayton, Author and Editor of Award-winning books;*
www.sacredwriting.com

"I highly recommend this engaging, informative, and surprisingly touching look at Transformative Imagery in all its manifestations, and encourage you to step on the path with this book as your guide."

—*Molly Roberts, M.D., Past President,*
American Holistic Medical Association

"This book is inspiring, revealing, and life-changing. I highly recommend that you read it, study it, and discover innovative ways to change your life and your practice."

—*Anna Halprin, Ph.D., Co-founder of Tamalpa Institute and Author of*
Returning to Health with Dance, Movement and Imagery

"This well-written book offers a comprehensive look at the power of imagery to transform our lives… I highly recommend this book to anyone wanting to explore this powerful path toward opening our heart and connecting with life in a deeper and richer way."

—*John Amodeo, Ph.D., Author of* Dancing with Fire

of related interest

Emerging Practice in Focusing-Oriented Psychotherapy
Innovative Theory and Applications
Edited by Greg Madison
Foreword by Mary Hendricks-Gendlin
ISBN 978 1 84905 371 6
eISBN 978 0 85700 722 3

Guided Imagery & Music (GIM) and Music Imagery
Methods for Individual and Group Therapy
Edited by Denise Grocke and Torben Moe
Foreword by Cathy McKinney
ISBN 978 1 84905 483 6
eISBN 978 0 85700 877 0

Shamanism and Spirituality in Therapeutic Practice
An Introduction
Christa Mackinnon
ISBN 978 1 84819 081 8
eISBN 978 0 85701 068 1

Mindfulness and the Arts Therapies
Theory and Practice
Edited by Laury Rappaport
ISBN 978 1 84905 909 1
eISBN 978 0 85700 688 2

Archetypal Imagery and the Spiritual Self
Techniques for Coaches and Therapists
Annabelle Nelson
ISBN 978 1 84819 220 1
eISBN 978 0 85701 169 5

The Compassionate Practitioner
How to create a successful and rewarding practice
Jane Wood
ISBN 978 1 84819 222 5
eISBN 978 0 85701 170 1

Cultivating the Imagination
for Healing, Change, and Growth

TRANSFORMATIVE
Imagery

EDITED BY LESLIE DAVENPORT
FOREWORD BY MARTIN L. ROSSMAN

Jessica Kingsley *Publishers*
London and Philadelphia

Chapter 2: Style by Rachel Naomi Remen also appeared in *Kitchen Table Wisdom: Stories That Heal* by Rachel Naomi Remen, M.D., copyright © 1996 by Rachel Naomi Remen, M.D. Used by permission of Riverhead, an imprint of Penguin Publishing Group, a division of Penguin Random House LLC.

Epigraph for the chapter "Mindful Advocacy: Imagery for Engaged Wisdom" used by permission of the Golden Sufi Center for Susan Murphy's quote, from the essay "The Koan of the Earth" in *Spiritual Ecology: The Cry of the Earth*, ed. by Llewellyn Vaughan-Lee (The Golden Sufi Center Publishing 2013), p.125.

For all material in Chapter 9, "C.G. Jung: Champion of the Imagination," that is cited from *The Collected Works of C. G. Jung*, permission is provided jointly from Routledge (UK) and Princeton University Press (USA).

First published in 2016
by Jessica Kingsley Publishers
73 Collier Street
London N1 9BE, UK
and
400 Market Street, Suite 400
Philadelphia, PA 19106, USA

www.jkp.com

Copyright © Jessica Kingsley Publishers 2016
Foreword copyright © Martin L. Rossman 2016

Cover art: Laury Rappaport, *Unfolding Beauty* (Watercolor, 2014)

Library of Congress Cataloging in Publication Data
Names: Davenport, Leslie, editor. Title: Transformative imagery : cultivating the imagination for healing, change and growth / edited by Leslie Davenport ; foreword by Martin L. Rossman. Description: London ; Philadelphia : Jessica Kingsley Publishers, 2016. | Includes index. Identifiers: LCCN 2015035237 | ISBN 9781849057424 (alk. paper) Subjects: LCSH: Imagery (Psychology)--Therapeutic use. | Change (Psychology) Classification: LCC RC489.F35 T73 2016 | DDC 153.3/2--dc23 LC record available at http://lccn.loc.gov/2015035237

British Library Cataloguing in Publication Data
A CIP catalogue record for this book is available from the British Library

ISBN 978 1 84905 742 4
eISBN 978 1 78450 175 4

Printed and bound in the United States

*This book is dedicated to the enduring
refuge and freedom of Home.*

*May the comfort of Home, built through loving
connections to yourself, life, and your given and chosen
family, sustain you, wherever you plant your feet.*

Contents

Part 2   Imagery for Health and Healing

Part 3   Imagery and Depth Psychology

PRÁCTICAS CON LA IMAGINASIÓN

GUIDED IMAGERY PRACTICES

All of the imagery practices that you'll find throughout this book are listed below and can be found in boxes in the chapters, for easy reference.

FOREWORD

Martin L. Rossman

There's nothing really important about mental imagery, except that, as Leslie Davenport points out, it is the Rosetta Stone of the body, mind, and spirit. Imagery, a sensory way of thinking, is the natural language of the subconscious mind, a way of symbolizing inner or outer reality that includes thinking, feeling, and sensing in a tapestry that can inform and move us on all these levels of being.

Imagery emerges spontaneously into consciousness in dreams, daydreams, visions, art, poetry, music, and in imagery-laden words and phrases. We can also learn to use it on purpose to open up a hidden treasure house of creativity, insight, and perspectives that can help us solve problems, avoid dangers, resolve conflicts and stimulate healing on emotional, psychological, spiritual and even physical levels.

As a medical doctor, my interest is in finding ways to help people prevent, recover from, or heal from illnesses and injuries. Imagery has proven useful for these purposes in a very wide range of medical conditions, which Dr. Dean Shrock and I review in one chapter of this inspiring book. Imagery can be used to help you relax, relieve pain, get better sleep, prepare for and recover from surgical and medical procedures and more. It is a great blessing that we can use our minds these ways, but these are not the imagination's most powerful ability.

Beyond symptom management, imagery is a mental processing language that can reveal or evoke a deeper shift in your approach to life. This is something that we see when we quietly and respectfully invite images into our awareness, and listen to what they have to communicate to us.

An image of a beautiful arched bridge in a Japanese garden appeared in a session with a highly anxious cancer patient. A kind, gentle Christ-like figure stood in the center of the bridge, hand extended toward her. At first she was a little scared, but gradually started feeling that everything was alright and that he was a source of safety. Hesitantly, she slowly stepped on the bridge, and as she drew nearer to him, she felt almost overwhelmingly filled with love and acceptance. Her pace quickened as she walked toward him and took his hand. She folded into his embrace and wept.

When she returned to her usual consciousness she told me that she had never before felt loved like that, and now felt completely reassured, whether the imagery meant she was going to recover or cross over from the this life to whatever follows. She said, "I really know that I am in God's hands, so what more could I ask?"

A spiritually-oriented person, whatever their faith, would probably take this experience at face value, while the skeptic might say that she simply took a dose of the opium of the masses. Her imagery-creating mind spoke to her in a language she understood and brought her not only comfort, but a lasting transformation from a lifetime of anxiety to a state of peacefulness that stayed with her for the duration of her survival.

Wish fulfillment? Spiritual enlightenment? From my doctor's perspective it doesn't matter. I am just grateful that I was able to introduce her to something in herself that was able to bring her deep peace and comfort.

Whether it is God or nature that guides us from within, it is clear to me after 45 years of working with thousands of patients in this deep way that we were not dropped off here at birth without a considerable amount of inner guidance. Some is acquired as we learn from our experiences, our education, and our role models, and some comes from programs that we are born with in order to survive. We inherit not only the physical organs and capabilities developed by our ancestors, but a good deal of the learning they acquired from hard experience, and it is coded into our genes and our brains. When we feel cut off from it, we can often access it by getting quiet, asking for help, and paying attention to the imagery that comes to mind.

This remarkable source of wisdom within reveals itself to us primarily in the deeply quiet moments that have become all too rare in these busy times. While our ancestors might venture naked in the woods for a week in order to seek the guidance of a vision, we might not take even a single quiet moment for many weeks or even months. When we do, we may be too exhausted to pay attention to the quiet guidance within. The pace of modern life, and the immense information flow we are exposed to every day fills our minds so completely with information that we may not be able to adequately process it, sort it, and differentiate between what is important and what is not. The demands of daily life in developed society take up so much time and storage space in the brain that many of us don't even get adequate sleep, further eroding our contact with our wise subconscious.

No wonder so many people are harried, overburdened and stressed. What a pleasure it is to have some quiet time, whether on a walk in nature, some quiet time alone or with a loved one, or during a nap or meditation. Along with the deep rest and renewal that comes in these times, they are times when our inner perceptions can come to mind, and inform us from a deeper and larger perspective. We owe it to not only ourselves, but to each other and the world we live in to make time for this informed quietude.

Much thanks and appreciation is owed to Leslie Davenport for her latest book, which assembles state-of-the-art theories and practices from a select group of imagery pioneers and luminaries. It will introduce you to or deepen your understanding of both the practical utility and deep transformative potential of imagery, and is a very welcome and important addition to the field.

Mill Valley, California
May 23 2015

Acknowledgements

I am deeply grateful for all the people and organizations that have offered their trust in me, and created openings for the transformative practice of guided imagery to be known and experienced. All have nourished the evolution that has led to the creation of this book.

Thanks first to Jessica Kingsley Publishers for their vision and commitment to publishing books that make a contribution to the world. I am honored that this book is included in their distinguished collection.

This book is as valuable as it is thanks to the breadth and depth of guided imagery expressed through the stellar collection of writings from authors who have generously contributed their expertise to this book. It is rare to have the brilliance and compassion of so many leaders from diverse fields converge and openly share their professional experience of guided imagery. I extend my heartfelt gratitude to all the acclaimed authors.

Much appreciation goes to those who offered their assistance and support to the writing process, including editorial clarity offered by Madeleine Fahrenwald and Simone Gorrindo. Laury Rappaport and Nancy Dunn brought fresh and valuable perspectives as the book was taking shape.

Several organizations took the risk of hosting my imagery work before it was fully recognized by the mainstream, and as a result, were influential in shifting the perception of guided imagery from being optional to becoming essential. The heart of my professional work was nourished within the Institute for Health & Healing (initially the Humanities Program), where I first launched a guided imagery program in a hospital setting in 1989. My 25 years with the Institute supported a truly integrative approach, as I learned from my colleagues and offered my imagery practices as part of a collaborative team.

Thanks in addition to Alta Bates Medical Center and Brookside Hospital where I launched imagery training programs. I am also so appreciative for being invited to teach guided imagery as faculty at Five Branches University, and currently, as founder of Certifications in Guided Imagery at John F. Kennedy University and the California Institute of Integral Studies.

But all of these settings have most importantly been a doorway to the hearts and minds of the clients and students that I have directly worked with. In the service of teaching, I have learned so much; in the practice of psychotherapy, I have grown so much.

A nod and a wink go to the late John O'Donohue, whose writings are a source of inspiration to me. I hope you feel his lyrical spirit in my poem, "Blessing for the Journey."

And my heart goes to my close family and friends, who so often see in me what I cannot always recognize in myself. The chance to reflect with each other what is real and what is possible, is priceless.

Introduction

There is a vibrant and elegant wholeness found deep within every human heart. The practice of transformative imagery plumbs the depths of our opening heart and brings us home to our essential, wholesome nature. Guided imagery invites symbols and impressions to rise like bubbles from beneath our conscious awareness and allows hidden aspects of ourselves to come into view. These images reveal our gifts, talents, and strengths as well as the dysfunctional beliefs, patterns, and dis-ease that have formed around our unresolved pain. As we explore these deep layers through guided imagery, we develop a clearer and more compassionate understanding of ourselves and others. We cultivate tools that will transform our lives so that we are healthier and more fulfilled.

Interpreting a language of symbols and images can at first seem confounding—but that impression is formed in the logical, most familiar part of our mind that is attempting to grasp that which can only be perceived through a different but equally natural way of knowing. Understanding the language of the imagination takes practice, but as we will discover in the essays in this book, it is a worthwhile endeavor that is vitally important to living in harmony with other humans and the natural world.

Imagery is like a Rosetta Stone that decodes and translates the deep undercurrents at the very center of our lives. When we open to the clarity that emerges through imagery practice, there is a growing experience of well-being, a visceral wisdom that surpasses ordinary logic. We experience wholeness regardless of the circumstances of our lives, and often discover fresh ways to improve the conditions we're in. We naturally begin to live in a qualitatively different way; more present and responsive to the moment-by-moment miracle of daily life.

The practice of imagery is a form of deep listening, like placing an ear on our innermost being. It is a remarkably faithful process of connecting us to the sacred pulse that animates life and which takes on a vast expression of forms. Images that appear through the practice are generous in their diversity, sometimes dawning quietly—a hint of remembering something profound but previously dormant, an undeniable flash of insight. At other times, the imagery arises dramatically as shimmering, bold symbols or iconic figures that transmit tangible and potent qualities of being. Simply being in the presence of these inner-wisdom symbols is transformative.

Imaginative experiences that bring wisdom and healing are available to everyone regardless of temperament, culture, age, and life experience, and imagery is as practical as it is numinous. But imagery is most easily understood through a direct experience of the process. Come with me and witness the transformative power of imagery in Amanda's[1] first experience with the practice.

Case Study: Amanda

A nurse in her late 30s, Amanda entered the medical field with an earnest desire to be of service to others. She arrived at the office dressed casually: navy-blue hoodie and jeans, her long blonde hair pinned back in a loose bun. As she sank into a chair, her rounded shoulders and cloudy gaze exposed the depletion and overwhelm she was about to describe. Amanda reported several sources of stress, a checklist that included escalating conflict with her roommate, longstanding tension with her Mom, and pressures at work. She had heard of guided imagery through her interactions with patients and thought it might help her deal with stress.

When I ask her to say more about her stress, she reveals what finally prompted her to make an appointment: she had a panic attack while running routine errands. Amanda feels like she was assaulted internally for no known reason, and now feels pursued by a threatening emotional predator she can't identify. She describes the experience as "bringing her to her knees" emotionally, and it continues to trigger recurring feelings of dread and a persistent inner voice that whispers, "What if this happens again? I couldn't bear it. I'd lose my job. It would destroy my life."

As she describes this pivotal experience, she becomes aware of feelings of weight and constriction in her chest. She agrees to explore these sensations with imagery. After several minutes of breath-work and progressive relaxation, I guide her to an imaginal environment of her choosing, a safe and supportive setting from which to explore the feelings. After a moment, she described in detail being at a rustic family cabin by a lake on a summer afternoon, a serene setting where she relaxes into safety and comfort.

"Now bring your awareness more deeply into your body, feeling again the weight and constriction in your chest from the inside out. Trace the edges of the strongest feelings with your awareness." I allow time for her to explore her experience and encourage her to continue. "Keeping your eyes closed, describe aloud what you are aware of."

Eyes still closed, she traces a circle in the air with her finger and says, "It feels like there is a metal pancake pressing down on my sternum; black, cast-iron, round. It's rough. It feels raw where the edges rub my body."

I encourage her to say more, and she continues, "The circle is cold, maybe a quarter of an inch thick, but heavier than it looks, as if something is pushing it down on me. It's hard to describe, but the feeling echoes in my back too, as if its shadow can be felt there. It's a little hard to breathe."

In spite of the discomfort, she is willing to continue, so I ask if the image has something it wants her to know. Her forehead creases in confusion as she receives an impression that the metal disk is there to help her. "It's protecting me, like a shield."

She finds this message surprising given how oppressive and painful the sensations are, so I encourage her to ask the image for greater clarification. There is a long pause, then she begins to reply in whispers, as though she is tiptoeing inside, treading very carefully. She tells me that she is peeling back the disk to peer underneath.

It is moments like this in the imagery process that so often begin the healing transformation. She is willing to look, at least glance, in the direction of a frightening and longstanding pain. Since she's spent a lifetime "looking the other way," this is a significant step for her.

A sweet tenderness and vulnerability spread across her face. She suddenly looks younger and more engaged than when she first entered the office. She continues softly, "It feels like cool air entering an old stuffy room inside my chest. It's dusty and hazy, as if it has been boarded up for a long time."

I follow her lead, sensing from her expression and tone of voice that she is now being guided from a place deep within herself that is wanting to be known. "Take your time to explore. What else do you notice in this dusty room?"

After a considerable pause, she begins to tear up. "I'm slumped in the corner with my head resting on my knees. I must be around seven or eight years old." We pause together, honoring this most unexpected and tender discovery.

"Would you like to greet this younger you?" I ask, allowing full permission for her to sense whatever feels appropriate.

"I already have. I'm sitting beside her now."

It is clear that she is following her inner impulses, trusting the process. The tears increase and quietly stream down her face.

"What needs to happen now?" I inquire, letting her take the lead.

She speaks with great confidence and strength, as if clearly recognizing the inherent truth of her imagery experience. She fills me in on what she is experiencing.

"When I first approached the little me, there was caution in her eyes, but I just stayed with her. I feel a lot of love for her. Then it switched, and her young eyes looked old and wise and very loving. I can barely tolerate the intensity of the love, but I'm still staying with her. It's hard to tell now which direction the love is flowing—we're just both in one big love burst."

After taking time to savor this experience, we gradually begin to close the imagery session. Amanda expresses gratitude and agrees to meet with her younger self again. I guide her to gently return to her safe imaginal place by the lake before bringing her focus back to the office.

When she opens her eyes, her expression is soft. "These feel like very old tears," she says simply. I ask her to notice her chest, and she describes feeling sore, "but a 'good sore,' like after an exercise class. I feel…empty—in a peaceful way, like I let go of something. Much better."

Over the next several imagery sessions, Amanda began to recognize how she left her own needs and desires out of her daily choices, and instead focused excessively on taking care of others, both personally and professionally. It became clear that Amanda's self-defeating pattern originated in her childhood as she struggled to grow up in a chaotic family with an alcoholic father and passive mother. She created a child's emotional survival strategy, believing that if she could take care of her parent's feelings and have no needs of her own, it would stabilize the family. This belief continued to function below her adult awareness. After several sessions, her panic attack was no longer mysterious to her: she now understood it as an indicator that there was a strong need for her to add self-care to her lifestyle and adjust her priorities.

Images have a way of bubbling up to just the right level within our psyche to address the aspects of ourselves that most need attention—much the same way our immune system sends just the right kind and combination of cells to a physical injury that requires healing. Amanda had an emotional wound that gave rise to specific healing images on the psychological level. But the wise and loving glance shared between the younger and the present-day parts of herself also unveiled Amanda's spiritual depths and opened up a path of growth that will take her beyond psychological roles, patterns, and ego traits.

How to Use this Book

Transformative Imagery marks the first time that both the breadth and depth of imagery practice has been assembled into a single book. It offers an understanding of how imagery resides at the heart of many different human endeavors, and will reveal both the science and the grace at work in it. Like holding a jewel up to the light, the chapters that follow will examine the many facets of imagery that illuminate the human path of transformation.

This book is divided into five sections that address different aspects and applications of guided imagery, including:

1. An overview of imagery and its historical foundations

2. The uses of imagery in medicine and healing

3. Imagery's contribution to the practice of depth psychology

4. Imagery used as a contemplative practice within spiritual and religious traditions

5. Examples of the application of imagery in other areas, including social transformation.

Each chapter weaves relevant details into the complex fabric of guided imagery to create a deep and cohesive understanding of imagery's transformative properties. You are invited to either turn directly to the author or topic that draws you, or take time with each section for the full voyage into depth imagery.

Part 1: Foundations of Guided Imagery: History and Overview

Imagery experiences have been an essential aspect of human life since the beginning of our time on earth.

- Michael F. Cantwell, M.D. launches our journey by defining imagery and naming key contributors to the field of imagery practice as we know it today.

- In Chapter 2 by Rachel Naomi Remen, M.D., we explore one of the central debates among imagery professionals: the benefits and drawbacks of scripted versus unscripted imagery.

- Emmet Miller, M.D. traces the threads of imagery from a mother's ancient lullaby to today's information highway.

- Gerald Epstein, M.D. describes the metaphysical history of imagery in the West.

Part 2: Imagery for Health and Healing

Images directly impact our physiology, and our bodies speak to us through imagery—as we will see in this brilliant collection of essays. Even those physiological systems that were previously believed to be inaccessible to conscious control, including the immune and autonomic nervous systems, respond to imagery. With practice our attunement increases, and by employing mind-body imagery we can reduce pain, boost immune function, lower blood pressure (Naparstek 1995) and optimize our health in a variety of ways.

In this section of *Transformative Imagery*, leaders who have spearheaded imagery work in the medical field offer us a deeper look.

- Bruce Roberts, M.D. offers a unique medical overview, weaving together the impact of the Cartesian split catalyzed by René Descartes, the astrological eras, the chakra system, energy work, and Western allopathic medicine.

- Martin L. Rossman, M.D. and Dean Shrock, Ph.D. have assembled an impressive list of medical research that verifies the efficacy of imagery for a range of health issues.

- Pain relief is one of the most sought-after medical applications of imagery, and it is frequently a part of the protocols at pain clinics. David Pincus, Ph.D. and Anees A. Sheikh, Ph.D. show us why imagery is so effective with pain management.

- And many patients first hear of imagery through self-help literature they encounter during cancer treatment. Grounded in the most recent cellular science, Sondra Barrett, Ph.D. gives us an updated approach to imagery for cancer treatment.

PART 3: IMAGERY AND DEPTH PSYCHOLOGY

When we practice imagery, the light of awareness shines on our mental and emotional realms, and old, faulty beliefs about ourselves and life itself begin to become clearer to us. Imagery gives us the opportunity to shed fear-based behaviors that no longer serve us, and to choose a life integrated with our deepest values.

- No work on the psychological benefits of imagery would be complete without referencing the work of Carl Gustav Jung. Brian Dietrich ushers us into the domain of Jung's archetypes and "active imagination."

- The most recent findings in neuroscience reveal the remarkable plasticity of the brain—and the potential for building new neural pathways that make possible a healthier mind and lifestyle. Imagery plays a key role in brain retraining, as Linda Graham, MFT shows us in her hands-on descriptions.

- While much that is written about guided imagery focuses on the mind, Glenn Hartelius, Ph.D. and Judith Goleman, MFT reveal the importance of embodied imagery, a somatic approach that locates the imaginal mind within our biological expression.

- And if you work with children, Charlotte Reznick, Ph.D. reminds us that imagination is the natural state of mind for kids. She offers keys for adapting guided imagery practices to the appropriate developmental phase for teens and younger children.

PART 4: SPIRITUAL IMAGERY IN WISDOM TRADITIONS

Because imagery is a natural contemplative process grounded in awareness, it has a rich and heritage that continues to thrive in many spiritual and religious traditions. This section of the book takes us into the realm of some of the lesser-known but very powerful imagery practices found in some of the ancient contemplative traditions.

- Michael Samuels, M.D. is a physician who is also a bear dancer with the Chumash Native American people. He gives us a rare insider look at his blend of medical practice and shamanic imagery and ritual.

- We are honored to include, for the first time in print, the internal alchemy of Daoist imagery from Master Zhongxian Wu.

- While Sufism is known for rich images, Llewellyn Vaughn-Lee, Ph.D. offers an esoteric yet accessible understanding of imagery as a bridge between Mystery and Visibility found within this exquisitely beautiful tradition.

- Alan Morinis, D.Phil., a leading interpreter of the 1000-year-old Mussar teachings found in the Jewish heritage, invites us to partake of these imagery practices to deepen our spiritual understanding.

- And Reverend Carolyn J. Stahl Bohler gives us a fresh perspective on Christian imagery, including the rare and surprising references to Goddess-worshipping cultures in the Bible.

PART 5: BOUNDLESS APPLICATIONS OF IMAGERY

Imagery surges throughout all human endeavors in much the same way it billows up within individuals. Like an underground water table that spills over as wellsprings across the terrain, imagery has surfaced within all times and cultures and flowed into every human discipline. If only this book could be a 12-volume series! The scope of *Transformative Imagery* cannot come close to encompassing the full range of imagery applications, but in this section you will get a sense how it can be an essential tool for healing and transformation across a vast range of endeavors.

- With environmental, economic, agricultural, and other crises escalating on our planet, my chapter on employing imagery for advocacy work and stewardship is an area that will become even more crucial in the coming years.

- The next trio of chapters explores the natural interface of imagery with creative endeavors: expressive arts, music, and writing with authors Laury Rappaport, Ph.D., Denise Grocke, Ph.D., and Ruth L. Schwartz, Ph.D.

- Olympic athletes have often used imagery to pursue excellence in their sport, and Phillip Post, Ph.D. shows us how they do it in his chapter on sports performance.

- As we learn more about PTSD and trauma from so many of our combat veterans, Judith A. Lyons, Ph.D. shapes the healing power of imagery to meet the specific needs of this population.

- Aftab Omer, Ph.D. stretches our awareness to witness the subtle but powerful impact of images in our education systems and society at large.

The Invitation

This book is an invitation to plumb the depths of the heart with imagery practices. Cultivating a spirit of curiosity and becoming comfortable with the unfolding process of imagery can become a gateway to life's greatest and most surprising gifts. When we pay attention using our imagination, we bear witness to life's essential nature as it translates into who we are and who we are becoming. We can learn to see with the eyes of our heart and witness the mystery of life that is always hiding in plain sight.

The practices found throughout this book and listed in the appendix are not only valuable for self-exploration, they also provide a clinical perspective that makes them appropriate for working with patients and clients. But even the best gardening tools are of little use when they are only stored in the shed. Writer Lawrence Durrell reminds us that, "Somewhere in the heart of experience there is an order and a coherence which might surprise us, if we were attentive enough, loving enough, or patient enough" (Durrell 1991, p.211). I invite you to engage deeply with the wonder of your days, and to use a diverse array of imagery tools to launch a transformative journey for yourself and those you work with.

Blessing for the Journey

When days rush past in a blur,
    may you pause to receive the simple gifts that life generously offers.
When you are overwhelmed,
    may you rest in the gentleness of your own heart.
When you are feeling hopeless,
    may your imagination hold a torch to unseen possibilities.
When your mind is drowning in details,
    may spaciousness arise, connecting you to the sacred mystery that
    you are.
When you are exhausted,
    may you be refreshed by vibrant life forces always present within
    and around you.
When you are overcome with grief,
    may precious tears bathe your heart with salty buoyancy and
    comfort.
When the world brushes you with harshness,
    may you realize that we're all works in progress, and life itself is a
    learning curve.
When nothing seems to be going your way,
    may you make room for the unknown, finding patience with your
    unfolding life.
When you are disheartened by the suffering in the world,
    may you find the courage and strength to stand for what you know
    is good.
When you believe that you are not good enough,
    may you discover your inherent value and place in the family of all
    things.
May you receive earth's bounty to nourish your body,
    kindness to nourish your heart
        wisdom to nourish your mind,
            and wonder to nourish your soul.

Leslie Davenport

ENDNOTE

1. The details of Amanda's story, including her name, have been altered and composites employed to protect client confidentiality.

References

Durrell, L. (2011) *Justine (Alexandria)* (Illustrated by R. Ryan). New York: Penguin.

Naparstek, B. (1995) *Staying Well with Guided Imagery.* New York: Warner Books.

Part 1
Foundations of Guided Imagery
History and Overview

Chapter 1

The Rise and Fall and Rise of Guided Imagery

Michael F. Cantwell

> *The conscious mind may be compared to a fountain playing in the sun and falling back into the great subterranean pool of subconscious from which it rises.*
>> Sigmund Freud (as cited in Thiessen 2012, p.258)

Guided imagery involves the use of images of all kinds that arise from within, including visual, tactile, aural, olfactory, gustatory, mental, spiritual, and impressionistic images. The imagery itself is both diagnostic— an indicator of physical, emotional, or spiritual aspects of our being that are seeking exploration and healing—and a living pool of therapeutic symbols that hold the key to transformation, which can be unlocked through the guided imagery process.

Imagery and guided imagery have been powerful and resilient holistic tools for millennia throughout humankind's history, and they will likely remain so for centuries into the future. From antiquity through the Middle Ages, our predominantly holistic worldview, low literacy rates, and strong reliance on oral traditions all served to place imagery at the center of healing, spirituality, and the predominant social mindset. The rise of rationalism, however, with its emphasis on the body and (conscious) mind, led to a dramatic decline in the importance of imagery. In the 20th century, the "rediscovery" of the subconscious mind and the resurgence of a more integrated, holistic view have ushered in an exciting new era in the use of imagery in healing and spiritual practices and across a range of disciplines. Up, down, up again—imagery has flowed along with the currents of our changing view of our human nature throughout the ages. It's been quite a ride, and it's a story worth telling.

Historical Holism

For most of our history, nearly every culture has embraced a holistic view, regarding life as an interaction between body, mind, and spirit. Ancient cultures like those of Egypt, Greece, China, India, and Tibet as well as most indigenous cultures had rich traditions and rituals that recognized and fostered this interconnection to promote healing and transformation. These cultures often used physical interventions including fasting, pilgrimages, detoxification and purification rituals, and sweat lodges to advance spiritual growth. Conversely, they also relied on spiritual interventions such as prayer, meditation, retreats, healing rituals, and shamanistic journeys to promote healing and sometimes produce "miraculous" cures. Even through the Middle Ages this holistic interplay between body, mind, and spirit was taken for granted. Illness, plagues, and famine were usually seen as acts of God, the "Evil Eye" could cause disease, the sick were prayed for, and the roles of healer and priest were often commingled.

In these holistic times, imagery naturally flourished and was an integral part of most oral traditions and religions. When literacy rates are very low and books are scarce, images, symbols, and the oral tradition become the most efficient and powerful ways to pass down complex metaphysical and existential concepts. Ancient medicine is rich in imagery, and almost every culture used religious imagery as part of its healing rites. Idols, relics, talismans, and charms were everywhere and were believed to hold power to heal body, mind, and soul. Spiritual visions, voices, prophecies, and revelations were highly valued for what they told us about both the route to salvation and how to heal disease. Medieval medicine and alchemy, the primary science of medieval West, viewed healing in terms of interactions between the divine realm and allegorical images, including the seasons, the Four Humors (black bile, yellow bile, phlegm, and blood), and their corresponding Four Elements (Earth, Fire, Water, and Air, respectively). Traditional Chinese Medicine similarly approached healing by way of images: for example, the balance between Yin and Yang, the flow of Qi through channels or meridians in the body, and the interplay of the Five Elements (Wood, Fire, Earth, Metal, and Water). In these cultures, images of body, mind, and spirit and of the interaction between spirituality and health were an integral part of daily life. In both Eastern and Western cultures, imagery and guided imagery were not practices that occurred in isolation or during scheduled sessions: rather, they were part of the dominant worldview essential for understanding and interacting with this world and the next.

The Rise of Rationalism

This holistic worldview was uprooted by the rise of rationalism, science, and empiricism during the Renaissance and the late 16th and 17th centuries in the West. In 1637, René Descartes declared, "Cognito ergo sum" ("I think therefore I am"), and in a stroke reduced our existential view to the physical world and the world of the conscious mind (Descartes 1637). This concept, fostered by prominent scientists and philosophers of the time such as Hobbes, Locke, Berkeley, and Hume, ushered in the Age of Empiricism, which was focused on discovering the laws governing the workings of the physical world. Spirituality and the subconscious mind no longer held the keys to understanding the world, and with their decline came the decline of imagery. After all, if the world could be understood through observation, deduction, and the rules of science, of what use were images, symbols, and traditional narratives?

There have been many triumphs during this Age of Empiricism. We made dramatic discoveries that include electricity and how to extract power from steam, fossil fuels, the sun, wind, and atoms. We came to a much deeper understanding of biological processes, genetics, chemistry, physics, and mathematics. In medicine, illness and disease came to be seen more physically and objectively, as the interplay of pathogens, genetics, organ systems, and immunity. Treatment increasingly focused on addressing these objective, physical aspects of health, with the main interventions relying on medications, surgery, vaccines, public health interventions, nutrition, and occasionally herbs and nutritional supplements. In many, many ways these interventions have been revolutionary and life-saving. Having been trained as an infectious disease specialist, for example, I can definitely say that I would rather treat bubonic plague and most infections with antibiotics rather than the anti-infectives of medieval medicine: garlic, herbal posies, blood-letting, rotten treacle, crushed emeralds, or bathing in urine or feces. In other ways, however, the rationalistic paradigm in medicine that has predominated through the early 21st century is simply too reductionistic.

Resurgence of Holism

We are not—as the Age of Empiricism would have us believe—simply bodies and conscious minds. Over time, we've realized (or rather remembered) that we are a complex mix of body, mind, and spirit. As any holistic practitioner will tell you, it is difficult if not impossible to facilitate transformation without taking into account the importance of the subconscious mind and of understanding and living out the spiritual meaning and purpose of our lives.

As the miracles of modern medicine took hold in the last century, we began to live longer—dramatically longer. The average life expectancy at birth in the U.S. climbed from 47 years in 1900 to 76 years in 2005 (Arias, Ronston, and Tejada-Vera 2010). Much of this improvement came from public health interventions such as improved sanitation and water treatment, better access to medical care, standardization of medical training, and vaccinations. Modern medical discoveries like antimicrobials and improved medications, anesthesia, and surgical techniques have further prolonged our lives.

But what did we do with all those extra years? These medical miracles and our greater longevity exposed a new epidemic, an epidemic of chronic stress. At present, the top causes of death in the U.S.—cardiovascular disease, cancer, diabetes, Alzheimer's Disease, accidents, suicide, murder, anxiety, depression, asthma, and autoimmune diseases—are all stress-related. Chronic stress undermines our health primarily by producing chronic inflammation and immune dysfunction. Trying to treat this new epidemic of chronic stress and the diseases associated with it using the tools of the age of empiricism—treating the body and the conscious mind—has been stunningly ineffective. One-fifth to one-quarter of all Americans take medication for attention deficit disorder, anxiety, depression, and other mood disorders (Medco 2011). Millions are in psychotherapy aimed at changing their conscious and subconscious thoughts, behaviors, and addictions. Yet despite these interventions, deaths from stress-related diseases continue to rise, and approximately two-thirds of all Americans still feel stressed (American Psychological Association 2014) and two-thirds are unhappy (Harris Interactive Polls 2013). Clearly we need a new approach and new tools to address this new epidemic, and imagery is one of the shiniest and most effective tools in our toolbox.

One of the main contributors to our epidemic of stress has been the rationalistic focus on treating our bodies and conscious minds while ignoring our subconscious minds and spirits. The recent resurgence of holistic care seeks to rediscover and reintegrate the subconscious mind and the spiritual aspects of health. This new holism strives to restore the truth that body, mind, and spirit are all interconnected and all influence our well-being. It challenges modern approaches to expand their scope, to diagnose and treat the roots of conditions wherever they may lie, not only in the body or conscious mind but in the subconscious mind or spirit as well.

Although it can be difficult to pinpoint the exact time when an old paradigm starts to fade and a new one begins, I propose that the beginning of the end of the age of rationalism and the resurgence of holism occurred in the early 20th century when Sigmund Freud "rediscovered" the subconscious mind. Although many of Freud's theories have not withstood the test of time, this rediscovery, combined with overwhelming subsequent research, firmly established not only the existence of subconscious thoughts, conditioned patterns, and behaviors but also their dramatic impact on our physical and emotional health. The scientific literature has consistently shown that most of the chronic stress resulting from prior traumas and psychological behaviors and patterns such as anger, fear, worry, guilt, regret, and the need for control arises from our subconscious minds.

Not surprisingly, one of the fastest-growing trends in psychological intervention over the last century has been the development of methods to diagnose and treat the subconscious roots of disease. Pioneered by Freud, classical psychoanalysis attempted to unearth these subconscious roots through probing discussion, free association, and dream and fantasy analysis. Other avenues for exploring the subconscious include somatic therapies like Erhard Seminars Training (EST), Rolfing, Emotionally Focused Therapy (EFT), Rosen Method bodywork, de-griefing techniques, Somatic Experiencing (based on the work of Peter A. Levine, Ph.D.), and the modality most germane to our current discourse, imagery. Freud, his daughter Anna, and Carl Jung laid the groundwork that established the vital role of imagery as the dominant language of the subconscious mind. Many, many psychotherapeutic techniques incorporating imagery emerged during the 20th century. Although it is beyond the scope of this chapter to list and describe all of these techniques, some of the most influential, in addition to those of Sigmund Freud and Carl Jung, have included the following along with highlights of their approaches:

- Pierre Janet—reverie states and substitution of images for "hysterical patients" (1890s)

- Anna Freud—free and guided imagination with children (1920s)

- Pierce Clark—images and "Fantasy Method" for facilitating countertransference in narcissistic patients and increasing access to childhood memories (1920s)

- Roberto Assagioli—"Psychosynthesis," a method that used imagery for healing childhood traumas and reintegrating the body, mind, and spirit (1920s)

- Carl Happich—imaginal settings, for example, meadows, mountains, seaside, and chapels, for diagnosing and treating negative psychological patterns and images (1920s)

- Robert Desoille—the "Waking Dream" state and a symbolic ascent and descent from imaginal settings to communicate with archetypal images and foster spiritual communication (1940s)

- Jacob Moreno—"Psychodrama" method, in which participants ("Auxiliary Egos") re-enact seminal events from the client's past (1940s)

- Hans Carl Leuner—"Guided Affective Imagery," a method involving standardized imaginal settings and catathymic imagery to increase awareness of emotions and repressed feelings (1950s–60s).

In the latter half of the twentieth century, the continued exploration and expansion of guided imagery in psychotherapy built upon the work of these pioneers (Schoettle 1980). But the really new—or rather, really old—frontier for imagery during this period was its expansion beyond treating the mind to treating the body as well. In the late 1960s, radiation oncologist O. Carl Simonton and his wife, psychologist Stephanie Simonton, presented cases of increased survival in cancer patients who had used guided imagery to improve their immune function. Working with the Simontons, psychologists Jeanne Achterberg and Frank Lawlis further advanced this field through more coordinated clinical trials and research into the efficacy of different types of guided imagery for cancer treatment. The work of these and other early pioneers stimulated great interest and extensive subsequent research in this new field of psychoneuroimmunology. These advances firmly established the strong linkage between body and mind, and specifically the linkage between guided imagery and immune function (Gruzelier 2002). Clinician-researchers such as Irving Oyle D.O., who adapted the use of the "Inner Advisor" to clinical practice, and Martin Rossman, M.D. and David Bresler, Ph.D., who pioneered the use of "Interactive Guided Imagerysm" and founded the Academy for Guided Imagery to standardize training in the field, expanded the clinical tools and methodologies available for applying guided imagery to an ever-widening spectrum of diseases. In current practice, the clinical scope of guided imagery extends far beyond the early work with cancer patients to encompass almost every stress- or immune-mediated disease. As Dr. Rossman so aptly puts it in his book, *Guided Imagery for Self-Healing*, "The evidence is now so strong that if imagery were a drug, doctors would have to prescribe it for anyone needing immune-system stimulation, or they would run the risk of malpractice" (Rossman 2000, p.227).

And so the current renaissance of holism and imagery continues. It all began with the "rediscovery" of the subconscious mind by Freud and the subsequent recognition of imagery in psychotherapy as one of the main therapeutic ways to communicate with and treat the subconscious mind. The realization continued into the medical world. First seen in cancer patients, it is now proven in a variety of stress and inflammation-mediated diseases that imagery is a powerful tool for healing both chronic stress and the immune system.

The next step in this holistic resurgence, our current frontier, is the reintegration of the spiritual aspects of health back into modern medicine and other therapeutic disciplines: the movement from body-mind medicine back to holistic body, mind, and spirit medicine. In this new approach, where spirituality and the purpose and meaning of one's life impact health at every level, imagery once again plays a central role. As one of the most important ways to talk about, diagnose, and treat spiritual issues and spiritual development, imagery will naturally take its place in the toolbox of this new, truly holistic spiritual medicine. The thoughts and insights of many of the pioneers of this rebirth of spiritually-based care, those at the forefront who are using imagery as a tool for reintegrating the body, mind, and spirit, can be found in this very book. This unique collection of insights and wisdom regarding imagery's role in the past, present, and future of healing makes this book an essential reference for anyone seeking to complete the circle and return to a fully integrated view of healing and transformation.

References

American Psychological Association (2014) *Stress in America: Are Teens Adopting Adults' Stress Habits?* Available at www.apa.org/news/press/releases/stress/2013/stress-report.pdf, accessed on June 8 2015.

Arias E., Ronston, B.L., and Tejada-Vera, B. (2010) "United States Life Tables, 2005." *National Vital Statistics Reports 58*, 10, 1–132.

Descartes, R. (1637) *Discourse on the Method (Part IV).* Available at www.gutenberg.org/files/59/59-h/59-h.htm, accessed on June 25 2015.

Gruzelier, J.H. (2002) "A Review of the Impact of Hypnosis, Relaxation, Guided Imagery and Individual Differences on Aspects of Immunity and Health." *Stress 5*, 2, 147–163.

Harris Interactive Polls (2013) "Are You Happy? It May Depend on Age, Race/Ethnicity, and Other Factors." *The Harris Poll 30*, May 30. Available at www.harrisinteractive.com/NewsRoom/HarrisPolls/tabid/447/ctl/ReadCustom%20Default/mid/1508/ArticleId/1200/Default.aspx, accessed on June 8 2015.

Medco (2011) *America's State of Mind: A Report by Medco.* Available at http://apps.who.int/medicinedocs/documents/s19032en/s19032en.pdf, accessed on June 8 2015.

Rossman, M.L. (2000) *Guided Imagery for Self-Healing: An Essential Resource for Anyone Seeking Wellness.* Novato, CA: New World Library.

Schoettle, U.C. (1980) "Guided Imagery—A Tool in Child Psychotherapy." *American Journal of Psychotherapy 34*, 2, 220–227.

Thiessen, D. (2012) *Bittersweet Destiny: The Stormy Evolution of Human Behavior.* New Brunswick, Canada: Transaction Publishers.

EDITOR'S NOTE TO CHAPTER 2: STYLE BY RACHEL NAOMI REMEN

Some of the most frequently asked questions by clients and clinicians alike are, "What is the most effective type of imagery? Should it be scripted or spontaneous? Should it be accompanied by music, or an approach that emphasizes the somatic or visualization aspects? Should the client recline or sit upright? What about particular breathing techniques to prepare for the imagery session?" The list of possible imagery technique refinements is a long one, and the queries are most often fueled by a genuine motivation to maximize the transformational benefits of the imagery experience. The answer to nearly all of these queries is "Yes!" There is considerable research[1] that endorses the efficacy of many different styles of guided imagery, as you will find described throughout this book. The style of imagery used can depend both on the needs of the client and the training and theoretical orientation of the practitioner.

The spectrum of guided imagery approaches can be broadly divided into two primary camps: scripted and non-scripted. Several of the chapters in this book, including those by Gerald Epstein and Mike Samuels, often emphasize a more directive, scripted style where the practitioner skillfully designs the imagery to produce an intended outcome. Other notable imagery leaders that promote a scripted style of imagery include Belleruth Naparstek and Jeanne Achterberg.

Examples from imagery experts who advocate the benefits of non-scripted or receptive imagery include Martin Rossman, Laury Rappaport, and as you'll read in this chapter, Rachel Naomi Remen. In receptive, non-scripted imagery, the images are generated from within the client, and the practitioner supports an exploration into the meaning of whatever symbols appear, facilitating the client's discovery of their own healing path.

Both the scripted and non-scripted guided imagery approaches have inherent strengths. The theory that favors a scripted imagery style maintains that a trained practitioner can effectively "install" a reparative physical and/or emotional system into the client using a very detailed and carefully shaped imagery script. A healthy body or mind may have been derailed through trauma, family or cultural conditioning, or a genetic malfunction, and the scripted imagery recalibrates the person's system to once again thrive.

For example, this excerpt from *Rituals of Healing: Using Imagery for Health and Wellness* is frequently used to help cancer patients integrate a new template of a healthy immune system:

> Imagine the macrophages…as the warning of an invader sounds, they swell up, becoming large and powerful, connecting with each other, moving in a flank. Watch as they approach an invader, reach out, lasso it with their armlike extensions, and inject it with potent enzymes. (Achterberg, Dossey, and Kolkmeier 1994, p.244)

This type of scripted approach has yielded excellent results in improving patients' medical and psychological conditions. Perhaps the most cited and influential research on scripted imagery consists of two hallmark studies out of the Cleveland Clinic. In the initial study, scripted imagery that provides guidance for imagining and "rehearsing" a successful surgical procedure and outcome was used in preparation for major colorectal surgery. The results showed 75 percent overall patient satisfaction, a 65 percent decrease in pain and anxiety, and 33 percent fewer side effects compared with the patients who did not have the imagery support (Tusek *et al.* 1997). A second study was conducted that provided imagery preparation to patients undergoing cardiothoracic surgery, with virtually identical results (Tusek, Cwynar, and Cosgrove 1999).

Non-scripted or receptive imagery recognizes that each person's symbolic imagery is infused with unique meanings. Because of the personalized nature of the imagery, the intuition of the client is entrusted to discover the most effective images for healing. For example, a scripted imagery session may direct the listener to imagine taking a walk on the beach for a relaxing, stress-reducing experience. But if the person listening to the script almost drowned in the ocean as a child, imagining the sounds of the waves could trigger unintended panic. Or if someone was raised in the Midwest and finds their greatest comfort by a lake, the invitation to the beachside may not be as soothing.

A non-scripted stress-reduction session would invite an image to form depicting a relaxing, safe environment that appeals to the client, and the practitioner would then facilitate a full vivification, exploration, and deepening of the client's imagery. Depending on the person, the imagined peaceful place could be a mountain-top, an ancient temple, or their own backyard. This receptive imagery approach can also be applied to a wide range of medical, psychological, and spiritual concerns.

Researching the effectiveness of non-scripted imagery is more challenging because of the increased variables that come with the open-ended nature of the process. A study out of California Pacific Medical Center in San Francisco tested a non-scripted, interactive style of imagery. The results found that the imagery sessions increased relaxation, provided patients with insight into the nature of their health problems, and assisted them in discovering and cultivating healing intentions (Scherwitz, McHenry, and Herrero 2005).

In Chapter 2: Style, Rachel Naomi Remen offers us an intimate glimpse into the tender nature of a non-scripted imagery approach. She shares the story of Jim, a cancer patient struggling to find healing imagery. Rachel gently guides his search as he sifts through imagery styles until he arrives at a surprising understanding that is both poignant and transformative.

ENDNOTES

1. Martin Rossman, M.D. and Dean Shrock, Ph.D. offer a literature review of the most current imagery research in Chapter 6. Additional resources for guided imagery research can be found in Appendix A.

References

Achterberg, J., Dossey, B., and Kolkmeier, L. (1994) *Rituals of Healing: Using Imagery for Health and Wellness*. New York, NY: Bantam Books.

Scherwitz, L.W., McHenry, P., and Herrero, R. (2005) "Interactive guided imagery[SM] therapy with medical patients: Predictors of health outcomes." *The Journal of Alternative and Complementary Medicine 11*, 1, 69–83.

Tusek, D., Church, J., Strong, S., Grass, J., and Fazio, V. (1997) "Guided imagery: A significant advance in the care of patients undergoing elective colorectal surgery." *Diseases of the Colon and Rectum 40*, 2, 172–178.

Tusek, D., Cwynar, R.E., and Cosgrove, D. (1999) "Effects of guided imagery length of stay, pain, and anxiety in cardiac surgery patients." *The Journal of Cardiovascular Management 10*, 22–28.

Chapter 2

Style

Rachel Naomi Remen

While an impulse toward wholeness is natural and exists in everyone, each of us heals in our own way. Some people heal because they have work to do. Others heal because they have been released from their work and the pressures and expectations that others place on them. Some people need music, others need silence, some need people around them, others heal alone. Many different things can activate and strengthen the life force in us. For each of us there are conditions of healing that are as unique as our fingerprints. Sometimes people ask me what I do in my sessions with patients. Often I just remind people of the possibility of healing and study their own way of healing with them.

Some time ago a young man was referred to me by an imagery training program for people with cancer. Despite a diagnosis of malignant melanoma, he had been so poorly motivated that only a month after completing the intensive training, he could not remember to do his daily imagery meditation. The referral had been clear: perhaps I could turn around his self-destructive tendencies and encourage him to fight for his life.

Jim was an air traffic controller at a major airport. He was a reserved and quiet man who might have been thought shy until you noticed the steadiness in his eyes. He told me with embarrassment that he was the only one in the imagery class who couldn't stick to the program. He didn't understand why. We talked for a while about his plans for his life and his reaction to his diagnosis. He certainly cared a great deal about getting well. He enjoyed his work, loved his family, and looked forward to raising his little boy. Not much self-destruction there. So I asked him to tell me about his imagery.

By way of an answer he unfolded a drawing of a shark. The shark's mouth was huge and open and filled with sharp, pointed teeth. For 15 minutes three times a day he was to imagine thousands of tiny sharks hunting through his body, savagely attacking and destroying any cancer cells they found. It was a fairly traditional pattern of immune system imagery, recommended by many self-help books and used by countless people. I asked him what seemed to prevent him from doing the meditation. With a sigh, he said he had found it boring.

The training had gone badly for him from the start. On the first day, the class had been asked to find an image for the immune system. In the subsequent discussion, he had discovered that he had not gotten the "right" sort of image. The whole class and the psychologist/leader had worked with him until he came up with this shark. I looked at the drawing on his lap. The contrast between it and this reserved man was striking.

Curious, I asked what his first image had been. Looking away, he mumbled, "Not vicious enough." It had been a catfish. I was intrigued. I knew nothing about catfish, had never seen one, and no one had ever talked about them in this healing role before. With growing enthusiasm he described what catfish do in an aquarium. Unlike other more aggressive and competitive fish, they are bottom feeders, sifting the sand through their gills, evaluating constantly, sorting waste from what is not waste, eating what no longer supports the life of the aquarium. They never sleep. They are able to make many rapid and accurate decisions. As an air traffic controller, he admired their ability to do this.

I asked him to describe the catfish for me in a few words. He came up with such words as "discerning," "vigilant," "impeccable," "thorough," "steadfast," and "trustworthy." "Not bad," I thought.

We talked for a while about the nature of the immune system. He had not known that the DNA of each of our billions of cells carries a highly individualized signature, a sort of personal logo. Our immune cells can recognize our own DNA logo and will consume any cell that does not carry it. Basically the immune system is the defender of our identity on the cellular level, patrolling the Self/Not Self boundary constantly, discerning what is Self from what is Other, never sleeping. Cancer cells have lost their DNA logo. The healthy immune system attacks them and destroys them. So in fact, his unconscious mind had offered him a particularly accurate image for the immune system.

As a medical student I had been involved in a study in which a micrograft, a tiny group of skin cells, was taken from one person and grafted onto the skin of a second person and I told him of these experiments. In 72 hours, the second person's immune system, searching through the billions of cells that carried his own DNA signature, would find this tiny group of cells which carried the wrong DNA signature and destroy them. I described the many ingenious things we did to hide or conceal the micrograft. Try as we might, we could not outwit the immune system. It found those cells and destroyed them every time.

He still seemed doubtful. The teacher and the class had talked of the importance of an aggressive "fighting spirit" and of the "killer motivation" of effective cancer-fighting imagery. He flushed again. "Is there something else?" I asked him. Nodding, he told me that the catfish grew big where he had been raised, and at certain times of the year they would "walk" across the roads. When he was a child this had struck him as a sort of miracle and he never tired of watching them. He had kept several as pets. "Jim," I said, "what is a pet?" He looked surprised, "Why, a pet is something that loves you, no matter what," he replied.

So I asked him to summarize his own imagery. Closing his eyes, he spoke of millions of catfish that never slept moving through his body, vigilant, untiring, dedicated, and discriminating, patiently examining every cell, passing by the ones that were healthy, eating the ones that were cancerous, motivated by a pet's unconditional love and devotion. They cared whether he lived or died. He was as special and unique to them as he was to his dog. He opened his eyes. "This may sound silly but I feel sort of grateful to them for their care," he said.

This imagery touched him deeply and it was not hard for him to remember it. Nor was it boring. He did his meditation daily for a year. Years later, after a full recovery, he continues this practice a few times a week. He says it reminds him that, on the deepest level, his body is on his side.

People can learn to study their own life force in the same way that a master gardener studies a rosebush. When its needs are met, a rosebush will make roses. Gardeners collaborate and provide conditions which favor this outcome. And as anyone who has ever pruned a rosebush knows, life flows through every rosebush in a slightly different way.

Chapter 3

The Cultural Evolution of Guided Imagery

Emmett Miller

When your thoughts, feelings, beliefs, and actions reflect your deepest truth, you have integrity, the core of healing, happiness, and peak performance. Lack of integrity produces dis-ease and failure.
                                                                    Emmett Miller

People have a way of referring to something that has been around for a very long time as being "old as the hills." Well, guided imagery *is* as old as the hills. Ever since the first mother discovered that she could quiet her child with an image-laden lullaby and guide them into a safe place where they could fall asleep, there has been guided imagery. Indeed, the love and security borne in those sounds and images enhanced the love with which the infant was held and protected.

By guided imagery, I am referring to the use of image-rich words and sounds clustered around a particular theme that evokes emotions appropriate to creating new neural pathways (synaptogenesis and neurogenesis) and brings about an intentional change in behavior of mind, body, and/or emotions. A professional uses guided imagery with their patient or client to bring about these very changes leading to healing, happiness, and success.

As humans, we currently appear to be poised atop a long chain of evolution. The first phase of our evolution took place at the genetic level and involved the development of the bodily organs and the remarkable central nervous system that organizes many of our behaviors in such an incredibly creative way that we have survived and thrived on our planet.

In the second phase, the job of evolution has been transferred from the incredibly slowly mutating genes to the rapidly metamorphosing social/cultural systems that humans have been developing. Whereas the reptilian and primitive mammalian parts of our nervous system are self-maintaining and operate from genetic blueprints, our neocortex, which contains extensive social programming, needs a different kind of ongoing guidance. This guidance is usually far more effective when it is wise and based on a clear understanding of the world, and enables people to live in ways that are healthy and happy for both the individual and all beings.

Just as we have evolved genetically and are continuing to master the art of physical survival on this planet, we have also evolved extremely intricate social, cultural, and global patterns of interaction that have produced such phenomena as Beethoven, Gandhi, the walk on the moon, and the ability to interact with the Internet through a cell phone.

Wise Guidance—the Wisdom of the Elders

Early in our development as a social species, we discovered that we needed family and tribe in order to survive. Then as now, the tribes that survived were those whose leaders were the tribe's elders, because it takes a great deal of experience with life to learn its wisdoms.

These wise and experienced leaders passed on their knowledge through teachings that always involved image-rich ritual, stories, and parables. They realized that the stories we hear, the music and songs we listen to and sing, the mental images we carry, and the ways we move our bodies have an enormous impact on our health, happiness, and productivity. They knew what kinds of experiences were needed by the members of the tribe, especially the youngest and most susceptible to learning.

So they transmitted stories, myths, songs, and dance to give form to their imagery and focus the attention of the tribe on valuable information about life passed down from prior generations. Their vehicle was metaphor (meta = between, phor = carry) that transferred meaning from the collected knowledge and wisdom of the tribe to each member of the succeeding generations.

The teachings of the elders contained different kinds of images that the members of the tribe most needed to focus on at particular times in order to survive and thrive. These shared images and values united people and made possible the miracles of cultural, scientific, and technological evolution. Throughout the most productive periods of the evolution of our cultures, caring elders taught valuable skills in this way; and although they did not realize it, they were modifying the neurochemistry of the brains of their followers.

Modern neuroscience has shown that relaxing images and feelings of belonging cause the brain to secrete higher levels of serotonin, dopamine, and oxytocin, all of which diminish anxiety, block cortisol, and enhance neuroplasticity. Similarly, images that are associated with negative emotions like fear and anger cause a different set of chemicals to be released that harm bodily tissues and functions when present for prolonged periods (Talbott 2007).

Historical Notes

ANCIENT ORIGINS OF IMAGERY

Throughout history we have records of the use of guided imagery-like techniques used for healing dating back 2500 years to ancient China and Egypt. Deep relaxation and guided imagery were employed in Egyptian "Sleep Temples." Built around the fourth century BCE, the Greek temple of Asclepius is still standing: following days of ritual fasting and bathing, patients would be approached by the temple priest who would describe how their illnesses would soon be healed and the good health they would enjoy. Then the priest would induce what was called the "Healing Sleep" (Tasman *et al.* 2015).

The church completely suppressed the explicit use of guided imagery techniques in healing and therapy during the Dark Ages (5th to 15th century): it was not seen again until after the Renaissance and the Age of Discovery. In the mid-1700s, Franz Mesmer appeared on the scene and is credited with the reintroduction of guided imagery-like techniques to our Western cultures. He discovered that people appeared to be healed of difficult illnesses when he simply painted a verbal picture; his technique resembled the following sequence:

I am going to magnetize this pile of iron scraps with "Animal Magnetism." Following this, you will have an opportunity to come, touch the pile, and then see and feel the magnetic energy flow into your body and heal you. You will feel your body contract into painless spasms, following which your aches, and pains, and diseases will melt away.

In this way he induced an altered state (called "Mesmerism") that often caused people's pain and dysfunction to ease. This basic technique of offering a powerful, imagery-rich story that could catalyze rapid healing has not changed since the days of Mesmer—although today we do not attempt to bamboozle our clients and patients with pseudo-science. Instead, we help them relax and then interest them in holding in mind images of possibilities that could come true in the future: a positive story together with a powerful emotional charge.

The scientists of that time evaluated the Mesmerism phenomenon superficially and decided there was no medical value to it. Gradually the movement faded away, and though it lost popularity there were still people studying such techniques "underground," as it were, and it was still practiced by traveling hucksters and stage performers.

Guided Imagery Is Reborn as "Hypnosis"

In the mid-1800s there was another flare of professional interest in approaches that utilized the techniques of guided imagery. Dr. James Braid watched a public demonstration of anesthesia being created through suggestion based on guided imagery, and he became convinced it could be used by the medical profession.

The procedures he developed proved to be enormously valuable in surgery. Instead of having to bite the bullet and bear the pain, a state of hypnoanesthesia could be induced in patients. The surgery and often the post-operative course would be painless, and the patient healed much more rapidly with less blood loss.

Braid called the phenomenon "hypnosis" (from Hypnos, Greek god of sleep), a name he invented after watching that first demonstration, and he is now known as the "father of modern hypnosis" (Kroger 1979). Braid soon regretted the name "hypnosis," because the state achieved is anything but sleep. In fact, it is a hyperaware state that he later tried to rename "Monoideaism" (Braid and Robertson 2009).

Soon, however, the easy-to-apply ether anesthesia was discovered: hypnoanesthesia, which required training of the physician and a fair amount of time to induce, lost out.

FREUD'S BRIEF FORAY INTO HYPNOSIS

Hypnosis once again attracted professional attention a century ago when the young Sigmund Freud studied the effects of having patients talk about their symptoms while in a hypnotic state. He later modified this technique by having his patients lie on a couch facing away from him and relating their symptoms and he would then converse with them outside their line of sight. Freud seemed unaware of the fact that this arrangement may induce trance, and he began to speak disparagingly of hypnosis. As psychoanalysis became more accepted as a method of healing, the formal practice of hypnosis slipped into the background. Once again these powerful tools disappeared from use, except for a few rare groups who continued to use and practice guided-imagery techniques (Bachner-Melman 2001).

JUNG AND ACTIVE IMAGINATION

Reason is the organ of truth, but imagination is the organ of meaning.

C.S. Lewis (1969, p.265)

It was Freud's student Carl Jung who in 1916 introduced to the West a powerful use of intentionally guided "active imagination" in his therapy to bridge the conscious and the unconscious mind. Unconscious material—like the characters and storyline of a dream—are translated using the imagination into images and entities that interact with each other in a spontaneously arising narrative. He insisted that one must have more than just an intellectual connection with one's story: "You yourself must enter into the process with your personal reactions…as if the drama being enacted before your eyes were real" (Stevens 1994, p.109). This kind of emotional participation has become a central element of modern guided imagery techniques.

Jung's work was never quite as accepted by the Western world as was Freud's, and active imagination was rarely used in mainstream psychology and psychiatry except by a small group of ardent adherents.

THE 1960S AND '70S: THE IMAGINATION AS AN ORGAN FOR UNDERSTANDING AND CREATION

Remarkably, these valuable tools remained obscure until they exploded into the mainstream in the 1960s and '70s. This era of dramatic change saw the empowerment of the individual, a serious social reaction to repression, resistance to war, and an upsurge in the globalization of information. Unlike ever before, the thinking of East and West came together, especially in the healing professions, as we began to incorporate such philosophies and practices as t'ai chi, yoga, and Buddhist meditation.

Those of us who recognized the potential of these approaches began to integrate them into what is now known as holistic medicine. We began to discover how we could wed these time-honored imagery techniques and the teachings of the East to the scientific accuracy and predictability of Western psychological and medical science. The new self-awareness movement, Eastern philosophies, the tools of hypnosis, and the new field of neuroscience all came together to give rise to an enormously powerful set of tools for tapping into personal power and transforming self, society, and the environment.

In the wake of this new energy of openness, experimentation, and compassion, we began to become aware of the significance of the beliefs and images we hold, and a new way of thinking began to dawn on a large segment of the population. Major changes in how we thought about ourselves—and in how we thought about thinking about ourselves—took place during these two decades. The segregation of blacks and whites was abolished, women were given control over their reproduction, LSD and marijuana demonstrated that by changing the condition of our thinking, we could dramatically change our experience of the world—and the human potential movement was born.

Being a part of this movement was exciting, and those of us involved in assembling the new tools into the technique we call guided imagery believed that we were witnessing a sea change in the field of psychophysical healthcare. I had entered medical school with the intention of discovering how the field could be transformed, how people could not only stop feeling pain but also learn how to be whole. It was not long before I realized the enormous impact that my patients' thoughts, emotions, stress, and lifestyle had on their health.

Relational Medicine

As a mathematician, I had been drawn to medicine because I realized that doctors were still using Newtonian-Cartesian thinking in their approach to patients. This paradigm—which in medicine sees the mind and body as separate and the body as a machine—had been replaced in many other fields of science and math by the idea of the world as consisting of interrelated complex systems. This paradigm shift had resulted in unprecedented growth in those fields. This was the soil out of which grew the notions of the holistic, integrative approach to mind, body, emotions, and behavior.

In my practice of general medicine, I had discovered that the relationship I created with my patients was often more important than a specific medication or surgery. It became clear that what we focus our awareness on and *how* we focus it and the intention we hold can make all the difference in how we experience our lives, how successful or happy we'll be, and in many cases, how physically healthy we will be.

In 1969 I started teaching at the Esalen Institute and collaborated with other pioneers who were also discovering a whole new universe of thought through the study of the philosophies and meditative practices of the East—which in many ways seemed to be the opposite of our Western philosophies. Stimulated by that experience and by my clinical experiments with altered states of consciousness such as hypnosis, meditation, and deep relaxation, I integrated all of these tools along with cognitive-behavioral techniques to help create the discipline we have come to call guided imagery. I also used meditation, autogenic training, prayer, hypnosis, and dance/movement therapy. Though these techniques had seldom if ever been used in clinical practice, they proved to be quite effective in the practice of medicine and psychology.

It was a thrilling period. Portable sound had come onto the scene in the form of audiocassettes that could carry the tones, rhythms, and other sound qualities of the imagery, and I included one with my new book. Now patients could record and listen repeatedly to the guided imagery we'd created during their office visit; because repetition of the imagery is crucial for creating new neural networks, the final link had been forged. Audiocassettes provided us with the perfect "guerrilla marketing system" for spreading these new perspectives and techniques to the culture as a whole. Healthcare professionals throughout the country began prescribing recorded sessions to their patients and attending training sessions to learn to use these techniques. Doctors Rossman and Bresler formed the Academy for Guided Imagery, and Jon Kabat Zinn demonstrated how mindfulness and relaxation techniques could manage illnesses that conventional medicine could not touch.

Guided imagery's day had come! The tools for harnessing the power of the mind through imagery combined with music designed to support relaxation could now be presented in a portable, easy-to-use form. Globalization had also created a distribution network that could reach everyone. At last we could present people with the basic tools for communicating with and bringing balance to the brain and mind and creating their own health and happiness.

The Information Highway to the Rescue

It's no secret that the most powerful tool in our world today is information. If the Native Americans had information on how to build a machine gun, the invading Europeans would never have subjugated them. If the Nazis had the information needed to break the Allies' code, D-Day would have failed. Having the right information is having power to do what you want. It was only with the advent of modern technology, especially the Internet, that information of all kinds became instantly available as it is today. Just as the vast volume of information on the Web is changing our day-to-day world, people are also awakening to the way our minds use the information we take in to create our experience. We are learning that our thoughts, beliefs, and mental images are the architects of our present and our future. Guided imagery has proven to be a powerful technique for enabling us to understand this principle and live in a wholesome way.

Change Your Belief System—Change Your Life

Our lives, our behavior, and our future are determined by how we answer three fundamental questions: who do we believe we are, what do we believe to be the nature of the world we live in, and what do we believe to be our proper relationship to that world? We make all of our decisions from these three foundations.

Therefore, at the root of most of our symptoms and distress are the decisions that we make on an ongoing basis in our minds. What we believe to be true creates our life experience, and that in turn influences our culture. A slight change in our answer to any of the three crucial questions can change our decisions and our lives very rapidly and to an enormous extent.

You are invited to explore your own core beliefs with the following imagery practice.

TRUE NATURE IMAGERY PRACTICE

Take a moment and tap into your imagination. Close your eyes and take a few clearing breaths. When you feel relaxed, ask yourself, "Who am I—at the deepest level?" Go beyond your title, your job, or your relationships, to the "spiritual" level. Invite an image to arise in response and explore whatever appears. What is the size, shape, color, and texture of the image? What qualities emanate from the symbol? What feelings arise from within you in the presence of this image? Does it have a message it wants you to receive? Reflect on this for several minutes with your eyes closed.

Continuing with your eyes still closed, ask, "What to me is the true nature of this world, personally, collectively, and materially? Allow a second image to arise in response, and explore it in a similar way, being especially attentive to the qualities it conveys. Does the true nature of the world appear as benign or dangerous? Does it appear to be random, or does it have spiritual purpose? Be receptive to whatever arises, even if it surprises you.

Take a few more minutes and inquire within, "How am I to act in this world: do I have a purpose or mission? What is my true relationship to the people, things, and ideas around me?" Once again, allow the answer to arise in the form of an expressive image, staying open to what it may want you to know.

Just as it is with primitive tribesmen, the information present in the "stories" we have heard and witnessed has been internalized and gives rise to our beliefs—and the way these beliefs guide our lives toward various degrees of health and happiness or illness and dysfunction, depending on the truth and wisdom of the information we have incorporated.

With neuroimaging devices such as functional MRIs and PET scans, we can look into the brain and observe what occurs there when a person is practicing guided imagery. By the way that different parts of the brain are reacting, we can clearly see that the parts of the brain corresponding to the unconscious mind cannot tell the difference between what is real and what is only being imagined (Ganis, Thompson, and Kosslyn 2004). For example, the limbic system responds exactly as though the event being imagined is actually occurring. So if you imagine sucking on a lemon, your brain acts like a lemon is actually present and triggers the involuntary behavior of salivation. If you imagine that you are being jabbed in the arm with a needle, the area of the brain that feels pain in the arm "lights up" just as if the needle were real. And when you imagine a relaxing day on the beach, your system relaxes and begins to recover from recent stresses.

The thoughts and images that continually pass through your mind each day produce similar, often more subtle inner changes. The sum and substance of all them determines our health, success, and happiness—yet most of us have not learned how to intentionally guide them.

Wise Guidance of Awareness

Where your awareness rests from moment-to-moment has an enormous effect on the quality of your life. The following awareness practice can be done with your eyes closed, or as an informal check-in throughout your day.

AWARENESS PRACTICE

Close your eyes and reflect on these questions: What is it that is guiding your awareness in this moment? Do you find any specific principles, emotions, or thoughts that are predominating and drawing most of your attention? Is your awareness focused or diffuse? If so, what images, sensations, or emotions accompany that? Do you find your awareness dominated by things in your external environment, such as sounds, light, and temperature, or to sensations within your body? What are the accompanying images? Is your mind drawn to events from the past, imaginings about the future, awareness of the present, or to a feeling of timelessness? Do this practice in the spirit of curiosity, with as little judgment of what you "should" be experiencing as possible.

Guided imagery offers a set of tools for making that choice—where your attention goes and what leads it—wisely and intentionally, from the highest level of your consciousness. Using your selective awareness, you can deliberately choose what images to cultivate and stories to tell yourself in order to promote a healthier perspective.

Selective awareness is the fundamental tool of consciousness that allows us to focus. Hypnosis has been defined as "suggestion during a focused state of consciousness (usually relaxation)" (Miller 1997, p.52). Selective awareness is also the function of the conscious mind that makes it possible for us to relax.

The principle is simple and powerful: what we focus our attention on and how we focus it—and the very ability we have to intentionally choose what to focus on—makes all the difference in how we experience our lives, how successful or happy we'll be, and in many cases how physically healthy we'll be.

LIFE SCRIPT IMAGERY

For a few moments, imagine that you possess the power to rewrite your life story by changing your beliefs about yourself and the world. Now close your eyes and invite an image to arise of a possible future, one that embodies your wholesome ideals. As it takes shape, even if it surprises you, "step into" your imagined future life. Notice what surrounds you, who you are with, and how it feels. Let the experience offer you insight into what your new story could be. Notice if you have a sense of the purpose and meaning. Once you have savored the experience, open your eyes and consider what beliefs and behaviors would need to change to move toward your healthy future.

Dare to answer honestly!

What is Guided Imagery?

Guided imagery is a conscious reworking of the images and their associations in our minds with the goal of rewiring the brain in a wholesome way. Guided imagery is designed to go right to the root of our symptoms and create new neural networks to replace defective ones—and transform our lives.

Although the tools of modern-day guided imagery have been developed in the laboratories of our clinical practice with patients, they have a much wider range of applications. They can assist coaches in helping athletes improve their ability to perform, and teachers to help students develop the confidence and ability to learn and think for themselves—just as they can help patients overcome a life trauma or support the body in healing from a physical illness. In fact, guided imagery is being incorporated into more fields all the time, from Olympic coaching and sales training to combat training and kindergarten classes. At least in the beginning, guided imagery is generally practiced in a relaxed state of mind in which we have a heightened awareness and responsiveness to ideas and images and an increased willingness to respond to those ideas. Once an image has arisen into awareness, it is fully explored to glean the beliefs it represents and the behaviors it drives. It becomes clear to us as this process unfolds that we are creating our future with our beliefs, especially those that are accompanied by passion, pain, or other strong emotions.

Guided Imagery as a Professional Field

Guided imagery is an extremely effective tool for health and helping professionals. Professionals also frequently provide education so that patients or clients can design effective imagery interventions for their own use in the future, targeted at specific issues they want to address.

One of the most important purposes of guided imagery education is to help the patient or client develop a different mode of conceptualizing (imagining) themselves and their world—in effect, to undergo a personal paradigm shift. Most people in our culture are trapped in a way of thinking that leads to suffering unnecessary stress, pain, dysfunction, and illness. Although in our culture the concept of "imagination" is not seen as a very important aspect of our lives (except for artists, musicians, poets, and other specialists), when we actually interact with our imagination we find an untapped potential that has atomic power. The guided imagery professional can help unleash this power by helping clients examine their "stories" and edit them by cultivating new images and ideas.

The guided imagery practitioner specializes in crafting images that produce a relaxed, receptive state, and in developing a series of inspiring, supportive images and imaginal stories that will produce positive change in the client's mind, body, emotion, and behavior. We introduce sensory-rich stimuli, words, music, and perhaps even touch (some of my most effective guided imagery has taken place while the recipient is being massaged). The positive qualities of relaxation, trust, empathy, and gratitude facilitate the release of chemicals into the brain that nurture the growth of new synapses and even new neurons (Siegel 2007). This growth virtually reprograms the subconscious mind so that new emotional and cognitive responses emerge in harmony and in ways that reflect the wisdom in the guided imagery.

Thus, instead of taking the usual allopathic route of attempting to openly confront and wrestle with a person's resistance, expectations, family messages, and fears, the patient/client is invited to "try on" new ideas while in a receptive state. If the ideas fit well, they can keep them "at the end of the story." This is a skillful way of bypassing our usual mind-chatter and inviting the person to enter a state of acceptance.

It is also valuable to ensure that these new ways of perceiving the world will be practiced regularly (for example, using recordings of guided imagery scripts). In this way we can literally help patients rewire their brains by installing powerful new neural networks that support the development of the life changes they most desire: achieving their potential, accepting themselves, creating health and wellness, and being happy.

The Challenge of Guided Imagery

Our challenge—and opportunity—in practicing guided imagery techniques is to guide the unconscious part of the mind, the paleocortex, to move beyond its dualistic way of approaching the world, as though our universe was composed of completely separate, competing objects and people. Instead, clients learn to see a world of interconnected systems, where the whole is greater than the sum of the parts. This enables them to discover emergent qualities of creativity, wisdom, and intention— qualities that appear only at the highest levels of our consciousness.

References

Bachner-Melman, R. (2001) "Freud's relevance to hypnosis: A reevaluation." *The American Journal of Clinical Hypnosis 44*, 1.

Braid, J. and Robertson, D. (eds) (2009) *The Discovery of Hypnosis: The Complete Writings of James Braid, the Father of Hypnotherapy.* Maidenhead: National Counsel for Hypnotherapy.

Ganis, G., Thompson, W.L., and Kosslyn, S.M. (2004) "Brain areas underlying visual mental imagery and visual perception: An fMRI study." *Cognitive Brain Research 20*, 2, 226–241.

Kroger, W.S. (1979) *Clinical and Experimental Hypnosis*, 2nd edition. Philadelphia, PA: J.B. Lippencott.

Lewis, C.S. (1969) *C.S. Lewis: Selected Literary Essays.* New York, NY: Cambridge University Press.

Miller, E. (1997) *Deep Healing: The Essence of Mind-Body Medicine.* Carlsbad: Hay House.

Siegel, D.J. (2007) *The Mindful Brain: Reflection and Attunement in the Cultivation of Well-Being.* New York, NY: W.W. Norton & Company.

Talbott, S. (2007) *The Cortisol Connection: Why Stress Makes You Fat and Ruins Your Health—And What You Can Do About It.* Cape Town: Hunter House.

Tasman, A., Kay, J., Lieberman, J.A., First, M.B., and Riba, M. (eds) (2015) *Psychiatry.* Hoboken, NJ: Wiley-Blackwell.

Stevens, A. (1994) *Jung: A Very Short Introduction.* Oxford: Oxford University Press.

Chapter 4

The Western Metaphysics of Mental Imagery and Its Clinical Applications

Gerald Epstein

The imaginal process of which mental imagery is a function provides us with a portal for self-discovery, healing, and creativity. By turning our senses inward, we can tap this inborn capacity to direct us in our lives. Unbound from time and space, this capacity is unconditional and serves as an access point to discovering our liberation and freedom. In this essay I outline the Western spiritual history and contemporary use of these methods as well as the 33 unique functions that I've observed in my years as a practitioner.

As clinicians it is vital that we understand the scope of the miseducation and faulty conditioning laid down in early childhood. One of their primary effects is a pattern of beliefs that assumes that our personal and communal freedom is dependent on forces *outside* ourselves, forces that presumably hold the key to our happiness, well-being, love, truth, power, and fulfillment. The key to achieving our ultimate freedom lies in expanding our worldview beyond materialism to include a spiritual matrix. In contrast to our shared everyday life of "visible reality," I refer to this matrix as the Invisible Reality. Others have called it Cosmic Consciousness, Divine Consciousness, God, the Absolute One Mind, or Macrocosmic Reality. A spiritual life is predicated on living as a self-authority free of external dependencies and contingencies that we believe we need to ensure our own independence and safety.

Spiritual life doesn't follow the rules and regulations of ordinary society whose primary values are the freedom-restrictive functions and applications of will: to take; to keep; to hold onto; to advance at the expense of others; to be great (a function of vanity). These "five dark currents of will" fulfill the desires of the individual with no consideration for the welfare and freedom of others. Spiritual life, on the other hand, reverses the way we use our will. Instead, we utilize our "light currents of will" to give, share, renounce, mentor, and be humble. Here we are self-directed from within, independent of external authorities.

I believe there are four dimensions of this spiritual freedom: faith, love, intuition, and imagination. *All of them are unconditional and do not require anything or anyone else to authenticate or validate their existence or truth.* This chapter focuses on the fourth dimension: imagination. In contrast to lexical, discursive thought and language, imagination is an unconditional language. It does not depend on a reference to anything in its environment to give it meaning or value or even to make sense out of it.

The Spiritual History of Mental Imagery in the West

The spiritual history of mental imagery and its "parent," imagination, is the history of the spiritual life as it developed in the Western tradition of monotheism through the patriarchs and matriarchs and the visionary experiences of the prophets and prophetesses, of whom Moses was the first. The Israelite prophets (circa 1200 BCE to 515 BCE) continued to receive sacred messages revealed through visionary experiences. The practices that these visionaries developed were passed down through the schools called "Sons of the Prophets" established by Samuel the Prophet/Judge (see, for example, 1 Samuel 10:2–5 and 2 Kings 2:3–7). These prophets would enter a visionary state where the spirit of God descended upon them (Price 1889). During the time of Rabbi Akiva in the first century CE this tradition was referred to as Merkabah Mysticism, or the Chariot Mysticism of Ezekiel. In the late Middle Ages, this type of practice came to be known as Theosophical Kabbalah or the Kabbalah of Light, founded by Rabbi Isaac the Blind of Provence, France, Jacob Ben Sheshet of Gerona,

Spain, and others.[1] In the 20th century, my teacher of blessed memory Mme. Colette Aboulker-Muscat was a master of this deeply healing and transcendent lineage.

Jesus and Mohammed, the founding prophets of the other strands of the Western monotheistic tradition, continued this visionary tradition as well. Christian champions of imagery include luminaries like Teresa of Avila, Ignatius of Loyola, and Hildegard of Bingen. In Islam, we have the monumental works of Ibn'Arabi, Shahāb al-Dīn Yahya ibn Habash Suhrawardī, and the grand Sufi mystical tradition arising from Rumi, the unparalleled love poet.

References to the primary language of image are made in Genesis (1:26), where it is stated that we are made in the *image* and likeness of God. The creation of the world is considered a work of art created by the Master Painter who created His unmatched visual spectacle. We emulate the Master when we use the corresponding gift we are born with called "imagination," of which mental imagery is one function. Thus our world was and continues to be birthed through this creative process. As is well documented, many geniuses have discovered solutions to problems through dreams and imagination.

Further along in Genesis we find the celestial messages that were conveyed to the patriarchs and matriarchs: for example, Jacob's dream of the celestial ladder and Moses' vision of the burning bush from which he hears the word of God. The most striking example within this tradition is Ezekiel's description of his inner journey to the throne of God in Ezekiel 1:1–28 (Sherman 2004). Prophesy means "mouthpiece:" a prophet's mission was to bring the presence and messages of God down to Earth. But what exactly is the metaphysical and time-space nature of this profound imaginal dimension and its messages?

Metaphysics of Imagination: Defining the Divine Language

The imaginal realm is a world of truth and reality as real as the world we occupy physically here on Earth. It is a repository of self-knowledge and wisdom that dwells in the Invisible Reality and is revealed to us where we reside, in our conscious, visible reality. My teacher Mme. Aboulker-Muscat taught that we receive divine images through the channel of communication called "mind." Mind conveys this information to us through the portal in our human form called "heart," which channels this information to be stored in the "brain." I call the imaginal experience "the intelligence of the heart."

These are some of the most important qualities and functions of this divine language:

- It is a universal, non-discursive, non-verbal, esoteric language that comes to us in pictorial form, as the hieroglyphs of our inner life.

- It is an inner natural language that can be translated and understood like any other exoteric spoken language.

- It communicates truth because it is not subject to the internal and external distortions of conditioning, associations, and other determinants arising from the ideas conveyed by exoteric language. Moreover, it is a free language and remains pure and unconditioned by other ideas and opinions applied to it. This latter point refutes the grievous error made by Freud in his misunderstanding of dreams as a "psychotic process" that require interpretation through associative and logical thought (Epstein 1981).

- This language is the foundation of the inner, silent "conversation between us and Source." The building of the Tower of Babel described in Genesis marks humanity's shift away from its connection to Source and its fall into the multitude of discursive, non-holy languages that reflects the fragmentation and strife between peoples in their quest to become omnipotent.

- The imaginal process bypasses the habitual verbal and logical functions of everyday life and goes directly to "the heart of the matter." It is the language of emotion given form—a pictorial analogue of the emotional state.

- It serves as a mirror or hologram of our thoughts, emotions, perceptions, and sensations. Images are a belief system given form.

- The imaginal process is the vehicle for traversing the vertical axis of freedom to create personal and collective change. Through this primal act of re-membering ourselves, we unite body and soul (Epstein 2004).

Located as it is in the sphere of cosmic consciousness, we can understand imagination as a precious gift that *is* its own language: it need not be associated with any other field of study like psychology to derive its validity, legitimacy, authenticity, and infinite value. It is our way to have

conversations with God, or with our inner or higher source of wisdom—
to reach out and be answered. All types of imaginal activities, be they
dreams, hallucinations, reveries, deliriums, visions, or imaginings of any
kind are as real as the time-space we occupy and call "objective reality."

It is crucial to develop the ability to discern the difference between
what is real and what is true. When I was a first-year psychiatric resident
on a locked/closed-door unit, a gentleman came up to me and told me
he was Jesus Christ. Ignorant then of what I later came to understand, I
immediately labeled him "crazy." What a mistake and missed opportunity!
What he was experiencing was real: but was it true as well? In retrospect,
I could have asked him whether he had changed the water at lunchtime
into wine and the bread into fish. Was he able to become the Master
of Christianity right before my eyes? Facing the truth might have been
beneficial to him, if painful—but less so than living in the pain of his
megalomaniac delusion. The truth can hurt, but that pain is ultimately
part of a process of growth, not the destructive, stunting pain of delusion.

Coming to grips with the existence of Cosmic Consciousness does
require shifting our fixed ideas of reality and truth. These truths can
only be known through our efforts to experiment with the "truisms" of
spirituality, to find out for ourselves if they are true. The materialistic
sciences are of no help here, because subjective reality is not measurable
in quantitative terms: it does not speak the language of natural science.
Qualitative precision, however, is useful, especially in defining the
language used to describe the imaginal functions.

IMAGERY AND FANTASY

Imagery and fantasy, for example, are not the same. Fantasy is time-
bound and references past and future. It is repetitive, ruminative, habitual,
and wish-fulfilling—whereas imaginal realities are spontaneous, non-
historical, and non-self-centered (Epstein 1981). Dreams and waking life
are defined differently but are equally real. To say, "Last night I dreamed
...*but* in reality..." is incorrect and is more accurately expressed as, "I
dreamed...*and* in my *waking reality*..." It requires a growing awareness to
break these imprecise habits of speech and thought.

IMAGERY AND MEDITATION

Imagery and meditation are often misunderstood as two interwoven
practices, when they are actually two processes of consciousness with
separate and distinct characteristics (Brown *et al.* 1982–1983). Imaginal
activity is *not* meditation. Imagery is a mental activity that plunges us
into another level of consciousness in order to make discoveries and

explore other dimensional worlds hidden behind this time-space reality we normally occupy. When I use the word "meditation," I refer to a familiar range of practices that have typically been adopted from the East. These meditational practices emphasize the stilling of thoughts, a dis-identification with the contents of mind, a heightened awareness of aspects of sensations, thoughts, and feelings, a relaxed sense of presence, and a general goal of mental clearing. To *imaginate* (my term) is altogether different: it means to become one with what is perceived, to actively become the embodiment of our experience of mental images.

IMAGERY AND HYPNOSIS

Likewise, hypnosis differs markedly from imagination, though the lines have been blurred in modern clinical practice. In conventional hypnotherapy, we are led into a deep relaxed state, near sleep, where a new set of suggestions is "programed" into us. In contrast, in the imaginal process we keep our will at the forefront, and after a light induction, we turn our senses inward in a hyper-attentive state. With our will at the forefront, it allows us to actively explore, discover, and objectify the subjective reality. Thus hypnosis is a process of surrendering our will to the will of an outside authority (the hypnotherapist), a process in which we are not free but rather remain dependent on the instructions, voice, and suggestions of another.

Imagery Practices

As mentioned above, to practice imagery is to dive into the depths of consciousness. The very senses by which we apprehend everyday tangible reality—our five senses of sight, hearing, touch, taste, smell—are *turned inward* to discover what lies within the subjective realities of the "invisible night worlds" that are obscured by the "visible day world." The senses are the keys that permit this transition to happen. In daily life, our senses bring us in contact with physical reality. We are all well aware from experience that we tend to go where our senses take us. They summon us, fill us with desire, and prompt us to relate to whatever they encounter. In imaginal work, our senses move away from the outer world. As the senses discover other realities, we explore these worlds in the same way we explore the physical world. Here, however, our five senses are attached to a sixth sense called imagination. Imagination is the inner light that guides the senses to pierce into the darkness of subjective reality so that what is there can be discovered. In this paradigm there is no unconscious—there is only the vast field of consciousness, that which we can illuminate and know for ourselves.

The term imagination actually defines three distinct functions: an inner sensory organ, an inner dimension of existence, and a technique for healing. Most of us consider our subjective reality to be our thoughts, fantasies, and emotions; but these are all conditioned states attached to known external life. What is discovered within has plasticity, mobility, and is ungoverned by the rules and laws that obtain here in day-consciousness—as anyone who has ever dreamed has experienced. This inner world is also limitless, a world without end that serves as an inspirational ground for creativity. We can create wings for our flights of discovery and be transported; we can plummet into the depths of self and achieve transcendent heights. All the potentials of our existence are just waiting for us to probe these unseen and heretofore unknown realms.

Let's take a look at the tools and methods that we use for our explorations. The primary tool is our imaginal sense, and there are three distinct methods I use in working with this sense:

1. Short exercises

2. Waking Dream

3. Guided exercises.

Before distinguishing between the various imagery methods, let me make a distinction between the processes described here and the more commonly used term "visualization." Visualization usually indicates a mere *visual* picture rather than a full sensory-awareness experience that includes hearing, touching, smelling, tasting, and other bodily sensations. This latter picture is *conjured* purposefully and projected onto the screen of our mind's eye. Creating an image in this manner is not the same as spontaneously discovering images. For greatest effect, the imagery process is to be freely lived, freely perceived, and freely explored.

Short Exercises: A Path to Self-Knowledge

Short exercises, generally taking from seconds to three minutes, are instructional keys that open the door to our subjective reality where the "explorer" discovers the precise image needed to create change, solve problems, and move toward healing, health, and wholeness. Aimed at solving daily, topical problems in health and relationships, it is the most common type of imagery used in clinical practice.

Short exercises are crafted with specific aims or intentions, and are comprised of detailed instructions to assist the explorer in the discovery process. No long sensory relaxation induction is necessary to enter into the experience because the focus is on the imagery, not on relaxation. The relaxation induction takes only several seconds and consists of a few rounds of long exhalations through the mouth followed by short inhalations through the nose.

While short imagery exercises can be descriptive, they are always jumping-off points for the imager to find his/her own healing images. For example, in the Green Leaf Exercise you'll find later in this chapter, if the imager opens his/her hand and spontaneously finds a fairy, this healing agent would be incorporated into the imagery. The emergence of these spontaneous, organic images indicates that the imagery has taken root in the person. Of course, clinicians need to remain open, without bias or preconception, to whatever is discovered in this realm of freedom.

These self-discoveries provide us with specific instructions for how to proceed or behave in ways that are different than we habitually enact. We recognize that our inner or higher source of wisdom is sending us messages from the subjective reality, messages that are more potent and impactful than those we receive from our outer objective reality. We are given new direction(s) for repairing relationships, creative inspiration, healing illness, changing destructive habits.

For example, in my practice I worked with a young man in his early 30s who was told by his doctors that he had a destructive liver disease that was "autoimmune" (in other words, his body was committing an act of physiological suicide). He was told that he would not live beyond a year because "nothing could be done to save him" (nothing, that is, within the limited scope of the current medical model). My client embarked on a course of imagery practice, and after several months new tests and a biopsy revealed no evidence of the disease process: he had healed.

Not only do our imaginal discoveries create change and revelation, they also act as a diagnostic tool, an inner source of wisdom that provides knowledge beneficial to us. For example, during an imagery exercise undertaken to repair her self-image, a young woman found out that she couldn't see as well from one eye as the other. She had not been aware of any difficulty with that eye or her vision in general. On my recommendation, she had an eye exam, which confirmed the eye weakness. This is but one of a host of instances where an image portends a difficulty that needs our attention or investigation.[2]

Imagery has a mental homeopathic impact, a micro-input that obtains a macro-output or result, in the process of which *we become the agent of our own change*. The following are some important tips for using this tool:

- Sit upright in a chair with spine erect, rather than lying down or sitting cross-legged as in meditation.

- Make the exercises short, meaning they can be practiced in a short span, from just seconds to one minute. The longer the imagery session, the less power it exerts because our minds can quickly become inured to the process and lose focus. The exercises are essentially short *shocks* delivered to the system to stimulate its innate healing capacities.

- It is helpful to give ourselves doses of imagery two or three times per day, similar to the way we consistently dose allopathic medications over a timeframe ranging from seven to 21 days.

Of critical importance in generating change and/or healing is the *attitude* we hold toward the process, rather than the goal or outcome. Concerns about the product negate the possibility of change. Learning that the outcome is not in our hands can be life-changing. We are instead establishing a healing relationship with the self that answers the ancient question attributed to Hillel the Elder, one of the developers of the Talmud: "If I am not for myself, who will be for me?" (Lieber and Scherman 1995, p.43). Practicing in this way builds a respectful, loving, kind, truthful, and generous way of living true to ourselves.

You are invited to try this short imagery exercise for self-healing.

Green Leaf

Close your eyes. Breathe out three full respiratory cycles with long exhalations through the mouth, each followed by normal inhalations through the nose. Imagine yourself in the backyard of a house in autumn. Leaves are falling from the trees. They are yellow, orange, and red. A leaf falls from the tree and touches you on the head as it falls to the ground. Pick it up and hold it in your left hand. Cover that hand with your right hand. Feel a pulsation there. Uncover it, and see the leaf turning partly green. Cover the left hand again. Feel the pulsation becoming stronger. Uncover the hand again. See that the leaf is now three-quarters green.

Cover the hand once more. Feel the pulsation getting stronger still. Remove your hand and see the leaf now fully green and alive.

Place the leaf over or into any part of your body that needs care or healing. Sense and feel the sap from the leaf entering into the affected area. See and know that the area is completely healed and looks just like the surrounding healthy tissue. Say *"Healing"* to yourself. Be aware of any feelings, bodily sensations, and images that accompany this. Breathe out and open your eyes.

I recommend that you do this practice for 30–45 seconds once a day in the morning for 21 days in order to realize the greatest benefits.

WAKING DREAM AND GUIDED EXERCISES: FROM SELF-KNOWLEDGE TO SELF-KNOWING

The other two methods of imaginal practice—Waking Dream and guided exercises—take us from the sphere of *self-knowledge* supplied by short exercises to the sphere of *self-knowing*. *Self-knowledge* provides a fixed endpoint to self-discovery, while *self-knowing* is an ongoing process of self-discovery. These explorations move us into our inner universe on the vertical axis of freedom.[3]

As a therapeutic practice, Waking Dream involves a *descent* into the deepest levels of self followed by an *ascent* to transcendent levels of self.[4] It is an extensive imagery adventure that lasts from one to two hours and is initially undertaken with the assistance of an experienced guide. The portal for entering is through a night dream chosen for its vivid or striking appeal or a vertical element such as a mountain, hill, cave, or staircase. Starting in the conscious waking state, with eyes closed and spine erect, the explorer is taken through a light induction that takes them back into the night dream to either the vivid or vertical element. Once back in the dream, the therapist guides the explorer through the experience. The explorer describes all that s/he sees, hears, feels, and senses. After the discovery phase of the journey, the explorer is led quickly back by the guide along the same route s/he has traversed, and exits the Waking Dream, breathing out once and opening the eyes. Generally, after several such journeys, explorers discover their inner guide (objectively discovered within their subjective reality) and can then enter the waking dream state on their own. The inner guide is a living presence that dwells in another dimensional reality and is unique to each traveler. These guides lead us into and through transcendent reality.

This process of traveling on a vertical axis of freedom reverses our attachment to our habitual and limiting horizontal time-space reality, where our suffering is always lying in wait and death beckons. To my knowledge, Waking Dream as taught by my teacher, Colette Aboulker-Muscat, is the only imaginal method that emphasizes the process of turning the senses inward and the exploration of the vertical axis to explore the depths of self and the heights of transcendence.

In the 20th century, psychologists attempted to integrate psychological theories with the ancient truths embodied in the Waking Dream practice. From my point of view, this mixing devalued the imaginal experience. Most notable among these practitioners were Carl Jung, Robert Desoille, and Hanscarl Leuner. Jung practiced a modified form of Waking Dream: he had his patients "complete" their night dream where it broke off, but without the full experience of exploring the vertical axis. Desoille used pre-defined Freudian themes of early childhood development as "plots" for his patients to explore. For example, men were asked to "Look at a sword (penis)" and women to "Look at/into a purse (vagina)" and then observe what occurred. He called his work "Directed Waking Dream" (*Rêve Eveillé Dirigé*). Leuner utilized Jungian archetypal "themes" for patients to explore. For example, facing a lion would allow the patient to confront aggression. He called his method "Guided Affective Imagery." Other contributors of some note have been Wolfgang Kretschmer, Carl Happich, and Roberto Assagioli. In America, Jerome Singer and Jeanne Achterberg were major proponents. However, the singular master of this method in modern times was my teacher, Mme. Aboulker-Muscat. The ancient tradition of the prophetic practices was passed down through her family line; and while she was not a prophetess herself, she maintained an unbroken lineage that had been transmitted through the millennia as far back as King David (Yehezkiel 2003).

The third intermediate technique called guided exercises takes 20–40 minutes to complete. The long guided exercises are forged from the experiences of our daily lives and have specific themes. I refer to them as "guided" because they are less structured than short exercises and thus require a "guide" to explore them.

These exercises can be used alone or as a preparatory process to stimulate striking or unusual night dreams. These night dreams are then used for a Waking Dream. Often, the dreams that emerge from these guided exercises characteristically include some visual *vertical* component such as a staircase or mountain (Epstein and Hogben 1980). We now have an organically connected experience: guided imaginal exercises → night dreams → Waking Dream. All unfold beautifully from within, free of biases or external influences, and form a road to personal freedom.

Examples of guided exercises follow. Some contain a vertical descent or ascent, but it is not a necessity as in Waking Dream explorations.

- Find three doors in front of you: one to the left, one in the center, one to the right. Choose one spontaneously, go through it, and explore what you discover there.

- Find a key in an open space, locate a door it opens, and go inside.

- Descend into a meadow, find a flower, and enter into it through the stem.

- Enter a library and select a book to make a discovery about the self.

- Clean a room and rearrange it to cleanse the self.

- Find your way out of a dark pit or similar depression/hole/cave.

- Enter a labyrinth using a ball of red thread to mark the way. Make your way to the center to find something of primal importance. Follow the thread to exit the labyrinth (Epstein and Hogben 1980, p.279).

In closing, I'd like to share a list of the 33 functions of mental imagery and imagination that I have discovered to date. This may help clinicians expand their conception of imagery so that it can become a limitless source of inspiration.

1. Healing physical, mental, or emotional disturbances (such as tumors, depression, or infections)

2. Rapidly relieving pain

3. Changing injurious conscious beliefs

4. Uncovering and de-creating hidden sabotaging beliefs

5. Ending slave mentality

6. Removing the inner terrorist

7. Reversing ingrained patterns of thought, mood, or behavior

8. Restoring balance after stressful shocks

9. Sourcing self-regulation internally, not externally

10. Ending "false emergencies" derived from our miseducation and faulty conditioning

11. Amplifying the potential that allows learning to emerge from within

12. Learning to trust oneself

13. Aligning with one's life path

14. Getting "to the bottom" of any issue

15. Feeling more alive

16. Accessing the passion to serve

17. Removing resistance to success

18. Living creatively

19. Manifesting what one needs

20. Clarity in decision-making

21. Optimizing learning capacity

22. Fulfilling sought-for aims or intentions

23. Bringing closure to the personal past

24. Resolving past or present relationship challenges

25. Understanding dreams

26. Learning morphological significance (face-reading: the external image)

27. Ending the pain of interpersonal competition

28. Ending isolation through connecting to a supportive universe

29. Reflecting and facilitating freedom for others

30. Learning to lead

31. Knowing the self by descending into the deepest layers

32. Cleansing our errors

33. Realizing the transcendent-spiritual dimensions of self to discover Self

All of these imaginal experiences allow us to deeply discover hidden and unrecognized aspects of ourselves that when brought to light can inform our lives in new ways and guide us toward wholeness.

ENDNOTES

1. Consult the writings of Eliot Wolfson, Joseph Dan, Moshe Idel, and Gershom Shalom for background information on these visionary traditions.
2. For more clinical examples, I refer the reader to my book *Healing Visualizations*.
3. I have explicated this method in detail in my book *Waking Dream Therapy*.
4. In addition to Ezekiel's journey, other examples of transcendent experiences include: St. Teresa De Avila's vision of the crystal globe in the shape of a castle, described in *The Interior Castle*; and Muhammad's ascent to the heavens in his "Night Journey" where he speaks with God.

References

Brown, D., Forte, M., Rich, P., and Epstein, G. (1982–1983) "Phenomenological Differences Among Mindfulness Meditation, Self-Hypnosis, and Waking Dream." *Imagination, Personality and Cognition 2*, 4, 291–309. Available at https://drjerryepstein.org/sites/default/files/Phenomenological_Differences.pdf, accessed on February 4 2016.

Epstein, G. (1981) *Waking Dream Therapy: Dream Process as Imagination*. New York, NY: Human Science Press.

Epstein, G. (1992) *Waking Dream Therapy: Unlocking the Secrets of Self Through Dreams and Imagination*. New York, NY: ACMI Press.

Epstein, G. (2004) "Mental Imagery: The Language of Spirit." *Advances 20*, 3, 5.

Epstein, G. and Hogben, G. (1980) "Visual Imagination and Dreaming." In G. Epstein (ed.) *Studies in Non-Deterministic Psychology*. New York, NY: Human Science Press.

Lieber, M. and Scherman, M. (eds) (1995) *The Pirkei Avos Treasury: Ethics of the Fathers. The Sages' Guide to Living, with an Anthologized Commentary and Anecdotes*. Brooklyn, NY: Mesorah Publications.

Price, I. M. (1889) "The Schools of the Sons of the Prophets." *The Old Testament Student 8*, 7. Available at www.jstor.org/stable/3156528, accessed on June 26 2015.

Scherman, Rabbi Nosson (ed.) (2004) *Tanach: The Torah/Prophets/Writings: The Twenty-Four Books of the Bible Newly Translated and Annotated*, 2nd edition. Brooklyn, NY: Mesorah Publications.

Yehezkiel, A. (2003) *The Davidic Families and the Genealogy of Colette Aboulker-Muscat*. Jerusalem: Aliza Yehezkiel Publisher.

Part 2

Imagery for Health and Healing

Chapter 5

Bringing Spirit Back into Medicine

Bruce Roberts

We are on the verge of a major evolutionary shift, a quantum leap if you will, in our development as a species. We are being brought to our knees as our relationship to each other and to our planet is becoming more and more out of balance. We can see this shift taking place on many different levels and from many different perspectives. In grand astrological terms, we are moving from Pisces, the age of dichotomies, to Aquarius, the age of synthesis. In the cosmology of our body's energy system, we are shifting from third-chakra thinking, with the focus on the individual will, to fourth-chakra thinking, with the focus on connection and interdependence. We are moving out of the Industrial Age, based on individual creativity and initiative, into the Information Age, which is based on the collective sharing of wisdom and knowledge. All of these changes involve a shift away from predominantly masculine, left-brain thinking toward a more balanced approach that embraces feminine, right-brain thinking as well.

Our medical system is on the verge of a major evolutionary shift as well. The traditional Western allopathic medical model is about to collapse under its own weight. The United States spends a higher percentage of its gross domestic product on healthcare than any other nation in the world—yet, according to the World Health Organization, we rank 37th in terms of our overall health (World Health Report 2000). We undoubtedly have the most technologically advanced medical system in the world, but somehow that has not translated into better health for our citizens. Chronic illnesses like cancer, heart disease, diabetes, obesity, chronic fatigue, fibromyalgia, and Alzheimer's disease are running rampant in our society today, and the current system of medicine is struggling to stem the tide.

The old model of "one disease, one remedy" that relied on discovering a silver bullet in the form of a pill, surgery, or radiation to destroy the disease does not work with these complex, multifactorial illnesses. We are finding that we are more than just a body with replaceable parts: there are physical, emotional, and spiritual aspects to all of these chronic diseases. It is estimated that 70–90 percent of visits to primary care providers are for stress-related problems (Rosch 1991), and physicians simply do not have the time nor the training to address these more holistic issues. Likewise, the spiritual aspects of who we are, the bigger picture that includes our connections to ourselves, to each other, to the world around us, to something bigger than ourselves, and to our sense of purpose, are not being addressed.

If we are going to have any hope of healing these complex holistic maladies, we will need to learn new tools. By helping to reduce stress, by bringing insight and perspective, and by tapping into the healing power of our mind, guided imagery serves as an invaluable tool for helping restore our bodies and, ultimately, the planet to a state of equilibrium and health.

The Cartesian Split

Before delving further into guided imagery, let's take a look at the bigger picture of this evolutionary process and how the practice of medicine became disconnected from the concept of spirit in the first place. In order to understand this disconnect, we must first travel back a few hundred years in time to Europe in the middle of the 17th century. It was a time of devastating disease. The bubonic plague, or "Black Death" as it was called back then, had been ravaging the continent off and on for centuries,[1] leaving whole communities decimated in its wake. There was nowhere to hide and no way to protect yourself from this terrible disease. As you can imagine, it must have been absolutely terrifying to watch your neighbors and loved ones being carried off in wheelbarrows and death carts to mass graves (you might not want to imagine this too vividly!).

In those days, illness was generally seen as a punishment from God for our sins or misdeeds. Our physical health and spiritual life were deeply intertwined, and living a good, righteous, and religiously orthodox life was felt to afford some measure of protection. The Black Death, however, was an equal-opportunity illness, attacking the righteous as well as the wicked. Priests and doctors were dying right alongside the thieves and the scoundrels.

With this devastating illness as the backdrop, the French philosopher and mathematician René Descartes was determined to take a new look at illness in particular and the ways of the world in general. He decided that it was time to question everything, even what the priests said was true. He didn't want to just guess how the body worked; he wanted scientists to open up the body and actually *see* how it worked. He didn't want to assume that we understood the causes of illness; instead, he wanted to assume that everything was unknown until research provided us with a better understanding. This left the responsibility for the mind and spirit in the hands of the Church, and responsibility for the body was gradually taken over by physicians and scientists. This new way of thinking eventually split the physical body from the spirit and created a momentous divide between medicine and religion (Robinson and Zalta 2003).

While Descartes was busy laying the foundations of scientific inquiry, the English physicist and mathematician Sir Isaac Newton was exploring new concepts about how forces interact in the physical world. Newtonian physics became the guiding light to a deeper understanding of the remarkable world we live in, while the same concepts were providing invaluable clues to the inner workings of the human body as well. These two synchronistic events—the Cartesian split and the development of Newtonian physics—marked the beginning of a new era in science, an evolutionary leap in how we view health, and the birth of Western allopathic medicine as we know it.

Pisces: The Age of Dichotomies

This shift in medicine took place during an era that astrologists referred to as the Age of Pisces. The symbol for Pisces, two fish swimming in opposite directions, was a good symbol for this age of dichotomies: it was a period during which the world and our social structures became more and more polarized. The great empires from the previous Age of Aries diverged into Eastern and Western cultures, with the Eastern culture honoring the more yin or feminine elements, while the Western culture honored the more yang or masculine elements. These cultures were further divided into many smaller countries with their own distinct and unique characteristics. The various races were socially and geographically isolated. Male and female roles were clearly defined, and we lived by a set of dualities: right or wrong, black or white, feminine or masculine, physical or emotional, mind or body, physical or spiritual.

This era can be thought of as our third-chakra developmental stage of separation and individuation, and was critical to the development of our unique human gifts and talents. It was dominated by left-brain masculine thinking. The left brain is reductionistic in nature and likes to take things apart and analyze them. It focuses on structure and details, but can lose sight of the bigger picture of how all the individual parts function together.

This process of analysis led to some incredible discoveries and advances that have deepened and enriched our understanding of each other and of the world we live in. When Henry Ford separated the automobile into its component parts, it led to the advent of the assembly line and ushered in the industrial revolution. Separating the body into its individual parts using Cartesian and Newtonian principles has allowed Western medicine to make incredible advances in our understanding of anatomy, physiology, and pathological processes. The human body has been dissected and analyzed down to its very DNA and molecular structure. We can manipulate genes and even clone new life. Many of our most serious illnesses have been conquered.

However, once we began applying the assembly line style reductionist mentality to the care of human beings, something vital was lost. As we continued to build a higher and more complex edifice of knowledge of the individual parts, we lost track of the bigger picture of who we are as human beings and our spirit was driven underground. Although we have made incredible progress in treating acute illness, we still have a lot to learn about healing the chronic maladies that are plaguing society. These must be addressed on a much more comprehensive mind, body, and spirit level.

The Age of Aquarius: Synthesis

As we move into the 21st century we are moving out of the Age of Pisces, the age of dichotomies, into the Age of Aquarius, the age of synthesis. We are moving from the third-chakra stage of separation and individuation to the fourth-chakra stage of interdependence. We are learning to honor the more feminine right-brain thinking that sees the bigger picture of how all the individual pieces function together as a whole.

We see evidence of the beginning stages of this evolutionary shift in some of the seminal events of the last 50 years. When the Dalai Lama was exiled from Tibet in 1959, he brought the more feminine Eastern philosophies of meditation and spirituality to the West. The advent of the Internet and global communication brought more masculine Western concepts to the East, resulting in increased material prosperity in those regions. The women's movement of the '60s broke down the rigid sex role stereotypes that had been so characteristic of our separation and individuation phase. Men became more comfortable in nurturing roles, and women have moved into the highest echelons of the workplace and government. Likewise, the civil rights movement has made great strides in breaking down racial barriers, while inter-marriage and mixed race children are serving to blur boundaries between the races even further. We are moving from a dualistic either/or mentality to a more unified both/and mentality.

While society is making great strides in many areas, Western medicine has been lagging behind. It continues to be driven, for the most part, by the limited utility of Newtonian physics that addresses only the physical aspects of the body while ignoring the bigger picture of who we are as energy-based spiritual beings. We already embrace the energetic aspects of our body for diagnostic purposes: for instance, we use EKGs to measure the energy coming from the heart and EEGs to measure the energy emanating from the brain. We use MRIs to measure the electromagnetic patterns of various body tissues in order to allow us to "see" the inner structures of the body. We are even beginning to recognize and acknowledge the quantum physics principle that the process of observation by the researcher influences the outcome of the study. Yet we still limit ourselves primarily to Newtonian physics in our attempts to heal the body.

Quantum physics has emerged over the past 100 years to help explain how the world works on an energetic level, it is beginning to blur the boundaries between the physical and the energetic, between science and spirituality. Einstein's famous equation $E=MC^2$ tells us that energy and matter are really the same thing: our body is an electromagnetic system. The physical body is simply that part of the energetic system that has slowed down to the point that our senses perceive it as being solid. Our eyes perceive only the visible spectrum of light, while the infrared and ultraviolet spectrums lie beyond our perception. Likewise, our physical body represents only a small portion of who we are as human beings while our emotional, mental, and spiritual bodies lie beyond the reach of our perceptions and of Newtonian physics. It is time to embrace the insights we have gained from quantum physics, heal the Cartesian split, and rejoin the physical and spiritual aspects of our human nature.

The Spirit Body and the Chakra System

There are medical systems that have been around for thousands of years that are more holistic by their very nature because they recognize that we are more than just physical beings. These systems have a great deal to teach us about what it means to be human, to be healthy, to be whole. Traditional Chinese Medicine, Ayurvedic medicine, and many Shamanic healing traditions recognize that we are both physical and spiritual beings, and they all describe strikingly similar cosmologies.

In the cosmology of these systems, the spirit body consists of seven chakras, or energy centers, starting at the base of the spine and ending at the crown of the head. Each successive chakra represents a higher frequency of energy and a higher level of psycho-spiritual development. For example, the third chakra is located at our solar plexus and represents our individual will, our sense of who we are separate from our families or tribes. The fourth chakra, at our heart, represents our ability to give and receive love, our connections to each other and to our community. This chakra lies at the center of our being and serves as a bridge between the lower three physical and the upper three spiritual chakras (Myss 1997).

Energy channels or meridians interconnect the major chakras. The energy that flows through these meridians is called *chi* by the Chinese, *prana* by East Indians, Vital Life Force by naturopaths, and simply "The Force" by that wise sensei, Yoda. This enigmatic energy that flows through our bodies is the difference between a cadaver and a live human being. It is the energy that animates us, that connects us to each other, our environment, and all living things.

As we go through life, physical and emotional stresses create blockages in the flow of chi through the spirit body. When you come up against one of these blockages, when your "buttons" are pushed, it triggers certain images, thoughts, or beliefs in the mental body. These thoughts and images trigger emotions in the emotional body, resulting in the fight-or-flight response and a cascade of biochemical reactions that directly impact the physical body. As we accumulate more and more blockages in the spirit body, the flow of chi is progressively diminished. We lose our resilience and our ability to maintain homeostasis. Our inherent ability to heal our self is diminished, and we develop dis-ease.

Another way of conceptualizing the cosmology of the body is to think of the physical body as your hard drive and the spirit body as your operating system. Blockages or "viruses" in the spirit body (operating system) create corruptions or dis-ease in the physical body (hard drive). You can run the disc defrag and disc cleanup programs *ad nauseum*, but until you clear the viruses or blockages from the operating system you will never "heal" the hard drive. Western medicine attempts to support the physical body by treating the symptoms in our hard drives, but does nothing to reprogram the platform—the physical, emotional, mental, or spiritual imbalances that caused the problem in the first place.

From a holistic perspective, the universe is always conspiring in our favor and working toward our healing. Symptoms are messages informing us of where things are out of balance in terms of body, mind, and spirit. The message may start as a small, quiet voice in our head, but most of us are too busy to pay attention. If we ignore the voice, it may then manifest as a twinge in our neck or indigestion in our belly. Ignore it even more and it will grow louder and stronger until it eventually stops us in our tracks, bringing us to our knees in the form of a heart attack, stroke, or cancer.

Just as our symptoms inform us about imbalances in ourselves as individuals, our planet has been giving us some pretty strong messages about where things are out of balance in the environment. Third-chakra, left-brained, masculine thinking says that we are separate from the environment, and that our individual needs take precedence over the collective. This has allowed us to pollute the air and water, destroy the ozone layer, and trigger global warming. We are increasingly witnessing the symptoms of these imbalances in the form of tsunamis, earthquakes, floods, and droughts. Many of our most serious health problems are also a result of our societal choices and decisions. In the last 50 years we have put 85,000 new chemicals into the environment, and we have corrupted our food supply with pesticides and genetically modified "frankenfoods." As a result, we are collectively being brought to our knees.

Guided Imagery

There is inevitably a certain amount of chaos as we transition from one developmental or evolutionary stage to another, and we can certainly see evidence of that chaos all around us. Our pendulum has moved too far in the direction of separation and individuation, to the point of alienation from our families, our neighbors, and our planet. It is time for the pendulum to swing back in the direction of connection and interdependence. As we transition to this next stage of our evolution as a species, we are going to need tools to address the bigger picture of who we are as physical and spiritual beings that are connected to each other and to the planet we live on. Guided imagery is one of these valuable tools, and it can play a significant role in addressing this process on multiple levels.

Guided imagery uses directed thoughts and suggestions to guide our imagination toward a more relaxed and focused state. This helps shift us out of the fight-or-flight response, a place of fear and constriction, into the relaxation response, a place of love and compassion. Since up to 90 percent of visits to the doctor are primarily stress related, by shifting us into the relaxation response, guided imagery has been shown to be beneficial in a wide variety of illnesses including physical conditions such as asthma (Olness 1981), diabetes (Surwit *et al.* 2002), and hypertension (Crowther 1983), as well as psychological issues such as anxiety (Finucane and Mecer 2006), depression (Jarvinen and Gold 1983), and eating disorders (Esplen *et al.* 1998).

Guided imagery also shifts us from our more masculine left brain into our more feminine right brain. Left-brain masculine energy is the energy of action and is a third-chakra function. It emphasizes the individual over the collective: it sees the trees, but may miss the bigger picture of the forest. Right-brain feminine energy is the energy of contemplation. It is intuitive and synthetic and is a fourth-chakra function. It emphasizes the collective over the individual: it sees the whole forest, but may miss some of the details of the individual trees.

Men and women, of course, possess both masculine and feminine energy, and one is not better than the other. In order for us to be healthy we need a "Sacred Marriage," a balance between the masculine and the feminine within each of us, between the yin and the yang, action and contemplation, the will and the heart. Contemplation without action does not serve ourselves or society, and action without contemplation is a recipe for disaster that we have seen played out over and over again throughout history. By facilitating a healthier balance between masculine and feminine energies, guided imagery helps assure that all of our third-chakra actions are first filtered through fourth-chakra contemplation in order to make sure that our actions are in right relationship with ourselves, our loved ones, our community, and our planet.

By helping move us into a more focused and relaxed state, guided imagery can also help quiet the noise in our head so that we can tune in to the intuitive voice of our inner healer that is trying to inform us where things are out of balance physically, emotionally, or spiritually in our lives. If we are eating the wrong foods, it will let us know. If we are holding onto anger, fear, guilt, shame, or resentment, it will let us know. If we are doing one thing and our soul is yearning for something else, it will let us know. We simply need to quiet our mind and pay attention before disaster strikes. Guided imagery is a low-cost diagnostic and therapeutic tool that can help us to see what the MRI fails to reveal and heal what penicillin cannot touch.

We have seen how physical and emotional stresses create blockages in the flow of chi in our spirit body, triggering thoughts and images in our mental body, leading to the fight-or-flight response in our emotional body, resulting in dis-ease in our physical body. Just as these unconscious negative thoughts and images create dis-ease, a conscious effort to cultivate positive imagery can result in healing. Our minds are extremely powerful. Our body cannot tell the difference between what is really happening and what we are simply imagining: it responds exactly the same way. If negative thoughts and images can make us sick, positive thoughts and images can make us well. Guided imagery helps us bring our negative images into consciousness where they can be dissolved by the light of awareness. Guided imagery can, in essence, serve as a powerful antivirus program that helps remove those disruptive, negative thoughts and images, and replaces them with more positive, healing alternatives.

Guided imagery can also move us beyond freedom from disease to a state of optimal wellness. Most of us live our lives by accident, allowing our subconscious negative thoughts, beliefs, and images to dictate our reality. Whatever we believe or imagine to be true is true. If we cannot picture or imagine a better life for ourselves or our planet, then we cannot possibly bring that into our reality. It is time for us to begin to live our lives on purpose by consciously choosing and guiding our thoughts and images to bring us the rich abundant life we truly desire.

René and Sir Isaac: with all due respect for the gifts you have brought to the world, it is time for us to move on. It is time to take the knowledge we have gained from third-chakra thinking and graduate to the fourth-chakra. We can no longer afford to see our bodies as separate from our spirit, and we can no longer afford to see ourselves as separate from our communities and our environment. The process of separation and individuation has brought us this far, but it can't take us the whole way. Our very survival depends on our ability to take that quantum leap to the next phase in our evolutionary process, one in which we recognize our connectedness and interdependence. It is time to imagine a better, healthier world, and guided imagery can help show us the way.

Endnotes

1. The Black Death had its greatest impact from 1346–1353, killing 60 percent of Europe's population. However, there continued to be ongoing outbreaks of bubonic plague, including a major epidemic in London in the 17th century.

References

Crowther, J. (1983) "Stress management training and relaxation imagery in the treatment of essential hypertension." *Journal of Behavioral Medicine 6*, 2, 169–187.

Esplen, M.J., Garfinkel, P.E., Olmsted, M., Gallop, R.M., and Kennedy, S.A. (1998) "A randomized controlled trial of guided imagery in bulimia nervosa." *Psychological Medicine 28*, 6, 1347–1357.

Finucane, A. and Mercer, S.W. (2006) "An exploratory mixed methods study of the acceptability and effectiveness of mindfulness-based cognitive therapy for patients with active depression and anxiety in primary care." *BioMed Central Psychiatry 7*, 6, 14.

Jarvinen, P.J. and Gold, S.R. (1983) "Imagery as an aid in reducing depression." *Journal of Clinical Psychology 37*, 3, 523–529.

Myss, C. (1997) *Anatomy of the Spirit: The Seven Stages of Power and Healing.* New York, NY: Harmony Books.

Olness, K., (1981) "Imagery (self-hypnosis) as adjunct therapy in childhood cancer." *American Journal of Pediatric Hematology/Oncology 3*, 3, 313–320.

The World Health Report (2000) "Health Systems: Improving Performance." Available at www.who.int/whr/2000/en, accessed on March 28 2015.

Robinson, H. and Zalta, E.N. (eds) (2015) "Dualism." *The Stanford Encyclopedia of Philosophy.* Available at http://plato.stanford.edu/entries/dualism, accessed on April 17 2015.

Rosch, P.J. (1991) "Job stress: America's leading adult health problem." *USA Magazine*, May, 42–44.

Surwit, R.S., van Tilburg, M.A., Zucker, N., McCaskill, C.C., *et al.* (2002) "Stress management improves long-term glycemic control in type 2 diabetes." *Diabetes Care 25*, 1, 30–34.

Chapter 6

Medical Applications of Guided Imagery

Martin L. Rossman and Dean Shrock

Guided imagery can have significant therapeutic effects in a wide range of medical applications. Mental imagery is an ancient form of information processing utilizing thoughts that can be seen, heard, smelled, or felt in the mind. Guided imagery practitioners evoke or suggest mental imagery to gain diagnostic information, help people better understand themselves, and positively influence psychology and physiology. This has been shown to be helpful in medical conditions as diverse as acute and chronic pain, sleep disorders, allergies, asthma, fertility and childbirth, anxiety, depression, stress management, cancer treatment, medical decision-making, preparing for and recovering from medical and surgical procedures, and more.

Imagery can be a potent way to influence patient attitudes, expectations, motivation for change, and ability to cope with difficult medical events. It can be a helpful diagnostic aid and a tool for engaging and empowering patients in their own care.

Imagery is the natural language of the human subconscious, a rich, sensory-based, and emotional coding language of the brain/mind that reveals itself in human culture through art, poetry, and drama. It is the language of dreams, visions, insights, intuitions, and creativity. Imagery allows us to access and work with our perceptions of both external and internal reality.

Imagery is often, perhaps always, the very first way we become conscious of our thoughts. Small children have rich, imagery-filled perceptions of the world around them long before they are able to articulate and express their desires and perceptions in words. Written language historically began with pictograms depicting objects and events that gradually came to take on symbolic meanings that could express increasingly abstract ideas like the future, past, possibilities, morals, and values.

In many ways, it is the human imagination that sets us apart from other life forms. Virtually everything created by humans, whether buildings, spaceships, computers, or gluten-free bread, first came into existence as an imagined idea.

Systems of Representation of Thought

University of California San Francisco Professor of Psychiatry, Mardi Horowitz explained that we represent reality to ourselves in three major modes: the verbal, the imaginal, and the somatic (enactive) (Horowitz 1978). In medical situations, patients typically try to explain their somatic experience by describing symptoms, complaints, and concerns to the doctor using words (the history), and the doctor attends both to their story and an examination of their body in an attempt to understand the problem.

In this chapter, we will show how learning the language of imagery can greatly expand a medical history and offer rapid and significant insight into the nature of medical problems and the patients who present with them. Imagery can help reduce stress and stimulate healing responses in the body. Learning to attend to and use imagery in medical settings can provide important insight into the psycho-emotional matrix that often underlies puzzling and distressing symptoms.

Here's a clinical example:

> A mother in her 30s presented with breast lumps. She was anxious that they were cancerous but hadn't yet had a biopsy. In our session she was invited to relax, focus her attention on the lumps, and invite an image to come to mind that could tell her something about them. She described an image of a stream with rocks obstructing part of the flow. She was asked to observe them, noticing what came to mind as she paid attention. Soon she volunteered that the rocks had a pearl-like luster, reminding her of pearls in oysters. She went on to say that the pearls were a way

that oysters protect themselves from irritants. When asked about irritants in her own life, she talked about the many obligations she had taken on in her work, her family, and volunteer positions at her children's school. She began sobbing as she talked about life being overwhelming because there wasn't enough time and energy for everything. She had been missing sleep, eating poorly, and drinking lots of coffee in an attempt to keep up. She felt exhausted.

When asked what she might do to relieve some of the stress and irritation, she talked about cutting back, saying "no" to some requests, improving her diet, and getting enough sleep. She emerged from the imagery session saying that she believed it had shown her the pattern that may have made her vulnerable to developing her symptoms. She felt confident that she could correct her course, whether the biopsy was benign or not. She felt that the image was a tangible signal from her body that it needed better care, and felt motivated now to give herself that care.

To her relief, her biopsy showed benign fibrocystic changes, but she went on to make the lifestyle changes she had imagined anyway. The breast lumps went away in a month or so.

Guided Imagery

Guided imagery is a process where imagery is used in a therapeutic way to create relaxation, increase blood flow, provide pain relief, improve sleep, and reduce anxiety and stress through imagery-based suggestion. The imagery can be created by the doctor or therapist or, more powerfully, it can be self-generated by patients in response to prompting questions. Guided imagery is a type of "directed daydream" that immerses patients in their imaginal worlds and can shift their physiology from one of stress and pain to relaxation and comfort in a relatively short time.

It is most accurate to think of guided imagery as a way to treat the patient, rather than as a way to treat symptoms or illness. It is not something that you can *do to* people, it is something you must *do with* them. In time, patients can learn to create and practice guided imagery on their own, which expands their coping skills and sense of self-efficacy. Relaxation, a sense of inner connectedness, and the experience of being able to do something to help one's self (self-efficacy) are all common experiences with guided imagery, and they all have therapeutic power of their own whatever the particular images involved.

Hypnosis and Guided Imagery

We have included many hypnosis studies in our review, because clinical hypnosis almost always involves the use of guided relaxation with imagery-based suggestions. Suggestions that most effectively modulate physiology nearly always include images.

The term "hypnosis" refers to a state of relaxed yet concentrated attention. The distinction between guided imagery and hypnosis is more semantic than practical or clinical. In practice, the processes of hypnosis and guided imagery often look very similar if not identical. The question of whether there is a distinct hypnotic state or if the effects of hypnosis are simply the result of imaginative engagement has been debated in the hypnosis literature for many years (Barber 1965).

The Scope of Our Review

Because of space limitations and the enormous amount of literature, we have decided to focus on the most important and widespread uses of guided imagery and hypnosis in medicine. These include anxiety, stress, pain, cancer and cancer treatment issues, sleep, and coping with medical and surgical interventions. Guided imagery is useful in almost any medical situation where stress is an issue. Unmanaged and prolonged stress can precipitate disease events and amplify and exacerbate symptoms. While stress does not cause all disease, it is almost always a significant co-morbidity factor. And, of course, having a serious illness is in itself stressful.

We also have limited our review to articles published since 2005, although there were literally thousands of studies published on guided imagery and hypnosis between 1975 and 2005. Many of these are reviewed in an excellent article by James Stewart, M.D. from the Mayo Clinic (Stewart 2005). Another good resource for earlier literature is *The Best Alternative Medicine* by Kenneth Pelletier, Ph.D., M.D., in which he states:

> Of all the CAM interventions, Mind Body medicine is supported by the greatest body of scientific evidence for the greatest number of conditions for the largest number of people. It has also gained the widest acceptance within the conventional healthcare system. (Pelletier 2002, p.59)

To offer a quick visual summary of this literature, we have organized the research in Table 6.1. Note that many of these articles are themselves meta-analyses or reviews.

Again, this is by no means a comprehensive review of the literature. There are many more studies, which address medical conditions as diverse as urge incontinence, migraine headaches, irritable bowel syndrome, and addiction issues.

Table 6.1: Summary of Clinical Research on
Guided Imagery or Hypnosis Since 2005

Condition	Author, year	Type
Pain	Bernardy *et al.* 2011	M, Rv
	Berger *et al.* 2010	Ra
	Butler *et al.* 2009	Ra
	Chen and Francis 2010	Pi
	Elkins, Jensen, and Patterson 2007 Elkins,	Rv
	Johnson, and Fisher 2012	Rv
	Hammond 2007	Rv
	Menzies *et al.* 2014	Ra
	Pölkki *et al.* 2008	Ra, Pi
	Rogovik and Goldman 2007	Rv
	Sheinfeld-Gorin *et al.* 2012	M
	Syrjala *et al.* 2014	Rv
Stress, anxiety, depression	Apóstolo and Kolcaba 2009	O
	Armitage 2012	Pc, Ra
	Arora *et al.* 2011	Pc, Ra, Pr
	Cardeña, Svensson, and Hejdström 2013	Ra
	Hammond 2010	Rv
	Iglesias *et al.* 2012	Pc, Ra
	Jain *et al.* 2012	Ra
	Kip *et al.* 2013	Ra
	Lee and Kwon 2013	Pc, Ra
	Marc *et al.* 2011	Rv
	Mizrahi *et al.* 2012	Ra, Pr
	Purohit *et al.* 2013	O
	Shih, Yang, and Koo 2009	M
	Spiegel 2013	Rv
	Watanabe *et al.* 2006	O

Sleep	Casement and Swanson 2012	M
	Cook *et al.* 2010	Pc, Ra
	Davis *et al.* 2011	Ra
	Escamilla *et al.* 2012	Rv
	Hansen *et al.* 2013	M
	Harb *et al.* 2012	O
	Harb *et al.* 2013	Rv
	Krakow and Zadra 2006	Rv
	Loft and Cameron 2013	Pc, Ra
	Long *et al.* 2011	O
	Margolies *et al.* 2013	Ra
	Nadorff, Lambdin, and Germain 2014	Rv
	Nappi *et al.* 2010	O
	Schaffer *et al.* 2013	O
	Schoenfeld, Deviva, and Manber 2012	Rv
	Thünker and Pietrowsky 2012	Ra
Cancer	Carlson, L.E., 2008	Rv
	Cramer *et al.* 2015	Rv
	Eremin *et al.* 2009	Ra
	Figueroa-Moseley *et al.* 2007	Rv
	Freeman *et al.* 2008	O
	Freeman, L.W., 2014	Ra
	Kang *et al.* 2011	O
	Kravits 2013	Rv
	Mayden 2012	Rv
	Montgomery *et al.* 2014	Ra
	Montgomery, Schnur, and Kravits 2013	Rv
	Nunes *et al.* 2007	Ra
	Sheinfeld-Gorin *et al.* 2012	M
Pediatrics	Adinolfi and Gava 2014	Rv
	Butler *et al.* 2005	Pc
	Huet *et al.* 2011	Pc
	Kuttner 2012	Rv
	Stein, Sonty, and Savoyan 2012	O, Rv
	St-Onge, Mercier, and De Koninck 2009	Ra
Infection/ immunity	Barabasz *et al.* 2010	Pi
	Eremin *et al.* 2009	Pc, Ra
	Jones *et al.* 2014	Ra
	Lengacher *et al.* 2008	Pi
	Trakhtenberg 2008	Rv
	Wahbeh *et al.* 2009	Rv

Medical procedures	Butler *et al.* 2005	Ra
	Catoire *et al.* 2013	Ra, Pr
	Flory, Salazar, and Lang 2007	M
	Griffiths 2014	O
	Iserson 2014	Rv
	Nelson *et al.* 2013	Rv
	Schnur *et al.* 2008	M
	Varga 2013	Rv
Pregnancy and childbirth	Beebe 2014	O
	Fink *et al.* 2011	Pc, Ra
	Granger 2012	O
	Jallo *et al.* 2009	Pc, Ra
	Jallo *et al.* 2014	Pr
	Marc *et al.* 2011	M
	Urech *et al.* 2010	Pc, Ra
Eating disorders/ weight loss	Hamilton *et al.* 2013	O, Pi
	May *et al.* 2010	O
	Somerville and Cooper 2007	O
	Tatham 2011	Rv
	Weigensberg *et al.* 2014	Ra, Pi
Preparation for and recovery from surgery	Broadbent *et al.* 2012	Ra
	Charette *et al.* 2014	Pi
	Diaz and Larsen 2005	Ra
	Gonzales *et al.* 2010	Ra, Pr
	Hildebrand and Anderson 2011	Rv
	Kekecs *et al.* 2014	Ra
	Kshettry *et al.* 2006	Ra
	Lim, Yobas, and Chen 2014	O
	Lin 2012	Pi
	Maddison *et al.* 2012	Ra
	Pellino *et al.* 2005	Ra
	Shenefelt 2013	Ra
	Schwab *et al.* 2007	O
	Stein *et al.* 2010	Pi
	Thomas and Sethares 2010	Ra
Rv=Review, M=Meta-analysis, Ra=Randomized, O=Observational, Pc=Placebo controlled, Pi=Pilot, Pr=Prospective		

Imagery-Laden Language in the Clinical Setting

It is important in guided imagery practice for clinicians to pay attention to the client's imagery-laden language in their history taking with patients. When people refer to their back as "irritated" or their headaches as "explosive," these terms may indicate emotional aspects involved in their symptoms and their management.

An extreme example is a patient who had been dealing rather successfully with a rare type of leukemia for over four years. He consulted one of the authors wondering if there were any nutritional or mind/body factors that could help him deal even more effectively with his disease. When giving his history, he twice referred to his oncologist as "Dr. Doom." When asked why he called him that, he said, "Every time I see him, he reminds me that no matter what I do, I will die from this disease." When asked how that affected him, he replied, "It's so depressing. It takes me days to recover from every visit with him." When asked why he continued to see him, he said, "Oh, he's really an expert in leukemia."

We informed him that there were many great doctors in our area who were experts in this type of leukemia, and who would be much more encouraging of his attempts to maintain and restore his health. We pointed out that if he didn't have to fight against that message all the time, he might have more energy to use for living well and taking good care of himself. He was immensely relieved and ultimately changed his oncologist to someone who addressed his disease expertly but also treated his whole person with respect and encouragement.

Safety Concerns

Guided imagery is generally a very safe intervention, but there are precautions that need to be observed. Patients with a history of psychosis or other mental illness who have difficulty differentiating the internal world of imagery from the external world need to be treated with expertise with respect to both imagery and the treatment of their condition. Patients who have dissociative disorders from traumatic etiology also need to be treated skillfully, and should work with someone with training and experience in both trauma therapy and guided imagery. Imagery can be very helpful but can also be disorganizing if explorative methods are used without adequate preparation and guidance. Patients with traumatic backgrounds may also become more anxious as they are invited to relax or even to close their eyes, which is a sign to ask about trauma and seek more expert care if imagery is to be used.

The only other significant risk of using imagery is the potential for minimizing the seriousness of symptoms or using imagery in lieu of necessary medical care. We have seen patients with treatable cancers who avoided medical or surgical treatment because they were convinced that they could cure the disease using only their thoughts and mind/body approaches. We advise making every effort to steer such clients at the very least into an intensive monitoring situation so that they do not ignore the progression of their disease until it is too late for appropriate medical treatment.

Imagery and guided imagery are mind/body approaches that can realistically encourage and empower patients in their own self-care and help them deal with multiple sources of stress in their lives and medical encounters. When used responsibly, they are safe interventions that are compatible with almost every other form of medicine and healing. Imagery is a relatively direct and easy-to-learn way to set healing goals, find healing paths, encourage confidence in the body's ability to heal, and adapt to any limitations or losses.

Guided imagery is useful in almost any medical situation where stress is an issue. Unmanaged and prolonged stress can precipitate disease events and amplify and exacerbate symptoms. While stress does not cause all disease, it is almost always a significant co-morbid factor, since being ill is stressful in itself.

Guided imagery can be learned from audio recordings, classes, or in one-on-one therapeutic relationships. It is such a useful adjunct to medical care that it should be part of the standard of care wherever medical care is provided.

References

Adinolfi, B. and Gava N. (2013) "Controlled outcome studies of child clinical hypnosis." *Acta Bio-medica 84*, 2, 94–7.

Apóstolo J.L. and Kolcaba, K. (2009) "The effects of guided imagery on comfort, depression, anxiety, and stress of psychiatric inpatients with depressive disorders." *Archives of Psychiatric Nursing 23*, 6, 403–411.

Armitage C.J. (2012) "Evidence that process simulations reduce anxiety in patients receiving dental treatment: Randomized exploratory trial." *Anxiety, Stress, and Coping 25*, 2, 155–165.

Arora, S., Aggarwal, R., Moran, A., Sirimanna, P., *et al.* (2011) "Mental practice: effective stress management training for novice surgeons." *Journal of American College of Surgeons 212*, 2, 225–233.

Barabasz, A., Higley, L., Christensen, C., and Barabasz, M. (2010) "Efficacy of hypnosis in the treatment of human papillomavirus (HPV) in women: Rural and urban samples." *International Journal of Clinical and Experimental Hypnosis 58*, 1, 102–121.

Barber, T.X. (1965) "Measuring 'hypnotic-like' suggestibility with and without hypnotic induction: Psychometric properties, norms, and variables influencing response to the Barber Suggestibility Scale (BSS)." *Psychological Reports 16*, Monograph Suppl. 3, 809–844.

Beebe, K.R. (2014) "Hypnotherapy for labor and birth." *Nursing for Women's Health 18*, 1, 48–58.

Berger, M.M., Davadant, M., Marin, C., Wasserfallen, J.B., *et al.* (2010) "Impact of a pain protocol including hypnosis in major burns." *Burns: Journal of the International Society for Burn Injuries 36*, 5, 639–646.

Bernardy, K., Füber, N., Klose, P., and Häuser, W. (2011) "Efficacy of hypnosis/guided imagery in fibromyalgia syndrome: A systematic review and meta-analysis of controlled trials." *Musculoskeletal Disorders 12*, 133.

Broadbent, E., Kahokehr, A., Booth, R.J., Thomas, J., *et al.* (2012) "A brief relaxation intervention reduces stress and improves surgical wound healing response: A randomised trial." *Brain, Behavior, and Immunity 26*, 2, 212–217.

Butler, L.D., Koopman, C., Neri, E., Giese-Davis, J., *et al.* (2009) "Effects of supportive-expressive group therapy on pain in women with metastatic breast cancer." *Health Psychology 28*, 5, 579–587.

Butler, L.D., Symons, B.K., Henderson, S.L., Shortliffe, L.D., and Spiegel, D. (2005) "Hypnosis reduces distress and duration of an invasive medical procedure for children." *Pediatrics 115*, 1, 77–85.

Cardeña, E., Svensson, C., and Hejdström, F. (2013) "Hypnotic tape intervention ameliorates stress: A randomized, control study." *International Journal of Clinical and Experimental Hypnosis 61*, 2, 125–145.

Carlson, L.E. and Bultz, B.D. (2008) "Mind-body interventions in oncology." *Current Treatment Options in Oncology 9*, 2–3, 127–134.

Casement, M.D. and Swanson, L.M. (2012) "A meta-analysis of imagery rehearsal for post-trauma nightmares: Effects on nightmare frequency, sleep quality, and posttraumatic stress." *Clinical Psychology Review 32*, 6, 566–574.

Catoire, P., Delaunay, L., Dannappel, T., Baracchini, D., *et al.* (2013) "Hypnosis versus diazepam for embryo transfer: A randomized controlled study." *American Journal of Clinical Hypnosis 55*, 4, 378–86.

Charette, S., Fiola, J.L., Charest, M.C., Villeneuve, E., *et al.* (2014) "Guided imagery for adolescent post-spinal fusion pain management: A pilot study." *Pain Management Nursing 16*, 3, 211–220.

Chen, Y.L., and Francis, A.J. (2010) "Relaxation and imagery for chronic, nonmalignant pain: Effects on pain symptoms, quality of life, and mental health." *Pain Management Nursing 11*, 3, 159–68.

Cook, J.M., Harb, G.C., Gehrman, P.R., Cary, M.S., *et al.* (2010) "Imagery rehearsal for posttraumatic nightmares: A randomized controlled trial." *Journal of Traumatic Stress 23*, 5, 553–563.

Cramer, H., Lauche, R., Paul, A., Langhorst, J., Kümmel, S., and Dobos, G.J. (2015) "Hypnosis in breast cancer care: A systematic review of randomized controlled trials." *Integrative Cancer Therapies 14*, 1, 5–15.

Davis, J.L., Rhudy, J.L., Pruiksma, K.E., Byrd, P., *et al.* (2011) "Physiological predictors of response to exposure, relaxation, and rescripting therapy for chronic nightmares in a randomized clinical trial." *Journal of Clinical Sleep Medicine 7*, 6, 622–631.

Diaz, M. and Larsen B. (2005) "Preparing for successful surgery: An implementation study." *The Permanente Journal 9*, 3, 23–27.

Elkins, G., Jensen, M.P., and Patterson, D.R. (2007) "Hypnotherapy for the management of chronic pain." *International Journal of Clinical and Experimental Hypnosis 55*, 3, 275–287.

Elkins, G., Johnson, A., and Fisher, W. (2012) "Cognitive hypnotherapy for pain management." *American Journal of Clinical Hypnosis 54*, 4, 294–310.

Eremin, O., Walker, M.B., Simpson, E., Heys, S.D., *et al.* (2009) "Immuno-modulatory effects of relaxation training and guided imagery in women with locally advanced breast cancer undergoing multimodality therapy: A randomised controlled trial." *Breast 18*, 1, 17–25.

Escamilla, M., LaVoy, M., Moore, B.A., and Krakow, B. (2012) "Management of post-traumatic nightmares: A review of pharmacologic and nonpharmacologic treatments since 2010." *Current Psychiatry Reports 14*, 5, 529–535.

Figueroa-Moseley, C., Jean-Pierre, P., Roscoe, J.A., Ryan, J.L., *et al.* (2007) "Behavioral interventions in treating anticipatory nausea and vomiting." *Journal of the National Comprehensive Cancer Network 5*, 1, 44–50.

Fink, N.S., Urech, C., Isabel, F., Meyer, A., *et al.* (2011) "Fetal response to abbreviated relaxation techniques: A randomized controlled study." *Journal of Early Human Development 87*, 2, 121–27.

Flory, N., Salazar, G.M., and Lang, E.V. (2007) "Hypnosis for acute distress management during medical procedures." *International Journal of Clinical and Experimental Hypnosis 55*, 3, 303–317.

Freeman, L., Cohen, L., Stewart, M., White, R., *et al.* (2008) "The experience of imagery as a post-treatment intervention in patients with breast cancer: Program, process, and patient recommendations." *Oncology Nursing Forum 35*, 6, E116–121.

Freeman, L.W., White, R., Ratcliff, C.G., Sutton, S., *et al.* (2014) "A randomized trial comparing live and telemedicine deliveries of an imagery-based behavioral intervention for breast cancer survivors: Reducing symptoms and barriers to care." *Psychooncology*. Available at www.ncbi.nlm.nih.gov/pubmed/25146413, accessed on June 27 2015.

Gonzales, E.A., Ledesma, R.J., McAllister, D.J., Perry, S.M., Dyer, C.A., and Maye, J.P. (2010) "Effects of guided imagery on postoperative outcomes in patients undergoing same-day surgical procedures: A randomized, single-blind study." *AANA Journal 78*, 3, 181–188.

Granger, S. (2012) "Hypnotherapy for childbirth." *The Practicing Midwife 15*, 8, S13–14.

Griffiths, M. (2014) "Hypnosis for dental anxiety." *Dental Update 41*, 1, 78–80, 83.

Hamilton, J., Fawson, S., May, J., Andrade, J., and Kavanagh, D.J. (2013) "Brief guided imagery and body scanning interventions reduce food cravings." *Appetite 71*, 158–162.

Hammond, D.C. (2007) "Review of the efficacy of clinical hypnosis with headaches and migraines." *International Journal of Clinical and Experimental Hypnosis 55*, 2, 207–219.

Hammond, D.C. (2010) "Hypnosis in the treatment of anxiety and stress-related disorders." *Expert Review of Neurotherapeutics 10*, 2, 263–273.

Hansen, K., Höfling, V., Kröner-Borowik, T., Stangier, U., and Steil, R. (2013) "Efficacy of psychological interventions aiming to reduce chronic nightmares: A meta-analysis." *Clinical Psychology Review 33*, 1, 146–155.

Harb, G.C., Phelps, A.J., Forbes, D., Ross, R.J., Gehrman, P.R., and Cook, J.M. (2013) "A critical review of the evidence base of imagery rehearsal for posttraumatic nightmares: Pointing the way for future research." *Journal of Traumatic Stress 26*, 5, 570–579.

Harb, G.C., Thompson, R., Ross, R.J., and Cook, J.M. (2012) "Combat-related PTSD nightmares and imagery rehearsal: Nightmare characteristics and relation to treatment outcome." *Journal of Traumatic Stress 25*, 5, 511–518.

Hildebrand, L.E., and Anderson, R.C. (2011) "Hypnosis and relaxation in the context of plastic surgery nursing." *Plastic Surgical Nursing 31*, 1, 5–8.

Horowitz, M.J. (1978) *Image Formation and Cognition,* 2nd edition. New York, NY: Appleton-Century-Crofts.

Huet, A., Lucas-Polomeni, M.M., Robert, J.C., Sixou, J.L., and Wodey, E. (2011) "Hypnosis and dental anesthesia in children: A prospective controlled study." *International Journal of Clinical and Experimental Hypnosis 59*, 4, 424–440.

Iglesias, S.L., Azzara, S., Argibay, J.C., Arnaiz, M.L., *et al.* (2012) "Psychological and physiological response of students to different types of stress management programs." *American Journal of Health Promotion 26*, 6, E149–158.

Iserson, K.V. (2014) "An hypnotic suggestion: Review of hypnosis for clinical emergency care." *Journal of Emergency Medicine 46*, 4, 588–596.

Jain, S., McMahon, G.F., Hasen, P., Kozub, M.P., *et al.* (2012) "Healing touch with guided imagery for PTSD in returning active duty military: A randomized controlled trial." *Military Medicine 177*, 9, 1015–1021.

Jallo, N., Bourguignon, C., Taylor, A.G., Ruiz, J., and Goehler, L. (2009) "The biobehavioral effects of relaxation guided imagery on maternal stress." *Advances in Mind Body Medicine 24*, 4, 12–22.

Jallo, N., Ruiz, R.J., Elswick, R.K. Jr., and French, E. (2014) "Guided imagery for stress and symptom management in pregnant African American women." *Evidence-Based Complementary and Alternative Medicine.* Available at www.ncbi.nlm.nih.gov/pmc/articles/PMC3955623, accessed on June 27 2015.

Jones, D., Owens, M., Kumar, M., Cook, R., and Weiss, S.M. (2014) "The effect of relaxation interventions on cortisol levels in HIV-seropositive women." *Journal of the International Association for Providing AIDS Care 13*, 4, 318–323.

Kang, D.H., McArdle, T., Park, N.J., Weaver, M.T., Smith, B., and Carpenter, J. (2011) "Dose effects of relaxation practice on immune responses in women newly diagnosed with breast cancer: An exploratory study." *Oncology Nursing Forum 38*, 3, E240–252.

Kekecs, Z., Jakubovits, E., Varga, K., and Gombos, K. (2014) "Effects of patient education and therapeutic suggestions on cataract surgery patients: A randomized controlled clinical trial." *Patient Education and Counseling 94*, 1, 116–122.

Kip, K.E., Rosenzweig, L., Hernandez, D.F., Shuman, A., Sullivan, K.L., *et al.* (2013) "Randomized controlled trial of accelerated resolution therapy (ART) for symptoms of combat-related post-traumatic stress disorder (PTSD)." *Military Medicine 178*, 12, 1298–1309.

Krakow, B. and Zadra, A. (2006) "Clinical management of chronic nightmares: Imagery rehearsal therapy." *Behavioral Sleep Medicine 4*, 1, 45–70.

Kravits, K. (2013) "Hypnosis: Adjunct therapy for cancer pain management." *Journal of the Advanced Practitioner of Oncology 4*, 2, 83–88.

Kshettry, V.R., Carole, L.F., Henly, S.J., Sendelbach, S., and Kummer, B. (2006) "Complementary alternative medical therapies for heart surgery patients: Feasibility, safety, and impact." *Annals of Thoracic Surgery 81*, 1201–1205.

Kuttner, L. (2012) "Pediatric hypnosis: pre-, peri-, and post-anesthesia." *Paediatric Anaesthesia 22*, 6, 573–577.

Lee. S.W., and Kwon, J.H. (2013) "The efficacy of imagery rescripting (IR) for social phobia: A randomized controlled trial." *Journal of Behavioral Therapy and Experimental Psychiatry 44*, 4, 351–360.

Lengacher, C.A., Bennett, M.P., Gonzalez, L., Gilvary, D., *et al.* (2008) "Immune responses to guided imagery during breast cancer treatment." *Biological Research for Nursing 9*, 3, 205–214.

Lim, Y.C., Yobas, P., and Chen, H.C. (2014) "Efficacy of relaxation intervention on pain, self-efficacy, and stress-related variables in patients following total knee replacement surgery." *Pain Management Nursing 15*, 4, 888–896.

Lin, P.C. (2012) "An evaluation of the effectiveness of relaxation therapy for patients receiving joint replacement surgery." *Journal of Clinical Nursing 21*, 5–6, 601–608.

Loft, M.H., and Cameron, L.D. (2013) "Using mental imagery to deliver self-regulation techniques to improve sleep behaviors." *Annals of Behavioral Medicine 46*, 3, 260–272.

Long, M.E., Hammons, M.E., Davis, J.L., Frueh, B.C., *et al.* (2011) "Imagery rescripting and exposure group treatment of posttraumatic nightmares in Veterans with PTSD." *Journal of Anxiety Disorders 25*, 4, 531–535.

Maddison, R., Prapavessis, H., Clatworthy, M., Hall, C., *et al.* (2012) "Guided imagery to improve functional outcomes post-anterior cruciate ligament repair: Randomized-controlled pilot trial." *Scandinavian Journal of Medical Science in Sports 22*, 6, 816–821.

Marc, I., Toureche, N., Ernst, E., Hodnett, E.D., *et al.* (2011) "Mind-body interventions during pregnancy for preventing or treating women's anxiety." *Cochrane Database Systems Review 7*, CD007559.

Margolies, S.O., Rybarczyk, B., Vrana, S.R., Leszczyszyn, D.J., and Lynch, J. (2013) "Efficacy of a cognitive-behavioral treatment for insomnia and nightmares in Afghanistan and Iraq veterans with PTSD." *Journal of Clinical Psychology 69*, 10, 1026–1042.

May, J., Andrade, J., Batey, H., Berry, L.M., and Kavanagh, D.J. (2010) "Less food for thought: Impact of attentional instructions on intrusive thoughts about snack foods." *Appetite 55*, 2, 279–287.

Mayden, K.D. (2012) "Mind-body therapies: Evidence and implications in advanced oncology practice." *Journal of the Advanced Practitioner in Oncology 3*, 6, 357–373.

Menzies, V., Lyon, D.E., Elswick, R.K. Jr., McCain, N.L., and Gray, D.P. (2014) "Effects of guided imagery on biobehavioral factors in women with fibromyalgia." *Journal of Behavioral Medicine 37*, 1, 70–80.

Mizrahi, M.C., Reicher-Atir, R., Levy, S., Haramati, S., *et al.* (2012) "Effects of guided imagery with relaxation training on anxiety and quality of life among patients with inflammatory bowel disease." *Psychology and Health 27*, 12, 1463–1479.

Montgomery, G.H., David, D., Kangas, M., Green, S., *et al.* (2014) "Randomized controlled trial of a cognitive-behavioral therapy plus hypnosis intervention to control fatigue in patients undergoing radiotherapy for breast cancer." *Journal of Clinical Oncology 32*, 6, 557–563.

Montgomery, G.H., Schnur, J.B., and Kravits, K. (2013) "Hypnosis for cancer care: Over 200 years young." *CA: A Cancer Journal for Clinicians 63*, 1, 31–44.

Nadorff, M.R., Lambdin, K.K., and Germain, A. (2014) "Pharmacological and non-pharmacological treatments for nightmare disorder." *International Review of Psychiatry 26*, 2, 225–236.

Nappi, C.M., Drummond, S.P., Thorp, S.R., and McQuaid, J.R. (2010) "Effectiveness of imagery rehearsal therapy for the treatment of combat-related nightmares in veterans." *Behavioral Therapy 41*, 2, 237–244.

Nelson, E.A., Dowsey, M.M., Knowles, S.R., Castle, D.J., *et al.* (2013) "Systematic review of the efficacy of pre-surgical mind-body based therapies on post-operative outcome measures." *Complementary Therapies in Medicine 21*, 6, 697–711.

Nunes, D.F., Rodriguez, A.L., da Silva Hoffmann, F., Luz, C., *et al.* (2007) "Relaxation and guided imagery program in patients with breast cancer undergoing radiotherapy is not associated with neuroimmunomodulatory effects." *Journal of Psychosomatic Research 63*, 6, 647–655.

Pelletier, K.R. (2002) *The Best Alternative Medicine*. New York, NY: Touchstone.

Pellino, T.A., Gordon, D.B., Engelke, Z.K., Busse, K.L., Collins, M.A., Silver, C.E., and Norcross, N.J. (2005) "Use of nonpharmacologic interventions for pain and anxiety after total hip and total knee arthroplasty." *Orthopedic Nursing 24*, 3, 182–190.

Pölkki, T., Pietilä, A.M., Vehviläinen-Julkunen, K., Laukkala, H., and Kiviluoma, K. (2008) "Imagery-induced relaxation in children's postoperative pain relief: A randomized pilot study." *Journal of Pediatric Nursing 23*, 3, 217–224.

Purohit, M.P., Wells, R.E., Zafonte, R., Davis, R.B., Yeh, G.Y., and Phillips, R.S. (2013) "Neuropsychiatric symptoms and the use of mind-body therapies." *Journal of Clinical Psychiatry 74*, 6, E520–526.

Rogovik, A.L., and Goldman, R.D. (2007) "Hypnosis for treatment of pain in children." *Canadian Family Physician 53*, 5, 823–825.

Schaffer, L., Jallo, N., Howland, L., James, K., Glaser, D., and Arnell, K. (2013) "Guided imagery: An innovative approach to improving maternal sleep quality." *Journal of Perinatal and Neonatal Nursing 27*, 2, 151–159.

Schnur, J.B., Kafer, I., Marcus, C., and Montgomery, G.H. (2008) "Hypnosis to manage distress related to medical procedures: A meta-analysis." *Contemporary Hypnosis 25*, 3–4, 114–128.

Schoenfeld, F.B., Deviva, J.C., and Manber, R. (2012) "Treatment of sleep disturbances in posttraumatic stress disorder: A review." *Journal of Rehabilitation Research and Development 49*, 5, 729–752.

Schwab, D., Davies, D., Bodtker, T., Anaya, L., Johnson, K., and Chaves, M. (2007) "A study of efficacy and cost-effectiveness of guided imagery as a portable, self-administered, presurgical intervention delivered by a health plan." *Advances in Mind Body Medicine 22*, 1, 8–14.

Sheinfeld-Gorin, S., Krebs, P., Badr, H., Janke, E.A., *et al.* (2012) "Meta-analysis of psychosocial interventions to reduce pain in patients with cancer." *Journal of Clinical Oncology 30*, 5, 539–547.

Shenefelt, P.D. (2013) "Anxiety reduction using hypnotic induction and self-guided imagery for relaxation during dermatologic procedures." *International Journal of Clinical and Experimental Hypnosis 61*, 3, 305–318.

Shih, M., Yang, Y.H., and Koo, M. (2009) "A meta-analysis of hypnosis in the treatment of depressive symptoms: A brief communication." *International Journal of Clinical and Experimental Hypnosis 57*, 4, 31–42.

Somerville, K. and Cooper, M. (2007) "Using imagery to identify and characterise core beliefs in women with bulimia nervosa, dieting and non-dieting women." *Eating Behaviors 8*, 4, 450–456.

Spiegel, D. (2013) "Tranceformations: Hypnosis in brain and body." *Depression and Anxiety 30*, 4, 342–352.

St-Onge, M., Mercier, P., and De Koninck, J. (2009) "Imagery rehearsal therapy for frequent nightmares in children." *Behavioral Sleep Medicine 7*, 2, 81–98.

Stein, T.R., Olivo, E.L., Grand, S.H., Namerow, P.B., Costa, J., and Oz, M.C. (2010) "A pilot study to assess the effects of a guided imagery audiotape intervention on psychological outcomes in patients undergoing coronary artery bypass graft surgery." *Holistic Nursing Practice 24*, 4, 213–222.

Stein, T.R., Sonty, N., and Saroyan, J.M. (2012) "Scratching beneath the surface: An integrative psychosocial approach to pediatric pruritus and pain." *Clinical Child Psychology and Psychiatry 17*, 1, 33–47.

Stewart, J.G. (2005) "Hypnosis in contemporary medicine." *Mayo Clinic Proceedings 80*, 4, 511–524.

Syrjala, K.L., Jensen, M.P., Mendoza, M.E., Yi, J.C., Fisher, H.M., and Keefe, F.J. (2014) "Psychological and behavioral approaches to cancer pain management." *Journal of Clinical Oncology 32*, 16, 1703–1711.

Tatham, M. (2011) "The role of imagery-based techniques in cognitive-behavioural therapy for adults with eating disorders." *Clinical Psychology Review 31*, 7, 1101–1109.

Thomas, K.M., and Sethares, K.A. (2010) "Is guided imagery effective in reducing pain and anxiety in the postoperative total joint arthroplasty patient?" *Orthopedic Nursing 29*, 6, 393–399.

Thünker, J. and Pietrowsky, R. (2012) "Effectiveness of a manualized imagery rehearsal therapy for patients suffering from nightmare disorders with and without a comorbidity of depression or PTSD." *Behaviour Research and Therapy 50*, 9, 558–564.

Trakhtenberg, E.C. (2008) "The effects of guided imagery on the immune system: A critical review." *International Journal of Neuroscience 118*, 6, 839–855.

Urech, C., Fink, N.S., Hoesli, I., Wilhelm, F.H., Bitzer, J., and Alder, J. (2010) "Effects of relaxation on psychobiological well-being during pregnancy: A randomized controlled trial." *Psychoneuroendocrinology 35*, 9, 1348–1355.

Varga, K. (2013) "Suggestive techniques connected to medical interventions." *Interventional Medicine and Applied Science 5*, 3, 95–100.

Wahbeh, H., Haywood, A., Kaufman, K., and Zwickey, H. (2009) "Mind-Body Medicine and Immune System Outcomes: A systematic review." *The Open Complementary Medicine Journal 1*, 25–34.

Watanabe, E., Fukuda, S., Hara, H., Maeda, Y., Ohira, H., and Shirakawa, T. (2006) "Differences in relaxation by means of guided imagery in a healthy community sample." *Alternative Therapies in Health and Medicine 12*, 2, 60–66.

Weigensberg, M.J., Lane, C.J., Ávila, Q., Konersman, K., *et al.* (2014) "Imagine HEALTH: Results from a randomized pilot lifestyle intervention for obese Latino adolescents using Interactive Guided Imagery^SM." *Complementary and Alternative Medicine 14*, 28.

Chapter 7

Relieving Pain Through Mental Imagery

David Pincus and Anees A. Sheikh

Pain is as strange as it is commonplace. Indeed, it is the most common complaint in primary medicine, and chronic pain impacts about one in every five people worldwide (Toth, Lander, and Wiebe 2009), costing $61.2 billion each year in lost productivity in the United States alone (Stewart *et al.* 2003). Beyond the chronic sufferers, we all experience pain from time to time; it is as ubiquitous as it is punishing. In modern Western societies, one's image of pain is almost invariably tied up with images of modern medical treatment, doctors, pills, medical technology, and so on. In the Western worldview, pain is associated with the body and is typically assumed to be a physical experience.

Yet pain is not entirely physical; it isn't even mostly physical. Pain experiences are essentially private and subjective. Certainly, our pain perception may emerge from damage to bodily tissue. But it can also emerge when there is no tissue damage whatsoever, as in *central pain* and *phantom pain* syndromes. In addition to tissue damage, our pain perception may be influenced by virtually any other subjective experience we are having, as long as that experience is connected to our emotional state or our sense of life's meaning (Melzack and Wall 1965, 1996). Levels of fatigue, anxiety, sadness, hope, self-concept, and interpersonal relationships have each been found to independently influence pain perception (for a review, see Pincus and Sheikh 2009).

Pain lies at the crux of the conflict between Cartesian dualism and modern medical assumptions on the one hand, and the uncommon allies of modern science and ancient wisdom on the other. The remnants of the absurd belief that mind and body are distinct still work within the culture of modern medicine to blind patients and practitioners alike to the fact that pain is *not* primarily caused by physical damage to the body; nor is it uniquely or ideally treated with material interventions alone. Buried deep beneath this fundamental conflict we can find the largely overlooked benefits of guided imagery for pain relief.

Imagination and "Physical Pain": Is It All in Your Head?

There are a fair number of empirical studies on a variety of clinical pain populations, each pointing to the conclusion that guided imagery is effective in reducing pain, increasing pain tolerance, and improving broader quality of life (see Pincus and Sheikh 2009 for a review). Nevertheless, from a skeptical modern health-science perspective, most of these studies can be correctly criticized as being outdated and methodologically crude when compared to the highest modern standards of clinical proof: repeated, large-scale, and well-controlled randomized clinical trials (RCTs).

On the other hand, proponents of guided imagery as an intervention for pain can rightly counter that:

- imagery for pain management tends to be neglected in this high-stakes health-science context

- a lack of testing at a modern level and scale only indicates an *absence* of evidence, not evidence *against* imagery

- the evidence that has been gathered should be considered in the meanwhile—and it is genuinely compelling.

Interestingly, the positive results of these smaller-scale applied studies become less convincing when read in greater detail. For example, in a pioneering study, Philips and Hunter (1981) treated a group of patients with chronic and severe headaches using relaxation training over an eight-week period: half of the patients used visual imagery along with the standard relaxation procedures (deep breathing and muscle contraction exercises). The study's goal was to determine if imagery worked better than relaxation alone. In dramatic fashion, the imagery-plus-relaxation group's headache intensity dropped by 300 percent, the number of headaches per week dropped by 100 percent, duration dropped by 25 percent, emotional distress dropped by 100 percent, avoiding activities and complaining about pain decreased by 75 percent, depression about pain dropped by 90 percent, and sense of control in reducing pain increased by 300 percent. Subsequent studies have shown similar magnitudes of positive change. Most clinicians would be pleased to observe results of this scale on average across their patients, particularly after only eight weeks of extremely simple guided imagery that is essentially focused on enhancing relaxation.

However, the only *statistical difference* they found between the groups was that the imagery group had more improvement in depression and sense of control over their pain. So in a strict scientific sense, imagery won over relaxation alone, but only in a very limited sense, and only by a nose. The reason for this apparent split between clinical and statistical significance lies in the fact that the researchers had only eight people in each group and the groups were highly heterogeneous (a sample of clinical headache pain patients with diverse etiologies, circumstances, and treatment responses). Small numbers and high variance both place tough limits on inferential statistics—even when clinical significance is robust.

Numerous other studies followed the same pattern through the next decade, producing consistent and promising results with respect to applied (external) validity, along with somewhat more limited statistical (internal) validity (for example, Achterberg, Kenner, and Lawlis 1988; Albright and Fischer 1990; Fors, Sexton, and Gotestam 2002; Gauron and Bowers 1986; Mannix *et al.* 1999; Manyande *et al.* 1995; Powers 1999; Raft, Smith, and Warren 1986; ter Kuile *et al.* 1994). In sum, research into the question, "Does it work?", including more recent systematic reviews of multiple small RCTs of guided imagery for pain, have consistently produced the conclusion that the results are *encouraging but inconclusive*—which we take as a strong endorsement for a relatively understudied, underutilized, underdog treatment like guided imagery (Baird, Murawski, and Jingwei 2010; Gansler *et al.* 2008; King 2010; Meeus *et al.* 2015; Posadzski and Ernst 2011; Posadzski *et al.* 2012; Thrane 2013).

How Does Guided Imagery Reduce Pain?

The first and most prominent modern scientific theory supporting the use of nonphysical interventions like guided imagery to reduce pain is the gate-control theory (Melzack and Wall 1965; 1996). The theory proposes that there is a physiological "gate" (the substantia gelatinosa) at the top of the spinal column that serves to regulate (open or close) pain signaling between the central (brain) and peripheral (body) nervous system. This gate theoretically opens and closes based on efferent psychological information about a person's state, specifically information from three channels: sensory/discriminative, motivational-affective, and cognitive-evaluative. This supports the notion of a variety of psychosocial etiologies of and interventions for pain. Based on this theory, any imagery technique that changes our focus of attention, emotional state, or sense of pain relevant meaning ought to have the potential to modify our experience of pain.

More recent and arguably more complex theoretical accounts have been proposed, including a broader physiological and self-regulatory theory by Melzack (1999). This is a novel theory that posits that the immune system is perceptual and is therefore able to instigate physiological corrections when our imagined health is better than our true physical health (Bedford 2012). There is also a systems-informed theory that we have developed that focuses on imagery's capacity to create open and integrated flows of biopsychosocial information that promote healing and resilience (Pincus and Sheikh 2009; Pincus and Metten 2010). These theoretical accounts are not necessarily exclusive, however, and each must accept the preponderance of evidence suggesting that pain is caused by a wide and unique array of biopsychosocial processes, including: behavioral learning, changes to sensation and perception of pain, improved pain management efficacy, improved emotional regulation, and alterations of pain-related schema (Pincus and Sheikh 2009). Changes within one or more of these psychological systems, depending on the unique presentation of each patient, may bring pain relief.

Approaches to Imagery for Pain

Guided imagery's potential when applied to pain is literally limitless, and the list of approaches that have already been formalized and disseminated to clinicians is massive—but it is also a bit scattered. Our text, *Imagery for Pain Relief*, was motivated in large part by our desire to assemble a large number of these approaches into a single source (Pincus and Sheikh 2009). Essentially, the existing approaches can be categorized by their depth, from simple techniques to the deepest techniques. The deepest techniques involve larger shifts in consciousness and more idiosyncratic patient responses. They include metaphor approaches developed by David Grove (Pincus and Sheikh 2011), eidetic psychotherapy (Ahsen 1984), Focusing (Gendlin 1996), and Ericksonian Hypnosis (Rossi 1994). Training in these approaches is well beyond the scope of this brief chapter, but descriptions can be found in Pincus and Sheikh (2009). Instead, we will focus here on understanding how clinicians can begin by using a simple approach and then make use of a variety of options for flexibly moving toward greater depth.

Simple imagery techniques for pain are the most often studied in clinical trials because they are relatively easy to standardize. They can be delivered by any qualified healthcare provider or even via audio recording. The most commonly used approach is probably relaxation, where the patient is guided through some imagined relaxation scenario. One may guide a patient to engage with the full sensory experience of a relaxing beach, to bathe in some healing substance (light or liquid), or to spend an evening in a remote mountain cabin, for those who prefer a warm fire in winter to the sun and sand of the beach.

Other simple approaches aim at simple sensory transformations (for example, Achterberg, Dossey, and Kolkmeier 1994; Barber 1996; Fernandez 1986; Syrjala and Abrams 2002), such as turning sharp pain into dull pain, inducing numbness, itchiness, or pressure instead of the presenting pain. Each of these simple sensory transformation options rely heavily on patient-compatible suggestion, and as such are virtually indistinguishable from hypnotic vignettes. In order to use sensory transformation techniques, patients must have good awareness of the sensory aspects of their pain; they also must be willing to apply attention to their pain without increased concern about the need to seek medical attention for the shifting pain experiences. For example, if numbness is experienced by some patients, they will fear that there is some further injury that is occurring, even if the imagery-induced numbness is effective in blocking out the pain. Furthermore, since the substitute sensation needs to be plausible to the patient, it cannot be too pleasant (Barber 1996). A sense of tickling, for example, is not likely to work as a replacement for a sharp stabbing pain.

With these caveats in mind, virtually any compatible suggestion can be used, and with a good working relationship, patient and guide can creatively explore many options. For example, the suggestions may aim to make pain more diffuse, spreading it to cover more body tissue, or even spreading it to the point where it fills the entire universe. Pain can be moved to different areas of the body or consciousness, or rolled into a ball that can then be manipulated in some way that is healing (for example, soaking it with water, spreading it flat, burning it, locking it up in a trunk, and burying it).

You should not be surprised if your patients go deeper than anticipated during these simple transformation procedures. Specifically, they may experience shifts within the motivation-affective or cognitive-evaluation dimensions of their pain as they are guided to examine their feelings about aspects of their imagery, or to examine what various images might mean. For example, a patient may experience a new sense of compassion and caring for herself, along with a sense of connection to important others in her life after being guided through a simple process of dulling a sense of pain with an imaginary salve. Patients may go further still, making broader self and relational shifts following changes in their pain sensations—especially if the pain is complex and if the imagery is relatively open-ended rather than scripted. As such, the sensory-discriminatory dimension of pain can be considered to serve as an entranceway into the pain system, and once inside we may find any number of relational and existential aspects that can be explicitly explored.

For patients who are prepared to go a bit further, several options are available for *deeper imagery* approaches to pain. Two of the most common approaches involve either taking a journey within the body and interacting with some bodily system to influence healing and relief, or having an encounter with the pain itself, embodied anthropomorphically as some sort of living creature. Neither approach is exclusive, of course, as it may be most practical to travel within the body to meet one's pain creature at the site where it lives within the body.

Furthermore, journeys within the imagination are outstanding methods for enhancing patient participation in and immersion within the imagery process. This is because journeys naturally engage our imagination. Such narratives will also tend to spontaneously include characters that occupy archetypal roles like hero and villain, along with morals, conflicts, and resolutions, each intrinsically related to an individual's ongoing meaning-making process of self and world. Indeed, when uncertainty is fully embraced, any number of inner journeys for relief and healing may emerge naturally and creatively during the treatment process.

The inner body travel techniques allow the individual to have direct access to physiological processes within the imagined body, by traveling in the imagination to visit pain sites. Once the patient has arrived at the pain site, many different direct or metaphoric techniques can be applied to promote relief and healing. These techniques usually begin with the instruction to step out of the body and to leave the resting or sleeping body behind, like crawling out of a shell. This technique uses an emanation: the new imagined self emanates from the original imagined self, resulting in two or more self-images. Once the individual has left the body behind, the emanation is instructed to shrink and then to enter the body through an opening like the mouth.

TRAVEL WITHIN THE BODY FOR PAIN RELIEF

Guide patients through a progressive relaxation process, such as paying attention to several deep breaths, progressive muscle relaxation, focused bodily attention with relaxation suggestions, or the equivalent. Then guide them to gradually leave their bodies and move toward a perspective outside the body where they can observe the body in its current relaxed state. It may be helpful to guide clients to notice details of the resting body, like clothing and hairstyle. Ask patients to observe this second, emanated self (that is currently outside the relaxed, inanimate body), noting clothing, hands, and other details to further increase the immersion.

Now guide patients to experience shrinking down to a size that is small enough to enter their inanimate body. Guide them through the process of entering the body through any means they prefer (for example, through an orifice like the mouth, nose, or ears; or by some creative means, like dissolving through the skin).

Guide patients on a reasonably anatomically correct journey through the body, arriving eventually at the pain site. Be sure to offer time to increase their immersion by attending to each of the various sense modalities along the way: sights, sounds, temperature, textures, wind, smells, and other perceptions. Once at the pain site, use passive guidance to inquire about any visible features of the pain itself: size, shape, texture, color, and any other features that the patient notices spontaneously.

Ask patients to make whatever interventions are necessary to improve these perceptible features of the pain. For example, if the pain is glowing bright red and hot, they may be guided to place it in a bucket of cool ice. If the pain is frozen and blue, patients can wrap it in warm towels. Ideas for transforming the pain object will ideally come from the patient though open-ended passive guidance, such as, "And what might this object need to become duller and cooler (or warmer and softer)?"

When the pain has subsided, gently guide the small-sized patients to exit their relaxed and comfortable body, leaving the pain relief intact. Guide the emanated self to reintegrate with the resting self, and gently direct them to open their eyes.

Examples from our own practice have included pain that is round and white like a soccer ball, pain in the lower back showing up as thick cables that are tied in a knot, or painful vertebrae from a slipped disc that were imaged as large, white pillowed sponges that had become dry, stiff, and cracked. Once the sensory images of the pain are clear, the transformation of those images becomes straightforward. For example, the soccer ball was eventually deflated and kicked into a goal outside of the body where it belonged; knotted cables in the lower back were loosened and untied; and pillowed sponges holding vertebrate in place were moistened and softened with a series of healing oils.

In addition to the transformation of imagery content within a journey narrative, patients can use these techniques to identify people, emotions, situations, and/or memories that are connected to the rigidities associated with the pain site. The following is a hypothetical example involving the identification and transformation of rigid and constrained emotional information through imagery.

Case Study: Michelle

Guide: As you find yourself becoming more and more relaxed, allow yourself to shrink down into your chest, shrinking smaller and smaller until you are small enough to enter the pain area. And now you are a tiny you inside your chest cavity, small enough to walk around and look at the inside of your chest and find the painful spot. As you explore this new area, notice the sounds you hear. Can you hear your heart beating? It is a relaxing thump, thump. Notice your breaths, slow and deep. Can you feel them swirl around you as you look for the painful place? You can see large thick bones, like dinosaur bones, and tendons like ropes stretching across your chest. And at last you find the site of the pain. Notice the colors and sounds that you see there. When the image becomes clear, can you describe what you see there?

Patient: I see a wall of muscle...no, it's like a woven quilt that's stretched tight. It's pulling from its edges, and in the center is a bright red bullseye where the pain is radiating. It's like a trampoline standing on its side, but it's stretched too tight. It's right in the center of my chest.

Guide: Now I want you to walk up to this bright red bullseye and touch it with your tiny finger. When you touch this bullseye, I want you to describe any sensations, feelings, thoughts, or memories that come to you.

Patient: It feels hot, and when I push it I feel like it will rip. It makes me feel angry and helpless.

Guide: Look around you to see what you can do to make the fabric looser and more flexible.

Patient: I can see a basket next to me full of fabric. I am weaving more fabric into the quilt so that it's larger and doesn't stretch so much.

Guide: And as you weave more and more fabric into the quilt, what happens to the bright red spot, to your feelings and your sensations?

Patient: The quilt is becoming looser and looser. The wind from my lungs is blowing it around, like a sheet on a clothesline. The red spot is cooling and softening. I feel calmer and the pain is decreasing.

In this example, the patient was able to quickly find a remedy in the basket of cloth. Any number of possibilities for creating healing experiences become possible once the person begins interacting with their pain site. For example, in the case above the patient could have been asked to probe for specific memories of anger and helplessness that emerged when the bullseye was pushed. Unleashing repressed emotions or transforming these imagery experiences in a meaningful way can result in a complete transformation of the imaginary landscape within the pain site, or it may simply be of psychosocial benefit to the patient, improving his or her relationships with self and others.

A common theme in the imagery literature and in our practice experience is pain that is easily represented as a pernicious creature of some sort. For example, Shone (1984) describes a detailed case study involving a patient who journeyed to the site of their pain and found a large black cat with huge teeth pulling at his spine. In this case, the patient was guided to begin a dialogue with the cat to find out what he was seeking. After several sessions, the cat became satisfied that his message had been heard, and then the cat died. Subsequent sessions were used to facilitate the healing process: images of white birds (i.e. white blood cells) devoured the cat's remains, and a crew of tiny workmen repaired the nerves.

For one of our patients, a young woman with early-onset atypical arthritis, the pain appeared as a creature similar to Golum from the *Lord of the Rings* series. After hiding and refusing to interact during an initial imagery session, the creature was later revealed to be frightened of the patient, and was only hurting her out of fear that she would cure her pain and thus kill him. With ongoing interactions with him—carried out via letters left for one another in a chest near her left hip bone—the creature was able to communicate a need for her to remember some very specific childhood memories involving her fear (for example, her first trip to the hospital as a young girl when she suffered a bad infection that preceded the onset of her arthritis). This allowed her to recommit herself to proper assertiveness and self-care now in her adulthood. After three imagery sessions, this patient reported a warm and caring relationship with her "pain Gollum." She came to appreciate that he was a displaced aspect of her inner child who was holding onto fearful memories that, when explored, would allow her to live more fully and meaningfully in adulthood. With these deeper resolutions, her arthritis flare-ups became significantly less frequent, less intense, and more manageable.

Most situations will call for a combination of simple exercises that eventually involve some aspects of the various inner-body journey techniques and interactions with pain just described. As a practitioner, your job is to provide an array of options to your patient, either in a structured discussion or during your actual imagery work. Like any relational journey, both structure and flexibility are important, as is the ability to appreciate both the destination and the trip itself.

On a professional level, each of us rare and fortunate imagery practitioners can be emboldened by the fact that the most rigorous evidence assembled within a highly constrained and resource-deprived medical research context suggests that even the most simple imagery experiences can significantly improve clinical pain. Moreover, guided imagery is perhaps the safest and most patient-empowering approach one can pursue in helping people in pain, while at the same time one of the most often ignored. With the support of science, history, and your patient's own healing resources, you can safely ask yourself, "If not me, who? If not now, when?" and take a leap of faith to explore the inner regions of your patients' imaginations. At a minimum, you can expect significant improvements in their pain, and perhaps you might also learn along with them some much deeper lessons about the true meanings bound up in our collective human experiences with pain and with suffering.

References

Achterberg, J., Dossey, B., and Kolkmeier, L. (1994) *Rituals of Healing: Using Imagery for Health and Wellness*. New York, NY: Bantam Books.

Achterberg, J., Kenner, C., and Lawlis, G.F. (1988) "Severe burn injury: A comparison of relaxation, imagery and biofeedback for pain management." *Journal of Mental Imagery 12*, 1, 71–88.

Ahsen, A. (1984) "ISM: The triple code model for imagery and psychophysiology." *Journal of Mental Imagery 8*, 4, 15–42.

Albright, G.L. and Fischer, A.A. (1990) "Effects of warming imagery aimed at trigger-point sites on tissue compliance, skin temperature, and pain sensitivity in biofeedback-trained patients with chronic pain: A preliminary study." *Perceptual and Motor Skills 71*, 1163–7770.

Baird, C.I., Murawski, M.M., and Wu, J. (2010) "Efficacy of guided imagery with relaxation for osteoarthritis symptoms and medication intake." *Pain Management Nursing 11*, 1, 56–65.

Barber, J. (1996) "Hypnotic Analgesia: Clinical Considerations." In J. Barber (ed.) *Hypnosis and Suggestion in the Treatment of Pain*. New York, NY: W.W. Norton & Company.

Bedford, F.I. (2012) "A perception theory in mind-body medicine: Guided imagery and mindful medication as cross-modal adaptation." *Psychonomic Bulletin Review 19*, 24–45.

Fernandez, E. (1986) "A classification system of cognitive coping strategies for pain." *Pain 26*, 141–151.

Fors, E.A., Sexton, H., and Gotestam, K.G. (2002) "The effect of guided imagery and amitriptyline on daily fibromyalgia pain: A prospective, randomized, controlled trial." *Journal of Psychiatric Research 36*, 179–187.

Gansler, T., Kaw, C., Crammer, C., and Smith, T. (2008) "A population-based study of prevalence of complementary methods use by cancer survivors: A report from the American Cancer Society's studies of cancer survivors." *Cancer 113*, 1048–1057.

Gauron, E.F. and Bowers, W.A. (1986) "Pain control techniques in college-age athletes." *Psychological Reports 59*, 1, 163–1169.

Gendlin, E.T. (1996) *Focusing-oriented Psychotherapy: A Manual of the Experiential Method*. New York; NY: Guilford Press.

King, K. (2010) "A review of the effects of guided imagery on cancer patients with pain." *Complementary Health Practice Review 15*, 2, 98–107.

Mannix, L.K., Chandurkar, R.S., Rybicki, L.A., Tusek, D.L., and Solomon, G.D. (1999) "Effect of guided imagery on quality of life for patients with chronic tension-type headache." *Headache 39*, 326–334.

Manyande, A., Berg, S., Gettins, D., Stanford, S.C., *et al.* (1995) "Preoperative rehearsal of active coping imagery influences subjective and hormonal responses to abdominal surgery." *Psychosomatic Medicine 57*, 177–182.

Meeus, M., Nijs, J, Vanderheiden, T., Baert, I., Descheemaeker, F., and Struyf, F. (2015) "The effect of relaxation therapy on autonomic functioning, symptoms, and daily functioning, in patients with chronic fatigue syndrome or fibromyalgia: A systematic review." *Clinical Rehabilitation 29*, 3, 221–233.

Melzack, R. (1999) "Pain and stress: A new perspective." In R.J. Gatchel and D. C. Turk (eds) *Psychosocial Factors in Pain: Critical Perspectives*. New York, NY: Guilford.

Melzack, R. and Wall, P.D. (1965) "Pain mechanisms: A new theory." *Science 150*, 971–979.

Melzack, R. and Wall, P.D. (1996) *The Challenge of Pain*, 2nd edition. London: Penguin Books.

Philips, H.C. and Hunter, M. (1981) "The treatment of tension headache: I. Muscular Abnormality and Biofeedback." *Behavior Research and Therapy 19*, 485–498.

Pincus, D. and Metten, A. (2010) "Nonlinear dynamics in biopsychosocial resilience." *Nonlinear Dynamics, Psychology, and Life Sciences 14*, 253–280.

Pincus, D. and Sheikh, A.A. (2009) *Imagery for Pain Relief: A Scientifically Grounded Guidebook for Clinicians*. New York, NY: Routledge.

Pincus, D. and Sheikh, A.A. (2011) "David Grove's metaphor therapy." *Imagination, Cognition, and Personality 30*, 259–288.

Posadzski, P. and Ernst, E. (2011) "Guided imagery for musculoskeletal pain: A systematic review of randomized clinical trials." *Clinical Journal of Pain 27*, 648–653.

Posadzski, P., Lewandowski, W., Rohini, T., Ernst, E., and Stearns, A. (2012) "Guided imagery for non-musculoskeletal pain: A systematic review of randomized clinical trials." *Journal of Pain and Symptom Management 44*, 1, 95–104.

Powers, S.W. (1999) "Empirically supported treatments in pediatric psychology: Procedure-related pain." *Journal of Pediatric Psychology 24*, 131–145.

Raft, D., Smith, R.H., and Warren, N. (1986) "Selection of imagery in the relief of chronic and acute clinical pain." *Journal of Psychosomatic Research 30*, 481–488.

Rossi, E.L. (1994) "Ericksonian Psychotherapy—Then and Now: New Fundamentals of the Naturalistic-utilization Approach." In J.K. Zeig (ed.) *Ericksonian Methods: The Essence of the Story*. Philadelphia, PA: Brunner/Mazel.

Shone, R. (1984) *Creative Vizualization: How to Use Imagery and Imagination for Self-Improvement*. New York, NY: Thorsons Publishers.

Stewart, W.F., Ricci, J.A., Chee, E., Morganstein, D., and Lipton, R. (2003) "Lost productive time and cost due to common pain conditions in the US workforce." *Journal of the American Medical Association 290*, 2443–2454.

Syrjala, K.L. and Abrams, J.R. (2002) "Hypnosis and Imagery in the Treatment of Pain." In R.J. Gatchel and D.C. Turk (eds) *Psychological Approaches to Pain Management: A Practitioner's Handbook*, 2nd edition. New York, NY: Guilford Press.

ter Kuile, M.M., Spinhoven, P., Linssen, A.C.G., Zitman, F.G., Van Dyck, R., and Rooijmans, H.G.M. (1994) "Autogenic training and cognitive self-hypnosis for the treatment of recurrent headaches in three different subject groups." *Pain 58*, 331–340.

Thrane, S. (2013) "Effectiveness of integrative modalities for pain and anxiety in children and adolescents with cancer: A systematic review." *Journal of Pediatric Oncology Nursing 20*, 6, 320–332.

Toth, C., Lander, J., and Wiebe, S. (2009) "The prevalence and impact of chronic pain with neuropathic pain symptoms in the general population." *Pain Medicine 10*, 918–929.

Chapter 8

New Cancer Imagery

Engaging Cellular Science and Ancient Wisdom

Sondra Barrett

Our scientific understanding of cancer has changed significantly since the early days, when imagery began to be used in the early 1970s as an adjunctive care strategy for cancer. The primary theory about cancer at that time, which most of us based our understanding and imagery on, was the "immune surveillance" theory. Developed by Nobel Laureate Sir Macfarlane Burnet, this model suggested that the reason we get cancer is that the immune system has become weak and can no longer recognize and destroy cancer cells. Then and now, guided imagery scripts typically focused on strengthening the immune cells to eliminate tumor cells. Pioneers Carl and Stephanie Simonton were among the first to popularize this idea of the mind-body connection and the immune system's role in cancer imagery (Simonton, Matthews-Simonton, and Creighton 1978). And while some clinical success was reported from their innovative program, research studies were lacking.

Science has now proven the immune surveillance theory to be flawed: healthy immune cells do not recognize most cancer cells because the antigenic identity of the cancer cell is no different than that of normal cells (Swann and Smyth 2007). The immune system is most effective at recognizing and protecting against tumors with a viral etiology, including melanoma, some lymphomas, and cervical cancer. In these cancers, the cancer cells often express new antigens so that immune cells can recognize them as foreign or "not-self" and will eliminate them. The common belief that cancer is the result of a single genetic error is also incorrect: we now know cancer is often the result of multiple genetic mutations (Bernstein *et al.* 2013).

The Biology of Cancer: What Is Cancer, Really?

The accepted understanding today about how cancer cells develop involves multiple genetic mutations of the growth-regulating genes, and gene expression is altered by a variety of means too complex to describe here. No wonder that imagery-enhanced immune cells did not have much impact on cancer cells. Granted, the data from numerous studies indicate that engaging in any form of cancer imagery certainly helped reduce stress, anxiety, pain, and many of the negative side effects of chemotherapy (Spiegel and Moore 1997); none showed increased lifespan or cancer reversal. More recent studies indicate that psychosocial support and imagery can provide comfort and improved quality of life (Kolcaba and Fox 1999; Roffe, Schmidt, and Ernst 2005).

I would like to propose that we begin using the latest biological understandings of cancer to inform our imagery exercises. I also integrate a psychological concept of "letting go" with biological process in my imagery exercises. Unfortunately, no research studies have yet been conducted to test the potency of any of these new imagery scripts, samples of which you'll find in this chapter. I invite you to test my ideas in your imagery practice: they may actually help people with cancer to eliminate abnormal cells, or at least to let go and soften their stress and fear using some new information and tools. I believe that by better understanding the biological processes involved in cancer, practitioners of guided imagery can write their own scripts to help their clients and patients.

THE GENE STORY: CORRECTING GENE ERRORS

Science now tells us that cancer cells arise due to genetic mutations of the growth-regulating genes. Often several gene errors may occur before a cell actually becomes a cancer cell. These cells may simply have an abnormal growth pattern. And we know that in human lung cancer, colon cancer, and breast cancer, at least five to six gene changes occur before a cell shifts from abnormal to malignant (Bernstein *et al.* 2013). Some cancers show up to 100 different genetic mutations before becoming malignant. Unfortunately, once a cell acquires numerous gene errors, it becomes unstable and is vulnerable to more gene mutations. Fortunately, at an early stage many gene errors are reversible.

Repairing DNA Mishaps

It is estimated that human cells experience an average of 10,000 mutations or instances of damage every day (Ames, Shigenaga, and Hagen 1993)—so apparently our DNA repair pathways are potent cell healers and useful strategies for eliminating potentially dangerous abnormal cells. One protective mechanism the cells use to reverse gene errors is the DNA repair process. A DNA repair pathway corrects a genetic mutation when it occurs; and if unable to repair the gene, this process causes the damaged cell to die (apoptosis). Apoptosis is actually programmed cell death, which is a property of normal genes. Yet a common error that occurs in the cancer process affects genes in the DNA repair system (Dietlein, Thelen, and Reinhardt 2014). In fact, in some human cancers the repair genes have a mutation that prevents them from programming cell death in the cancer cells. With no programmed death, the cells become immortal. The unfortunate clinical result of this mutation is that a much more aggressive therapeutic course is required to eradicate the cancer cells. Clinical research is beginning to show beneficial results with individualized immunotherapy that targets specific DNA repair defects (Dietlein *et al.* 2014). Is it possible that focusing our cancer imagery on DNA repair could change the clinical course of the illness?

Stress, Our Genes, and DNA Repair

Studies from China have shown that a daily Qigong practice improved the rate of DNA repair in cancer patients (Ming *et al.* 1993). We already know that Qigong, the parent of tai chi, and similar meditative movement practices reduce stress (Barrett 2013). We also know that stress impairs the DNA repair rate while increasing the inflammatory response (Gouin and Kiecolt-Glaser 2011). Stress reduction has been demonstrated to improve overall health and healing—so that one way Qigong may help with gene repair is by decreasing stress (Kiecolt-Glaser and Glaser 2010). And since we know that practicing imagery can also reduce stress, by adding the DNA repair option as the focus, we may be able to create a win-win set of cancer-fighting imagery exercises.

The Internal Environment: Loosening Up, Tension, Our Genes, and Letting Go

Many things in our body, mind, and the environment influence how genes are expressed. Keep in mind that all of the cells in your body have the same genes, but not all are expressed by every cell. Heart cells don't need to use the genetic information that kidney cells use, nor do the kidney cells express heart genes. So inherent in the biological nature of our cells is the ability to turn on and off different genes. A variety of factors regulates the expression of our genes: chemical messages, hormones, the physical environment, mechanical-cellular tension, food, the seasons, and even the changing shape of our cells. One basic imagery script could simply suggest that only the genes necessary for our health be expressed, and that genes be turned off if they don't contribute to our survival and good health.

Exciting research into the connections linking gene expression, mechanical tension, and regulation of cell growth was conducted in Dr. Donald Ingber's lab at Harvard University (Ingber 1998). Ingber showed that when normal cells are put in a petri dish, they attach themselves to the dish and begin to grow and stretch out to cover the surface of the dish. When they are stretched at maximum mechanical tension, they express the genes for growth and reproduction: they keep making more cells. When some of that mechanical tension is released, they let go of their tight attachment to the dish and no longer reproduce. These cells turn off the growth genes and turn on the genes they need to mature. How like a Buddhist principle: let go of attachments in order to mature (spiritually). When our cells begin to express the properties of mature cells, they no longer need to keep repeating the reproductive pattern. And when cells completely release their rigidity, mechanical tension, and attachment to the petri dish, they express another gene, which programs them to die. What might cells growing in a petri dish tell us about cancer? Rigidly attached cells are stretched, which triggers them to make more of themselves, to reproduce. Cells that soften up and let go of their tension stop growing, and they either become mature cells or program themselves to die.

Many years ago I interviewed a man who ran attitudinal-healing support groups for cancer patients. I asked him if he saw any patterns in people who remained in remission for long periods, or who experienced "unexpected" remissions. His observation was that they all had *let go of something big* like a troubled marriage or an unfulfilling job. This included my informant, who had survived stage IV lymphoma. That conversation set my mind on a course to find a healing principle in cell behavior. My *aha!* moment came when I realized that letting go emotionally could soften the body so that the cancer cells could also let go. They would no longer express growth genes, and instead could "maturely" express genes that would trigger cell death. Dr. Valerie Weaver at the University of California takes research—about how the physical environment our cells inhabit affects their gene expression—one step further. She showed that normal breast cells that are grown in hard, rigid environments become breast cancer cells; whereas breast cells grown on a rubbery, softer environment grew normally (Weaver *et al.* 1997). In fact, research is now showing that as the matrix or environment surrounding a tumor stiffens, this pushes the cells' growth further toward malignancy (Kandice *et al.* 2009). In clinical settings, research is now underway to see whether placing different materials around the tumor will affect its growth pattern. (Weaver *et al.* 1997; Ingber 2008). This is fertile ground for developing cancer-fighting imagery. See an example of the imagery exercise later in the chapter.

The property of a cell's structural tension was named *tensegrity* by Buckminster Fuller (1961). *Tensegrity* refers to any structure that maintains its integrity by balancing the forces and tensions inside and outside. The geodesic dome is a man-made structure that depends on this principle. Cells are in a constant state of movement, continuously changing their shape and balancing internal and environmental tensions—all of which intimately affects the genes that will be expressed. As we've seen, tightness sends one message to the cell, while letting go, softness, and relaxation send a different message.

Sample Imagery Scripts

I am offering several options that will allow you to interweave the current biological understandings of cancer into your own guided imagery scripts. You can easily build from these foundations and create your own metaphors:

- *Change the immune identity of the cancer cells.* In order to fulfill the requirement for immune cells to be able to eliminate cancer cells, the cancer cells must reveal new membrane markers that identify them as foreign "not-self" cells. Immune cells are then able to recognize these newly revealed foreign antigens and destroy the cells. This is apparently the case for the cancers that meet some immune destruction like melanoma or some lymphomas.

- *Fix cells for DNA repair and program cell death.* Either fix the genes for repair, or make new genes that can fix the gene mutations; or instead, program cell death of all the abnormal and cancer cells.

- *Change the internal environment* surrounding and supporting the cancer cells, softening it so that the cells no longer reproduce; and soften even more to help the cells initiate cell death.

Here are some sample exercises for beginning and ending guided visualizations that I am sure you can embellish and improve with your own perspective.

RELAXATION INDUCTION
(Prior to the imagery)

I invite you to get comfortable, find a quiet, safe place to sit or lie down. Have close at hand some drawing materials to use after your imagery journey. Close your eyes and feel where your body touches the chair or floor; feel your feet on the floor. Pay attention to your breath. Notice the flow of your breath in and out of your nostrils. With each exhalation, let go of any thoughts or tensions. Notice the temperature of your hands. Feel the flow of your breath by putting one hand on your belly and the other on your chest: notice which hand moves more. You are creating an awareness of how your body feels now, to compare with when you complete the imagery. Relax, feel your body being held by the earth, the chair, and the floor. Feel supported and safe, and know that what you experience here will do no harm. We ask for guidance for your healing to take place in the best possible way.

Go to the place in your body that feels like your center, your core. It could be your heart, your belly: you know what feels like your center. Breathe into that place. Next, bring your attention to what feels like your outside edge. Does your outer boundary stop at your skin, or does it go beyond your skin? There is no right or wrong, only what you experience, sense, or imagine. Now sense both your inner core and outer edge, and as you breathe, imagine or sense them connecting together. (This ends the basic induction section that should be used to launch the following imagery exercise samples.)

CHANGING IMMUNE IDENTITY
(Continue after the induction above)

Now imagine that the edges of any cancer cells in your body are changing their identification markings so that they reveal a new bumpy edge; this will let the immune cells instantly detect their presence and eliminate them. See your immune cells becoming aware of these abnormal and cancerous cells and eliminating them. Sense or imagine all abnormal cells leaving your body, and that you're now whole and healthy. Go once more to your center and your outer edges. Become aware that all your normal, healthy cells have strong boundaries, and any cancer cells have been removed. Sense yourself breathing from your core and to your outer edges. Thank your body for doing such a good job for you.

CHANGING GENES AND IMMUNE
IDENTITY FROM INSIDE OUT
(Continue after the induction above)

Sense or imagine that a flexible, shimmering fabric composed of strands of strings and tubes connects both your inner core and outer edges. The tension and pull exerted by this fabric can modify the expression of your genes. Sense or imagine which genes your cancer cells need to change. It could be that you tug on the genes so that they express new identity markers on their outer edges, so that the immune cells can detect their presence and destroy them. If you choose this option, sense or imagine that the outer edges of all your cancer cells exhibit new detectable markings. You might even see what these ID characteristics are: their symbols, shape, colors.

GENE DNA REPAIR
(Continue after the induction above)

Now focus your attention inward and notice if there is any part of your body that feels tense or painful. Ask that area if it needs anything from you, and listen to the response. Using your intuitive instincts, try to find any abnormal cells in your body. If you sense abnormal or cancer cells, bring your attention to their core where the DNA is spiraling inside those cells. Bring a laser light to the top of the DNA molecule and see its light traveling down the center of the DNA core, correcting any and all errors that may exist there as it moved downward. You can also ask the abnormal or cancer cells to program themselves to die and leave your body, making all the corrections necessary for your health. Imagine that any abnormal cells remaining have regained their ability to repair themselves and all their DNA.

See that all your cells are healthy, and that only the healthy ones are thriving. And when you are ready, bring your awareness to your breath, feel your hands, and anchor this imagery by touching two fingers together. When you're ready, slowly open your eyes. If any images came to mind, take a few minutes to draw them or write about them.

Changing the Internal Environment
(Continue after the induction above)

Take some time to enter the inner space of your body. Close your eyes and let your breath move deeper into your belly and lungs. Breathe so that you receive the life-giving oxygen your cells need. Now imagine yourself as one giant cell that knows the core and wisdom of your entire cell-self. Breathe into that core and then sense the outside edges of your cell-self. If you know that there are abnormal areas hiding within your body or you even suspect it, imagine or sense these abnormal molecules or cells. Continue to breathe normally.

When you feel ready, imagine or pretend that any abnormal cells are becoming less rigid. Know that the strings of your cells can vibrate and set the strings in nearby cells vibrating as well, all in resonance, shifting shapes and tension. Instead of holding tight to the tissues where they are now spending time, they soften up as though they are relaxing on a soft mattress. The genes in these cells have now been altered and are unable to reproduce any more. Imagine your cancer cells letting go of their attachments to your body, releasing tensions and leaving your body. Instead of clinging to their tight anchor, they relax and turn on their "time to die" signal. Allow yourself to experience the inner journey of these genes for as long as you like.

When you're ready, bring your awareness and breathe back to your cell-self and begin humming "mmmmm" to fill the space where the cancer or abnormal cells were with healing energy. You don't have to know the specifics of where they were or what they looked like: just know that you and they have let go of the hold they had on your body and spirit. Hum, drum; ring a Tibetan bowl to fill you with vibrating energy, peace, and love. Thank your cell-self for taking such good care of you, and thank yourself for changing your mind and taking on a new program.

PROGRAM CELL DEATH THROUGH
THE INNER BUBBLE
(Continue after the induction above)

Feel or sense where there may be cancer cells in your body. What do they look like? What is their shape and color, and do they have a sound associated with them? Now imagine that an invisible bubble penetrates the cancer cells' surface, both puncturing it and facilitating its death—a gentle, bubbling death. Imagine or sense the cell bursting and being quickly eliminated from your body. Is there a picture or sound that came to mind? If so, draw it, say it, and see all the abnormal cells eliminated.

BASIC ENDING TO ANY OF THE SCRIPTS

Thank your body for helping you heal. Now take a few minutes to be aware of how you feel; feel yourself in the room, on the chair or floor, feel your breath. Rub your hands together, noticing their temperature. Bring them up to your face for a few moments and then put them in you lap or to your sides. When you are ready open your eyes. Take some time to write or draw any insights you got from this journey.

As medical research brings more understanding to the many ways that genes can change that lead to cancer, we can also become more empowered to explore the inner healing modalities based on the science. We know that healing happens at many levels; that the emotions and imagination are two powerful doorways into the healing treasures within you. Of course, one key is to know how to quiet the mind and listen for the wisdom within.

I invite you to take time to explore these basic ideas from the standpoint of the new biology, and please add your own spin and expertise to these scripts. Together we can build on this evolving understanding and help our patients heal.

References

Ames, B.N., Shigenaga, M.K., and Hagen, T.M. (1993) "Oxidants, antioxidants, and the degenerative diseases of aging." *Proceedings of the National Academy Science USA 90*, 17, 7915–7922.

Barrett, S. (2013) *Secrets of Your Cells: Discovering Your Body's Inner Intelligence.* Boulder, CO: Sounds True.

Bernstein, C., Prasad, A.R., Nonsam, V., and Berstein, H. (2013) "DNA Damage, DNA Repair and Cancer." In C. Chen (ed.) *New Research Directions in DNA Repair.* Rijeka, Croatia: InTech.

Burnet, F.M. (1957) "Cancer—A biological approach. I. The process of control." *British Medical Journal 1*, 779-782.

Dietlein, T., Thelen, L., and Reinhardt H.C. (2014) "Cancer-specific defects in DNA repair pathways as targets for personalized therapeutic approaches." *Trends in Genetics 30*, 8, 326–339.

Fuller, R.B. (1961) "Tensegrity." *Portfolio and Art News Annual 4*, 112-127, 144, 148.

Gouin, J.P. and Kiecolt-Glaser, J.K. (2011) "The impact of psychological stress on wound healing: Methods and mechanisms." *Immunology and Allergy Clinics of North America 31*, 81–93.

Ingber, D.E. (1998) "The architecture of life." *Scientific American 278*, 48–57.

Ingber, D.E. (2008) "Can cancer be reversed by engineering the tumor microenvironment?" *Seminars in Cancer Biology 18*, 5, 356–364.

Kandice, R., Leventhal, R., Hongmei, Y., Kass, L., *et al.* (2009) "Matrix crosslinking forces tumor progression by enhancing integrin signaling." *Cell 139*, 891–906.

Kiecolt-Glaser, J.K. and Glaser, R. (2010) "Psychological stress, telomeres, and telomerase." *Brain, Behavior, and Immunity 24*, 529–530.

Kolcaba, K. and Fox, C. (1999) "The effects of guided imagery on comfort of women with early stage breast cancer undergoing radiation therapy." *Oncology Nurse Forum 26*, 67–72.

Ming, Y., *et al.* (1993) "Stress-reducing practice of qigong improved DNA repair in cancer patients." Proceedings from the 2nd World Conference on Academic Exchange of Medical Qigong, Shanghai Qigong Institute.

Roffe, L., Schmidt, K., and Ernst, E. (2005) "A systematic review of guided imagery as an adjuvant cancer therapy." *Psycho-oncology 14*, 8, 607–617.

Simonton, C., Matthews-Simonton, M., and Creighton, J. (1978) *Getting Well Again: A Step-by-Step, Self-Help Guide to Overcoming Cancer for Patients and Their Families.* New York; NY: Tarcher.

Spiegel, D. and Moore, R. (1997) "Imagery and hypnosis in the treatment of cancer patients." *Oncology 11*, 8, 1179–1195.

Swann, J.B. and Smyth, M.J. (2007) "Immune surveillance of tumors." *Journal of Clinical Investigation 117*, 5, 1137–1146.

Weaver, V.M., Petersen, O.W., Wang, F., Larabell, C.W., *et al.* (1997) "Reversion of the malignant phenotype of human breast cells in three-dimensional culture and in vivo by integrin blocking antibodies." *Journal of Cell Biology 137*, 231–245.

Part 3

Imagery and Depth Psychology

Chapter 9

C.G. Jung

Champion of the Imagination

Brian Dietrich

Variously described as an empirical scientist, a philosopher, theologian, gnostic, occultist, artist, and poet, Carl Jung is arguably one of the two great Western psychologists of the modern era—the other of course is Freud, the founder of psychoanalysis (Bair 2003). Inaugurating the first system of transpersonal psychology, Jung was a champion of images and the imagination. His theoretical insights and innovative methods not only established the legitimacy of the imagination as a valid means of producing knowledge, they also substantiated the use of imagination— understood as a bridge linking the conscious and unconscious, sense perception and ideas, matter and mind—as an essential component of mind/body medicine.

There are far-reaching spiritual implications at the heart of Jung's work (Corbett 1996). Recognizing that images of the imagination share the same level of reality as sense perceptions of the physical body and ideas of the intellect, Jung's method of active imagination constitutes a core spiritual technology capable of providing sacred visions and direct experiences of the divine.

At their deepest level, Jung's imaginal[1] discoveries hold the potential of healing modernity's violent desacralization of the natural world (Tarnas 2006). By suturing together the Cartesian incision cleaving matter from mind, and supplanting the Newtonian image of nature as a lifeless machine with the personified image of the Great Mother, Jungian active imagination restores a collective appreciation and reverence for the *Anima Mundi*, the living soul of the world.

With certain notable exceptions (Singer 1974; Hall *et al.* 2006; and Pincus and Sheikh 2009), Jung is seldom credited or fully acknowledged for his groundbreaking work with images and imagination. Nevertheless, imagery practitioners have much to gain by situating their various practices in the context of Jungian depth psychology. Superseding the scientific materialism that insists all that can be known is observable, measurable, and predictable, Jungian psychology offers an alternative imaginal ontology (a foundational theory of being and existence) that Jung (1960a) called *"esse in anima"* (p.328), or being in soul, and an epistemology (theory of knowledge) based on images and the imagination.

Beyond the Freudian Unconscious

Freud (1974) recognized Jung as the heir apparent to the psychoanalytic movement, anointing him his "successor and crown prince" (p.218). Because he fundamentally disagreed with Freud's reductive views regarding spirituality and the nature of the unconscious, however, Jung's coronation never came to pass.

Whereas Freud dismissed religion and spirituality as a regressive "black tide...mud...of occultism" (cited in Jung 1963a, p.150) and attributed humanity's highest spiritual aspirations and cultural achievements to nothing more than repressed sexuality (Jung 1961, p.781), Jung affirmed that the psyche possesses an inherently religious function (1968, p.13) and regarded *religious truths* as imaginatively real *psychological facts* mediated by the psyche's spiritually charged images.

Equally impoverished, Jung believed, was Freud's view that the unconscious is nothing but a repository of entirely personal contents, including forgotten memories, repressed emotions, and conflictual desires. According to Jung, underlying this superficial layer, which he called "the personal unconscious" (1959b, p.3), is a second, far deeper, and more mysterious stratum, which is of an entirely impersonal and objective nature. Jung (1966) named this transpersonal dimension of the objective psyche "the collective unconscious" (p.95) and understood it to be the wellspring of all psychic creativity.

Archetypes

Although Jung described archetypes in a number of different ways, he resisted attempts to limit their meaning to any single definition. Nonetheless, one helpful way of describing them is to say that archetypes are universal patterns of the psyche (Jung 1967). Existing across cultures and throughout time, these transcendent forms without content (Hobson 2013) metaphorically reside in the collective unconscious. As such, they cannot be directly experienced or fully known. Their existence, however, can be inferred from *archetypal images* appearing in mythology, dreams, and nondirective forms of guided imagery.

Jung identified two different categories of archetypes: archetypes of transformation (or process) such as rebirth, the path toward wholeness, and the transformative dark night of the soul; and archetypes appearing as personified figures in fantasies, dreams, myths, and fairytales. From his clinical work and mythological research, Jung identified certain archetypes he thought exerted the most influence on conscious experience:

- the Persona—a social mask adopted to seek approval through conformity (Jung 1966)

- the Shadow—the inferior aspects of the personality disavowed, repressed, and projected onto others (Jung 1959b)

- the Anima/Animus—contrasexual soul-figures in men and women that establish a relationship between the conscious and unconscious, transmitting the creative psyche's images to the conscious mind

- the Mother—the Anima in her maternal aspect

- the Child—who represents the original wholeness of the psyche

- the Wise Old Man/Woman—a source of wisdom outside the ego's rational intelligence

- the Self—which Jung (1959a) referred to as "the god image in man" (p.40). Representing psychic totality, the Self may be understood as the greater personality beyond ordinary ego consciousness. As the archetype of order, integrating the conscious and unconscious, the Self stands behind the other archetypes and brings them into appropriate relationship within the psyche.

Individuation

Jung recognized that the archetypes serve a *teleological function*, which is to say they are purposeful and prospective: they propel a process of self-realization that he called *individuation*, which is the full and unique development of the personality. The teleological function of the psyche suggests that organisms possess an inherent drive toward health and wholeness.

Transcending Dualism

In his later writing Jung argued archetypes were *psychoid* in nature, which means they are both psychological, manifesting in the psyche, and at the same time physical, embedded in the material world of sensual nature and biological instinct. His realization that archetypes are not merely psychological phenomena but also constitute a tangible material reality permeating the entire cosmos led Jung (1960a) to conclude that, "psyche and matter...are two different aspects of one and the same thing" (p.215), which only appear divided due to the limitations of ego consciousness. Jung's idea of the psychoid archetype as point of union where psyche and matter are one and the same provides a theoretical foundation for guided imagery and an imaginal locus for the mechanism of healing in mind/body medicine.

Diverging Methods

Freud employed a method of *free association*, in which patients passively observe and give voice to their stream of consciousness and reveal their repressed personal secrets and hidden wishes. Jung's method of active imagination[2] brings the ego and the autonomous archetypes into dialogical relationship and provides a means of accessing the collective unconscious. This facilitates the process of individuation: the path toward wholeness and the full integration of the personality.

Fantasy and Active Imagination

Jung (1971) originally used the term *fantasy,* to describe what he called "a vital process [and] continuously creative act [that]...creates reality every day" (p.52). Distinguishing two varieties of fantasy, *active* and *passive,* he described active fantasies as products of the intuition tuned to perceive unconscious contents in order to bring them into clear visual form. Passive fantasies, in contrast, are basically idle daydreams (Jung 1971). For Jung, active fantasies generated by the interplay between the conscious ego and the unconscious personality are a superior form of psychic activity because they demonstrate the essential psychic unity of a person's individuality (Jung 1971).

According to Jung, the relationship between the ego and the unconscious evinced through images and fantasy is of the greatest importance because that collaboration expresses the Self archetype, which orders and balances the psyche. Jung (1977) later clarified his terms and asserted that, "Fantasy is more or less your own invention, and remains on the surface of personal things and conscious expectations…[while] active imagination…means the images have a life of their own and that symbolic events develop according to their own logic" (p.171).

Neither Jung's (1960a) method nor his theoretical understanding of it resulted from a logical or rational process. Rather, they emerged from a long, drawn-out, and at times painful process that he called his "confrontation with the unconscious" (p.88), which consisted of a series of tumultuous imaginal experiences he recorded in journals and later elaborated in his *Red Book*.

Jung's Imaginal Method

Jung's (1960a) active imagination consists of inviting the unconscious to arise and then "coming to terms with the unconscious" (p.88). Unconscious activity is encouraged through a suspension or relaxation of the rational mind. In the first stage, the unconscious takes the lead while ego bears witness to arising images. In the second stage, consciousness leads: the ego engages and interacts with images and emotions flowing from the creative unconscious (Jung 1960a). Jung emphasized the second stage, *coming to terms with the unconscious*, because it involves integrating the imaginal experience and deriving meaning from it. We then ground the experience by transforming the insights or wisdom gained into committed action in the outer world. For example, an anxiously attached young man unsure about "the nature of true love" experienced an image of a plastic treasure chest in an aquarium. Pressure increased inside the chest as it filled with air bubbles until the lid swung open and the bubbles rushed to the surface. The young man viscerally understood this image of release to mean that true love is a process of "fullness and flow forever letting go." Beyond mere aesthetic appreciation, he experienced this image as a kind of ethical imperative to love others by setting them free. Informed by this insight, he worked at reducing his anxious fears of abandonment, which improved his relationships.

Coming to terms with the unconscious also includes the amplification of symbols wherein the psyche's images are associatively linked to similar images or motifs appearing in myths, folklore, and fairy tales across cultures and throughout the human history (Chodorow 1997). Contextualizing symbolic imagery in this way often provides a person with a sense of greater dimensionality and depth. Most essential to the process of active imagination is that the ego surrenders having a plan and allows the process to unfold on its own terms.

Jung's Imaginal Knowledge

Jung's life and work provides a canonical example of the imagination's ability to produce knowledge. His prolonged engagement with spontaneously arising unconscious contents and autonomous psychic figures formed the basis of his *Red Book*, which he created to contain, honor, and elaborate his numinous (spiritual) experiences with the careful attention and dutiful consideration of sincere religious devotion. The imaginal experiences he creatively expressed in the book also provided him with the *prima materia* (the foundational building blocks) that became the basis of his *Collected Works*. Confirming this point in his quasi-autobiographical work *Memories, Dream, Reflections,* Jung (1963a) wrote:

> All my works, all my creative activity, has come from those initial fantasies and dreams. Everything that I accomplished in later life was already contained in them...in the form of emotions and images. (p.192)

Through his imaginal dialogues with spiritually charged personified figures arising from the objective psyche, Jung (1963a) realized that, "There [are] things in the psyche...[he did] not produce, but which produce[d] themselves and [had] their own life" (p.183). Crucial to Jung's process of discovery through active imagination was his reclamation of soul or Anima, the feminine personification of soul, which serves as a mediating gateway between the conscious and the unconscious (Jung 1963a). Although Jung's long-repressed Anima, personified as Salome, exhibited a harsh and wrathful attitude toward him, Jung (2009) nevertheless wrote, "When the mystery [of the soul] draws near to you... [your] heart awakens...things happen around you like miracles...[and] your world begins to become wonderful" (p.264). This is because, "Man belongs not only to an ordered world. He also belongs to the wonder-world of his soul" (p.264).

Elaborating the idea of the soul's mediating function, Avens (1980) writes, "In Jungian psychology soul is [not] based on matter...nor on mind or metaphysics, but is a 'third [psychic] reality' *between* all these 'entities'" (p.189). This third psychic reality he contends is "the creative realm of emotions, fantasies, moods, visions, and dreams; and its language is that of images, metaphors, and symbols" (p.189). Jung's direct experience with objective *others* within the psyche (1969) led to his foundational understanding that "Every psychic process is an image and an imagining" (p.544). It is this understanding that forms the keystone to the edifice of his entire psychology.

Restoring the World Soul

Drawing upon his study of medieval alchemy, which located its transformational processes in the imagination, "an intermediate realm between mind and matter...a psychic realm of subtle bodies whose characteristic it is to manifest themselves in a mental as well as a material form" (Jung 1968, pp.278–279), Jung conjectured that the archetypes must exist along a continuum linking psyche and matter (1960a). He reasoned that just as the instincts are embedded in and express the central nervous system's biophysical processes, so too do the archetypes possess a psychoid (non-psychic) basis, "which is immediately rooted in the stuff of organism" (p.216). For Jung (1973), archetypes do not just reside in an intrapsychic realm that is somehow separate from the world; nor does the psyche exist as a discrete entity encapsulated solely in our human skulls. He argued instead that we are surrounded by the psyche like "an atmosphere in which we live" (p.433), which means that "the psyche is a universal substrate" (p.433), which is present in the environment.

Recognizing and reestablishing a fundamental unity between matter and mind, Jung (1960a) ultimately deduced that the archetypes of the collective unconscious form "a bridge to matter in general" (p.216). Experienced transrationally as an evolved form of *participation mystique* (imaginally *participating* in and not merely *observing* phenomena), Jung's notion of an archetypal span linking psyche and matter transcends monotheistic rationalism's hellish alienation and restores to human consciousness an ecological awareness of the unity of all life and humankind's place in the natural order.

Jung's idea that there exists but one psyche encompassing the interiority of human beings, nature, and the cosmos harkens back to the original Platonic idea of the Anima Mundi, the world soul. It also references the ancient hermetic concept of the *Unis Mundus, one world* or *one cosmos*. According to Jung (1963b), "The background of our empirical world... appears to be...a *Unis Mundis* [sic]" (p.538), because there exists a fundamental "identity of the psychic and the physical" (p.537). Although it may appear there are two distinct spheres of inner and outer, when one peers into the depths of the archetypal psyche, these distinctions dissolve into an undifferentiated unity.

Imagery and Spirituality
The Numinous

For Jung, all spiritual experience is an expression of the Self archetype. Despite the fact that the Self archetype cannot be directly known nor its mysteries fully fathomed, we can discern whether or not we are in contact with the archetypal unconscious, or transpersonal Self, by a distinct quality of experience that Frederick Otto (1950) describes as *numinous*, meaning:

> A state of mind which is...perfectly *sui generis* and irreducible to any other [mental state]... Like every absolutely primary and elementary datum [that]...cannot be strictly defined...it can only be evoked [or] awakened in the mind; as everything that comes "of the spirit" must be awakened. (p.7)

Otto (1950) characterizes the numinous as a *"mysterium tremendum et facinans"* (p.12), which means a mystery that is both tremendous and fascinating. Other words used to portray numinous experience include *stunning, astonishing,* and *wonderful,* but also *overwhelming, dreadful,* and *frightening.* Recognizing that numinous experience has been linked to metaphysical and religious ideas from ancient times, Jung (1963b) observed that in all attempts to understand it, "use must be made of certain parallel religious or metaphysical ideas...to formulate and elucidate it" (p.547). Hence, words such as *holy, spiritual, divine, mystical,* and *sacred* are necessarily used to point to, though not fully define, its ineffability.

The Numinosum

Numinous experience emanates from and is made possible by the *numinosum,* which Jung (1969) defines in his essay "Psychology and Religion" as:

> A dynamic agency or effect not caused by an arbitrary act of will... The *numinosum*—whatever its cause may be—is an experience of the subject independent of his will... The *numinosum* is either a quality belonging to a visible object or the influence of an invisible presence that causes a peculiar alteration of consciousness. (p.7)

Similar in kind and character to the mystical experience that confers a sense of oneness through sympathy with all beings—or a sense of participation *in*, not separation *from*, phenomena—the numinosum can be disclosed in a variety of ways: through dreams, arising from the depths; through experiences of nature in which dualistic and illusory categories of subjects and objects fall away; through embodied experiences such as ecstatic dance, somatic forms of spiritual practice, and sacred sexuality; through the mystery of love and intimate relationship; and even more esoteric forms such as vocational passion, immersive creativity, and ritual—all of which to some degree obviate ego consciousness (Corbett 2007). Reflecting a relatively unmediated experience of the archetypes, in Jungian depth psychology the numinosum is ultimately an expression of the intrapsychic divinity that is their source: the Self.

DIRECT EXPERIENCE OF THE DIVINE

It was Jung's (1970) contention that people who consider faith to be the essence of "true religious experience" (p.265), fail to consider that faith itself might be a "secondary phenomena" (p.265) predicated on a particular individual's direct experience of the numinosum, the veracity of which understandably inspired his or her original trust and abiding loyalty. Faith in this context may be understood as a disconnected commemorative homage to another person's direct experience.

Jung's approach to spirituality gives no credence to beliefs that lack a personal experience of divine revelation. As he famously suggested in a 1959 BBC television interview, one does not have to *believe* if through direct experience of the numinosum one *knows* (Jung 1960b). Questions of religious faith versus secular doubt become irrelevant in Jung's spiritual psychology, because, try as one might, there is no denying one's direct personal experiences of the divine, even if others find such experiences to be incredulous.

Because in Jung's (1970) view, "Belief is no adequate substitute for inner experience" (p.265), active imagination and guided imagery offer ways of living a spiritually rich and meaningful life without embracing any particular theology or religious dogma. Emphasizing the direct experience of the sacred, Jungian depth psychology offers an experiential form of spirituality that neither defines nor dictates for others what form the divine should take. Absent an imperative to proselytize or definitively enshrine a particular image of the ineffable underlying all idiosyncratic images of the divine, the depth psychological approach to spirituality instead leads to an open and ecumenical respect for the many ways the sacred presents itself to individual consciousness.

Contrasts, Complements, and Future Research

Although Jung's influence on the various modalities of guided imagery has not been fully explored, there is potentially much to gain by situating guided imagery in the tradition of Jungian depth psychology. Jung's transpersonal psychology offers guided imagery practitioners a well-established theory of knowledge based on images and imagination. It supports the use of imagination as an essential feature of authentic spiritual practice, providing a method of tapping into the psyche's transcendent potentials through direct experience of the divine. And— similar to innovative theories in modern physics and systems theory— it identifies the inseparability and essential unity of mind and matter, psyche and cosmos. Transcending modernity's toxic blend of dualism and mechanistic determinism, Jung's psychology restores the *world's soul*, resacralizes nature, and fosters a deeper sense of connection to self, others, and the natural world.

A number of differences exist between interactive forms of guided imagery and Jungian active imagination. The most obvious is that guided imagery typically takes place in a relational context in which a client interacts with spontaneous images emerging from the unconscious while also interacting (though to a lesser degree) with an imagery guide (facilitator) who holds space for the client's exploration and provides gentle encouragement for the client's sustained imaginal engagement and inquiry. Exciting opportunities for further research are suggested by this distinction, exploring the various ways that guided imagery and Jungian depth psychology may inform each other. It may be that undertaking imaginal experience in a relational context enhances Jungian active imagination, providing it with greater sensual dimensionality, affective resonance, and depth.

One Final Note and a Suggestion

Aside from Jung's peculiar formulation—he advised clients to undertake active imagination alone, outside of the therapeutic container—an additional feature of his overall approach distinguishing it from most other current forms of imagery practice is Jung's emphasis on the sovereign nature of the unconscious and its status as an objective *other* within the psyche. From the perspective of Jungian and archetypal psychology, many new-age forms of guided imagery chiefly address outer-world concerns over and against the inner imperatives of the soul. The question hinges on a person's attitude toward the imaginal world: in Martin Buber's (1937) terms, whether one is having an I-it experience *of* it or an I-thou relationship *with* it—which is to ask, is one experiencing a thing (albeit a fascinating one) that may be used and exploited? Or is one relating to a sentient form of living indigenous wisdom? Humankind's relationship to non-human nature graphically illustrates the starkly contrasting poles of this dynamic.

Take, for example, the majestic elephant Satao, the African "tusker" roaming Kenya's Tsavo East National Park. Having encountered the great elephant in the bush with his guide, the *Telegraph's* Robin Page (2014) declared it was "a deep and emotional experience connecting us to a time when the world was young—something that will live with us for the rest of our lives (para. 6)." Contrast his attitude of reverential gratitude with that of the poachers who shot Satao with a poison arrow, killing him, and then hacking away his tusks for black market sale and profit.

These extremes illustrate the divergent attitudes Buber defined in relationship to what I describe as a delicate ecology between worlds. From the perspective of soul, it is important to consider if one is venturing into the imaginal world with a loving and open heart and a commitment to "stick with the image" (Hillman 1983, p.21)—or if one seeks only to colonize and exploit the imaginal realm for outer-world gain.

In Jungian active imagination, it is important that one possess humility, a capacity to tolerate irrational processes, and an ability to humbly ask for and receive guidance from *other* psychic forces beyond ego consciousness. In this way, the conscious and unconscious psyche come together to produce enlivened images that lead to greater psychic integration and higher levels of being (Jung 1960a).

After much discussion of the imaginal realm, active imagination, and Jung's emphasis on the creative nature of the unconscious, the reader may wish to have a direct experience of it by trying the following exercise.

ACTIVE IMAGINATION EXERCISE

Communicating open-hearted goodwill, allow yourself to enter into the imaginal realm—however you imagine it to be—in whatever way feels most effective for you. In so doing, recognize that you are consciously entering into relationship with a form of wild indigenous life and timeless wisdom. Take all the time you need to fully arrive there, or simply bring your attention fully to bear on whatever you do experience. You may invite an image to present itself. Or simply remain present to whatever *is* in the moment. If nothing presents itself immediately, be patient and wait. Take all the time you need and accept what comes, even if it is nothing. Use all the subtle senses of the imagination and allow yourself to fully register your experience, taking note of all you see, hear, smell, taste, and feel. Let your awareness be drawn to wherever it wants to go, without will or intention. Experience whatever image or images arise, with no agenda beyond your commitment to be fully present to your experience and to whatever reveals itself to you. If you wish, allow yourself to respond (or not respond) to any part of your experience in whatever ways feel appropriate. Take all the time you need to simply listen, observe, and reside in your experience. When you feel your inner exploration is complete, or at any other time you desire, bring your inner experience to a close. Give thanks in a way that feels true to who you are, and allow yourself to return to the outer-world in a way that is comfortable for you. Take time to reflect on the experience.

ENDNOTES

1. Henry Corbin, a scholar of Islamic mysticism and a contemporary of Jung's, coined the term *imaginal* to differentiate it from the word *imaginary*, suggesting unreal or fanciful. The imaginal, in contrast, represents a separate ontological reality that mediates sense perceptions and ideas, and requires for its apprehension the organ human of imagination.

2. Jung first used the term "active imagination," designating his psychotherapeutic method at his 1935 "Tavistock Lectures" in London. Information about the method, which he previously described as "active fantasy," can be found in the *Collected Works* in "The Aims of Psychotherapy," "The Transcendent Function," "On the Nature of the Psyche," *Two Essays on Analytical Psychology*, and *Mysterium Coniunctionis*.

References

Avens, R. (1980) "James Hillman: Toward a poetic psychology." *Journal of Religion and Health 19*, 3, 186–202.

Bair, D. (2003) *Jung: A Biography*. Boston, MA: Little, Brown and Co.

Buber, M. (1937) *I and Thou*. Mansfield Centre, CT: Martino Publishing.

Chodorow J. (ed.) (1997) *Jung on Active Imagination*. Princeton, NJ: Princeton University Press.

Corbett, L. (1996) *The Religious Function of the Psyche*. Florence, KY: Taylor and Francis/Routledge.

Corbett, L. (2007) *Psyche and the Sacred: Spirituality Beyond Religion*. New Orleans, LA: Spring Journal Books.

Freud, S. (1974) *The Freud Jung Letters: The Correspondence Between Sigmund Freud and C.G. Jung*. Translated by R. Meinheim and R.F.C. Hull. Princeton, NJ: Princeton University Press.

Hall, E., Hall, C., Stradling, P., and Young, D. (2006) *Guided Imagery: Creative Interventions in Counseling and Psychotherapy*, 1st edition. London: SAGE Publications Ltd.

Hillman, J. (1983) *Archetypal Psychology: A Brief Account*. Woodstock, CT: Spring Publications.

Hobson, R.F. (2013) "The Archetypes of the Collective Unconscious." In M. Fordham, R. Gordon, and J. Hubback (eds) *Analytical Psychology: A Modern Science*. Oxford: Butterworth-Heinemann.

Jung, C.G. (1959a) "Aion: Researches into the phenomenology of the self." In R.F.C. Hull (trans.) *The Collected Works of C.G. Jung*, vol. 9, ii. Princeton, NJ: Princeton University Press.

Jung, C.G. (1959b) "The Archetypes of the Collective Unconscious." In R.F.C. Hull (trans.) *The Collected Works of C.G. Jung*, vol. 9, i. Princeton, NJ: Princeton University Press.

Jung, C.G. (1960a) "Structure and Dynamics of the Psyche." In R.F.C. Hull (trans.) *The Collected Works of C.G. Jung*, vol. 8. Princeton, NJ: Princeton University Press.

Jung, C.G. (1960b) Carl Jung's letter to The Listener, January 21, 1960. Temple Illuminatus. Available at www.templeilluminatus.com/group/carl-jung-s-red-book/forum/topics/carl-jung-s-letter-to-the-listener-january-21-1960, accessed on March 12 2012.

Jung, C.G. (1961) "Freud and Psychoanalysis." In R.F.C. Hull (trans.) *The Collected Works of C.G. Jung*, vol. 4. Princeton, NJ: Princeton University Press. (Original work published in 1931).

Jung, C.G. (1963a) *Memories, Dreams, Reflections*. New York, NY: Pantheon Books.

Jung, C.G. (1963b) "Mysterium Coniunctionis." In R.F.C. Hull (trans.) *The Collected Works of C.G. Jung*, vol. 14. Princeton, NJ: Princeton University Press.

Jung, C.G. (1966) "Two Essays on Analytical Psychology." In R.F.C. Hull (trans.) *The Collected Works of C.G. Jung*, vol. 7. Princeton, NJ: Princeton University Press.

Jung, C.G. (1967) "Symbols of transformation." In R.F.C. Hull (trans.) *The Collected Works of C.G. Jung*, vol. 5. Princeton, NJ: Princeton University Press.

Jung, C.G. (1968) "Psychology and Alchemy." In R.F.C. Hull (trans.) *The Collected Works of C.G. Jung*, vol. 12. Princeton, NJ: Princeton University Press.

Jung, C.G. (1969) "Psychology and Religion: West and East." In R.F.C. Hull (trans.) *The Collected Works of C.J. Jung*, vol. 11. Princeton, NJ: Princeton University Press.

Jung, C.G. (1970) "Civilization in Transition." In R.F.C. Hull (trans.) *The Collected Works of C.G. Jung*, vol. 10. Princeton, NJ: Princeton University Press.

Jung, C.G. (1971) "Psychological Types." In R.F.C. Hull (trans.) *The Collected Works of C.G. Jung*, vol. 6. Princeton, NJ: Princeton University Press.

Jung, C.G. (1973) *Letters*, vol. 1, 1906–1950. Translated by R.F.C. Hull. Princeton, NJ: Princeton University Press.

Jung, C.G. (1977) "The Symbolic Life: Miscellaneous writings." In R.F.C. Hull (trans.) *The Collected Works of C.G. Jung*, vol. 18. Princeton, NJ: Princeton University Press. (Original work published 1921.)

Jung, C.G. (2009) *The Red Book: Liber Novus*. Translated by S. Shamdasani (ed.). New York, NY: W.W. Norton.

Otto, R. (1950) *The Idea of the Holy: An Inquiry into the Non-rational Factor in the Idea of the Divine and its Relation to the Rational*. Translated by J.W. Harvey. Oxford: Oxford University Press.

Page, R. (2014) "Country Diary: RIP Satao, Kenya's biggest 'tusker.'" *The Telegraph*, July 22. Available at www.telegraph.co.uk/news/earth/earthcomment/country-diary/10980830/Country-Diary-RIP-Satao-Kenyas-biggest-tusker.html, accessed on April 7 2015.

Pincus, D. and Sheikh, A.A. (2009) *Imagery for Pain Relief: A Scientifically Grounded Guidebook for Clinicians*, 1st edition. New York, NY: Routledge.

Singer, J.L. (1974) *Imagery and Daydream Methods in Psychotherapy and Behavior Modification*. New York, NY: Academic Press.

Tarnas, R. (2006) *Cosmos and Psyche: Intimations of a New World View*. New York, NY: Viking.

Chapter 10

Using Guided Imagery to Create Brain Change

Linda Graham

The brain learns—and rewires itself throughout our lives—from experience. Any experience at all, positive or negative, causes neurons in the brain to "fire": to activate and send messages to up to 5000 other neurons in the brain, 50 times per second (Siegel 2012). The human brain has evolved to store and reconnect those messages in the forms of thoughts, feelings, and images that, in turn, become new experiences themselves that can trigger new changes in the brain.

Now that neuroscientists are able to track neural firing in the human brain, we are learning from their discoveries that changes in the brain are the rule of our human experience rather than the exception (Davidson and Begley 2012). When we intentionally and wisely choose the experiences that we want to use to rewire our brain's habitual patterns of response to experience, we can create important changes in our behaviors, our attitudes, our relationships to ourselves and our stories about ourselves, our judgments about others, and how we navigate the complexities and challenges of our world.

Guided imagery is a powerful tool for creating brain change. When we imagine a banana, the same neurons fire in our visual cortex as when we are looking at a real banana (Siegel 2012). When we reimagine how a brief encounter between ourselves and another could have gone, or when we rehearse how an important encounter with another could go, we are priming changes in our brain's patterns of neural firing that allow us to relate to ourselves and to others, even to our history with others, with more resilience (Ecker 2012).

In this chapter I'll explore four mechanisms of brain change—self-directed neuroplasticity—and how guided imagery can be effectively incorporated into each of them:

1. Conditioning: How the brain encodes patterns of response—learning—in the first place.

2. New conditioning: How new experiences create new patterns that, over time, become new habits of response.

3. Reconditioning: How the juxtaposition of positive experiences or memories with negative experiences or memories can, when the positive is strong enough, rewire the circuitry of the old memory, often instantly and often permanently.

4. Deconditioning: How we can use imagination to create a mental play space that allows the grip of old patterns to loosen up. The brain can make new associations and connect the dots in new ways that better serve us.

The three prerequisites that allow these mechanisms to work safely, efficiently, and effectively are:

1. Presence: Showing up, coming out of distraction, denial, dissociation, and engaging with the experience of the present moment, even as we are choosing to shape that experience in the moment. Presence primes the neuroplasticity of the brain and allows changes to register in our brain as our conscious awareness.

2. Intention: Stating a wished-for goal or outcome activates the receptivity of the brain to register and install the new learning; intention creates a file folder in the mind, so to speak, where new information can be stored.

3. Perseverance: The brain learns through repetition—repeated experiences, repeated neural firings. Neuroscientists do not agree on how many times an experience must be repeated in order for the brain to encode the new learning in its circuitry and transfer the patterns of firing to long-term storage: but "little and often" (Gilbert 2009) is what is recommended for new

learning to "stick," in other words, to become a new automatic pattern that—like learning how to ride a bicycle—once we know it, we don't have to think about it anymore.

Conditioning

Donald Hebb, a Canadian neuroscientist, tells us that neurons that fire together, wire together (Siegel 2012), describing how the brain converts experiences into learning and memory. Every single experience causes neurons in the brain to fire. Repeated experiences mean repeated neural firings. Repeated firings strengthen the connections among neurons across the synaptic gap between them, making it more likely that the same, similar, or even new experiences will cause those same neurons to fire together again. Repeated firings and stronger connections create the neural circuitry and pathways that become the brain's way of remembering and recalling previous experience.

The conditioning process itself is neutral. We can exhibit problematic ways of responding to an experience happening now as the result of the conditioning of negative or traumatizing experiences in the past; we can exhibit flexible and adaptive ways of responding to our current experience from the optimal conditioning of experiences that validated our competence and worth in the past. Conditioning is nature's way of being efficient. About 80 percent of the time, we operate from our conditioned implicit memory so that our higher conscious brains are free to write symphonies, create governments, and solve global warming. This process of conditioning is going to continue in the brain now, every moment we draw breath, for the rest of our life.

What's required of us is that we become aware and accepting of our previous conditioning. We can learn to see our previous conditioning clearly, regulate any reactivity arising from with compassion, and rewire our brain's automatic learned habits going forward. We may become aware of our conditioning in the form of powerful images or visual memories. We can hold those images now in a conscious, compassionate relationship, observing and reflecting, allowing and accepting, without pushing them away or becoming hijacked by them. We can use new guided imagery to change or amplify that learning from the past.

NOTICING AND NAMING

Imagine that you're walking down the sidewalk in the neighborhood where you live. You notice a friend walking toward you on the sidewalk on the other side of the somewhat busy street. You call out and wave "hello!" but there's no response. Notice your own split-second reaction to that "no response" in your own body: a contraction, a drop in energy. Notice whatever thoughts might begin to cascade in response to your body's reaction. "Hmm, that's unusual. I'd better try again." Or, "Whew! He has a lot on his mind. I wonder if I should even bother him?" Notice any reactivity to those thoughts. "Gee, he seems a little stuck up today." Or, "Oh, no! What have I done wrong?" Notice if your thoughts follow a pattern that you've observed in the past: feeling bad about yourself or wanting to reach out even more, for example.

Now imagine that your friend suddenly sees you, calls out, and waves "hello!" to you. Again, notice the split-second reaction in your body to the friend connecting with you: a smile, an uplift in energy. Bring awareness to any shifts in your body, notice any shifts in your thoughts. "He noticed me!" "I'm glad we weren't disconnected after all." As you reflect on your experience, notice if your thoughts follow a pattern that you've noticed before, perhaps relief or gratitude.

Take a moment to name the reactions and the patterns you discovered, with compassion for any reactions that may have been triggered by what you noticed. With every moment of this practice of noticing and naming, you are strengthening the parts of your brain that do the noticing. And by pausing to do this, you are conditioning your brain to create choice points, which give you a chance to respond with more flexibility and choose a different response the next time.

Mindfulness and empathy are two of the most powerful agents of brain change known to science (Lazar 2007). We can use these practices to consciously be with the conditioning that has already occurred and implement the other three mechanisms of brain change to transform it when necessary.

New Conditioning

Because any new experience will catalyze changes in our brain, when we carefully choose among the experiences that we will use to create brain change, we can intentionally send our brain's re-education in a wise and wholesome direction (Davidson and Begley 2012).

The last 20 years of behavioral science research in the positive psychology movement (feeling good and flourishing) have paralleled the same 20 years of research in cognitive and affective neuroscience (thoughts and feelings). Scientists in both fields have discovered that deliberately cultivating experiences of positive, pro-social emotions create remarkable changes in our resilience, creativity, and well-being, in part because they create remarkable changes in our brains.

Experiencing a positive emotion—gratitude, kindness, compassion, serenity, awe, delight, love—provides an immediate antidote in the present moment to the brain's innate negativity bias (Fredrickson 2004). We are hardwired by evolution to react very quickly and very unconsciously to any sense of danger or life threat with our automatic survival responses of fight-flight-freeze-numb out-collapse. We may experience these responses as anger, fear, anxiety, grief, or shutting down and not feeling anything at all. If we can remember a moment of calm and equanimity or encouragement from a trusted friend, or to stop and inquire, "What's right in the midst of this wrong?", it can help put the brakes on our automatic negative responses. Even the briefest image of a friend hugging us, of the sunset that touched our soul last night, of our own space at home where we can feel safe and begin to regroup, helps us come out of contraction and a narrowed view to find the space to breathe and respond differently.

Positive emotions also have a long-term effect on the brain. Neuroscientists have found that experiencing positive emotions causes a "left shift" in the brain: in their scanners, they see more real-time neural activity lighting up in the left hemisphere of the brain. This activity does not necessarily involve language and abstract thinking; it seems to indicate a shift into the "approach" stance of the left hemisphere rather than remaining in the "avoid" stance of the right hemisphere (Davidson 2004). This left shift allows us to be more open to the experiences of the moment, enabling us to shift our view to the bigger picture, encouraging collaboration with others and, as we discern more options, fostering more resilience.

These long-term effects on the brain show up in the outcome data from studies of people who cultivate a daily positive emotion practice (Emmons 2008):

- less stress, less anxiety, less depression

- more friendships and social support

- more collaboration with colleagues

- more productivity, more creativity, fewer mistakes at work

- better sleep, better health, longer life expectancy

- more resilience and thriving.

Gratitude is one of those positive emotions practices that create such powerful changes in our brains and our behaviors. Here is a simple gratitude practice that can easily be done every day and shared with others at the end of the day.

GRATITUDE PRACTICE

Evoke visual images of the people (or pets) in your life you are grateful for. Make each image as specific and concrete as possible: the dimple in your child's smile; the grin of the co-worker who showed up at your door with homemade lasagna the day you were home with the flu; your dog's ecstatic stretching as he waits for a belly-rub.

With each image, allow a feeling of warmth to flow out from your heart; notice the feelings and where you feel them in your body. Amplify these feelings so that you sense them even more strongly. Really savor them, so that their goodness doesn't simply wash through your brain like water through a sieve.

Linger with the feelings for 30 seconds so that your brain has time to translate the feelings into patterns of neural firing it can encode in long-term memory.

Repeat this practice three times a day for 30 days ("little and often"). The images may change; the feeling of gratitude becomes stronger; the activation in your brain becomes more reliable and enduring. You are creating a resource for resilience and for further brain change.

Sharing these feelings with someone at the end of the day—in person with a family member or friend, sending a text or email to a gratitude buddy, recording them in a gratitude journal—primes your brain to notice these moments as they happen throughout the day, anticipating that you will happily share them later.

Reconditioning

Neuroscientists have been able to view the mechanism of memory deconsolidation–reconsolidation in their fMRI scanners for the past seven years (Ecker 2012). Briefly, when the neural network that holds an implicit memory (outside of awareness) is made to fall apart, it can be rewired again differently just a split second later. This is how memories (conditioning) can change over time. Neuropsychologists have discovered that juxtaposing one memory that directly disconfirms or contradicts another memory can cause that second memory to deconsolidate or fall apart. When the new, contradictory memory is stronger in its patterns of neural firing, it can rewire the old memory, often instantly and permanently. This is the neural basis of all trauma therapy: that a new positive memory can rewire an old negative one.

I teach an exercise in my workshops called Wished-for Outcome, a guided visualization that reconditions a sense of failure, inadequacy, or shame into a sense of self-acceptance, efficacy, and pride. The exercise is based on the transformative power of this mechanism of memory deconsolidation–reconsolidation.

Practices that cultivate mindfulness and compassion help lay the foundation of safety needed for an experiential exercise like Wished-for Outcome. This exercise can be done using your own mindful empathy, if it is strongly established, or with the help of the mindful empathy of a good friend or therapist.

WISHED-FOR OUTCOME

Sit comfortably in your chair or lie comfortably on the floor or bed. Focus your attention on your breath, breathing calmly and deeply into your heart-center. Call to mind a particular moment of ease and well-being. Or a particular sense of your own goodness. Or a particular moment when you felt safe, loved, connected, cherished. Or specific people who love you, who believe in you. Remember one of these moments in as much detail as you can, in as many levels of your body-brain as you can: visual images, the feelings that the memory evokes, where you feel those feelings in your body, any thoughts you have about yourself now as you remember the sweetness of that moment. Let yourself savor this moment in a mindful and compassionate "holding" of the memory. (You're creating a positive neural resource to help contain the process of neural firing and rewiring.)

When you feel bathed in the good feelings and are still anchored in the larger awareness of safety in the present moment, call to mind a moment of experience when things went awry between you and another person, however slight or terrible, a hiccup or a hurricane. But chunk down the "terrible" to a small size: start with a small storm and work up to the hurricane. Maintain an observer role, even as you go back into the memory of that moment, imagining what was happening quite vividly. The observer role allows you to "hold" the memory in your awareness rather than getting sucked into the experience again. Evoke this memory to light up all the neural networks: visual images, body sensations, emotions, thoughts or beliefs at the time. Memories of what you said and did, what someone else said or did; who else was there; how old you both were; what each person was wearing. Maybe you wish you could have said or done something differently at the time, but didn't. Maybe you wish someone else had done something different, even if that would never have happened in real life. Remember the moment, the feelings of the moment, in as much detail as you can.

Then, in your imagination, begin to visualize a wished-for outcome. What you wish would have happened differently. What you would have said or done differently. What the other person could have done differently, even if this never would have happened in real life. What someone else who didn't even appear in the original scenario might have said or done. Perhaps you even wish that none of it had happened at all. You can imagine what would have happened if this event had never happened. Imagine the new scenario in as much detail as you can. Let the new story unfold as you would have wished it to, coming to a new and better resolution. You are creating a scenario that completely disconfirms or contradicts what happened in the past.

Hold the two scenarios in your awareness at the same time, or toggle back and forth between them, always refreshing and strengthening the newer, more positive scenario. After a few moments, "let go" of the old memory and let your attention rest in the new scenario. Let your mind play out this new scenario, then notice how you feel. Notice any emotions or thoughts or beliefs about yourself that come up, and if they are more positive and resilient, let them soak in.

Holding the wished-for outcome clearly in your awareness, briefly touch base again with the older, more negative memory. Notice any difference in the "charge" or energy of the original memory.

Again, let go of the original, more problematic memory and focus your awareness on the newer, wished-for outcome. Then bring your awareness back to the present moment.

Reflect on any changes you notice in your present sense of yourself. You can repeat this exercise as many times as needed, for as many different memories as needed, in order to rewire your sense of yourself and your relationship to yourself.

The Wished-for Outcome exercise doesn't change what happened, but it does change our relationship to what happened. The exercise does not rewrite history, but it does rewire the brain and thus our sense of ourselves going forward.

Deconditioning

The two mechanisms of brain change described above—new conditioning and reconditioning—are focused modes of processing in the brain. We are intentionally setting a goal and repeatedly focusing our efforts. We are conscious of the process; we hope to be conscious of the results.

Deconditioning happens when we relax the guardianship of our mind's efforts; we relax into a kind of daydream or reverie; we let our stream of consciousness flow; we allow our imagination to play without trying to control or predict the results (Siegel 2010). Often this defocused mode of processing happens when we're out in nature, when we're in the timeless flow of a work project, when we're first waking up or just about to fall asleep. This defocused mode seems to be the neural foundation for insights, epiphanies, "Aha!" moments. Neuroscientists are just beginning to research this mode of processing. It's much harder to observe in their scanners than when they are asking the brain to perform a task and then monitoring the structures of the brain that "light up" while performing that task.

Here is an exercise I've led many times in workshops to evoke this defocused mode of processing and facilitate the deconditioning of our deeply held beliefs about ourselves and others to relax and expand a bit. The sense of expansion can inform, even transform, our previously conditioned beliefs. The exercise is done silently with a partner. You may want to record the instructions or ask a third person to guide you through the steps.

Brahma Viharas

The *Brahma Viharas*—loving kindness, compassion, sympathetic joy, equanimity—are considered to be "the divine abodes" in the Buddhist wisdom tradition: states of consciousness we embody as we move toward enlightenment. The four Brahma Viharas are also states of being that we actively cultivate to further us on the path toward enlightenment.

This exercise is done with a partner, entirely in noble silence. Invite a friend to do this guided meditation with you. Sit across from each other so that you can easily maintain eye contact. Decide who will be partner A and who will be partner B.

Begin by simply gazing into each other's eyes, allowing yourself to see in your partner the nobility of their true nature. See their innate goodness and radiance of their being; their sincere wishes for peace, happiness, and well-being.

Partner A closes her eyes. Partner B begins to silently wish her well, sending her sincere expressions of loving kindness: "May you know the deepest happiness, may you have ease of mind and heart." Partner A, let yourself know that your partner is sending you expressions of loving kindness; let yourself receive and take in the kindness being offered you.

Partner B closes his eyes; both partners sit in silence, reflecting on the experience of giving and receiving wishes for loving kindness, happiness, peace, and ease.

Partner A opens her eyes; partner B keeps his eyes closed. Partner A begins to silently wish Partner B well, sending him sincere expressions of loving kindness: "May you know the deepest happiness, may you have ease of mind and heart." Partner B, let yourself know that your partner is sending you expressions of loving kindness; let yourself receive and take in the kindness being offered you.

Partner A closes her eyes; both partners sit in silence, reflecting on the experience and giving and receiving wishes for kindness and happiness, peace and ease.

Partner B opens his eyes; Partner A's eyes remain closed. Partner B begins to imagine what human sorrows Partner A might have experienced on her journey, what losses, what griefs, what pain of the human condition. Partner B silently begins to send Partner A expressions of compassion: "May your sorrows be held in loving awareness, may your sorrows ease; may your sorrows cease. May you be free of suffering, and all causes of suffering, and from causing any suffering." Partner A, let yourself take in the care and compassion being offered to you.

Partner B closes his eyes; both partners sit in silence, reflecting on the experience of giving and receiving compassion and care for sorrows and suffering.

Partner A opens her eyes; Partner B's eyes remain closed. Partner A begins to imagine what human sorrows Partner B might have experienced on his journey, what losses, what griefs, what pain of the human condition. Partner A silently begins to send Partner B expressions of compassion: "May your sorrows be held in loving awareness, may your sorrows ease; may your sorrows cease. May you be free of suffering, and all causes of suffering, and from causing any suffering." Partner B, let yourself take in the care and compassion being offered to you.

Partner A closes her eyes; both partners sit in silence, reflecting on the experience of giving and receiving compassion and care for sorrows and suffering.

Partner B opens his eyes; Partner A's eyes remain closed. Partner B begins to imagine what human joys Partner A may have experienced on her journey. What accomplishments and competencies she might have achieved, what blessings of abundance and love she might have experienced. Partner B begins to silently send her expressions of sympathetic joy, happiness for her happiness: "May you fully delight in your delight; may you feel your joy deeply." Partner A, let yourself receive and take in the delight in your delight being offered to you.

Partner B closes his eyes; both partners sit in silence, reflecting on the experience of giving and receiving joy and delight.

Partner A opens her eyes; Partner B's eyes remain closed. Partner A begins to imagine what human joys Partner B may have experienced on his journey. What accomplishments and competencies he might have achieved, what blessings of abundance and love he might have experienced. Partner A begins to silently send him expressions of sympathetic joy, happiness for his happiness: "May you fully delight in your delight; may you feel your joy deeply." Partner B, let yourself receive and take in the delight in your delight being offered to you.

Partner A closes her eyes: both partners sit in silence, reflecting on the experience of giving and receiving joy and delight.

Partner B opens his eyes; Partner A's eyes remain closed. Partner B begins to imagine what ups and downs Partner A might have experienced in her life, what twists and turns. Partner B begins to send her wishes for equanimity, for a calm abiding in centeredness and groundedness as she rides the waves of life. Partner A, let yourself receive these wishes for equanimity, balance, and deep inner peace.

Partner B closes his eyes: both partners sit in silence, reflecting on the experience of giving and receiving wishes for calm, for equanimity, for deep inner peace.

Partner A opens her eyes; Partner B's eyes remain closed. Partner A begins to imagine what ups and downs Partner B might have experienced in his life; what twists and turns. And begins to send him wishes for equanimity, for a calm abiding in centeredness and groundedness as he rides the waves of life. Partner B, let yourself receive these wishes for equanimity, balance, and deep inner peace.

Partner A closes her eyes; both partners sit in silence, reflecting on the experience of giving and receiving wishes for calm, for equanimity, for deep inner peace.

With eyes remaining closed, both partners simply bring awareness to this entire experience, reflecting on the giving and receiving of kindness, compassion, joy, and equanimity. Notice any changes in your sense of yourself or of your partner.

Both partners open their eyes and gaze into the eyes of the person you have shared this experience with. Offer a bow of thanks and gratitude for creating this experience together.

Guided imagery is a powerful tool for creating change in our lives because it reliably creates the desired change directly in our brains. We can use guided imagery to produce new experiences that will evoke new patterns of neural firing in our brains and result in new patterns of relating to ourselves and navigating our lives.

References

Davidson, R. (2004) "Well-being and affective style: Neural substrates and biobehavioural correlates." *Philosophical Transactions of the Royal Society of London B, Biological Sciences 359*, 1395–1411.

Davidson, R. and Begley, S. (2012) *The Emotional Life of Your Brain: How Its Unique Patterns Affect the Way You Think, Feel, and Live—and How You Can Change Them.* New York, NY: Penguin Books.

Ecker, B. (2012) *Unlocking the Emotional Brain: Eliminating Symptoms at Their Roots Using Memory Reconsolidation.* New York, NY: Routledge.

Emmons, R. (2008) *Thanks! How Practicing Gratitude Can Make You Happier.* New York, NY: Houghton Mifflin.

Fredrickson, B. (2004) "The broaden-and-build theory of positive emotions." *Philosophical Transactions of the Royal Society of London B, Biological Sciences 359*, 1367–1378.

Gilbert, P. (2009) *The Compassionate Mind: A New Approach to Life's Challenges.* Oakland, CA: New Harbinger Publications.

Lazar, S. (2007) "The mindful brain: Reflections and attunement and the neuroplasticity of mindful practice." Paper presented at conference *Mindfulness and Psychotherapy.* Lifespan Learning Institute, Los Angeles, CA, October 6 2007.

Siegel, D. (2010) *The Mindful Therapist: A Clinician's Guide to Mindsight and Neural Integration.* New York, NY: W.W. Norton.

Siegel, D. (2012) *The Developing Mind: How Relationships and the Brain Interact to Shape Who We Are.* New York, NY: Guilford Press.

Chapter 11

Imagery as a Therapeutic Tool for Children[1]

Charlotte Reznick

> *I like imagery because it gives me a chance to relax and settle down. It helped me to not lose my temper or get frustrated when I don't do my work right.*
>
> Fourth-grade boy

For as long as I can remember, my imagination helped me through my childhood. It was there to keep me company on lonely nights when my parents were working, it was there to cheer me up when other kids made fun of my name, and it was there to help me picture a better world I longed for.

Years later I became a psychologist in the inner city schools of south Los Angeles. The kids were from the lowest socioeconomic levels, violence and abuse at home were the norm, and there was little to look forward to, as hopelessness and despair were ever-present. My goal was to heal the hearts of these innocents and help them see their inner light. I wanted to create a safe, loving environment where kids could thrive and be their best selves.

A couple of years into my sojourn, life presented opportunities to draw on my childhood imagination by introducing me to guided imagery and created the seeds for developing *Imagery For Kids*[2] and the Nine Tools I wrote about in *The Power of Your Child's Imagination* (2009). My first foray into imagery came when I attended a psychology conference in 1981 where a group from Paradise Unified School District presented their findings from a three-year study involving several hundred elementary students. The treatment variable was weekly classroom guided imagery exercises. Compared to a control group, statistically significant effects occurred over the school year; behavior referrals to the office decreased, attendance increased, and academic achievement on standardized tests improved.[3]

Following their data presentation, the researchers had us draw a forest scene—mine was primitive and limited. Then they conducted an evocative guided imagery that included all our senses and we drew again. What a difference in my picture! The second one was lovely and much richer. My mind and heart were touched.

I started researching guided imagery as a potential therapeutic tool to use with children. I read every book, every article I could get my hands on, and attended every relevant conference. The people I studied with all worked with adults, yet I found a way to make it succeed with my kids.

Perhaps it was synchronicity when my personal path led to learning traditional meditation practices—because over the years I combined both modalities. But what was most exciting for me was that there was a core group (e.g. Bresler 1979; Naparstek 1994; Rossman 1987) who so valued the imagination and the mind-body connection early on, that we realized we could affect personal change by tapping into that vast resource.

Although guided imagery had been around for quite some time, it was primarily used with adults in sports and in medicine (e.g. Simonton, Matthews-Simonton, and Creighton 1978), and was not yet popular as an intervention for children. There were a few books that stood out and described similar processes, though they didn't always name it "imagery."

The Centering Book's (Hendricks 1975) goal was to "center" and calm kids, but it didn't refer to the many helpful scripts as "guided imageries," even though that's basically what they were. Deborah Rozman's *Meditation for Children* (1977) included several wonderful guided journeys, but the public school system would not tolerate the word "meditation." *Hypnosis and Hypnotherapy with Children* (Olness and Kohen 1996) is an important textbook that provides protocols for many medical concerns (like migraine, stomach pain, surgery, tics, and grief), but "hypnosis" was another unacceptable word in public schools. Yet these texts, from supposedly different disciplines, were basically on the same track.

Today, "mindfulness" is the popular buzz technique, pioneered for adults by Jon Kabat-Zinn (1990, 1995, 2013) and more recently for kids by Greenland (2010). I believe that Americans have embraced this particular form of meditation because the word "mind" is included—and the word "meditation" is not. Classic mindfulness teachers might say that mindfulness is not guided imagery: mindfulness is being aware without judgment or scripted words. However, when working with kids, my experience shows me that mindfulness practitioners are often actually using guided imagery.

Hypnosis (the most directed), guided imagery and mindfulness (middle of the road), and meditation (the least directed)—are all variations on the theme of quieting our minds and connecting to our inner resources.

My underlying assumptions working with children and teens are that kids (like adults) possess wisdom that can be accessed once they are quiet, centered, and open to connect with their intuition; that intuition can be developed through meditation, the power of the imagination, and expressive outlets such as drawing and writing; and that imagery has a way of bypassing our internal defense system and connecting us to our intuitive, creative side.

It's important to make the imagery experiences fun, light, and relevant to kids' lives. You'll be more successful if they buy into the new system. It's pretty easy to do if you start with their concerns, which are not necessarily on their parents' agenda. Ask yes-oriented questions. For example, one girl complained about not being able to fall asleep and being exhausted in the morning. I asked if she would like to fall asleep more easily: "Yes." Then I wondered what her life *will* be like when she *can* fall asleep quickly. At that point, she didn't need any prompting: but if a child can't easily describe their new life, be ready to offer some choices (in this case, rested, better mood, happier). Her final "yes" told me that she was ready to learn some new techniques to reach her goal.

I'm here to help kids achieve their dreams, whatever they are, as long as they aren't hurting anyone. I'm secure in the knowledge that we can do this together. I may not be sure exactly how, or how long it will take, but I know we will be successful. I've done this hundreds of times. My clarity and confidence may provide a partial placebo effect, but what's important is achieving positive results in a loving, heart-centered way.

My 15 years in the inner city and another 15-plus years with middle- to upper-class kids confirmed that imagery (and its cousins mentioned above) can be highly effective no matter the age, developmental level, or economic status. The main differences lie in the language we use to teach these skills.

Imagery is beneficial for a variety of concerns, including:

- reducing stress

- overcoming anxiety and fears

- decreasing anger, aggression, and acting-out behaviors

- healing somatic illness (headaches, stomachaches, tics)

- minimizing pain

- reducing sleep disorders (falling asleep, staying asleep, bedwetting)

- coping with loss (divorce, death)

- healing past abuse (physical, emotional, sexual)

- enhancing concentration

- calming hyperactivity

- increasing academic/sports performance

- expanding creative expression

- living peacefully with family and friends

- developing self-esteem and self-worth

- creating transpersonal/spiritual applications.

We can approach imagery as a therapeutic tool in many different ways. In those early years I offered simple guided journeys to lovely special places, with the goal of creating a safe sanctuary, a mini-vacation from the stresses of everyday life. The children relaxed, but what emerged were not always peaceful feelings. As their defenses dissipated, for some children the horrors of their lives came to the fore and gory pictorials exploded. One fifth-grade boy drew himself drowning in a lake while his dad stood by on land. "Could anyone help?" I questioned. "Yes, my dad could throw me a life rope and pull me out." It's showing kids how to connect with their resources that is critical. Life contains so many challenges, but as long as we can teach our kids to get help, either from inside or outside, there's hope that they'll be okay.

Not everyone can easily access intuitive wisdom. When working in a group, other kids can be a strong support. In *Windows to Our Children* (1988), Violet Oaklander offers an exercise in which we imagine ourselves as a flower or bush as a metaphor for how we see ourselves. In one

Kindergarten class, most kids pictured lush flowers, but one lonely boy said he couldn't. His flowers were limp and dying. "Could anything help?" I asked. "No," was his reply. So I brought the group in; they were happy to suggest watering the plant, showering it with sunshine, and adding nutritious food. Then he closed his eyes, and taking in all his peers loving thoughts, he imagined his flower growing healthy and himself being calmer and happier.

Today I lead group and individual guided imageries/meditations or create personal interactive scenarios based on both general and specific issues. I often use music as a background, with drawing as a follow-up activity. Music can deepen the relaxation response and create a natural healing environment. Sometimes kids get lost in the music and don't hear my words: they go to a deeper restorative place inside themselves. That's perfectly fine. Drawing is frequently cathartic and is a great way to express inner images. It's also a safe way to start a conversation and process the imagery experience.

A basic approach is to teach kids how to relax and connect. In a group, it's important to leave the directed imagery open enough for children to make decisions within their reverie so they feel in control. When working with individuals, it's easier to interact and see what's happening in the moment. Your intention may be simple relaxation to a pleasant place, or you may want to reach a specific goal, heal physical concerns, or address life issues. There are several scripts on a variety of topics in *The Power of Your Child's Imagination* (Reznick 2009).

Once I had a group of preteen and adolescent boys with different physical complaints: headache, stomachache, and canker sores. I guided them through *Creating a Magical Garden and Healing Pond* (Reznick 2005), where the garden was a metaphor for a healthy budding body. While their gardens were growing, they rested in healing waters to take away any physical, emotional, or spiritual pain. When we were done, both the headache and stomachache were gone, and the canker sores didn't hurt so much. The boy with the canker sores listened nightly to the recording he made during our session, and the next week he reported that the sores went away in half their usual time.

Group Guided Imagery Process

1. Start the children with slow breathing just below the navel ("Balloon Breath").

2. Practice progressive muscle relaxation (toes to head) to quiet squirmy bodies.

3. Use a deepening induction of white light (or rainbow or another calming color) coming from the sky through their entire body from top to bottom to begin the relaxation and prepare for their inner journey.

4. Take them through a guided imagery (reminding them they are in control and can change any words or pictures they are not comfortable with).

5. Have them return and ground by being aware of their breath, feet/toes, hands/fingers, then slowly open their eyes.

6. Process what happened: draw or write about the experience.

7. Group discussion and individual follow-up as needed.

Over the years, I've refined this simple group process and developed a Nine Tool system that can be mixed and matched to help kids confront and conquer many issues in order to create a happy and healthy life.

The Nine Tools
THE FOUNDATION TOOLS
The basis for all our imagery work is to build a strong foundation that can hold big emotions and manage resistance.

The Balloon Breath
A simple, basic meditation breath; breathing in slowly (1…2…3…) about one to two inches below the navel centers and calms us. It's easy even for the youngest because of the visual: when we breathe into a balloon it expands, and it flattens as we breathe out. I'll start with having the kids put their hands on their bellies so they can actually feel their breath going in and out. Or I'll have them lie down and place a dime or a small stuffed animal on their bellies that they can watch rise and fall.

For the older ones, I might call the exercise "deep breathing." I asked one teen if she had ever done yoga or meditation, and she almost shouted, "Oh no, my mom does that!" So I said, "Good, we'll just be doing some deep breathing." I also tell teens that I don't have their answers for them: my job is to assist them in finding their own.

Start with three Balloon Breaths with eyes open, then three with eyes closed. This helps ease into the closed-eye inner work. If a child is uncomfortable shutting her eyes, I suggest lowering the eyelids slightly and looking down with a soft focus. Most tell me they feel more relaxed when they take a risk and close their eyes.

Then I'll time how "few" breaths they can do in a minute; that becomes their "Take Care of Me Homework"—find one minute twice a day to practice. We add another 30 seconds every two weeks or so, and before long they're up to five/eight/ten minutes of meditation twice a day. Longer practice usually occurs when they are listening to a guided journey I've recorded for them on their Voice Memos, or listening to one of my guided-meditation/imagery CDs. This inner time is a necessary balance to all the stimulation from their outer world.

Discovering Your Special Place

The second foundation Tool is to learn to create a sanctuary where they can be themselves, feel safe and loved, chill out, and do "inner work." They can imagine whatever makes them feel good: it can be a meadow, beach, forest, their comfy room, or even Disneyland. They can be on their own or invite friends, family, and pets. A caveat is that once someone steps through the door, they love and accept them just the way they are: that helps manage previous squabbles or arguments. One nine-year-old boy used a remote covered with numerous colored dots that would take him to a variety of inner-work places depending on what color he pressed. Blue was for water places, green for nature, yellow for warm spots, and so on. Another girl had a special place with several rooms, including a kitchen, bedroom, and a "main" room with a table and two chairs where she did her inner work with one of her helpers.

CHECKING IN WITH INNER GUIDES

The next group of Tools helps kids connect to their inner wisdom.

Meeting a Wise Animal Friend

For younger kids, Animal Friends are a great way in. They are loving, protective, caring creatures that have your best interests at heart and show up to help you through life's challenges. Shamans have used "power animals" for centuries, and contemporary imagery practices can build on that. Animal Friends can be any sort: wild beast, gentle lamb, even a beloved dog or cat. An inventive six-year-old boy created his own combo of a dog and chicken.

One 11-year-old girl had the hardest time falling asleep because of nighttime fears. She was sure she and her family were not safe and that someone was going to break into her home, even though they had an alarm system and a barking dog. What worked? She imagined a giant white dragon, Valcor, wrapped around her bed, and a tiger by her door for extra security. This helped her feel safe enough to close her eyes, relax her body, and drift off to sleep.

When she started worrying about the safety of her parents and younger brother several weeks later, she just sent Valcor's cousins to take care of them. This was all she needed. One friend made fun of her, "It's just your imagination; how can that help?" This now confident girl declared, "My fears come from my imagination, so I had to go into that realm to fix it."

Encountering a Personal Wizard

Sometimes Animal Friends aren't enough. Resistance pops up and sends them on vacation, leaving the child in the lurch. Or perhaps extra magic is needed. A Personal Wizard can be just the ticket, and with Harry Potter's fame, wizards are quite popular. Wizards are master teachers in human form. Variations include goddesses and superheroes, fairies and angels. Wizards can function as an all-around Everything Wizard, or they can have special abilities. One harried teen conjured up a Time-Management Wizard, while an active seven-year-old imagined a Focus Wizard with a green crystal wand to calm his body and who told him to "stay focused." Sleep Wizards and their potions also crop up a lot.

If a child isn't into Wizards, I'll incorporate a Wise Person or their Older and Wiser Self who has already conquered the problem and is here to advise them. A six-year-old bed-wetter was encouraged by his Older and Wiser Self, "Don't give up; never give up."

Both Animal Friends and Wizards offer their wise counsel in the form of...

Gifts

A Gift can be anything that will help with the issue at hand. Gifts are either "real" imaginary gifts, advice a guide gives you, or something they show you. One 13-year-old received a significant book, *Becoming a Better You*, from her Wizard as she entered adolescence. An anxious nine-year-old boy went into a Cave of Wisdom to help him with his troubles. There he received three Gifts from his panther Animal Friend: a golden eggshell to remind him that he's permanently protected, a stuffed toy panther to let him know his Animal Friend is always with him, and a neon-green snorkel set to remember his happy beach place.

CONNECTING WITH THE WISDOM OF THE BODY

The next step moves into wisdom that is truly inside—inside the body. Many kids find it easier to imagine someone who seems to be "outside" offering advice (Animal Friends, Wizards, Wise People): that's why I usually teach these first. Yet these guides *are* inner guides, because they come from the person's own imagination. The physical body offers another way in.

Checking in with Heart and Belly

This Tool is similar to life's tried-and-true wisdom that asks us to "listen to your heart" and "what does your gut tell you?" Our heart and belly both contain their own form of brain. There are anecdotal reports from people who've received heart transplants that they've started to like a particular food or activity that the heart donor did, suggesting a possible cellular memory transfer (Childre and Martin 1999). And it seems that our brain's neuropeptides, which talk in their own way to other parts of our body, also live in our intestinal tract, leading to the idea of a belly-brain (Pert 1997). By connecting the mind with our heart- and belly-brains, we get a much richer response.

My own meditation practice is heart-centered, and when a child is connected to the wisdom and love in their heart, fear and anger can dissipate. A simple way to teach children to listen to the heart is to start with the Balloon Breath, and then have them put a hand on the center of their chest at heart level: the heart-center. Then they can close their eyes and ask what their heart wants to tell them. The response can be a general message or it can pertain to a specific concern. I'll suggest that if the child is not used to talking with their heart, the heart might be shy, so please be patient. This takes away any discomfort from the unfamiliarity of such a request. Messages can vary, from a teen boy worried about fitting in who hears, "Be yourself" to a shy young gal's, "Let your heart sing" and a chronically negative 12-year-old's, "Focus on what brings you joy."

Connecting to belly-wisdom is similar. I'll have children put their hand over their lower abdomen and ask, "What does my belly say?" Sometimes I'll get giggles and hear, "It's hungry," and other times there's a clear message. One girl's fear of throwing up had her belly offering, "You will be okay no matter what." At other times, heart and belly have a conversation. One nine-year-old had knots in his gut because he didn't make the soccer team while his best friend did. His belly let him know, "It's not fair," but his stronger heart said "You'll get your turn next session."

Talking to Other Body Parts

Every part of our body has information to offer us. I look at this Tool as many-tiered and as a way to explore body awareness. Where do we keep our emotions? Where do love, anger, fear, worry, joy, bravery, and all the rest hang out? We'll regularly start by doing a body-feeling self-portrait, where kids imagine and draw what color, shape, or face their feelings have, without then adding clothes or facial features.

One seven-year-old was mad about her younger brother's birth. When she closed her eyes, I suggested she might be surprised at what was *under* her anger: it turned out that sadness was hiding there. She said she was sad because she missed the attention and time she used to have with Mom. Once she got to this core emotion, we made a plan to release and make peace. In her case it was to spend more time with Mom by helping with the baby.

We also explore how their feelings interact with each other, how they affect the child's life, and maximize the positive by bringing in and blending with the next Tool.

Using Color for Healing

An angry eight-year-old, often in trouble for tormenting his younger sister at home and behaving horribly with his peers at school, came into my office furious. He described his anger as red-hot in his belly. When working with a negative feeling, I recommend using two positive ones as an antidote. Depending on the child, either he or you can suggest some opposite emotions. I asked this boy where his calm feelings were: they were blue circles in his shoulders. Next I instructed him to breathe the positive calm blue into the anger and then throughout his entire body, and notice if there were any shifts or changes. For this little terror, calm blue smoothed itself over his anger and quieted its roar. When I asked him to find where "love" lived, it was white, inside his heart. And when he breathed love into anger, followed by filling up his whole body with love—that turned the tide. Love exploded his anger and it disappeared.

This sort of imagery work can touch kids on a deep level; I regularly see a turn-around in attitude and behavior. I like to anchor that shift into the body by offering a tiny heart to keep and hold as a reminder of the importance of their heart, their love, and all their feelings.

ACCESSING ENERGY FOR HEALING

Tapping into Energy

The final frontier for me was learning the concept of accessing energy for healing. Although I practiced energy work that I'd learned from my Buddhist/Taoist meditation teacher early on, I didn't talk about it much as a ninth Tool until recently. My 30-plus years of meditation have shown me that energy effects are real, and when combined with traditional imagery, we have a potent tool to incorporate into a healing repertoire. Jeanne

Achtenberg and her colleagues' research on energy healing demonstrated the efficacy of distant healing with adults (2005). A seminal study headed by Miranda Van Tilberg (2009) with children's chronic stomach pain confirmed the validity of teaching kids to send loving, warm energy through their hands as they place them on their tummies for comfort and pain reduction. Her team also established the positive effects of guided imagery over standard medical care for significantly reducing pain (73 percent of the treatment group reported their pain decreased by half compared to 27 percent of the controls).

Here's a sample case study that provides an overview of the Nine Tools Imagery Therapeutic Kit and how you can use it:

Case Study: Deva[4]

At ten, Deva appeared to have everything—she was brilliant in school, a natural artist, and an amazing dancer. But inside, something was off. Deva's attitude had soured—toward herself, her family, and her friends. A formerly loving and generous girl, she seemed to change overnight into a selfish bully.

Deva had a long list of complaints: "I hate my life, I have too much to do, I can't sleep, and I'm jealous of my brother. My friends don't let me choose games and now they won't play with me." Deva had no clue that her ungracious behavior impacted how others responded to her; she was just in pain.

When I first met Deva, she admitted she felt pressure to be perfect. I wondered what the pressure looked like. Deva envisioned herself with locks on her shoulders, hips, and feet. We asked for a loving Animal Friend to relieve her suffering. An Orangutan sat next to a shady tree holding the key to Deva's locks, while nearby was a pile of locks he'd already opened. He proceeded to release the rest.

Once that initial pressure subsided, Deva began to openly experience and express negative feelings she thought she'd been hiding, like anger and resentment. Her parents asked her to be a bit more positive, but she just couldn't. I asked her to draw what was going on inside. On one side she drew an angel, on the other, a devil. A big black X separated them, and blotches of black paint all over the paper revealed her distress. That day we did a combination of imagery and energy work. While she calmed herself with Balloon Breath, I placed my hands in her energy field, three to six inches above her body. I asked if she'd like to imagine letting go of her bad feelings and replacing them with love; she did.

Afterwards she offered, "When your hands were over my heart, I heard it talking: 'Don't be negative,' it said, 'think of happy things.' When your hands moved over my belly, a voice whispered, 'Things will be okay. Don't worry.'"

When I reached her legs, Deva said she felt the bad feelings being sucked out. She sensed an angel nearby, always ready to comfort her.

Like a blocked well, Deva's dark outlook had prevented her kind and loving feelings from surfacing. Once she felt the energy help to release her negativity, she could experience her goodness and her generous heart that were there all along. The encouraging voice and the angel she imagined seemed to remind her that healing and forgiveness were possible. Deva painted four brightly colored patched hearts for each family member. She whispered, "I do love my family."

In another session, Orangutan reappeared and gave Deva a Gift of a multicolored marker. His advice: "If you're angry, you can let it out in your pictures." The marker made her sketches come alive, and getting it out on paper somehow made her feel better. One day her Angel Wizard showed up with a magic eraser. "It erases my hateful thoughts," Deva explained.

After several months, Deva created an inner garden filled with edible flowers of love and kindness. She imagined slowly chewing them, filling her heart with love. I asked if she could extend that love throughout her body with her breath and intention. The deep peace it brought her translated into caring at home and sharing with her friends.

What a pleasure to witness these transformations! My hope is that your therapeutic path using imagery with children will bring you such joy and more.

ENDNOTES

1. Information for this chapter is based on my *Imagery For Kids*™ program and my book *The Power of Your Child's Imagination* (2009). All stories are composites or are disguised to protect privacy.
2. See www.imageryforkids.com
3. Paradise Unified School District. Personal communication with author, California Association of School Psychologists Annual Conference (1981).
4. Deva's story is similar to one in my book *The Power of Your Child's Imagination* (2009), where a fuller account can be found.

References

Achterberg, J., Cooke, K., Richards, T., Standish, L., Kozak, L., and Lake, J. (2005) "Evidence for correlations between distant intentionality and brain function in recipients: A functional magnetic resonance imaging analysis." *The Journal of Alternative and Complementary Medicine 11*, 6, 965–971.

Bresler, D. (1979) *Free Yourself From Pain*. New York, NY: Simon & Schuster.

Childre, D. and Martin, H. (1999) *The HeartMath Solution*. New York, NY: Harper Collins.

Greenland, S.K. (2010) *The Mindful Child: How to Help Your Kid Manage Stress and Become Happier, Kinder, and More Compassionate*. New York, NY: Atria Books.

Hendricks, G. (1975) *The Centering Book: Awareness Activities for Children, Parents, and Teachers*. Saddle River, NJ: Prentice Hall Trade.

Kabat-Zinn, J. (1990, 2013 revised edition) *Full Catastrophe Living: Using the Wisdom of Your Body and Mind to Face Stress, Pain, and Illness*. New York, NY: Bantam.

Kabat-Zinn, J. (1995) *Wherever You Go, There You Are: Mindfulness Meditation for Everyday Life*. Burbank, CA: Hyperion.

Naparstek, B. (1994) *Staying Well With Guided Imagery*. New York, NY: Warner Books.

Oaklander, V. (1988) *Windows to Our Children: A Gestalt Therapy Approach to Children and Adolescents*. Gouldsboro, ME: The Gestalt Journal Press.

Olness, K. and Kohen, D. (1996) *Hypnosis and Hypnotherapy With Children*. New York, NY: Guilford Press.

Pert, C. (1997) *Molecules of Emotion: The Science Behind Mind-Body Medicine*. New York, NY: Scribner.

Reznick, C. (2005) *Creating a Magical Garden and Healing Pond* CD. Los Angeles, CA: Imagery For Kids.

Reznick, C. (2009) *The Power of Your Child's Imagination: How to Transform Stress and Anxiety into Joy and Success*. New York, NY: Perigee/Penguin Group.

Rossman, M. (1987) *Healing Yourself: A Step-By-Step Program for Better Health Through Imagery*. New York, NY: Walker & Co.

Rozman, D. (1977) *Meditation for Children*. Berkeley, CA: Celestial Arts.

Simonton, C., Matthews-Simonton, S., and Creighton, J. (1978) *Getting Well Again: A Step-By-Step Self-Help Guide to Overcoming Cancer for Patients and Their Families*. Los Angeles, CA: JP Tarcher, Inc.

Van Tilburg, M., Chitkara, D., Palsson, O., Turner, M., Blois-Martin, N., Ulshen, M., and Whitehead, W. (2009) "Audio-recorded guided imagery treatment reduces abdominal pain in children: A pilot study." *Journal of Pediatrics 124*, 5, 890–897.

Chapter 12

Body Felt Imagery

Thoughts of the Radically Embodied Mind

Glenn Hartelius and Judith Goleman

Maureen's story (not her real name) will serve as an introductory example of what body felt imagery can accomplish. Maureen came for help with her relationship, but in the course of therapy she mentioned that she had been suffering from debilitating neck pain and muscular tension. When she brought her attention into the pain, what came to her mind were current issues she was having with a family member. As Maureen talked about these issues, she was gradually able to acknowledge how painful they were to her—something she had not been giving herself permission to feel. By the end of the session, as she realized that this family member was a "pain in the neck," the tension in her neck had begun to ease. Over the next several days the pain resolved. This illustrates the way that body felt images deeply reflect the realities of both body and mind, so that shifts in the imagery lead to actual changes in the whole embodied person.

We define body felt imagery as the process of internal image production in which emotionally significant images are seen and affectively experienced as occurring in or near the trunk of the body. This type of imagery appears to be similar to kinesthetic imagery, which is associated with sensorimotor experience rather than rational cognitive experience (cf. Glenberg 2010)—but it is focused more on sensations associated with emotional experience than on those associated with bodily movement. Body felt images may be spontaneous (e.g. Osman *et al.* 2004), they may be elicited (e.g. Arntz 2011), they may be guided (e.g. Leuner 1977, 1984; Achterberg 2013), or they may be intrusive (e.g. Brewin *et al.* 2010). They are always important because they can facilitate profound psychophysical transformation.

Stories of spontaneous healing like Maureen's are common in the literature of guided imagery, and it is clear that guided imagery is quite different than conventional imagery that an individual might use, for example, to remember the color of their car or where they last placed their keys. What is lacking are precise descriptions of what constitutes this difference, or how we can be sure that the more transformative forms of imagery are being accessed. Without a clear distinction, someone new to this work might unwittingly access a form of imagination that is more closely linked to their established cognitive belief systems, internalized social conventions, and constructed narratives about their identity and history—rather than eliciting images that reach deeply into those body-based reservoirs of lived experience that are not under ego's direction. By defining body felt imagery in terms of particular states of consciousness, or a range of states, a more precise distinction can perhaps be made between imagery that pertains to the domain of egoic imagination and imagery that directly represents unscripted, somatically bound trauma. This may help to promote greater accuracy in the description, study, and clinical use of imagery.

Body felt imagery seems to signal a shift in states of consciousness because it occurs in the context of a specific mode of mental functioning that is quite different from either ordinary thought or conventional imagination. A clear articulation of this associated state of consciousness could be the key to distinguishing between body felt imagery and imagery that may be useful for purposes other than healing. The challenge with this approach is that to date there has been no demonstrably reliable method for defining such states in a scientific manner (Rock, Friedman, and Jamieson 2013).

Early efforts such as those by Ludwig (1969), Krippner (1972), Tart (1969, 1975), and Singer (1977) proposed that states of consciousness should be defined either in terms of patterns of phenomenal properties or by the intensity of phenomenological experience—but they did not offer any methods for measuring these qualities nor a way of determining how much difference might be required to distinguish one state of consciousness from another. Along these lines, Rock and Krippner (2007) have proposed that the term "altered state of consciousness" be replaced by *altered pattern of phenomenal properties.*

One method for measuring both patterns and intensity of phenomenal properties, the Pekala Consciousness Inventory (PCI), was developed by Pekala (1991) as a way to measure 12 major and 14 minor dimensions of phenomenological experience (Pekala, Steinberg, and Kumar 1986; Pekala and Wenger 1983) and represented them graphically so that the patterns of phenomenal properties from one condition of lived experience can be easily compared with those of another condition (e.g. Rock and Storm 2010). This capacity to show a measurable difference between two states of consciousness may be the greatest strength of the PCI.

While the PCI is perhaps the most developed tool for measuring phenomenological experience, there are several problems with this approach. Most basically, the extensive list of phenomenological variables that is the strength of the PCI is also its liability. While any particular lived experience can be retrospectively mapped into a unique pattern of phenomenal properties, there seems to be no elegant way to classify these results into a meaningful taxonomy. A related issue is that the complexity of the patterns in PCI results makes the task of determining how much difference between patterns is sufficient to distinguish between one state and another nearly impossible (Rock and Krippner 2007). The simple criterion offered by Krippner (1972), namely, that either an individual or an observer is able to detect "a difference" (p.1) in state, leaves in doubt a potentially wide range of variability in terms of how various subjects or observers might discern, describe, or value difference—and many observable differences would likely make little visible difference in a visual display of PCI results.

In addition, the PCI is so complex that it is unlikely to be able to describe the lived experience of different states or patterns in a meaningful way. Finally, while Pekala has developed another scale to quantify descriptions of attention, the Dimensions of Attention Questionnaire (DAQ; Pekala 1991), it is possible that unless these two instruments are used together, significant differences in attentional states would not be adequately reflected in a thoroughgoing analysis of phenomenological experiences. This is also a weakness of the definition offered by Rock and Krippner (2007), which is based only on phenomenology and not on attentional state. Preliminary research shows that changes in attentional state may be reflected in electrocephalogram (EEG) measurements, supporting the potential importance of attentional variables in defining states of consciousness (Hinterberger, Zlabinger, and Blaser 2014).

Somatic phenomenology as described by Hartelius (2007, 2015) may be able to supplement tools like the PCI by offering a simple way to represent states of consciousness in terms of *attentional posture*: that is, the way that the phenomenal markers of attention are deployed within the lived experience of the body. One way to understand this is to imagine a driver sitting at an intersection waiting for the traffic light to turn from red to green. This driver's attention is focused on the red light. We can imagine this attention as an arrow extending from the driver up to the traffic light. Yet it is not just the business end of the arrow that has a specific location—the arrow also emanates from a particular part of the driver's body. In this case, we probably imagine the arrow originating from the driver's head—perhaps even specifically from the eyes.

There is indeed some preliminary evidence that many people may have the experience that their sense of "I" sits in a specific location in their head (Bertossa et al. 2008; cf. Strawson 1997). In other words, when we direct our attention outward at some object, it feels like our attention is arising from a particular location inside our head. In the language of somatic phenomenology, in this example the phenomenal markers of attention are located in the head, indicating a head-located attentional posture. Try this exercise as a way to experience your attentional posture (adapted from Bertossa et al. 2008).

ATTENTIONAL POSTURE PRACTICE

Choose an object to gaze at, and focus your attention on some specific part of it. For example, if you choose a pencil, focus on the eraser—or if you select a chair, focus your attention on the bottom of a chair leg or the end of an armrest. Notice the part of you that is paying attention—the "I" who is focusing—and ask yourself whether it would be possible, if you got up and physically moved your body, to bring this "I" closer to the point you are focused on. Now notice whether this "I," the part of you that is focusing, is closer to your knee or to your throat. If it is closer to your throat—which is more typical—notice whether this "I" is above your throat or below it. Then notice whether your "I" is at the front of your body, at the back of your body, or in the center of your body. Is it on your left side, your right side, or in the center? Finally, take one finger and point directly to where your "I" is. This is the location of your attention—your attentional posture.

Yet when we are in other states of consciousness, attention arises from other bodily locations, and so attention arising from a location in the head is just one of many possible attentional postures (Hartelius 2015). For example, preliminary somatic phenomenological research on flow-like states suggests that in these states attention arises from the trunk of the body, often from near the center of the chest (Marolt-Sender 2014). In addition, Hartelius (2015) has proposed that attentional posture may be a variable that distinguishes important differences between a cognitive-behavioral version of mindfulness (e.g. Hayes, Strosahl, and Wilson 2012) and a neo-traditional form of mindfulness (e.g. Kabat-Zinn 2003a, b)—a distinction that the language of cognitive process may be unable to capture.

From the perspective of somatic phenomenology, descriptions of cognitive-behavioral mindfulness are more consistent with a head-located attentional posture, while those of neo-traditional mindfulness suggest a belly-located attentional posture. This difference between attention arising in the head and attention arising in the trunk of the body may be a variable that can help distinguish between cognitive states and embodied states. This distinction deserves to be tested for possible correlations with neural measurement (Hartelius 2015).

Radical Embodiment and Attentional Posture

After the advent of behaviorism in the early 20th century came cognitive psychology, which then joined with neuroscience to create the field of cognitive neuroscience. If there is a next wave of development, it may be science's embrace of the embodiment of mind. In a sense, embodiment is not so much a new wave as it is a backwash from neuroscience—for if the mind is located within human biology, then that biology must surely be reflected in the functions and processes of mind.

Despite the self-evident nature of this concept, embodied mind can have a variety of meanings. With respect to human beings (as opposed to artificial intelligence), embodied mind can mean something that is limited to living, organismic bodies that are self-directing and self-shaping (Ziemke 2003; cf. von Uexküll 1982; Maturana and Varela 1980). A second version of embodiment describes abstract thought as based in experiences of bodily activity, such that cognition is metaphorically saturated with the bodily experience (Glenberg 2010; cf. Gallese and Lakoff 2005). In a third version, mental symbols are not unified abstractions but rather are composed of discrete components of neural activity—for example, the separate streams of visual and auditory information arising from the perception of some object—that together constitute a perceptual symbol system (Barsalou 1999). According to this model, the mind reconstitutes perceptual symbols by a sort of reenactment in each of the relevant sensory systems (Glenberg 2010). In a fourth version, cognitive representations are informed by bodily action as well as by sensory systems (Glenberg and Kaschak 2002). The social embodiment model, a fifth variant, suggests that mind is shaped not only by the functions and actions of one's own body but also by social stimuli and by perceiving and mimicking the bodily states of others (Barsalou *et al.* 2003). One might contemplate a sixth version that includes input from bodily-located responses known as somatic markers (Bechara and Damasio 2005).

Yet there is one version of embodiment that is more radical still. This model proposes that mind is grounded in the entirety of the body, and that body and mind are interconnected as reciprocally influencing facets of a single system. Evidence for this view comes from work by Pert, Dreher, and Ruff (1998), suggesting that the brain is not a unique or isolated biological system but is part of a psychosomatic information processing network that extends "to every molecular corner of the body" (p.30). Their research documented the fact that the scores of neurohormones in the human system move back and forth between the central and autonomic nervous systems and bodily networks like the endocrine, cardiovascular, digestive, is biologically and functionally interwoven with all the systems of the body—including exchanges of the sorts of neurohormones thought to be associated with mental processes in the brain—then conceptually there is little rationale for limiting mind to the brain. The entire contents of human physiology can perhaps be seen as potential biological correlates of mind just as much as the brain—even if they serve a wide range of different functions.

It may be that the conventional head-located attentional posture, which is common and perhaps even normative in mainstream Western culture, encourages the belief that mind resides only in the brain. If relatively common and accessible experiences such as flow-like states and meditative states can easily be created by shifting our locus of attention— the location from which attention arises—out of the head and into the trunk of the body, then perhaps mind exists throughout the body rather than just in the brain. Changing our attentional posture out of the head and into the trunk of the body could then reasonably be seen as conscious activation of other portions of a body-wide psychosomatic network.

In this context of a body-wide mind, embodiment can mean not only the ways that biology affects mind but also to those states of consciousness in which the attention that normally arises from the head is now deployed from the central structures of the body—as if the self that is conventionally centered in the head is now located in the trunk of the body. We are suggesting that body felt imagery may reflect mental activity occurring in an embodied state that is emerging from the many underused capacities of a radically embodied mind.

Related processes such as active imagination (Jung 1969; Chodorow 2015), guided imagery (Achterberg 2013), imagery used with Gendlin's felt sense-based focusing process (1980, 1996, 1999), hypnagogic/hypnopompic imagery (Sherwood 2002), and kinesthetic imagery (Guillot and Collet 2008) are thought to involve a similar shift to an embodied attentional state—either partially or wholly. There is some evidence that nondirective meditation—an activity that is considered to be similar to the processes just listed—activates neural areas that are associated with memory retrieval and with emotional processing (Xu *et al.* 2014).

The Potential Value of Body Felt Imagery

Kinesthetic imagery—that is, mentally simulating an action with no actual movement of the body—activates the same sensorimotor networks in the brain that would be activated if the imagined activity were actually performed (Guillot *et al.* 2009). For this reason, kinesthetic imagery is used not only to enhance performance in sports (Suinn 1997); it also seems to be as effective as perceptual-motor training for children with motor clumsiness (Wilson, Thomas, and Maruff 2002), it may enhance the performance of musicians and vocalists (Lotze 2013), and it appears to improve motor function in recovering stroke victims (de Vries and Mulder 2007; Stevens and Stoykov 2003). Kinesthetic imagery, but not conventional visual imagery, helps to normalize electrophysiological activity in individuals with Parkinson's disease (Lim *et al.* 2006). This type of imagery, then, appears to be effective because it impacts non-cognitive somatic processes in a way that the more conventional cognitive activities or mental imagery cannot.

We expect that the therapeutic uses of body felt imagery will prove to be as effective as kinesthetic imagery, though its applications are likely to be slightly different. We hope to see research that demonstrates that it can positively influence disruptive forms of body felt imagery, including the intrusive imagery prominently associated with depression, psychosis, eating disorders, and anxiety disorders, including posttraumatic stress disorder (PTSD) and obsessive-compulsive disorder (Brewin, Gregory, Lipton, and Burgess 2010). When used as guided imagery, studies to date find that body felt imagery appears to provide access to non-cognitive somatically held belief systems (Arntz 2011), reduce post-surgical pain (Tusek, Church, and Fazio 1997), reduce pain in some fibromyalgia sufferers (Wickramasekera 2011), and enhance immune system functioning (Trakhtenberg 2008). Through spontaneous imagery, it may also give access to somatically held emotional issues that may not be fully conscious to the cognitive mind (Reyher 1977; Wild, Hackmann, and Clark 2008).

The Practice of Body Felt Imagery

The successful practice of body felt imagery in therapeutic contexts typically includes four steps: intention, activation, invitation, and engagement. It is important that the client begins with conscious intent and interest in addressing potential body-held trauma; without openness and receptivity to the process, the risk is that re-experiencing a trauma may re-traumatize the person. From the therapist's side, the first and most basic condition is a reassuring therapeutic presence.

It is useful to begin with a cognitive exploration of the nature of the early trauma, its context and associated events. This helps direct the mind toward portions of the trauma that may not have been fully faced and comforted, and that may be reflected in tensions and somatic blockages. In order to frame the presenting issues in a constructive light, one might say to a client, "These issues have signaled distress to your cognitive mind because they are ready to be approached for healing." Invitation occurs by shifting into a more embodied state and inviting a metaphorical image to arise—an image associated with the trauma that safely reflects what the client is ready to re-contact. This might be explained to the client by saying, "Images that arise from uncomfortable physical sensations represent emotions that are being held by your body, because your cognitive mind has not been ready to look at them."

The shift into an embodied state can be realized simply by directing the client's attention toward sensations in the trunk of the body, a process that may be facilitated by open-monitoring forms of meditation (cf. Lutz *et al.* 2008) such as Kabat-Zinn's (2003a, b) mindfulness, through Gendlin's (1996) focusing process, or through somatic relaxation (Jacobson 1987) or guided imagery processes (Achterberg 2013). Gently ask the client to stay with the somatic feeling that will soon transform to an image or a memory that has been avoided. It may be helpful to say, "If it is alright with you, please stay with the [describe the sensation that the client has reported]." Once an image arises—typically from the body rather than the head, but always associated with a more embodied state—beneficial change can often be effected simply by remaining present and attending to the image, noting any body felt sensations that accompany the image, and observing any shifts in either the image or the associated sensations.

With childhood sexual molestation victims or others who have experienced particularly traumatic events, it is important that the therapist take steps to prevent a re-traumatizing experience. This can occur if the client goes directly to the memory of the experience without first entering a therapeutic container with the therapist. This container is created and strengthened by the therapist's reassuring presence; by a conscious intention to recall the experience by choice, for the sake of healing on a deep level; by giving the client permission to stop the therapeutic process at any time; and by the deliberate shift of attentional posture out of the head and into an embodied state. This latter step is greatly facilitated when the therapist is able to establish a felt rapport with the client and then shift into an embodied state, so that therapist and client move into somatic experience together.

Body felt images appear to give the client and therapist direct access to non-cognitive, somatically held belief systems and the traumatic events that may have helped to establish them. These traumas and beliefs often seem to be the actual determinants of our inner emotional lives and outer behavior. Moving toward these images and what they embody by choice, in a therapeutic context, can bring early traumatic experiences into somatic integration with the many safe experiences that have occurred since the early trauma. When this is achieved, the client is able to relate to current life experiences with whole-body clarity and freedom. In the words of the late John Heider (personal communication with second author), "Awareness itself is healing."

References

Achterberg, J. (2013) *Imagery in Healing: Shamanism and Modern Medicine*. Boston, MA: Shambhala.

Arntz, A. (2011) "Imagery rescripting for personality disorders." *Cognitive and Behavioral Practice 18*, 466–481.

Barsalou, L.W. (1999) "Perceptual symbol systems." *Behavioral and Brain Sciences 22*, 577–660.

Barsalou, L.W., Niedenthal, P.M., Barbey, A.K., and Ruppert, J.A. (2003) "Social Embodiment." In B.H. Ross (ed.) *The Psychology of Learning and Motivation*. Amsterdam: Elsevier.

Bechara, A. and Damasio, A.R. (2005) "The somatic marker hypothesis: A neural theory of economic decision." *Games and Economic Behavior 52*, 336–372.

Bertossa, F., Besa, M., Ferrari, R., and Ferri, F. (2008) "Point zero: A phenomenological inquiry into the seat of consciousness." *Perceptual and Motor Skills 107*, 323–335.

Brewin, C.R., Gregory, J.D., Lipton, M., and Burgess, N. (2010) "Intrusive images in psychological disorders: Characteristics, neural mechanisms, and treatment implications." *Psychological Review 117*, 1, 210–232.

Chodorow, J. (2015) *Encountering Jung on Active Imagination*. Princeton, NJ: Princeton University Press.

de Vries, S. and Mulder, T. (2007) "Motor imagery and stroke rehabilitation: A critical discussion." *Journal of Rehabilitation Medicine 39*, 5–13.

Gallese, V. and Lakoff, G. (2005) "The brain's concepts: The role of the sensory-motor system in conceptual knowledge." *Cognitive Neuropsychology 22*, 455–479.

Gendlin, E.T. (1980) "Imagery is More Powerful with Focusing: Theory and Practice." In J.E. Shorr, G.E. Sobel, P. Robin, and J.A. Connella (eds) *Imagery: Its Many Dimensions and Applications*. New York, NY: Plenum Press.

Gendlin, E.T. (1996) *An Introduction to Focusing: Six Steps*. New York, NY: Focusing Institute.

Gendlin, E.T. (1999) "A new model." *Journal of Consciousness Studies 6*, 2–3, 232–237.

Glenberg, A.M. (2010) "Embodiment as a unifying perspective for psychology." *WIREs Cognitive Science 1*, 586–596.

Glenberg, A.M. and Kaschak, M.P. (2002) "Grounding language in action." *Psychonomic Bulletin and Review 9*, 558–565.

Guillot, A. and Collet, C. (2008) "Construction of the motor imagery integrative model in sport: A review and theoretical investigation of motor imagery use." *International Review of Sport and Exercise Physiology 1*, 1, 31–44.

Guillot, A., Collet, C., Nguyen, V.A., Malouin, F., Richards, C., and Doyon, J. (2009) "Brain activation during visual versus kinesthetic imagery: An fMRI study." *Human Brain Mapping 30*, 2157–2172.

Hartelius, G. (2007) "Quantitative somatic phenomenology: Toward an epistemology of subjective experience." *Journal of Consciousness Studies 14*, 12, 24–56.

Hartelius, G. (2015). "Body maps of attention: Phenomenal markers for two varieties of mindfulness." *Mindfulness*, February 3, 1–11.

Hayes, S.C., Strosahl, K.D., and Wilson, K.G. (2012) *Acceptance and Commitment Therapy: The Process and Practice of Mindful Change*, 2nd edition. New York, NY: Guilford Press.

Hinterberger, T., Zlabinger, M., and Blaser, K. (2014) "Neurophysiological correlates of various mental perspectives." *Frontiers in Human Neuroscience 8*, Article 637, 100–115.

Jacobson, E. (1987) "Progressive relaxation." *American Journal of Psychology 100*, 3–4, 523–537.

Jung, C.G. (1969) "The Concept of the Collective Unconscious." In R.F.C. Hull (trans.) *The Collected Works of C.G. Jung*, vol. 9, part 1. Princeton, NJ: Bollingen.

Kabat-Zinn, J. (2003a) "Mindfulness-based interventions in context: Past, present, and future." *Clinical Psychology: Science and Practice 10*, 2, 144–156.

Kabat-Zinn, J. (2003b) "Mindfulness-based stress reduction (MBSR)." *Constructivism in the Human Sciences 8*, 2, 73–107.

Krippner, S. (1972) "Altered states of consciousness." In J. White (ed.) *The Highest State of Consciousness*. Garden City, NY: Doubleday.

Leuner, H. (1977) "Guided affective imagery: An account of its developmental history." *Journal of Mental Imagery 1*, 73–92.

Leuner, H. (1984) *Guided Affective Imagery*. New York, NY: Wiley.

Lim, V.K., Polych, M.A., Holländer, A., Byblow, W.D., Kirk, I.J., and Hamm, J.P. (2006) "Kinesthetic but not visual imagery assists in normalizing the CNV in Parkinson's disease." *Clinical Neurophysiology 117*, 2, 308–2314.

Lotze, M. (2013) "Kinesthetic imagery of musical performance." *Frontiers in Human Neuroscience 7*, article 290, 1–9.

Ludwig, A.M. (1969) "Altered states of consciousness." In C.T. Tart (ed.) *Altered States of Consciousness*. New York, NY: Free Press.

Lutz, A., Slagter, H.A., Dunne, J.D., and Davidson, R.J. (2008) "Attention regulation and monitoring in meditation." *Trends in Cognitive Science 12*, 4, 163–169.

Marolt-Sender, M. (2014) "A phenomenological inquiry into the attention postures of flow-like states." Doctoral dissertation. Sofia University, Palo Alto, CA.

Maturana, H. and Varela, F. (1980) *Autopoiesis and Cognition*. Dordrecht: Reidel.

Osman, S., Cooper, M., Hackmann, A., and Veale, D. (2004) "Spontaneously occurring images and early memories in people with body dysmorphic disorder." *Memory 12*, 4, 428–436.

Pekala, R.J. (1991) *Quantifying Consciousness: An Empirical Approach*. New York, NY: Plenum Press.

Pekala, R.J., Steinberg, J., and Kumar, C.K. (1986) "Measurement of phenomenological experience: Phenomenology of Consciousness Inventory." *Perceptual and Motor Skills 63*, 983–989.

Pekala, R.J. and Wenger, C.F. (1983) "Retrospective phenomenological assessment: Mapping consciousness in reference to specific stimulus conditions." *Journal of Mind and Behavior 4*, 2, 247–274.

Pert, C.B., Dreher, H.E., and Ruff, M.R. (1998) "The psychosomatic network: Foundations of mind-body medicine." *Alternative Therapies 4*, 4, 30–41.

Reyher, J. (1977) "Spontaneous visual imagery: Implications for psychoanalysis, psychopathology, and psychotherapy." *Journal of Mental Imagery 1*, 2, 253–273.

Rock, A.J., Friedman, H.L., and Jamieson, G.A. (2013) "Operationalizing psi-Conducive Altered States: Integrating Insights from Consciousness Studies into Parapsychology." In S. Krippner, A.J. Rock, J. Beischel, H.L. Friedman, and C.L. Fracasso (eds) *Advances in Parapsychology*. Jefferson, NC: MacFarland.

Rock, A.J. and Krippner, S. (2007) "Does the concept of 'altered states of consciousness' rest on a mistake?" *International Journal of Transpersonal Studies 26*, 33–40.

Rock, A.J. and Storm, L. (2010) "Shamanic-like journeying and psi: II. Mental boundaries, phenomenology, and the picture-identification task." *Australian Journal of Parapsychology 10*, 1, 41–68.

Sherwood, S.J. (2002) "Relationship between the hypnagogic/hypnopompic states and reports of anomalous experiences." *Journal of Parapsychology 66*, 2, 127–150.

Singer, J.L. (1977) "Ongoing Thought: The Normative Baseline for Alternate States of Consciousness." In N.E. Zinberg (ed.) *Altered States of Consciousness*. New York, NY: Free Press.

Stevens, J.A. and Stoykov, M.E.P. (2003) "Using motor imagery in the rehabilitation of hemiparesis." *Archives of Physical Medicine and Rehabilitation 84*, 7, 1090–1092.

Strawson, G. (1997) "The self." *Journal of Consciousness Studies 4*, 5–6, 405–428.

Suinn, R.M. (1997) "Mental practice in sport psychology: Where have we been, where do we go?" *Clinical Psychology: Science and Practice 4*, 189–207.

Tart, C.T. (1969) "Introduction." In C.T. Tart (ed.) *Altered States of Consciousness*. New York, NY: Wiley.

Tart, C.T. (1975) *States of Consciousness*. New York, NY: E.P. Dutton.

Trakhtenberg, E.C. (2008) "The effects of guided imagery on the immune system: A critical review." *International Journal of Neuroscience 118*, 839–855.

Tusek, D., Church, J.M., and Fazio, V.W. (1997) "Guided imagery as a coping strategy for perioperative patients." *AORN Journal 66*, 4, 644–649.

Uexküll, J. (1982) "The theory of meaning." *Semiotica 42*, 1, 25–82.

Wickramasekera, I. (2011) "Efficacy of hypnosis/guided imagery in fibromyalgia syndrome: A review of the international literature." *American Journal of Clinical Hypnosis 54*, 159–163.

Wild, J., Hackmann, A., and Clark, D.M. (2008) "Rescripting early memories linked to negative memories in social phobia: A pilot study." *Behavior Therapy 39*, 47–56.

Wilson, P.H., Thomas, P.R., and Maruff, P. (2002) "Motor imagery training ameliorates motor clumsiness in children." *Journal of Child Neurology 17*, 491–498.

Xu, J., Vik, A., Groote, I.R., Lagopoulos, J., Holen, A., Ellingsen, O., and Davanger, S. (2014) "Nondirective meditation activates default mode network and areas associated with memory retrieval and emotional processing." *Frontiers in Human Neuroscience 8*, article 86, 79–88.

Ziemke, T. (2003) "What's that thing called embodiment?" In *Proceedings of the 25th Annual Meeting of the Cognitive Science Society.* Mahwah, NJ: Lawrence Erlbaum, 1305–1310.

Part 4
Spiritual Images in Wisdom Traditions

Chapter 13

Four Shamanic Journeys with Guided Imagery

Michael Samuels

Close your eyes. Take several deep breaths and let yourself relax. Let your abdomen rise as you breathe in and fall as you breathe out. Now let yourself open to what is around you. Invite any spirit guides, spirit animals, angels, ancestors, and energies that heal you and keep you well to come to you. Let them come to you and be with you. You don't have to see them, just know that they are there with you always when you go into this guided imagery space.

As you rest in this space with your helpers around you, protecting you and keeping you safe, enter these four guided imagery experiences. Try not to analyze, judge, or understand them in words. Just feel and experience them.

IMAGERY INVITATION:
BEAR DANCE CEREMONY

It is after midnight. You are in the high desert of California on sacred Native American land. You are at a bear dance to heal people who are ill, to heal community and the earth. You are sitting on a chair, and in front of you is a large circle of stones. Inside the circle is a huge fire, drummers, and dancing bears. You can see the shadows of the bears as they move around the fire. See how the bears dance: they growl, step high, sometimes stand and raise their paws to the stars. Know that these spirit bears can move up and down the levels in the sky, making new cells, finding spirits that need to leave, taking them out, and adding in their bear energy. The bears circle over and over again. See, hear, and feel the ancient drumbeat and the songs of bears, men with eagle wings, and mother earth and father sky. Now see people coming into the circle to be healed. There can be many of them, 20 to 50. Know that they have cancer, chronic pain, arthritis, life crises, drug addiction, grieving for loss, any problem or disease. They come from as far away as Mexico and are of many tribes. Some are not Native Americans—there were many invited to come to this sacred healing bear dance. Know that the bears do not know the names of their ailments. They do not ask. See the bears go up to each person who offered tobacco to the leader for a healing. See the bears go around each person, maybe sniffing them, maybe looking in their eyes. Suddenly you see a bear go right up to someone. He growls, whacks them with a paw, not gently, and then he goes to the huge fire and throws up and then goes back to the people again, taking out what needs to be taken out, facilitating release of what needs to leave. Then in peace he may put his huge paw on them and let come in what needs to enter. Slowly as in a dream you can see the bears buzzing with energy as they fill up what was empty in each person. The bears may even do what seem to be unusual things, sometimes making star channels, sometimes dancing with the person, sometimes hugging them, but always putting in their bear energy, always something new and surprising...

The next day, after the dance, a woman comes up to me and thanks me. She tells me she has had osteoarthritis in her hand for many years and was in chronic pain and on many medicines. She tells me I came up to her and touched her with the bear claw, right on the place where she hurt the most, and she immediately released the pain and has been pain-free now for several days. It is the first time she is pain-free in years.

I do not know or remember any of this. I did not do it. What my bear does in that sacred circle is his own business. I carry him, he is my partner; that is all. I have no memory of the woman or what happened in that circle in the night around the fire with the drumming.

I am a bear dancer with the Chumash Native American people. We do a healing bear dance three times a year to heal people who are ill, and to heal the community and the earth. It is ancient, sacred, and beautiful. In this dance I do not heal anyone: my bear does it. I carry bear only. I wear a bear skin (a real skin with claws, head, ears) and to ancient bear songs I circle in the ring with 12 to 24 other bears, with ten men carrying eagle wings, with ten drummer/singers, and several men tending the fire. Everyone there, all the Native American people who come to the dance, know the story. The story is this: the illness goes from them to bear spirit, and the eagle swoops it away to Creator. It's a simple story. When bear comes up to them, they let the illness go, and sometimes it is hard to let it go: they faint, fall to the earth, go the fire, and throw up repeatedly, or just stand there, or cry. Then they often experience deep healings from many conditions.

What does this have to do with shamanism and guided imagery? In my day job, I am a physician who sees people with cancer, life-threatening illnesses, life crises, fertility problems, and those who seek personal growth to help them through their grieving, depression, or other painful afflictions. Before I began using guided imagery and shamanic processes, I was a family physician working on the Hopi reservation, and I also ran a holistic clinic in a nearby small town. I was trained by Rolling Thunder in using guided imagery to heal in the shamanic tradition and was trained by Turtle Hawk in bear dancing. I use many techniques including sacred listening, guided imagery, and if appropriate, shamanic Native American tools. I have done this for over 40 years, and my guided imagery has changed over the years to become more mystical, shamanic, and sacred.

The people in the circle who come to be healed hold this simple story: the illness goes to bear spirit, eagle swoops it away with his wing, and Creator takes it home. That for them is a basic underlying guided imagery. It is not a guided imagery exercise: it is a prayer. In all indigenous cultures the people held a story, a myth, a visionary reality that was also a powerful guided imagery. The imagery was made much richer with the use of music, dance, visual arts, and words. Taken together, these art forms created sacred ceremonies for transformation and healing.

The imagery is further deepened by the sacred culture, sacred space, prayers, and religious beliefs. The Native Americans that come to the dance for healing believe in animal spirits, in Creator and Mother Earth, in the four directions. As bear touches them, they feel their story, their prayer, and their guided imagery become real, physical, and embodied. The guided imagery exercise is actually a vision of a bear taking away their illness. They are truly in it. The illness leaves to bear, and they can see, hear, and actually touch the bear's fur. The bear is real, the illness is seen and felt to leave, and now they are different and new. Guided imagery and reality merge powerfully in sacred ceremony.

For me as a physician, the experience was more complex. To dance as a bear, I needed to shift, to release my male doctor control role and surrender to something beyond myself. I too need to fully believe in bear spirit, eagles, and Creator with my whole being with no doubt whatsoever in order to do this. Yet none of this is really so strange. In my healing work with guided imagery, I also believe with my whole being in another, more scientific story. I used to ask the people I worked with to relax and then invite an image to appear. Many of us working with guided imagery in the 1970s would start, for example, with white blood cells eating cancer cells, and that image would turn into an animal eating darkness, or what I used to call metaphorical imagery. But some of the people I worked with didn't want to picture white blood cells eating cancer cells, and they would very naturally move into another kind of imagery experience where they would see helpers like spirit guides, spirit animals, light and darkness, goddesses, and angels. We do not know from whence where these images arise: perhaps from the inner imagination, or from angels, or from genetic memory. Psychologists have been speculating on the origin of our imagery since the writings of William James and Carl Jung. But when a person hears the voice of an ancestor telling them they are loved and sees their grandmother's face, that experience is beyond reason.

In the bear dance, I carry bear, that is, an image in my mind, and then I surrender—just as the people I work with surrender—to the autonomous imagery that comes from deepest spirit/soul to heal us. I am allowing imagery to come to me from spirit, and my physician-observer self just watches bear do his thing.

IMAGERY INVITATION: TEMPLE OF ARTEMIS

Now picture yourself in Delos, Greece. You are on an island in the Aegean Sea. It is summer, it is hot and windy, and there is the brightest light you have ever seen all around you. You may know that Delos is an archeological site that for 3000 years, from about 2000 BCE to 1000 CE, attracted tens of thousands of people on pilgrimage for transformation and healing. In Greek mythology, Delos was the most powerful healing site in the Aegean Sea. It was the island that was the birthplace of Apollo, god of the sun, and Artemis, goddess of the moon.

See yourself in the marble remains of the temple of Artemis. Today it is only a square of marble stones, the remains of the foundation, but in your mind's eye you see it as an elegant columned temple. In this temple, as in all Greek temples, the statue of the god or goddess stood in the center. See the sculpture of Artemis in the center of the room. Now see the sacred priestesses in white diaphanous gowns bathing the statue, feeding it, anointing it with oils and perfumes, dressing it in gorgeous gowns, covering it with jewelry. They do this because they know the goddess Artemis actually lives there and they are beautifying her. This sacred temple is her home, the statue called them to her, she lives here and…when appealed to in ceremony and prayer, she heals and transforms their lives.

Now see women coming to this temple for help conceiving a baby, for help with labor, with help with moon energy, with their lovers, with their lost divine feminine power. They come after a difficult pilgrimage, over stormy dangerous seas, they bring offerings, gifts. When they arrive on the island, see them led by sacred female dancers in a snake dance to the temple. See the priestess sing and dance, and see her send their prayers to the goddess who would heal them.

Once again, we see the power of story. The people had a story that they all believed in: the goddess Artemis—goddess of the moon, childbirth, labor, woman's freedom, animals, nature, the hunt—would actually heed their prayers. Here the complex guided imagery had its origin deep in the animistic Hellenic religious beliefs, magnified by art (the statue) so that it could be seen, felt, and embodied by all to invoke a real, lived experience.

As a physician healer, I bring women to this temple, invite them to sit on a marble stone, tell them the story…and today it still has the power to heal. In their guided imagery space, they see, feel, and hear Artemis come to them, they ask her for their divine feminine soul back, and she gives it to them. When they feel HER enter their body, they gasp, cry, and know their life is different now.

They carry the guided imagery of the story of Artemis, they surrender to it, they live the guided imagery deeply. They too are making a pilgrimage, perhaps as difficult as in ancient times. These women are *in* and feel this ancient sacred site, the same wind, same hot sun, same bright light, the same sacred stillness that healed women two thousand years ago. They are benefiting from the healing energy and prayers of all that came before them in this sacred site to power their guided imagery/prayers and heal their souls.

Mercia Eliade described shamanism as the use of ecstasy to heal soul (Eliade, Trask, and Doniger 2004). This is not a trivial idea. Guided imagery is not only deeply relaxing: all it takes to shift our consciousness is to picture in the mind's eye a healing image. As discussed in other essays in this book, the neurophysiology of this is fascinating and complex. Images of illness and trauma that are held as mental images in the memory areas of the brain are stimulated by the guided imagery to heal.

People begin in the darkness, alone with the image of trauma that is bringing them to see the guided imagery professional. Then the images of trauma are actually replaced by images of sacred grace, of spirit animals, spirit guides, goddesses, angels, colors, light. They are mythological, symbolic, metaphoric images that are the stuff of shamanic healing and guided imagery therapy. New studies at Massachusetts Institute of Technology (MIT) (Hall 2013) illustrate how memory is replaced when a traumatic image is remembered while at the same time a new image is introduced. When we let go of what needs to leave and invite what needs to come in, we make new neuronal circuits that replace the circuits that held the trauma memory, and we restructure our brains: this is called healing.

It's interesting that guided imagery excites things like brain structures, hormones, neurotransmitters, but in my practice it always has been much more than that. Guided imagery is an experience beyond words; it takes place in parts of the brain that are different from the areas that hold our words. It takes place in visual, movement, auditory, and sensation areas. This pure experience beyond words is unfathomable. It is in the realm of soul stuff, of what is beyond analysis.

The shaman takes out the spirits that caused illness, brings in animal helpers who perform the healings, and bring back the soul that was lost. The guided imagery therapist does much the same. They help their clients go into a trance, the same state of consciousness as the shaman's trance, and they invite healing images, healing figures, animals and guides to come, and they let them perform the healing. Like bear, the images from inner soul that heal are autonomous and homeostatic. Bear comes when we invite him in ceremony, Artemis comes when we invite her in ceremony, and healing images arise when we facilitate an entrance into deep trance and then see what is there that will heal.

I believe that all of the elements of guided imagery as we practice it today are shamanic and ancient. The visions are the same as those received on a vision quest by a teenage Native American in the wilderness. The animal helpers are the same animals seen by shamans. The ancestors are the same ones prayed to by indigenous people. Guided imagery is prayer, prayer for images to come to you and heal.

IMAGERY INVITATION:
MOUNT TAMALPAIS HEALING

Now you are on the top of Mount Tamalpais in Marin County, California. It is sunset, you can see the Pacific Ocean spread out far below you. You see the fog clouds laid out over the ocean like a soft blanket. You see the woman I am working with. You know that she comes to me for guided imagery to heal her chronic pain from rheumatoid arthritis. She was on many medicines, she has severe contractures, and had many surgeries. She is laying in a shallow concave stone depression made of rock. She is covered in rose petals. The soft red light of the setting sun illuminates the petals, and her face looks like an angel. She is so beautiful.

Now you see me in my bear skin standing over her. You know that we have had previous guided imagery sessions where she found her spirit guides, spirit animals, and helpers. See them with her now on this mountain. Glimpse her helpers around her as she dreams and has visions. Know that she has worked with my bear for a year now, and the bear has touched her on each visit. She knows the story of letting go of the illness, giving it to bear, it is part of her visionary experience. The soft pink-white rose petals that cover her body are from her lover, they take care of her. The spirit animals are there with her at sunset.

Now see her come down from the mountain. Now her pain is gone. See her move on, change her life, move to a new city, get a new job. Know that she might have had years of surgery to repair her joint deformities, but her crisis is over and she is new.

During guided imagery sessions in my office, this woman had a vision of herself giving birth to the earth. She drew an image of it and brought it the next time she came to see me. With that vision, she knew she would be healed. It was a vision of excitement, physical balance, and power, an image she found for herself that connected her to the earth, to mothers, to the divine feminine, and to her soul. This image brought back her soul. I did not do it. I facilitated the space where her soul received this image to heal. In previous guided imagery exercises with me, she had glimpsed her spirit guides and spirit animals. They told her to do certain things, change her diet, do new physical exercises, and pray. She made art, which always makes the images easier to see and embody. (I now use art all the time with guided imagery).

For me, guided imagery is a portal to a sacred space of visions and dreams. It is a doorway to receive messages from deep soul, from spirit: they are exactly the messages a person needs to heal. As imagery therapists, we don't know what these image will be for each person. We can listen, even see them when we work with a client, but the shamanic images are theirs to invite, see, experience, and work with to create transformation. Shamanism has always been about transformation. Guided imagery and shamanism are about moving from the place of ordinary reality, physical space and time to non-ordinary reality, the place of space-time of the fourth dimension, a place of spirit. Illness is healed differently in this space. It is soul healing. Do you feel this?

IMAGERY INVITATION: YOUR PERSONAL JOURNEY

Now in your imagery space invite your own ancestors, spirit guides, spirit animals, teachers, those that love you, and rest with them a moment. Feel their beauty, energy, and love. Let what needs to leave you leave, and what needs to fill you come in. Receive the energy of the stars, of ancestors, of animals, and of celestial figures. Now come back to the room, to the book, and keep your helpers with you as you move on with your day.

This final exercise like all of the exercises in this chapter were intentionally created to be experiential, not theoretical. These prayers are your opportunity to experience being in the world of shamanic guided imagery. Guided imagery is the way we utilize our consciousness to go elsewhere, to travel to spirit realms that are completely real in the shamanic worlds. The people who work with me to transform their cancer, life crises, fertility, and chronic pain and to make life changes come to expand their realities with guided imagery, ceremony, and prayer into realms beyond ordinary healing methods. The people who come to the bear dance to be healed expect to have their illness leave and be taken by bear spirit, and their guided-imagery shamanic experience is deep and beyond words. Guided imagery is spirit speaking.

References

Eliade, M., Trask, W.R., and Doniger, W. (2004) *Shamanism: Archaic Techniques of Ecstasy*. Princeton, NJ: Princeton University Press.

Hall, S.S. (2013) "Repairing bad memories." *MIT Technology Review.* Available at www.technologyreview.com/featuredstory/515981/repairing-bad-memories, accessed on March 30 2015.

Chapter 14

Imagination

A Bridge to the Soul

Llewellyn Vaughan-Lee

> *The Human Imagination...throwing off the temporal that the eternal might be established.*
> William Blake in Keynes (1966, p.606)[1]

Entering the Symbolic World

The imagination is a powerful means of accessing and working with the inner world. Through the faculty of the imagination we can move from the world of the senses to an interior dimension, the symbolic realm of the soul. But we have forgotten this higher potential of the imagination, just as we have forgotten the potency of the symbols of the inner world. We need to reclaim the faculty of the imagination and understand its deeper purpose. In Sufism, this inner world of the imagination is seen as a bridge or "intermediary between the world of Mystery (*'alam al-ghayb*) and the world of Visibility (*'alam al-shahadat*)" (Corbin 1969, p.189). Through the imagination we are given access to an intermediary symbolic world. The use of the imagination in this tradition causes the symbolic essence of a material form—as it exists in the world of Mystery—to be perceived, uniting the inner and outer worlds.

The psychologist Carl Jung discovered this interior world through the dreams of his patients. He stressed the importance of its symbols, which belong to our collective history. According to Jung, the symbolic or archetypal realm and its collective psychology is "the powerful factor, the factor which changes our whole life, which changes the surface of our known world, which makes history" (Jacobi 1973, p.39).

Jung developed a technique of "active imagination" to consciously explore the inner world. In contrast to the dream state, where the symbolic is experienced solely at the unconscious level, in "active imagination" the individual *consciously* relates with the figures that inhabit the archetypal world—the wise old man or woman, the inner magician and healer, the gods and goddesses (Johnson 2009, p.138).[2]

Jung discovered "active imagination" in his own personal encounters with the collective unconscious, but he subsequently grounded this technique in his discovery of the use of the imagination in alchemy. The alchemists made the important distinction between *Imaginatio* and *Phantasia*. In *Imaginatio*, the individual consciously participates in the imaginative process, while *Phantasia* is merely the spinning of aimless or groundless fantasies. While fantasy or daydreaming is a passive process, like watching pictures on a screen, an encounter with the archetypal world demands that an individual consciously take part in the inner drama, which must be a fully-felt experience. Alchemists used *Imaginatio* in the work of transformation as a means of exploring the deeper mysteries of the psyche.

In both Sufism and alchemy, the symbolic world is understood as an objective inner reality that underlies our conscious, physical world. Through working with symbols and archetypal figures, we can reconnect with this deep interior and allow its numinous and transformative energy into our lives. Symbols are not just images: rather, they have a power that belongs to this inner world, and through them we can access the meaning of our soul and its divine purpose. Without this inner connection, we easily remain stumbling in the surface world of our contemporary culture, guided only by the ego and its desires.

Working with Inner Energies

The symbolic world has always been with us, silently calling, inviting us into the dynamic inner dimension of the soul. This inner connection can be used to empower ourselves, heal our addictions, and bring a sacred dimension to our lives.

But if we approach these inner energies only from the perspective of our individual well-being, we will see only a small fragment of the whole, and our imaginative capacity will remain imprisoned. As we turn our attention away from the individual self, our imagination will open its doors and we will begin to see the whole spectrum: the multidimensional psychic structure of life. Through the correct use of the imagination, we can learn to work with life's primal powers, and then real healing can begin.

While there are many techniques to access the inner worlds—active imagination, dream work, and other spiritual practices—there are specific guidelines that must be followed. Shamans, for example, who are adept at journeying through the inner dimensions, are always trained to be in service to the tribe or to the spirits or gods themselves. In order to work within these realms, we must follow their example. Like the shaman, our orientation must be beyond our own needs alone, in service to something greater.

As with all real work, our attitude is a powerful determining force. On one occasion, through active imagination, an archetypal figure explained to me the importance of entering their world with the right attitude:[3]

Each time you come from your world to this inner world, and you come with love and understanding rather than greed, then a grain of sand crosses the great divide. However small it may be, that grain of sand has immense meaning, for it comes with love. It forms part of an immense pattern like a mandala, and when this pattern is complete there will be a healing beyond all healing as the outer returns to the inner and the Self reveals itself. Then a new life will be upon your earth and upon my earth, and there will be a flowering as there has not been for thousands of years.

The inner world is waiting to be transformed. If we come with the right attitude, if we are attentive and watch and listen with respect, the inner world will take us by the hand and instruct us on how to redeem what we have damaged and desecrated.

But the inner realms are tremendously powerful. To enter, we need the humility to ask for help, and we need willingness to follow guidance. Shamans rely on power animals and other spirit helpers. Like Jung's archetypal symbols, power animals or spirit guides are living images through which the meaning and energy of the inner world are made accessible.[4] In the Sufi tradition, the imaginal guides belong more to the angelic world, accessed by the imagination through prayer or meditation. The angelic also helps us to experience and understand the spiritual inner worlds. There is a Sufi tradition that we each have a "heavenly twin," our "witness in heaven" (shâhid fil-samâ) who sees with the eyes of God and can guide and help us on our spiritual journey.

We need guidance to traverse the inner mountains and deserts, to return to the sacred source of life. We can learn about the inner world itself, its inhabitants, their sorrows and joys, their potential and problems. Too often we discover that they have been waiting to speak with us, to share their wisdom and power. Unable to directly cross into our world, they need us to come to them, to consciously choose to communicate. Like planets circling in their fixed orbits, these ancient powers cannot move freely in order to connect with their own source of healing. They need us, and if our motives are pure, we can travel freely in the imaginal world. They can give us a magical sword for power and discrimination, an invisible cloak for protection, a crystal sphere of light for wisdom. Through our conscious participation in the inner world, the temples of the imagination can be rebuilt, the sacred nature of our soul reestablished. We can once again reclaim our magical heritage and live in the sacred world of our ancestors.

The Desecration of the Inner Worlds

Before we begin working with the inner world, we need to understand the extent of the destruction we have caused. We live in a civilization whose rational and materialistic values have denied even the existence of the inner reality that permeates all of creation. We have no understanding of how this denial, together with our greed and desires, have made a wasteland of the inner. So many places of refuge have been lost, temples of the imaginal destroyed, sacred groves felled by the clear-cutting of our rational mind.

As a result, modern civilization has become stranded on the shores of our conscious self, cut off from our individual soul and also the World Soul, the *Anima Mundi*. And yet as recently as the medieval age, people lived in a richly symbolic world, as can be seen in the iconography of their cathedrals, the symbolism of the stained glass, the maze on the nave of Chartres cathedral. In their consciousness, the outer, physical world had its roots in the symbolic, and all of creation was part of the Great Chain of Being that links together the visible and invisible realms. This richly symbolic world was again honored during the Renaissance.

Nature was permeated by life, divinity, and numinous mystery, a vital expression of the World Soul and the living powers of creation. In the words of Richard Tarnas (1993), "The garden of the world was again enchanted, with magical powers and transcendent meaning implicit in every part of nature" (Fideler 2014, p.95).[5]

During the Renaissance, artists sought to channel the World Soul as a creative principle through their work. Their art was based on the same sacred proportions they saw in nature, and they understood the imagination as a magical power that can "lure and channel the energies of the *anima mundi*" (Fideler 2014, p.108).

Sadly, the birth of science drew us into a very different world-as-machine whose disembodied workings human beings could rationally understand and master. The magical world of creative mystery infused with divine spirit became a dream belonging only to poets and the laboratories and symbolic writings of the alchemists.

However, the Sufi tradition has kept alive a deep understanding of the inner worlds. In the 13th century, the great Sufi master Ibn ʿArabî wrote extensively about the imaginal, based upon his own visionary experiences. There is not the space here to describe in any detail the richness of his imaginal experiences—his meetings with embodied spirits (Chittick 1994), the landscapes of a celestial Earth with gardens and animals (Corbin 1989)—but he provided a depth of understanding of these interior realities that became part of the Sufi heritage. Since the last century, particularly through the work of Henry Corbin, these spiritual teachings have become more widely known in the West.[6]

The Sufi path leads the wayfarer away from the ego into the innermost mysteries of the heart. In complete contrast, when in the West we began to have access to techniques allowing us into the symbolic world, our commercialism quickly penetrated the inner, through the "secret" use of imagination as a way to manifest our desires. We have prostituted the sacred for personal gain. Spiritual teachings and stories have long warned us against this,[7] but our disregard for anything except the desires of the ego has desecrated the inner world to the point that it can no longer so easily give meaning to our life.

Yet it is important to understand that, as degraded as they are, the inner worlds dominate our experience more than we realize. For example, if we look closely, we can recognize the archetypes at work even within the predominant myth of materialism. We can see a primal masculine power drive fueling the objectification and domination of nature, which is a key component of our materialistic culture. And less obvious but just as powerful is the way in which the dark side of the rejected feminine has caught us in her web of desires. For what is materialism but the worship of matter, which is none other than the domain of the goddess?

Sadly, in our present-day culture we are not taught to revere these underlying powers, nor do we know how to relate to them. Our contemporary consciousness hardly even knows of their existence. We live on the surface of our lives, unaware of the depths that are in fact the real determining factors. How many people when they go to the mall realize that they are worshipping on the altar of the dark goddess?

Unknowingly we are caught in this shadow-land, and our lack of awareness only makes us more entrapped. But as the monster of materialism and the insatiable tyrant of economic growth continue to destroy our well-being and undermine the health of our entire planet, there is a vital need to awake from this nightmare and return to an ensouled world. As Thomas Berry wrote:

> There is now a single issue before us: survival. Not merely physical survival, but survival in a world of fulfillment, survival in a living world, where the violets bloom in the springtime, where the stars shine down in all their mystery, survival in a world of meaning. (Tucker 2009, p.172)

Real care and concern for the inner world will help heal it and restore meaning to our collective experience. The need for healing is real. A deep sorrow reigns in much of the inner world. In particular, our treatment of the feminine, and of the body of the world and its soul, has inflicted a grievous wound that needs our attention. It has created a veil of tears around the goddess, and spread a sense of isolation and desolation throughout the inner world.

Anyone who has journeyed there will have experienced this pain; it has an endless quality that belongs to the timeless nature of the archetypal world. Something essential to life and existence is missing: the colors of creation that are formed in the inner world are losing their vibrancy, its pure and sparkling rivers are growing murkier, and even some of its inhabitants have forgotten their divine purpose. Our forgetfulness, our loss of connection with our own souls, has affected the inner world and has gradually caused it, too, to forget. Our connection is their connection. The inner world cannot flourish without our conscious remembrance.

Remembrance is central to Sufism. Through the practice of the *dhikr*, the repetition of a sacred phrase or the name of God,[8] we remember our Beloved. For lovers of God this is the remembrance of the heart, which brings the sweetness "that was before honey or bee" (traditional Sufi saying) from the eternal world of the soul into everyday life. Remembrance reconnects the inner and outer worlds.

Our most precious gift to the inner realm is our remembrance of its sacred nature. The sweetness of our remembrance can help life's sacred purpose to be reborn. And then the inner world can flower again and spring can come again to barren wastelands—an unexpected spring that will catch us by surprise, even if we have been waiting and longing for it. The inner world will wake up and its song will be heard, first in the inner and then in the outer.

The song of the inner world is the music of life and all that is hidden within life; it contains the purpose of creation and the wonder of being alive. And it comes from the depths of existence, from the forces that give birth to life. Once this song is heard again, the rivers of life will flow with joy and the beings of all the worlds will be nourished. And this is just the beginning.

Walking in Both Worlds

Life is a mystery. Every step we make, like every breath we take, is a meeting of the inner and outer worlds. We may not consciously know it, but at every moment we are alive in both worlds. The inner is the ground from which our soul draws its sustenance, not in some abstract sense but in a very real way. We could not live if we did not walk continually in the inner. We have been conditioned to believe that we live only in the world we perceive through our senses, but a simple recognition of how our fantasies, fears, and imaginings influence us reveals that we also inhabit a less tangible world. We are driven by desires and demons, longings and fears, most of which have their origin in the inner world rather than our outer reality.[9] We are creatures of our own psyche and the vaster maze of the collective unconscious, nourished as much by our dreams and fears as we are by food and water.

It is time to acknowledge the presence and power of the inner realm, to see how it moves us, to welcome its presence. We breathe the air of both worlds. Sometimes a hidden fragrance from the inner world will catch our attention and lead us down unexpected avenues, around corners we never thought to turn, giving us a brief glimpse of life's inner dimension.

The pestilence of the inner world can also affect us, though we rarely recognize the ways its darkness draws us—we walk for the most part as though the tangible ground were all we tread upon, as if the emissions of our automobiles and our industries were the only bad air we breathe.[10]

Only when we understand the mysterious coming together of the inner and outer worlds can we live a grounded and meaningful life. We may have been told that to be "grounded" means to be fully present in the physical, everyday world, but this is only another myth. The real ground is the inner, which infuses and underlies the physical, as every earlier culture understood.

The advent of psychology has helped us become aware of the hidden powers at work throughout our own personal psyche. We have realized that there may be disturbances that come from within, from emotional or psychic wounds. This image of the inner does not begin to encompass the larger world of the collective unconscious we also inhabit. We rarely acknowledge our collective dreaming, the myths and stories that we live, and we do not consider just how much our outer actions are driven or determined by these larger forces of the inner world.

But it is time to wake up, to accept the very real existence of both worlds. We cannot not afford to pretend any longer: our collective fears are becoming too dark, our material fantasies too destructive. We have to accept that the inner worlds were never really banished by the Age of Reason, and that we are still frightened of their darkness just as we are seduced by their siren-like temptations. We may be projecting our fears on the next terrorist attack, our hopes on a new job, our soul on a romantic partner; but until we understand that these outer expressions are signs, symbols, and invitations into a much more powerful dimension, we will be living on the surface of our lives. Can all of our security measures help us when the real threat is an inner demon? Similarly, can all our striving really fulfill our dreams, when the source of our desires is an ethereal temptress or a deep longing of the soul?

In Sufism there is a rich tradition of working with the inner worlds through dreams, visions, and spiritual practices. We learn both to purify the darkness and be nourished by the images that come to us— the fragrance of the interior garden of the soul. The imagination is the gateway to these places of healing and redemption. Through the use of creative imagination, we can once again consciously walk in the hidden realms and reclaim the knowledge of how to work with the symbols and primal energies that underlie our physical existence. Then the wisdom and energy that are within us can emerge into the outer world, and we can be nourished from the source of life and the meaning that comes from the soul.

Uniting Inner and Outer

The union of inner and outer can be a creative opportunity, an awakening to a hidden magic within life in which life's symbolic dimension comes alive. When we experience the inner, symbolic world as a living reality, when symbols come alive in our everyday existence, a whole new spectrum of life comes into consciousness. Everyday activities that have become meaningless and routine reveal themselves as part of life's mystery and draw us into its deeper purpose.

We can glimpse the most profound symbolic reality in activities that we take for granted and in this way utterly change our experience. When we connect to the Internet, for example, we have the opportunity to be aware of directly connecting to a web of life and consciousness around the planet, a web that is continually moving, changing, developing. In this instant we can experience our individual self as part of a dynamic whole, of patterns of relationship flowing across the world.

What would it mean for the symbolic world to become fully alive? Our everyday life would lose its grayness and take on a new vibrancy. We would notice a dawn begin to break—an unexpected dawn infused with hues of colors we did not know existed. We would no longer need to satisfy an inner hunger with addictions or the accumulation of possessions, because we would be nourished directly from life, from its sacred substance that communicates through the symbolic. We would no longer need to search, often despairingly, for meaning; meaning would be all around us. Life would open to us its book of meaning and on its pages we could more easily read the purpose of our individual existence. Life would speak to us directly about why we are here, and we could participate in life as it really is, in the joy of our real nature and purpose.

Of course there will still be difficulties and struggles, challenges and the search for answers. There will be shadows, darkness and light, and temptations. However, because life is now alive, it will speak to us, reveal to us its sacred dimension. We will no longer have to make a deep and demanding inner journey to find meaning, because the inner and outer will come together; the meaning will be *here*. This coming together is the *coniunctio* promised by the alchemists, the alchemical marriage from which a child is born. And this child is none other than our real self, a self that breathes with our every breath that walks in this world with every step we take. The future that is being born *is* this child, a way to live our real self in everyday life. This is something so simple and so wonderful that it is almost unimaginable.

We have lived for too long without the real nourishment of the inner worlds; we have grown pale and anemic. Deprived of the sacred substance within life that is our real sustenance, we have struggled and fought to acquire a few crumbs from the table of life, a few temporary pleasures. Life is so much more than what we have asked of it: it is the divine becoming manifest, a wonder being revealed. The Garden of Eden from which we have been exiled is not heaven, but life. This is the world of divine presence into which we can be welcomed.

The power of the imagination both reveals the symbolic world and mediates our direct experience of the divine. It allows the divine to come into our life without overwhelming us with its unlimited power. On the Sufi journey it helps the wayfarer make the transition from the outer world of the senses to the inner worlds of pure light and love that belong to our spiritual self. One of the most powerful archetypal figures for the Sufi is Khidr, symbol of the direct revelation of the divine, who often appears a most ordinary figure. When the symbolic world is experienced as part of our everyday life, we will be nourished and guided in unexpected ways. Its *manna* will be our daily bread.

The child of this union is waiting to come alive, a promise that needs to be lived. She will show us how we are a part of life, not as survivors, but as celebrants. We are all part of a tremendous intimacy we call creation, a beautiful, violent, erotic explosion made of stardust and love. Our motion is bonded to the motion of the moon and the sun, of the galaxy, of a spider spinning its web in the corner of a room or between blades of grass.

When the inner and outer worlds start to dance together, the patterns of creation will change. They will come alive with the consciousness of humanity in a new way. They will respond to our vision and help us to recreate our world. If we let them, they can help us redeem the damage that we have done; cleanse the waters of toxins and our thought-forms of greed. Then, once again, we can walk and breathe in the sacred mystery of both worlds united into one.

ENDNOTES

1. Blake, W. (1966) "A Vision of the Last Judgment." In G. Keynes (ed.) *Blake Complete Writings*. Oxford: Oxford University Press, p.606.

2. A simple process of beginning "active imagination" is to enter into a dialogue with the images and figures that arise in your imagination: Instead of going into a dream you enter into your imagination while you are awake. You allow the images to rise up out of the unconscious, and they come to you on the level of the imagination just as they would come to you in dream if you were asleep. In your imagination you begin to talk to your images and interact with them. They answer back (Robert Johnson, *Inner Work*, p.138). One can also meditate on an image or symbol that has been given in a dream, allowing the symbol to communicate its meaning and numinous energy to one's conscious self.

3. For seven years beginning in 1987, I led a series of "Archetypal Journeys," imaginative ventures into the inner world and experiences with the archetypal energies that live there. Through these journeys I learned about the archetypal world and how our neglect has affected it. (http://archetypaljourneys.wordpress.com)

4. In some shamanic practices, these inner beings are not imaginal forces but rather are actual elemental or spirit beings that belong to a different realm and function in a different way. Working with the elemental world is very different to imaginal work, and requires a specific shamanic training.

5. Referenced from R. Tarnas (1991) *The Passion of the Western Mind*. New York: Harmony Books, p.213.

6. Corbin's seminal work, *Creative Imagination in the Sufism of Ibn 'Arabî*, was very influential, particularly for James Hillman and the school of Archetypal Psychology.

7. The Sufi story of *Moshkel Gosha* tells of a woodcutter who misuses the magical stones from the inner world for personal gain, and ends up destitute and in prison. The story teaches discrimination between need (the need of the soul) and

want (the desires of the ego)—"If you need enough and want little enough you will find your way."

8. In some Sufi orders the *dhikr* (which is frequently the phrase *La ilâha illâ 'llah* [There is no God but God] or the single word Allah) is chanted audibly in group meetings, often inducing a state of spiritual intoxication. In the Naqshbandi order the *dhikr* is practiced silently throughout the day.

9. I often wonder if our irrational and endless desire for "more stuff" is a fruitless attempt to placate deeper unmet needs of the soul, an inner longing for the sacred which alone can give us real nourishment, and which is scarcely present in today's materialistic culture. Or are we just feeding the monster of consumerism and greed that we have created in our collective psyche but do not dare to face?

10. Do we fully acknowledge the fears that fester beneath the surface, unexpectedly surfacing, as in the unrealistic panic in the United States in 2014 over the West African Ebola outbreak, which led one comedian to suggest that we could catch this fear just by watching the news for five minutes. What is this primal anxiety that pulls us toward panic? Is it a sense of the fragility of all our outer security, the house of cards that is our financial institutions? Or just a deep rooted fear that something is fundamentally unbalanced in our culture?

References

Blake, W. and Keynes, G. (1966) *Blake: Complete Writings with Variant Reading*. Oxford: Oxford University Press.

Chittick, W. (1994) *Imaginal Worlds: Ibn al-'Arabi and the Problem of Religious Diversity*. Albany, NY: SUNY Press.

Corbin, H. (1969) *Creative Imagination in the Sufism of Ibn 'Arabi*. Princeton, NJ: Princeton University Press.

Corbin, H. (1989) *Spiritual Body and Celestial Earth*. Princeton, NJ: Princeton University Press.

Fideler, D. (2014) *Restoring the Soul of the World: Our Living Bond with Nature's Intelligence*. Rochester, VT: Inner Traditions.

Jacobi, J. (ed.) (1973) *C.G. Jung: Psychological Reflections. A New Anthology of His Writings, 1905–1961*. Princeton, NJ: Princeton University Press.

Johnson, R.A. (2009) *Inner Work*. New York, NY: Harper Collins.

Tarnas, R. (1993) *The Passion of the Western Mind: Understanding the Ideas That Have Shaped Our Worldview*. New York, NY: Harmony Books.

Tucker, M.E. (ed.) (2009) *The Sacred Universe: Earth, Spirituality, and Religion in the 21st Century*. New York, NY: Columbia University Press.

Chapter 15

Daoist Imagery and Internal Alchemy

Master Zhongxian Wu

You Shang Ji You Xia

有上即有下

As above, so below

Wang Zong Yue 王宗岳,
TaiJi Quan Jing: *The Classics of TaiJi Martial Arts*

DaoJia 道家, or Daoism (also spelled "Taoism" using the Wade-Giles Romanization system),[1] is a traditional Chinese philosophy that values the inherent harmony of being, from the macrocosmic (the universe) to the microcosmic (all the organisms that exist within this great mystery we call life). Through the power of deep inner and outer observation, ancient Chinese sages realized that patterns of movements and behavior in the cosmos and the natural world are mirrored within our own bodies. The teachings of *DaoJia* (which include calligraphy, cosmology, feng shui, internal alchemy, numerology, martial arts, medicine, music, painting, philosophy, symbology, Taiji, Qigong, and more) guide students to incorporate the underlying philosophy into the ins and outs of their daily lives. Dedicated practitioners of Daoist internal cultivation techniques believe that through a daily practice of one or more of these arts, we humans are able to live in harmony with the Dao 道, the Great Way of Nature. Regardless of which Daoist art one devotes themselves to, high-level practitioners work toward the same result—*DeDao* 得道, attaining the Dao. The most important yet most secret element (and therefore widely missing in modern Daoist philosophy and arts) of all Daoist studies is *XiangFa* 象瀍, or applied imagery.

In order to better understand the importance of Daoist imagery and its use in internal alchemy in the Daoist arts, I will begin this article with some essential background information: the concept of Dao, Daoist cosmology, and the imagery of cosmology. Next, I will discuss the fundamental principles of Daoist imagery as they relate to Chinese medicine and internal alchemy. Lastly, I will share a powerful Daoist imagery practice, the Dragon Body internal alchemy method from the *XinYi* 心意 heart-mind lineage.

I hope this chapter will call attention to *Xiang* 象, Daoist imagery, as the key ingredient (often missing) in Daoist internal cultivation techniques. Through the proper use of *Xiang*, the devoted practitioner will be able to access and attain oneness with the Dao.

WenYiZaiDao 文以載道
The Pattern Carries the Dao

This traditional saying suggests that written characters are vehicles for connecting with nature and channeling universal wisdom. Accordingly, we are able to garner great insight from the ancient sages by studying Chinese graphemes (Wu and Taylor Wu 2014). The Chinese character 道 (Dao) has many meanings: it can signify a trail, road, or path on which to walk; it also can also be used to mean guide, lead, rule, law, way, method, express, speak, justice, and moral. In classical Chinese philosophy, the Dao refers to the way of nature or the universal law. The Dao also contains deeper profundities that cannot be expressed through words. However, words could lead one to discover the way of experiencing the wordless Dao if one recognizes that Chinese characters are patterns or images that can be used in cultivation practice.

We delve more deeply into the meanings within the meaning when we explore the imagery of the Dao as written in Oracle bone script, the oldest known Chinese written pattern and ancestor to the modern

Chinese writing system. Using my calligraphy as a reference (Figure 15.1), let us now explore how the characters within the characters express the meaning of Dao.

Figure 15.1: Dao in Oracle bone script
Fu 符 (talisman calligraphy) by Master Zhongxian Wu

For guidance on how to use the talisman for healing or creating harmonious feng shui energy, please see the *DaoFu* practice box.

In Oracle bone script, the Chinese character Dao 𦥑 is composed of three radicals:

1. *Xing* 彳 is the image of an intersection and symbolizes the connection of all energies and all directions. It is the same symbol used for "Element" in Five Elements philosophy. The other two radicals are found inside the strokes of the Xing portion of the character.

2. Found directly in the center is *Shou* 首, a pattern of a head, symbolizing observation, thought, decision, and wisdom.

3. *Zhi* 止 is a picture of a foot and is located at the bottom of the character. It represents walking, movement, or taking action.

From my perspective as a Daoist practitioner, the ancient symbol for the Dao is a portrait of a high-level martial artist or Qigong master with her feet rooted deeply into the earth, head upright and connecting with heaven, and entire body physically and spiritually open and merging with the universe. The character is an illustration of the ultimate state referred to in all classical Chinese arts: *TianRenHeYi* 天人合一, the oneness between human beings and nature (Wu 2014).

Oneness represents the Dao. The Chinese character *Yi* 一, which means the number one or oneness, is also commonly used as a symbol for the universe. LaoZi describes the Dao as the origin of the primordial universe in Chapter 25 of his *DaoDeJing*:[2]

YuWuHunCheng XianTianDiSheng
JiXiLiaoXi DuLiErBuGai ZhouXingErBuDai
KeYiWeiTianDiMu WuBuZhiQiMing ZiZhiYueDao

有物混成 先天地生
寂兮寥兮 獨立而不改 周行而不殆
可以為天下母 吾不知其名 字之曰道

Something unfathomable created
Birthed before heaven and earth
Within the silence and void
Standing alone and unchanging
Revolving without exhausting
May be the mother of heaven and earth
I do not know her name
I call her Dao

LaoZi

In the Daoist classic *QingJingJing* 清靜經,[3] LaoZi describes the Dao as the both the source and driving force of nature:

DaDaoWuXing ShengYüTianDi
DaDaoWuQing YunXingRiYue
DaDaoWuMing ChangYangWanWu
WuBuZhiQiMing QiangMingYueDao

大道無形 生育天地
大道無情 運行日月
大道無名 長養萬物
吾不知其名 強名曰道

The Great Dao is formless, giving birth to heaven and earth
The Great Dao is emotionless, conveying the motion of the sun
    and the moon

> The Great Dao is nameless, raising and nourishing the Ten-Thousand-Things
> I do not know her name—I call her Dao

> LaoZi

In the *DaoDeJing*, LaoZi includes many descriptions of the Dao to help us study the fundaments of Daoist philosophy. As this writing is meant to be just one chapter, I will not go more deeply into the *DaoDeJing* with you here. Of course there are many English interpretations of the *DaoDeJing* if you are interested in reading more! I will now shift focus a little to introduce Daoist cosmology in the following section.

Daoist Cosmology

Is it possible to substantiate that the Dao is the origin of the universe and the source and drive of everything in existence? The Daoist answer is *yes*. Practitioners who cultivate their *Qi* 氣 (vital energy) through Daoist internal cultivation methods discover that their bodies are indeed high-tech instruments of sensate knowing that allow them to directly experience the Dao.

Qi is the vital energy—the breath of the Dao—that creates all things and keeps all beings alive. According to Daoist cosmology, the primordial state of our universe consisted only of one swirling mass of *Qi*. Within this mass, there were two different qualities of *Qi*: *Yin* 陰 *Qi* (heavy, turbid, and chaotic) and *Yang* 陽 *Qi* (light, clear, and pure). After a very long time, all of the *Yin Qi* settled downward and formed the Earth while all *Yang Qi* rose upward to form Heaven. However, the Heavenly *Qi* and Earthly *Qi* are by nature attracted to each other, and the interaction between them generated all the life energy (including all living beings) that resides between Heaven and Earth.

In Daoist mythology, this evolution of nature is illustrated through the phrase *YiQiHuaSanQing* 一氣化三清, one *Qi* transforms to the Three Purities. It is said that the one mass of primordial *Qi* transformed to the three Gods of Purity (Supreme Purity, Jade Purity, and Utmost Purity) and that these three Purities in turn created the universe.

The Daoist cosmological structure of trinity, *SanCai* 三才, is modeled after these three layers of the universe. As described in my book, *XinYi WuDao* (Wu 2014), *SanCai* literally means three materials or three intelligences. It represents the trinity within one: every object, phenomenon, or event in the universe is composed of three parts. We commonly refer to these three layers as *Jing* 精, *Qi* 氣, and *Shen* 神 (I will discuss *Jing, Qi,* and *Shen* in more detail later). Each of these components is also made of three components (subcomponents, if you will), *ad infinitum*. Table 15.1 provides a conceptual example.

Table 15.1: The Daoist Cosmological Structure of Trinity

		Sun
	Heaven	Stars
		Moon
Oneness (Dao; our universe)	Human being (all life energy)	*Shen*
		Qi
		Jing
		Fire
	Earth	Wind
		Water

From the perspective of Daoist cosmology, everything exists within this same structure of trinity, and each object can be seen in relation to one another as macrocosm or microcosm. For instance, the galaxy is seen as microcosm when related to the universe and is seen as macrocosm when related to our solar system, our planet, or the human body. While the concept of trinity is the basis of all Daoist arts, it is easiest to experience when you work directly with your *Qi* through your Qigong or internal alchemy practice.

Qi creates everything that exists, and *Qi* brings life energy to all things. A specific aspect of *Qi* called *DaoQi* 道氣 (the vital breath of the Dao) is what keeps the trinity of all things in harmony. In order to help people understand the concept of *DaoQi*, we commonly explain it using the symbolism and mythology of the Chinese dragon.

Daoist Symbolism and *Long* 龍 (Dragon)

Figure 15.2: Dragon calligraphy

Fu 符 (talisman calligraphy) by Master Zhongxian Wu

For guidance on how to use the talisman for healing or creating harmonious feng shui energy, please see the *DaoFu* practice box.

In Daoist mythology *Long* 龍, the Chinese dragon, is the rainmaker and master of transformation. Here is a brief description of the symbolism of the Chinese dragon, as discussed in my book *Fire Dragon Meridian Qigong*:

> Dragon represents power, life energy, transformation, communication, connection, freedom, and the universal way. According to Chinese mythology, dragon is the rainmaker, has magic powers that allow it to change natural formations, and can easily fly between Heaven and Earth. Dragon can penetrate through rock with ease, as dragon makes its home in the rock, just as fish live in water and human beings live in air. If we want to find a dragon, we simply look to the sky. Confucius disclosed the way to seek the dragon in one of his *Ten Wings of Yijing*, *WenYan* 文言: *YunCongLong* 雲從龍, which means that the

clouds follow the dragon. The clouds are like the dragons' "groupies," and observing the clouds helps us learn the rich symbolic meaning of dragon on deeper and deeper levels. (Wu and Taylor Wu 2012, p.22)

FengTiaoYuShun 風調雨順
Harmonious Wind and Flowing Rain

Traditionally, "harmonious wind and flowing rain" is how Chinese portray a balanced state within our living environment. In other words, rain is recognized as a gauge for measuring the balance between human beings and nature. According to myth, the dragon draws in water from the earth, rides the clouds up to heaven, and sprays the water from its mouth to make rain. Too little or too much rain is an indication of disharmony between human beings and nature. A sick or angry dragon may make no rain or too much rain, while a peaceful dragon makes the perfect amount of rain and maintains harmony within the heaven, earth, and human being trinity. It is human behavior that influences the dragon's rainmaking. For instance, we may make the dragon sick by polluting the air or make the dragon angry by our methods of mass deforestation. The Chinese believe that human beings must respect and follow the way of nature in order for a peaceful dragon to maintain world balance.

The influence the dragon has on the world is similar to the influence that a person living in or out of resonance with harmonious *DaoQi* has on the world. When we are like the imbalanced dragon, we may find ourselves living in a state of reactivity, in constant upset with ourselves, our family, and our environment, or we may experience illness: this can be a disaster! However, when we are like the peaceful dragon, we resonate with *DaoQi* and experience a sense of oneness and well-being, feeling at ease and connection with ourselves and the world at large.

A peaceful dragon is essential for a harmonious external world—and creating a peaceful dragon within is one of the greatest benefits of having Daoist healing and internal cultivation practices. One of the primary goals of our practice is to transform *Jing* to *Qi* and *Qi* to *Shen* (again, I will discuss this in more detail later). Practitioners can use power of the dragon, the master of transformation, to help support this metamorphosis.

Now, let us turn our attentions to our bodies.

The Principles of Cultivation

As I mentioned, the workings of the universe can be seen as the macrocosm of the microcosmic workings of the body. The energetic patterns of human beings mirror those of the universe. If the same patterns are reproduced in all levels of the cosmos, from the largest, macrocosmic scale (universal level) to the smallest, microcosmic scale (human cells and the organelles within them), then it must follow that the flow of *Qi* in the human body is just like that found in nature: the ceaseless rotations of the sun, moon, and stars, for example, or the flow of a water through the evaporation/condensation cycle. As we see a balanced flow in a healthy landscape, the fundamental experience of balance in the human being is when the *Qi* is flowing freely throughout the body.

THE TRADITIONAL CONCEPT OF MEDICINE

The ancient Chinese concept of medicine differs vastly from that of modern-day medicine. We can begin to understand these differences by studying the symbolic meanings of *Yao* 藥, the traditional Chinese character for medicine. *Yao* 藥 is made of two Chinese characters: 艸 (*Cao*) and 樂 (with two pronunciations, *Yue* or *Le*). *Cao* means grass, *Jing* 精 (essence), herbal medicine, and new life energy. If you imagine an ordinary weed, you will connect with the power of strong life energy. People spend a lot of resources trying to make their gardens and farm fields free of weeds, but it is an endless process—they eventually come back! I am continually amazed by the strong life-*Qi* of grass every time I see green color peeking out from under snow and ice here in Sweden. *Yue* 樂 means music, *Qi*, and harmony, while *Le* 樂 means joy, peace, and uplifted spirit. The original character for 樂 is 𐙿, which creates an image of silk strings atop a piece of wood. This is the image of the *GuQin* 古琴, or the ancient Chinese musical instrument (similar to a zither). I believe that everyone has had the experience of being deeply moved by music that generates feelings of great joy within. Thinking about this, you will have a sense for why the same character for music (*Yue* 樂) means both harmony and joyful peace.

Is the ancient concept of medicine the combination of grass and a musical instrument? Yes! From a Daoist perspective, medicine is any thing or activity that generates in you the three qualities:

- strong life energy/vitalized *Qi*

- emotional balance

- uplifted, joyful spirit.

It is this concept of medicine that we carry into our internal alchemy practices.

In internal alchemy, the trinity structure of the body is *Jing* 精, *Qi* 氣, and *Shen* 神. All traditional Daoist teachings refer to these three as *SanBao* 三寶 (Three Treasures). They are *DaYao* 大藥, Great Medicine. We consider *Jing*, *Qi*, and *Shen* to be the best medicine in the world. *Jing* means essence and represents our physical body and Earth (on a macrocosmic scale). *Qi* means vital energy and it is related to our breath and energetic body and to all living beings. *Shen* means spirit, and is your spiritual body, higher consciousness, and also represents Heaven. No matter what traditional art we are practicing, we always work with these three Great Medicines.

However, in modern times most practitioners only pay attention to the *Jing* (physical) level of study, missing the *Qi* (energetic) and *Shen* (spiritual) levels entirely. Traditionally, the Daoist teaching method is known as *KouChuanXinShou* 口傳心授, or passing through the mouth and transmitting through the heart. In other words, we do not only teach the physical format of an art to students, we also train them to master the energetic and spiritual layers of the art. These more subtle teachings are passed from teacher to student through the heart and through special visualization techniques. In my decades of teaching experience, people have a very hard time understanding this traditional teaching method. Most students stick to their old ways of thinking and consider themselves "advanced" when they start to tally up the number of physical forms they can perform.

I often use a car as a metaphor for the traditional style of teaching. We are able to perform a physical form when we know the *Jing* layer of the form: it is like owning a nice car. However, if you do not know the functions of the car nor how to drive it, you will end up with a fancy car sitting in your driveway yet you will not be able to go anywhere in it! Learning the *Qi* layer of the form is akin to learning all the functions of the car, while developing the *Shen* layer of the form is analogous to your driving skill. The Daoist journey truly begins after mastering the *Qi* and *Shen* part of whichever art form you are practicing. Once you have good driving skills, it will be very easy for you to figure out how to drive a new car. Likewise, once you can access the *Shen* of one art form, it often becomes easier to access the *Shen* of another.

Awakening the *Shen* component (*Shen* medicine) of an art can be challenging because it is elusive, yet it is the *Shen* that brings the greatest benefits to your healing and cultivation practice. Regardless of the art we are learning, using visualization techniques connects us with *Shen* medicine (the spirit), thereby deepening the effectiveness of all three medicines. Next, I will discuss *Jing*, *Qi*, and *Shen* medicine as though they are separate phenomena for the purpose of simplification. In truth, the principle of trinity includes the trinity within the trinity. In other words, in life, *Jing*, *Qi*, and *Shen* are inseparable and each have *Jing*, *Qi*, and *Shen* layers within them.

When working with the physical component (*Jing*)—for example, learning the physical movements of a Qigong form, the notes to a piece of music, the strokes of a calligraphy character, or helping someone who has a physical ailment—we must use visualizations to hone our physical skill. We do not just stand with our feet planted firmly on the ground: we imagine that we are a tree with roots burrowing deeply into the earth. We do not simply play certain notes in a mechanical order, but we imagine our hands are dragonflies skimming the surface of the water. We do not put brush to paper without also imagining that our ink will penetrate deep into the calligraphy table. We cannot help move the body into physical balance without also assessing the flow of *Qi* and emotional state. When we are working with the vital energy of an art form (*Qi* medicine), we envision the *Qi* field created by all the lineage masters before us and we connect our breath to a specific image: for example, a long, unbroken silk string, moving clouds, rising mist, the acupuncture needle. We connect to the spirit of the art form through *Shen* medicine typically by visualizing light (sunlight, moonlight, the northern lights, or candle light), enlightened beings, our ancestors, the vast open sky, or specific colors.

It is also important to realize that a single object can serve as *Shen* medicine (the image) for all three components of an art form. For instance, when we are practicing a Tiger Qigong form, we imagine becoming the tiger. In this way, we draw upon the physical power of the tiger to bring strength to our physical movements; we connect with Tiger *Qi* by imitating the tiger's breathing patterns; we access the heart-mind of the tiger as we imagine seeing through its eyes. Each traditional Daoist art and internal alchemy practice carries many images to help us strengthen the three medicines within.

In Daoism, we also use *Fu* 符 (talisman calligraphy) as a great medicine for healing and for bringing harmony, joy, and prosperity into our lives. An authentic *Fu* is not simply a picture; it is a vehicle that carries *Jing*, *Qi*, and *Shen*. The master will create the physical image while channeling specific qualities of *Qi* and sealing them into the *Fu* with visualization techniques. Most often, creating an authentic *Fu* is a skill that requires many years of training with your master. Different *Fu* may have different functions. For instance, the moment I created the Dao *Fu*, I summoned strong harmonious *Qi* and penetrated them into the *Fu*. Perhaps you can resonate with that special *Qi* even as it is replicated in this book? Would you like to try this medicine now?

DaoFu

Please return and gaze at the image of the *DaoFu* (Figure 15.1) for a few moments. Then relax your eyelids and your body and adjust your breathing to be slow, smooth, deep, and even. At the same time, imagine sunlight radiating from the image and filling your whole body with light. Spend at least a few minutes bathing your body, breath, and mind in the sunlight before opening your eyes again.

You can also try this practice using the Dragon *Fu* (Figure 15.2).

Internal Alchemy Practice

In Daoist internal alchemy practices, water is often used to symbolize the Dao. Quiet observation of the various forms of water in nature helps us experience the Dao. In Chapter 40 of *DaoDeJing*, LaoZi states that the reverse way is the momentum of the Dao:

FanZheDaoZhiDong

反者道之動

The reverse way is the momentum of the Dao

LaoZi

As we all know, water has a natural tendency to move to the lower position. However, it would be disastrous for us if water only stayed down on Earth and never returned to Heaven! Nature's magic dragon helps the water move from Earth (evaporation) to Heaven (condensation) and back down again (precipitation). Now you may better understand why misty or cloudy landscapes are often depicted in Chinese arts as *XianJing* 仙境 (Immortal's Land). This harmonious circulation of water in nature is the model of our Daoist internal alchemy practice, where we work with the various forms of water, especially steam, and the reverse pattern of nature.

Honoring the trinity principle, any authentic Daoist cultivation practice, regardless of the school, system, or form, must include these three fundamental steps:

Step 1: *LianJingHuaQi* 煉精化氣: Refining the *Jing* and transforming it to *Qi*.

Jing is liquid. As is the Earth, your body is made up of over 70 percent water. *Jing* is both the source and reservoir of life energy in your body. To strengthen your physical body, you must work with your body fluid. We call this step *LianYe* 煉液, "refine your liquid."

In this step, we focus on igniting our inner fire to refine *Jing* and transform it to *Qi*. This practice emulates solid ice melting to liquid and then changing to steam. During this step, it is common to experience tremendous amounts of body heat and other *Qi* sensations.

Step 2: *LianQiHuaShen* 煉氣化神: Refining the *Qi* to transform to *Shen*.

Qi is the vital energy of your body and it is connected to your breath. In this step, we pay close attention to the breath. We nourish and balance different stages of our emotion (*Shen*), with different breathing techniques.

This step is like rising clouds and mist moving from Earth to Heaven. You may feel warm currents moving in your body.

Step 3: *LianShenHuanXu* 煉神還虛: Refining the *Shen* and returning to *Xu* 虛 (emptiness).

True emptiness is not actually empty but embraces all things. It is the deep spiritual wisdom that informs our daily lives.

This step is like rain falling down from the Heavens to nourish life on Earth. You may produce copious amounts of saliva in your mouth (which you should swallow), and feel sweat coming down from your head.

This internal alchemy principle allows us to gradually awaken our consciousness and understand how to live with the Dao.

Transforming Your Dragon Body

The Dao, when discussed in any language, loses its original meaning. To understand the Dao, we must take action. I will now share two special cultivation methods from my book *XinYi WuDao*, in hopes that they will help you discover your inner peaceful dragon. When done correctly, the following practices will help you experience the three fundamental steps of internal alchemy described above.

QianLongZaiYuan 潛龍在淵
Dragon Hidden within the Abyss
MOVEMENT (*JING* MEDICINE)

Standing with feet together, naturally straighten your body and imagine you have the body of a dragon. Bend your knees slightly, tuck your tailbone in, and tighten your bottom muscles. Curve your back and close your shoulders by bringing them close together in front of your body and sucking in your chest. Bring your forearms and hands together in front of your body (the pinky edge of your hands are together) with your palms facing forward. The back of your hands rest on your thighs as you hold your arms as close to your body as you can. Keep your head upright and eyesight horizontal. Hold the posture as long as you can (see Figure 15.3).

Figure 15.3: *QianLongZaiYuan* 潛龍在淵
—Dragon Hidden Within the Abyss

BREATH (Qi MEDICINE)

With each breath, feel as though you are breathing with your lungs, your skin, and your navel. On inhalation, imagine that all the pores of your skin are open and allow the universal *Qi*, like sunlight, to enter into your body and gather at your navel. With each exhalation, imagine the *Qi* descending from your navel to your *DanTian* 丹田 (the "elixir field" in your lower belly).

VISUALIZATION (SHEN MEDICINE)

Imagine your body is coiled like a dragon and sinking deeper and deeper into a great abyss. At the same time, feel each of your Three Hearts: *DingXin* 頂心, the heart of your head, located at *BaiHui* 百會 (also known as GV20), an important acupuncture point on the top of your head; *ShouXin* 手心, the heart of your hand, which is found on *LaoGong* 勞宮 (the acupuncture point known as PC8), located in the central area of your palm; and *ZuXin* 足心, the heart of your foot (also known as *YongQuan* 湧泉 or KD1, which lies in the center of the ball of your foot) connecting to your *DanTian*.

FeiLongZaiTian 飛龍在
Dragon Stretches to the Sky
MOVEMENT (JING MEDICINE)

Starting from previous posture, slowly straighten your body and turn your hands so that your palms touch your lower belly. As you straighten your body, grab the floor with your toes with continued force, lift and tighten your perineum, and keep your teeth and mouth closed. As you ascend, feel the pressure on the top of your head. In this posture, your body is *DingTianLiDi* 頂天立地—pushing up heaven whilst rooting deep into the earth. Hold the posture as long as you can (see Figure 15.4).

Figure 15.4: *FeiLongZaiTian* 飛龍在天
—Dragon Stretches to the Sky

Breath (*Qi* Medicine)

Exhale, allowing the *Qi* from your *DanTian* to fill up your entire body as you straighten. Then regulate your breathing to be slow, smooth, deep, and even.

Visualization (*Shen* Medicine)

Imagine that your body is a dragon unfurling out of the deep abyss and stretching into the sky as you straighten your body. Feel taut and powerful in your Three Hearts as your body expands with *Qi*.

TianChuiXiang XianJi Xiong ShengRenXiangZhi

天垂象 見吉凶 聖人象之

Nature shows its patterns
Indicating auspicious and inauspicious
Sages apply them as imagery

Confucius (551–479 BCE)
Yijing XiCi (Appended statements)

In Chapter 2 of his *DaoDeJing*, LaoZi tells us that the teachings from an enlightened master are wordless:

> *XingBuYanZhiJiao*
>
> 行不言之教
>
> Conduct the wordless teaching
>
> LaoZi

As the eternal Dao is wordless, we must follow the wordless method—*XiangFa*, Daoist applied imagery—in order to experience it. Daoist imagery is used as a vehicle to channel different universal energies for healing, divination, and internal cultivation. In Daoism, the process of inner transformation is only possible when we use the correct visualization techniques. The *Shen* helps us gain access to the wisdom of nature and move toward mastery of our art. I hope this article will inspire you to find a teacher to help you explore authentic Daoist wisdom traditions. May you ride the dragon and attain peace and harmony in your daily life!

Acknowledgements

Dr. Karin Taylor Wu provided editorial assistance and valuable insight during the writing of this chapter.

ENDNOTES

1. I have chosen to capitalize and italicize all Chinese PinYin words and phrases throughout this article. At first introduction, each will appear translated into English alongside the appropriate Chinese characters.
2. *DaoDeJing* is a classical Chinese text written around the sixth century BCE by the sage LaoZi. The Chinese citations in this article are based on a reprinted version entitled 中国气功四大经典 (*Four Qigong Classics*) published by ZheJiang GuJi ChuBanShe in 1988, translated into English for this article by the author, Master Zhongxian Wu.
3. QinjingJing is one of the most important Daoist classics. Orally transmitted for generations, the earliest written version to date was by 葛玄, Daoist Master GeXuan (164–244 CE). The Chinese citation for this article is based on the author's memory and translated into English by the author, Master Zhongxian Wu.

References

Wu, Z. (2014) *XinYi WuDao: Heart Mind—The Dao of Martial Arts*. London: Singing Dragon.

Wu, Z. and Taylor Wu, K. (2012) *Fire Dragon Meridian Qigong—Essential NeiGong for Health and Spiritual Transformation*. London: Singing Dragon.

Wu, Z. and Taylor Wu, K. (2014) *Heavenly Stems and Earthly Branches: TianGan DiZhi—The Heart of Chinese Wisdom Traditions*. London: Singing Dragon.

Chapter 16

What You See Is Who You Become

Imagery in the Jewish Tradition of Mussar

Alan Morinis

Mussar is a thousand-year-old Jewish tradition of personal study and practice that provides a path to awareness, wisdom, and transformation. Mussar involves the student in meditation, contemplation, exercises in the real, and chanting and visualization. It embraces a diversity of practices that are supported and united by a single concept: that it is not intellectual ideas but rather experience that has the power to transform us.

This is a surprising and remarkable principle, given the fact that the teachers who developed and propagated the Mussar tradition and practices have, for the most part, been Orthodox rabbis with a tremendous investment in the study of the Talmud. It is a profoundly intellectual discipline, but somewhere along the way they must have discovered limitations in their intense focus on study. For example, discovering that those who know all the theoretical nuances involved in the definition of humility might not necessarily be humble, or that someone who understands all the laws of the rewards that are held out to one who gives charity may not be open-handed themselves.

While the Mussar teachers affirmed the role of direct experience in the process of personal change, they were still very firmly rooted in the mind. The mind has an important role to play in Mussar practice because only the mind can grasp the ideal toward which one can aspire, and the mind is the tool that guides the process. The well-defined ideals of humility, gratitude, generosity, anger, and other traits are to be grasped in the mind as goals, and then pursued experientially. It is also the mind that registers experiences. But the Mussar method makes a priority of internalizing what is comprehended mentally, etching it into the metaphoric "heart" that is the very core of our being. This idea is so central and fundamental to Mussar practice that one relatively recent teacher in the tradition, Rabbi Elya Lopian (1872–1970), defined the goal of Mussar as being, "to make the heart feel what the mind knows" (Lopian 1975, p.1).

Because our mind must grasp the ideal that eventually will become our goal, the first step in Mussar practice involves study, which is an intellectual activity. Many Mussar books have been written through the centuries, and the ones that suit this practice best are those that analyze our inner traits. These traits are part of our vocabulary of everyday life, but for the most part they are unexamined and only understood as fuzzy concepts. Through studying a 16th-century text like *Orchot Tzaddikim* (*Ways of the Righteous*) or *Path of the Just* from the 18th century, we can gain a clear working definition of key inner experiences like patience and impatience, worry and trust, joy and sadness, kindness and cruelty.

That depth of study is necessary in order to understand and set our goals of practice. Our minds also play a key role in setting up the format that the practice will take.

But the actual transformative impact—the change the practitioner seeks to bring about in him or herself—comes not directly from the intellectual processes but from experience, whether derived from an encounter with the outer world or from wide range of contemplative practices that the teachers developed. The Torah itself alludes to this two-step process when it instructs us, with respect to God's commandments, to "lay these words upon your heart and upon your soul" (Deuteronomy 11:18).[1]

A Trace on the Soul

In the terminology of the Mussar tradition, every experience, and hence every instance of experiential practice, leaves a "trace on the soul." The technical term in Hebrew is *kibbutz roshmim*, which means "accumulation of impressions." All experience gives rise to internal impressions, which register and accumulate over time: but the impressions that are evoked

through practice stimulate specific experiences that even
personal transformation in the direction of an ideal, which
the practitioner will have defined at the outset. In the words (
century Mussar text, *Orchot Tzaddikim*, "It may be that a pe.
a certain trait to be of value to him, and worthy of pursuit so that he
practiced it until it became implanted in his heart" (Zaloshinsky and
Silverstein 1995, p.9).

This concept is clearly articulated by Rabbi Yisrael Salanter (1810–
1882), who led a movement based on Mussar in 19th-century Lithuania.
He wrote:

> Let a person's heart not despair if he studies Mussar and is not
> awakened, or if he feels no impression on his soul motivating him to
> change his path. It is known with certainty that even if the physical eye
> does not perceive the impression, the eyes of the mind nevertheless
> perceive it. Through an abundance of [Mussar] study over an extended
> period of time, the hidden impressions will accumulate, and he will
> be transformed into a different person. (Miller 2005, Letter 10, p.210)

Although the Mussar teachers of long ago were not clinical researchers,
they realized through empirical observation that sensory experience plays
an influential role in bringing about the kinds of deep and lasting changes
that would warrant calling someone "a different person." We see that
understanding showing up in an exercise prescribed by Rabbi Shlomo
Wolbe (1914–2005), a very recent proponent of the tradition, which he
based on a verse from Isaiah (40:26) that reads, "Lift up your eyes and
look to the heavens: Who created all these? The One who brings out the
starry host one by one and calls forth each of them by name."

With this verse as the foundation, Rabbi Wolbe assigns his students the
practice of simply visually observing something from the realm of nature,
be it a leaf, a flower, or a fruit. He acknowledges that the act of "bare
seeing" may perplex the student, and he cautions against retreating to
an intellectual approach that may be more familiar, because he attributes
enormous power to the impact of the visual impressions themselves. He
writes:

> Without doubt, one who practices in this way over the course of
> many days stands perplexed, wondering, "What will I derive from this
> looking activity?" This seeing doesn't say anything to him. He will try
> to return to the instructions for doing this exercise, or to the verses
> from Isaiah, "Lift your eyes and see who created this," and so on, but
> the words remain arid. There is nothing to that—continue every day to

contemplate, and make effort only to impress on oneself that which his eyes see. Slowly, slowly, his heart will open. (Wolbe 1974, p.272)

These ideas taught by Mussar teachers through the centuries help us understand the Mussar practice of visualization, which involves contemplating specific images that are conjured in the mind, just as in a guided imagery session in a clinical setting. The practitioner sets aside a period of time (often no more than five minutes) during which he or she focuses their imagination (*dimyon*) on specific images that are chosen according to the change in inner traits the person seeks, whether to become more or less humble, more or less generous, and the like. The images are meant to be visualized in the mind so vividly that they stimulate strong emotions and sensations, almost as real as if the person were in the actual situation itself. The goal is not to generate a new idea or to solve a problem, but rather to create sensory impressions that "leave their trace on the soul." With each repetition of the visualization, more traces are deposited, until the foundation of a new way of seeing and being has been laid down.

A leading proponent of visualization as spiritual cultivation in the Mussar world was Rabbi Simcha Zissel Ziv (1824–1898). He founded an academy (*yeshiva*) in the Lithuanian town of Kelm, which led to him being known as the Alter ("Elder") of Kelm. Rabbi Ziv was a primary disciple of Rabbi Salanter and played a leading role in the establishment of an institutional form for Mussar practice in his generation.

Visualization and Transformation

The Alter of Kelm taught a practice of controlled visualization in which consistent repetition of images and imagined experiences are seen to be a pathway to personal change (Ziv 2009). He placed so much emphasis on the impact of visualization that when his student, Rabbi Yechezkiel Levenstein (1895–1974) asked, "What is the difference between a righteous person and a sinner?" he responded with what he himself called "a surprising answer" from the Alter of Kelm, "It is the ability to picture things in one's mind as if they were real" (Morinis 2009, p.33).

This tenet underlies one of visualization's three main purposes in Mussar practice: preparation for the kinds of tests (*nisyonot*) and trials everyone faces throughout their lives, with the primary aim of avoiding transgression. In a teaching from the Mishnah[2] (Pirke Avot 2:13), a rabbi asks a number of his students to name the one quality that is most important for a human being to possess in life. Rabbi Shimon answers,

"To be one who sees what will be born,"[3] by which he means being able to foresee the consequences of our actions.

A classic way this visualization is given form in Mussar practice is to imaginatively envision oneself in the circumstances that are likely to arise as a consequence of wrong-doing. A person who knows that he or she may be tempted to steal something, or commit adultery, or utter a lie and the like, is guided to call to mind a vivid image of being humiliated in court, or being thrown out of the house by their spouse, or feeling the hot-faced shame of by being caught out in a lie. A source for this form of practice is found in the Talmud (Sotah 36b) where it says that Joseph was able to resist the temptation of Potiphar's wife (Genesis 39:1–20) because a vision of his father's face appeared before him. It was his father and all he symbolized that allowed Joseph to resist wrong-doing at the critical moment of extreme temptation.

MUSSAR IMAGERY PRACTICE: GUIDING CHOICE BY VISUALIZING CONSEQUENCES

Try it now. Close your eyes and call to mind a temptation that you have struggled with in the last few months. It should be something that really tempts you and for which you know that there are likely to be negative consequences. Picture very vividly the object or option that tempts you. You can taste it, or feel it, or see it happening in your mind as though it is almost real.

Once you have accomplished that visualization, create an equally vivid mental image of the negative consequence likely to be visited upon you because of that action. Is it your health that suffers? Picture the details of the health consequences. Or will someone be disappointed in you? Or angry? Hear the words and know how it feels to receive their tongue-lashing. Whatever the negative outcome might be, bring it to mind in full color and detail, and see yourself being dealt that consequence as a result of the choice you made.

Once you have done that, examine what effect the visualization has had on your feeling of temptation itself.

A few intense episodes of visualizing the adverse results your behavior might bring upon you are sure to reduce your temptation to transgress. This principle was stated clearly by the Alter of Kelm, Rabbi Simcha Zissel Ziv, when he was asked the question, "What's the difference between a righteous person and an evildoer?" His answer: "It is the ability to picture things in one's mind as if they were real."

Imaginatively envisioning and feeling the consequences of our choices can be an effective way to strengthen our will to resist should the actual situation occur. This form of visualization, with its vivid images and intense accompanying emotions, is a mental rehearsal that prepares a person to meet a test in a way that will avoid a habitual pattern of behavior or succumbing to a desire. The essential point is that the preparation does not involve rehearsing a stratagem but rather imprinting images that will result in a different intuitive impulse arising when the situation itself occurs.

A related teaching is also found in Pirkei Avot (2:1) that reads, "Visualize (*histakel*) three things, and you will not come to sin: Know that above you is a seeing eye, a hearing ear, and all of your deeds are written down in a book." In this case, the imagery that generates an emotional and hence transformative response is of images (eye, ear, book) that represent not the earthly but the eternal consequences of our actions.

Rabbi Eliyahu Dessler (1892–1953), who was trained in the Kelm yeshiva in the next generation after its founder, Rabbi Simcha Zissel Ziv, summarized three types of imaging that could be used in practice to transformative effect, the first of which was "preparation for spiritual or moral challenges by living them out in our minds before they happen," as I have just described.

The other two imagery practices in Mussar tradition that he identified are:

- Transforming abstract concepts into vivid images

- Taking advantage of life experience to enhance our spiritual imagery.

These types of imagery can be invoked in practice through specific prescribed visualizations for the purpose of cultivating ideal inner traits (called *middot* in Hebrew). A primary concern of the Mussar practitioner is to focus effort on changing specific inner traits that may be lacking but that might have the potential to grow at that point in life. Once we have identified such a trait, and learned from traditional sources what the nature of the ideal is, then the contemplation of images can be used to imprint those images of the ideal in our heart. Rabbi Dessler concluded with finality, "It is clear without the slightest doubt that without the power of mental imagery and analogy it is impossible under any circumstances to strengthen, focus, and bring to heart the spiritual matters a person learned" (Dessler 1965, p.145).

Someone who has become aware that they could stand to develop more generosity, for example, might practice visualizing the image of an open hand. Repeating this visualization over a period of time creates a deep imprint of that image, until it comes to pass that when that person encounters an open hand (actual or metaphorical) being extended in their direction, they find that their response is influenced by the image and concept of the open hand. The appeal being made to them triggers the mind to call up the image of the open hand that they had placed in their consciousness, and that image returning to their mind presents them with the option of acting in accord with their chosen ideal of generosity.

To give another example, a person is seeking to strengthen their quality of compassion. They can draw on a teaching given by Rabbi Moshe Cordovero in *Palm Tree of Deborah*, his 16th-century classic Mussar text. In Chapter 1, he says:

> Even if a person cannot find a reason for showing love and compassion to his fellows, he should say, "There was surely a time when they had not yet sinned, and in that time or in former days they were worthy." For their sake, he should recall the love of "those just weaned from milk and torn away from the breast (Isaiah 28:9)." This way, he will not find a single person unworthy of kindness, prayers, or compassion. (Cordovero in Miller 1993)

This teaching suggests a visualization that helps us develop more compassion for a specific individual. It focuses on envisioning that person as an innocent baby being denied succor at the breast. Images of the denial and its emotional impact on the baby (and hence on the adult) is held vividly in mind. Each instance of practice might last only five minutes, but the same images are visualized in repeated sessions until feelings of compassion for that person come to penetrate the heart of the practitioner.

The Alter of Kelm appreciated that visualization could also be used to inspire. He once gave a talk in which he called on his listeners to imagine that the dead of their town had all been granted one more day of life. He expounded at length on images of the earth tearing open and the dead rising in their white burial shrouds, slowly moving into town knowing that they had been given the inconceivably precious gift of just one more day of life. How will they spend that day? The imagery he created sharpened the question he wanted to drive home to his audience: are you living according to your truest priorities?

Mussar Visualizations: The Practice of Transformation

Mussar visualizations like these have been practiced for centuries because they have been found to be effective. The Mussar teachers observed that the repetitive practice of contemplating images could have a lasting transformative impact, bringing about change in a person's thinking, feeling, and behavior. Today we have the scientific knowledge that explains the phenomena they observed. Visual experience, whether generated by the eyes or the mind, stimulates neural activity. As the same images are repeatedly brought to mind, they stimulate the same neural synapses, and over time immature circuits are transformed into the organized connections that constitute adult brain function. When those new circuits become defined pathways, the brain has changed in both physical structure (anatomy) and functional organization (physiology). Current research has demonstrated that the adult brain can and does change in response to sensory experience.[4] Recognizing that the impact of imagery can be so profound as to change the structure and function of the brain brings validation to the claim the Mussar teachers have long made: that one who practices in this way will transform their heart and mind and so become a different person.

ENDNOTES

1. All biblical verses have been translated from Hebrew by the author, Alan Morinis.
2. The first major written version of the Jewish oral teachings and the first major work of rabbinic literature, dating from about 200 CE.
3. Pirke Avot translated from Hebrew by author, Alan Morinis.
4. For example, N. Doidge (2007) *The Brain That Changes Itself: Stories of Personal Triumph from the Frontiers of Brain Science.* New York: Viking; and J. Schwartz and S. Begley (2002) *The Mind and the Brain: Neuroplasticity and the Power of Mental Force.* New York: Harper Collins.

References

Cordovero, M. (1993) *Palm Tree of Deborah.* Translated by Rabbi Moshe Miller. Southfield, MI: Targum/Feldheim.

Dessler, E.E. (1964) *Michtav Me'Eliyahu,* vol. 5. Tel Aviv: Sifriati.

Lopian, E. (1975) *Lev Eliyahu.* Translated by B.D. Klien. Jerusalem: K. Pinski.

Miller, Z. (trans.) (2005) *Ohr Yisrael: The Classic Writings of Rac Yisrael Salanter and His Disciple Rav Yitzchak Blazer.* Nanuet, NY: Feldheim Publishers.

Morinis, A. (2009) *Everyday Holiness: The Jewish Spiritual Path of Mussar.* Boston, MA: Trumpeter Press.

Wolbe, S. (1974) *Alei Shur II.* Jerusalem: Bais Hamussar.

Zaloshinsky, G. (ed.) and Silverstein, S. (trans.) (1995) *Ways of the Tzaddikim: Orchos Tzaddikin*. Nanuet, NY: Feldheim Publishers.

Ziv, S.Z. (2009) *Kitvei HaSaba veTalmidav miKelm*. Bnei Brak, Israel: Siftei Chachamim, Va'ad l'''hiphtzat Torah u'Mussar.

Chapter 17

Christian Imaginative Spirit

Metaphors and Parables

Carolyn J. Stahl Bohler

Christian imagination is rooted in the imagery of the Hebrew Bible, yet it has been affected, both subtly and intentionally, by the diverse contexts in which Christianity was born and has lived. Jesus taught with parables that asked people to imagine all sorts of circumstances, hypothetical situations that provided conundrums requiring them to think seriously while also encouraging them to behave lovingly. Jesus enlisted the imagination as he taught his followers what he believed about God, as well as the way he thought humans should relate to each other—with an ethic of compassionate, self-transcending love.

Throughout history, icons, paintings, stained glass windows, liturgical resources, creeds, hymns, evocative sermons, and diverse forms of meditation and prayer have utilized imagination. These visual and aural images were intended both to cultivate the experience of the Spirit of God in people's lives and to maintain the status quo or, in other times and places, to promote social transformation. In Christianity there is no prohibition on naming God: names given to God are in a sense nicknames, metaphors that clarify some aspect of what God is believed to be like, but at the same time hint that God is, of course, not exactly like the metaphor.

This process of metaphor-making and the creative evocation of image-rich ideas is alive today in Christianity, and there is now a broader and more inclusive set of image-makers than in previous centuries.

For this chapter, which could cover volumes, I will focus on some of the ways that imagery has been transformative for individuals within the Christian tradition and other ways that social change was either fostered or stifled by those who had the power to construct images or define them for whole communities.

Creation Stories

Religious creation stories matter—they set a mood for entire worldviews. For example, the world is perceived as being a joyous or a hostile environment. Creation stories define the order of things, affecting our sense of responsibility in the world as well as our relationship to the divine. What is the purpose of us creatures and the natural world, and how are we to interact? Is there an ethic implied in creation itself? Although many Christians unconsciously merge the "*adam* made in the image of God" and the "the rib of *adam*" stories, these are two separate lengthy creation texts in Genesis 1:1–2:4a and 2:4b–3:24. We will look at the first account, which depicts God as creating the heavens and the earth.

At one point "God said, 'Let there be light'; and there was light. And God saw that the light was good" (New Revised Standard Version of the Bible (NRSV) 1:3–4a). This strikingly imaginative creation narrative culminates with even more potent imagery: "God said, 'Let us make humankind (*adam*) in our image, according to our likeness; and let them have dominion...'"; "God created humankind (*adam*) in his image, in the image of God he created them; male and female he created them" (NRSV 1:27); and "God saw everything that he had made, and indeed, it was very good" (NRSV 1:31). Christian imagery, from the beginning of the Hebrew Bible, affirms the goodness of creation. God speaks of creating "*adam*" ("human") in "our" image, according to "our" likeness. God's self seems to have a plural dimension, and God as plural creates humans—male and female (Bird 1995).

Throughout most of Christian history, those humans who have had the power to name God have named God as male. Poet/lyricist/theologian Brian Wren bemoans that, "though there are other rich metaphors," God has been "pictured, worshipped, and encountered by the human imagination" using "the dominant metaphor system," which Wren calls "KINGAFAP—the King-G-d-Almighty-Father-Protector" (Wren 1989a, p.119).

We know that the earliest humans to have God-representations had female ones, which is not too surprising because when you do not know how pregnancy and birth occur, it's pretty Goddess-like to be fecund. The earth at springtime and females have a lot in common. Not only did early humans think of God as female, our foremothers and forefathers who did so tended to have a different view of divine and human power and responsibility: less power-over, more empowerment; less competition, more cooperation; less earth-conquering, more earth-embracing (Stone 1976).

Cultures with polytheistic religions existed alongside early Judaism and then Christianity. These religions often began with a Goddess-led pantheon that included masculine deities, some of which were depicted as the consort of a Goddess. Over centuries, as Indo-European invasions led to a more militaristic and less agricultural neighborhood of cultures, many of these male Gods became the dominant deity (Swidler 1979; Stone 1976).

Most Christians are surprised to discover a number of references to Goddess-worshipping cultures in the Bible itself. For example, the reason foreign wives were not to be taken was that these women were often adherents of neighboring Goddess-worshipping religions. Whenever we come across (usually a derogatory) reference to "Baal worshippers," these peoples were likely following Anath, Astarte, or Asherah, all Goddesses who were linked to the male god Baal (Swidler 1979; Stone 1976).

In the Jewish tradition, God is beyond limitation, including gender. However, God was envisioned primarily with masculine images and characteristics. God was father, jealous husband, warrior, and lord. Yet there was feminine divine imagery, too. The Divine Feminine is present when God is referred to as Wisdom (*Hokmah* in Hebrew, *Sophia* in Greek) and as Presence (*Shekinah*) (Swidler 1979).

Parables

The traditions that grew up around the birth of Jesus are laden with imagery: shepherds, stars, angels, a manger, animals, the magi in search of the child, even poinsettias. These imagery-laden birth narratives are not uncommon in other major religions. *Jesus sought personal and social change and used transformative imagery to foster that change.* When religious followers embrace a brand new consciousness, they understandably use transformative imagination to live into their faith— and to explain it to others.

Some religious teachers are known from their written treatises. Jesus is known for and followed largely because of his engagement with people's imagination through his use of parables. Jesus' parables are sometimes introduced by a phrase such as, "He told them a parable," or, "Jesus spoke up and said to them..." (For example, Luke 5:36, "He also told them a parable: 'No one tears a piece from a new garment and sews it on an old garment.'") Other parables follow a question that Jesus has asked rhetorically or that someone else has asked him. (Luke 7:31, "To what then will I compare the people of this generation, and what are they like? They are like children...") (NRSV 1989).

Jesus taught that it is not enough to simply *do* the right thing, to be ethical. What is needed is to love, to *intend* love. One must love the other, not just do right by them. To command oneself to love (or to forgive) is quite a challenge; it often seems impossible, rationally and emotionally. However, Jesus sought to cultivate this self-transcending love through engaging his listeners' imagination. Jesus used parables to help his people *visualize* ways they could relate to everyone based on radical love.

Contemporary Christian Imagery

In the mid-1970s there was a heightened interest in guided imagery in secular settings. Since I held a unique position at the time to "explore spirituality and share that exploration with local churches" for Claremont School of Theology in California, I wrote a book of guided imagery based on Scripture. Due to an ever-growing demand for guided imagery, the book was expanded and revised 20 years later. These meditations were to be used for personal or group reflection or within a worship setting. The following is a shortened and hence adapted version of a meditation entitled "The Gift of Reconciliation."

THE GIFT OF RECONCILIATION

Reading: "So when you are offering your gift at the altar, if you remember that your brother or sister has something against you, leave your gift there before the altar and go; first be reconciled to your brother or sister, and then come and offer your gift" (Matthew 5:23–24).

Note: This is an example of Jesus' concern for what is inside the person, their motives and attitudes, in addition to their outward behavior.

Relax, Breath, and then Imagine: Get a sense of yourself in a sacred place. Notice the colors, fragrances, and people who are there… Now become aware that you have a gift in your hand. Move to a place where you can offer your gift. Beginning to let go of the gift, consider whether there is anyone with whom you have "unfinished business"—something that has not yet been fully dealt with. In your imagination, go and find that person, and do whatever you need to do to seek peace and closure. Take whatever time you need. Knowing that you can always return to this person in your imagination at another time, return to the sacred place, aware again of the gift you wish to offer. Reflect again to see whether there is anyone else with whom you do not have inner peace. If so, go out again and communicate with that person. When that encounter feels complete for now, again return to the sacred place. Sense God's all-pervading love moving through you. Now offer your gift and experience it being accepted. When you feel ready, in your imagination leave your sacred place. Become particularly aware of your current surroundings, and open your eyes.

Debriefing: You may practice this imagery meditation several times, each time finding more resolution or clarity! Notice that Matthew used the word "reconciled" rather than "forgiveness." This meditation is not to force forgiveness. Forgiveness is not an act of the will; we cannot make forgiveness happen. Usually we ponder, re-feel a situation, experience anger, try to gain a larger perspective, imagine ourselves into the life of the other, and then eventually realize that we have in large measure forgiven. Forgiveness and reconciliation are processes like physical scars, improving regularly but always "having been there" (Bohler 1996, pp.74–75).

The Image of Trinity

The Trinity, prayer to Saints, and Mariology are developments of Christian's spiritual imagination that have helped followers experience the nearness of what has often been perceived to be a transcendent God.

The Christian Trinity is not actually named as such in the Bible, nor does anyone depicted in the Bible ever say that we should think of God as three-in-one. Following informal references to different aspects of divinity, the Christian Trinity was declared by early Church Councils, most clearly by the Council of Nicea in 325 of the Common Era and the Council of Constantinople in 381 CE.

The Trinity as a transformative image is tricky to convey, for the Christian church has been fairly clear that all three really are one. I find the analogy to the sun to be helpful. The sun is just one thing: however, it provides *energy, light,* and *heat* simultaneously, each of which has a different way of working. Energy, light, and heat are different aspects of the sun and are actually quite different. Solar energy could potentially meet all of our needs for energy. Via photosynthesis, plants turn the sun's light into food. The sun's heat has provided a reasonable set of temperatures within which the creatures of Earth have flourished. The sun is one, and yet it works and affects us in different ways.

In much church liturgy, the Trinity is named the "Father, Son, and Holy Spirit." This particular naming is a choice, because the Trinity itself is not biblical. However, many Christians are so accustomed to hearing this naming that it has become, for them, "the way it is." This is in large measure due to the fact that those church leaders with the power to name have maintained this status quo. A number of clergy name the Trinity now with their theological intent, saying, "In the name of the Creator, Redeemer, and Sustainer." I often say, "In the name of the God who created you and claims your life good; in the name of the Prince of Peace; and in the name of the Holy Spirit, which is with you every step of your journey."

Mary

For Roman Catholics, praying to the saints and to Mary expanded their imagery options. Although it has been emphasized that God alone answers prayer, many Christians have felt more secure praying to a saint or to Mary, wanting those compassionate ones to "ask" God on their behalf. Imagining Mary's participation has enabled millions of Christians to visualize a responsive, caring spiritual dimension as receiving their pleas as well as their gratitude.

The "Hail Mary" is the best-loved prayer in the Roman Catholic world. Once, on Superbowl Sunday, I preached a sermon entitled, "Prayer: Throwing a Hail Mary?" (Bohler 2013). I had recently overheard the announcer of a football game say something like, "He's likely to throw a Hail Mary Pass." I was stunned. It's not that unusual for a preacher to use sports imagery, but this sports announcer was using religious imagery! I checked with my husband and learned that I had indeed heard correctly. I later discovered that Dallas Cowboys' quarterback Roger Staubach (who is Roman Catholic) had described his game-winning touchdown pass to wide receiver Drew Person in a 1975 playoff game this way, "I closed my eyes and said a Hail Mary" (Staubach 2000). After that, this transformative image became widespread. This image is a thought-teaser that has become understood in our culture to mean that if we are desperate, when nothing else seems reasonable, we might as well pray (or throw the ball), just in case there is someone (Mary, in prayer; a receiver in football) out there to catch the prayer (or ball) and carry it forward.

Prayer: Enlisting the Imagination

Prayer nearly always involves the imagination: imagining what prayer is and does, with whom or Whom it is engaged, visualizing what one might be grateful for, a situation in which one seeks guidance, or something that one is open to receiving. Not all prayers begin by addressing the divine, but many do—and however one addresses the Recipient, the One Whom is addressed is "named" by a metaphor.

However, there is a genre of Christian prayer that intends visualization through its very style. Four centuries ago, Saint Ignatius taught the Bible using guided imagery. He chose passages such as the Incarnation, Jesus at the Temple, the Last Supper, the Passion, and the Resurrection for "mental image" meditations. Ignatius suggested projectively moving into the biblical episode—being there, listening, watching, and even conversing with the people within the scene. He did not use his imagination exercises just to help people understand the biblical teachings: he explicitly expected personal growth, too (Mottola 1964).

Theologian John Cobb points out that if God is truly incarnate—present in the world—it follows that God is not limited to one human faculty (reason, emotion, will, or imagination) or to a single book. Rather, God can be known here and now through an appropriate integration of all human faculties. "The wholeness most worth striving for is one in which the maximum complexity of aspects of existence is united...indeed, the spirit in all its aspects is peculiarly dependent on imagination" (Cobb 1975).

THE WOMAN WITH THE JAR

Reading: Gospel of Thomas 97:6–14. Jesus said, "The Kingdom of the [Father] is like a woman who was carrying a jar full of meal. While she was walking [on a] distant road, the handle of the jar broke. The meal streamed out behind her on the road. She did not know [it], she had noticed no accident. After she came into her house, she put the jar down, she found it empty" (Guillaumont *et al.* 1959, pp.49–51).

Note: The following parable from Jesus is likely to be unfamiliar because it is found in the *Gospel of Thomas*, which was not included in the Christian biblical canon. Therefore, it is an exciting opportunity for imagery prayer as it has yet to be interpreted in sermons by preachers or taught in many Sunday Schools.[1]

Relax, Breathe, and then Imagine: Try imagining the parable above, reading it several times; sense yourself inhabiting the scene from various viewpoints. 1) Take the perspective of one who is watching the woman walking by. 2) Take the woman's perspective as she begins walking with the jar full of meal. 3) Experience yourself as the woman as she walks along the path, heading homeward. 4) Imagine becoming the jar itself, and then the meal. 5) Finally, be the woman as she arrives home and realizes there is no meal left in her jar. Then hear the words, "The Kingdom of the [Father] is like this." Give yourself time, reflect, doodle, write, imagine, feel, and ponder.

Debriefing: You might want to sketch these perspectives, with words or images; ponder and question. You might create a jar that is "full" and one that is "empty." Keep them in your daily purview for a while, taking notes on more thoughts that occur to you.

Metaphors (and Similes) for the Divine

Numerous examples could be given of *visual images* of the deity in myriad art museums around the world, all of which affect our view of ourselves and the divine, often without our conscious awareness. Think of the early 16th-century image of Michelangelo on the Sistine Chapel's ceiling. God is painted as a huge white male figure reaching out and down. What a powerful impact this visual image has had upon the human psyche!

Theologian Mary Daly's 1973 book, *Beyond God the Father: Toward a Philosophy of Women's Liberation*, helped to usher in several decades of social transformation by drawing attention to the power of naming. Naming God almost exclusively as "Father" has made an enormous impression on us. For one thing, males' greater power is legitimized, especially the power to name. Daly insists, "It is the creative potential itself in human beings that is the image of God" (Daly 1973, p.29). Theologian Major Jones articulates the importance of imagery for people of all colors, "Everyone colors God in the hues of relevancy, no less so Black people" (Jones 1987, p.39). In her very successful 1975 drama *for colored girls who have considered suicide/when the rainbow is enuf,* playwright Ntozake Shange presents women who are searching for meaning. One woman arrives at the point where she declares, "I found god in myself & I loved her/I loved her fiercely" (Shange 1975, p.67).

Hymns

Hymnals represent communal decisions by denominational decision-making bodies to evoke certain images and not others. For example, when the most recent *United Methodist Hymnal* (UMH) was published in 1989, the committee responsible for the final decisions did not include any *metaphors* for the deity that were female-oriented, but they did include some female-oriented *similes*. Hence, the hymn "The Care the Eagle Gives Her Young" (Postlethwaite) is included in the hymnal with this comparison: "The care the eagle gives her young…is *like* the tender love of God…" (Postlethwaite in UMH, 1989, #118). However, the hymn "Bring Many Names," by lyricist Brian Wren (1989b), is not included because it refers to "Strong mother God," without the word "like" or "as" that would make the "strong mother God" metaphor into a simile. God as female "eagle" in the first hymn is a simile; "strong mother God" in the second is a full-fledged metaphor. When *The Faith We Sing*, the supplement to the official *United Methodist Hymnal*, was published in 2000, the requirement for male-only metaphors for the deity was not in force, and "Bring Many Names" was included with its original lyrics (Hickman 2000, #2047).

This example illustrates in a very concrete way how imagery is expected to transform personal lives and to bring about social change. Therefore, when certain transformations are not desired by those with the majority vote, or those with the power to name, certain imagery may be intentionally stifled. Brian Wren is a prominent poet-lyricist who is passionate about using hymnal and poetic imagery to bring about a transformation toward more justice for individuals and society as a whole. "Patriarchal Christianity is in danger of worshipping an idol, and we are not protected from idolatry by the fact that much of our God-language is biblical" (Wren 1989a). More recently, Wren encouraged readers to question and to change lyrics that do not reflect God's love for every human being, whenever feasible. He confessed, "Everything I learn about justice in language comes from others who correct me" (Wren 2000, p.179).

REFLECTION ON A HYMN

Think of a hymn that you know "by heart," browse through a hymnal or look online until you come across a song you enjoy. Notice the images that the hymn includes. What metaphors (or similes) are used for the divine? How are humans portrayed? Do you *believe* the words you're singing? Do the images evoke justice for all? How might the hymn be altered to articulate what is congruent with what you currently believe?

Preaching and Leading Worship

Those who lead others in *guided imagery*, either as a group or one-on-one, know that choosing just how much guidance to offer is a delicate balance. The decision is both one of caring and ethics: how much to use our power as introducer of images, and how much to foster space for the other(s) to imagine on their own?

I consider preaching to be a source of "transformative imagery for personal and social change" because—whether it supports the status quo or change—preaching has the potential to exert a major influence on individuals and communities. When I preach, I am very intentional about the imagery I select. On a purely practical level, I try to reach diverse listeners by using examples from many aspects of life. However, I also use my preaching authority to refer to God with thought-provoking metaphors. In my 2008 book, *God the What? What our Metaphors for God Reveal About Our Beliefs in God*, I share examples from dialogues with people in diverse settings to show how important divine metaphors can be for our personal authenticity and for social justice. I want people to use God-metaphors that are truly congruent with what they believe, especially with regard to *divine and human power and responsibility*. To find congruence, we need to explore, to question, to wonder.

This exploration toward serious, if playful, theology requires imagination. If God can be described as "writing on the wall" (as in the Hebrew Bible, *Daniel*, Chapter 5), then could we consider God a Graffiti Artist, helping us to get clues for guidance in our daily walk? Or do we expect God to jump in to solve our problems, even if we barely take action ourselves? That is, do we behave as though God were a Helicopter God, taking charge like an over-involved parent? Alternatively, perhaps God is like a Divine Jazz-Band Leader, leading all, making music God's self, but also pointing to us when it's our turn to play a "riff." This metaphor implies that we have genuine freedom; God is not in complete control—

and so for the sake of all, we need to be responsible. God as Graffiti Artist, Helicopter God, or Divine Jazz-Band Leader: these images express profoundly different views of Godly and human power and responsibility. The metaphor matters.

From creation stories that set a mood to contemporary metaphors for God, imagery has been an essential element of personal faith and—less obvious but just as vital—of social transformation. Jesus used parables to help people entertain and visualize radical love. Christian hymn lyrics, prayers, and varied art forms have attempted to nurture our experience of the Creative Spirit's Love.

ENDNOTE

1. This exercise is a greatly reduced and adapted meditation from Bohler 1996, pp.163–166.

References

Bird, P.A. (1995) "Sexual Differentiation and Divine Image in the Genesis Creation Texts." In K.E. Borresen (ed.) *The Image of God: Gender Models in Judaeo-Christian Tradition*. Minneapolis, MN: Fortress Press.

Bohler, C. (formerly Stahl) (1996) *Opening to God: Guided Imagery Meditation on Scripture, Completely Revised and Expanded*. Nashville, TN: Upper Room Books.

Bohler, C. (2008) *God the What? What Our Metaphors for God Reveal About Our Beliefs in God*. Woodstock, VT: SkyLight Paths.

Bohler, C. (2013) *Prayer: Throwing a Hail Mary?* Sermon delivered on February 3 2013, Redlands, CA at Redlands First United Methodist Church.

Cobb, J., Jr. "Strengthening the Spirit." *Union Seminary Quarterly Review XXX*, Winter–Summer 1975, 133, 136.

Daly, M. (1973) *Beyond God the Father: Toward a Philosophy of Women's Liberation*. Boston, MA: Beacon Press.

Guillaumont, A., Puech, H., Quispel, G., Till, W., and 'Abd Al Masih, Y. (1959) *The Gospel According to Thomas: Coptic Text Established and Translated*. New York, NY: Harper & Row.

Hickman, H.L. (ed.) (2000) *The Faith We Sing*. Nashville, TN: Abingdom Press.

Jones, M.J. (1987) *The Color of God: The Concept of God in Afro-American Thought*. Macon, GA: Mercer University Press.

Mottola, A. (trans.) (1964) *The Spiritual Exercises of St. Ignatius*. Garden City, NY: Imagery Books.

New Revised Standard Version of the Bible (NRSV) (1989) Division of Christian Education of the National Council of the Churches of Christ in the USA.

Postlethwaite, R.D. (1989) "The Care the Eagle Gives Her Young," *The United Methodist Hymnal: Book of United Methodist Worship* #118. Nashville, TN: The United Methodist Publishing House.

Shange, N. (1975) *for colored girls who have considered suicide/when the rainbow is enuf*. New York, NY: Bantam Books.

Staubach, R. (2000) *Pro Football Hall of Fame, History Release,* chat transcript. Available at www.profootballhof.com/history/release.aspx?release_id=771, accessed on April 10 2015.

Stone, M. (1976) *When God was a Woman.* New York, NY: Harcourt Brace Jovanovich.

Swidler, L. (1979) *Biblical Affirmations of Woman.* Philadelphia, PA: Westminster Press.

Wren, B. (1989a) *What Language Shall I Borrow? God-Talk in Worship: A Male Response to Feminist Theology.* New York, NY: Crossroad.

Wren, B. (1989b) *Bring Many Names.* Carol Stream, IL: Hope Publishing Co.

Wren, B. (2000) *Praying Twice: The Music and Words of Congregational Song.* Louisville, KY: Westminster John Knox Press.

Part 5

Boundless Applications of Imagery

Chapter 18

Mindful Advocacy

Imagery for Engaged Wisdom

Leslie Davenport

And when the stakes are life on earth, all else is a diversion.
                                                     Susan Murphy Roshi[1]

We are a culture of information consumers, but facts too often skid over the surface of our souls. The statistics have been around for a long time: a child dies every ten seconds from causes related to inadequate nutrition or starvation (Alexander 2013); FBI records document an average of one murder every 31 minutes, a rape every six, and aggravated assault each 27 seconds (Federal Bureau of Investigation 2011); more than two million people are forced into labor, often sexual exploitation, as a result of human trafficking (United Nations 2010); and scientists warn that we are on the brink of a mass extinction (Barnosky 2014), with NASA reporting extreme weather events on the rise (Finneran 2013).

Here in the West, we root our beliefs in each person's unalienable rights to life, liberty, and the pursuit of happiness—but we need to take care of our home, our planet, in order to live out these ideals. We suffer from a critical lack of awareness: that the right to happiness must be paired with a duty to stewardship. With our planet's health faltering and our current lifestyles growing increasingly unsustainable, we need to make change happen. This kind of change begins with vision and continues with potent, mindful action—and the practice of guided imagery offers us a doorway to internal clarity and a path to engaged and wise action.

While there have always been wars, poverty, illness, and the full challenge of living, scientists around the world are issuing a stark warning that the current climate changes could lead to an erosion of the existing food supply, increased poverty, and the very real potential of a planet that is inhospitable to human life (Barnosky 2014). The realities of our time are painful to face, and they will eventually impact us all. So this is not a roll call of saints, flimsy sentimentalism, or an invitation to berate yourself for enjoying what modern life has to offer. It is instead a call for an ongoing, evolving practice of engaged wisdom in daily life that reveals a deeper recognition: that we are inseparable from the world and all its inhabitants. Our interdependent nature reveals that how we think and what we believe influences what we create; what we choose impacts others and the environment more deeply than we have yet to imagine.

Why Guided Imagery?

Guided imagery is an indispensable ally: it's a doorway to the kind of internal clarity we need in order to envision change, a catalyst for self growth, and a guide for wise action. As you will discover through the practices offered in this chapter, imagery provides us with a way to look inside ourselves and reconnect with our most authentic values and discover ways to live out those ideals.

Our contemporary Western culture highly prizes achievement and logical analysis. While we certainly wouldn't want to be without our rationality, there are equally valuable ways of knowing that shed light on aspects of life inaccessible to the logical mind. With guided imagery, we can expand our doors of perception to include creativity, intuition, mindful awareness, contemplative insight, synergistic impressions, "gut feelings," empathy, hunches, and a body-based "felt sense" that have become weak from disuse in a society that doesn't value whole-brain, whole-self education. Albert Einstein is said to have commented on our contemporary condition: "The intuitive mind is a sacred gift, and the rational mind is a faithful servant. We have created a society that honors the servant and has forgotten the gift" (Samples 1976, p.26).

The rational and intuitive parts of the mind are like two legs that keep us moving forward—so why would we set out on a lifelong journey with one leg becoming excessively muscle-bound and the other atrophying?

We need to strengthen and utilize everything we're made of. If we want change—if we want to come back into balance—we must understand how we got here and begin to develop the neglected aspects of ourselves. "Problems cannot be solved by the same consciousness that created them,"[2] is another astute insight attributed to Einstein.

And yet it is not just about accessing our different ways of knowing. As we increasingly gain skill in navigating through our many thresholds of perception, a deep congruence develops—an integration of what previously seemed paradoxical and the emergence of a hidden existence that infuses our physical world with vibrancy and meaning. This internal clarity gradually becomes the new foundation for living a way of life anchored in wisdom.

At the heart of our problems lies our collective blindness to the delicate balance expressed in the very laws of nature. Living things and the environment depend on one another for survival (Sterner 2002). Our world is a dynamic web: for example, the food that nourishes us comes from millions of years of evolution, and yet the industrialized world has introduced radically artificial forms of food production that are creating severe health problems as well as depleting our natural resources (Pollan 2008). Our tendency to disrupt the essential laws of nature without anticipating the potentially destructive outcomes is just one consequence of our lopsided thinking.

Guided imagery is a powerful way to become and remain connected with the essential pulse of life, which can help us make decisions that support a more balanced lifestyle. The part of the brain from which imagery arises generates "big-picture" thinking: it helps us grasp a larger context. Where logical analysis looks at sequential parts, imagistic consciousness sees connections and patterns, and processes the same information differently. The imagery perspective allows us to put ideas together in a fresh way, often creating new solutions to old problems.

While imagistic consciousness can seem mysterious, it is immensely practical when skillfully directed. There are four guided imagery practices in this chapter that can help you gain clarity about your unique talents and calling and help map the steps for expressing them in effective action. In the words of Pierre Teilhard de Chardin, "The actual task is to integrate the two threads of one's life...the within and the without."[3] Discovering and contributing your particular skills is part of building a planet-wide foundation of mindful advocacy and stewardship that will heal ourselves and our world.

Each exercise requires about 20 minutes of undisturbed time when you can safely step away from any potential interruptions. Since most of the practices are done with your eyes closed, you may first want to make an audio recording of the instructions on your phone or digital recorder and then play them while you enter the experience. It can also be valuable to have an imagery partner; you can take turns reading the instructions and discuss any insights that surface together at the end. The exercises are designed to build the strength and fluency of those underused parts of ourselves and integrate imagistic awareness so that it is readily accessible in our day-to-day lives.

Because who we are cannot be separated from what we do, I've also included two imagery practices that give us a clear vision of our inner gifts and true nature (Remembering and Intention), and two that support ways to express our mindful advocacy talents in the world (Balance and Connection).

Imagery Visioning Practices

While there are wonderful role models we can learn from, our charge is not to become another Martin Luther King or Gandhi. Our responsibility is to discover who we are and actuate our unique way of participating in and nurturing the web of life.

Maybe you're the person who helps someone resolve their public-speaking phobia when their challenge is to present a climate change keynote address at a 3000-seat auditorium podium. Or you support one of the cooks who provides a nourishing meal after a human rights rally. Maybe you're a full-time mom committed to raising a health-conscious family, who manages to find time when the house is quiet to sign petitions for the concerns you are most aligned with. You may be the grandfather who encourages their 20-something grandchild to pursue their dream of becoming an organic farmer, in spite of the financial risks. Perhaps you have the savvy and financial resources to back important candidates that you believe have the vision and fortitude to fight for change in the political arena. There are as many ways to serve in this world as there are people on the planet. Just as biodiversity nourishes the health of an ecosystem, the collective synergy of our gifts and talents is fuel for transformation.

Know, too, that there will doubtless be a variety of ways you will participate, given that mindful awareness and action can only arise together in the present moment. Notice your simple everyday choices: what and how you eat; your modes of transportation; the stories and images that your mind cultivates. A beautiful stained glass window is created by shaping just one tiny piece of colored glass at a time—and your daily choices all coalesce into one vibrant and creative expression of your values.

As you explore these imagery practices, know that this work is a process. You will probably need to enter into the imagery more than once to distill the messages that arise. In addition, the imagery is likely to evolve and change over time in parallel with your own development. In preparation for these practices, let your inner critic take a nap and set aside your perfectionism and the pressure to "do it right." Don't worry if what appears in your imagery doesn't seem practical. The time to decide how and when to take action will happen in a later part of the process. For now, let yourself dream. Let yourself imagine.

REMEMBERING: BE TRUE TO YOURSELF

Each of our particular gifts and talents has been with us since our first breath, and they are all still part of us. The poet Rumi reminds us, "You wander from room to room hunting for the diamond necklace that is already around your neck."[4] This imagery practice is a path to remembering and reconnecting with aspects of ourselves that may have been relegated to the shadows, and to ushering them into the light of being.

The instructions for entering into, exploring, and transitioning out of the exercise can be added to the other more briefly described imagery practices that follow.

PREPARATION FOR ALL THE IMAGERY PRACTICES

Set aside 20 minutes and sit or recline in a way that is supportive and comfortable, and allows your breath to flow freely. You may want to close your eyes to help you shift from focusing on the environment around you and tune into yourself more deeply. Each time you inhale, welcome the fresh new oxygen that is nourishing your body. Each time you exhale, invite your body to relax even more deeply. Take several minutes with this breathing, allowing the waves of breath to roll through your body. If you notice any pockets of tension or discomfort, spend a few moments sending ease and comfort to those areas, while also being kind and accepting toward your body for whatever sensations remain.

Send the same invitation for your emotions to rest, accompanied by kind acceptance toward whatever you are experiencing. It's natural for the mind to become distracted with planning, or worrying, or problem-solving. When you notice this occurring, acknowledge it and then gently but firmly redirect your focus to your breath and relaxation. Take several minutes with simply relaxing and being present with yourself, ever more aware, ever more relaxed.[5] (Continue with the imagery practices.)

REMEMBERING YOUR TRUE SELF

Begin with the imagery preparation described above. Now let your mind float back to a time when your heart felt expansive, connected to life, a place where your mind, heart, and body unanimously said "yes" to the moment. It may be a time when you participated in a significant event, or perhaps it was a quiet moment by yourself when the mystery and wonder of life was palpable. It may be six months, two years, five years, ten years ago or more; however long ago you experienced this doesn't matter. Simply trust that your innate intelligence will guide you to a time and place worthy of exploring the theme of your true nature.

Journey to a time when you felt free to be yourself without pressures or expectations. Let it be a time you experienced a feeling of belonging in life, of offering your own presence and gifts to the larger world—a time when the details of daily living dropped away to reveal the deeper awe of life. Once an impression begins to form, notice the colors, shapes, and texture of the environment. Reenter it now. Notice the temperature, the sounds. Are there any particular aromas? Allow this remembered experience to become vivid. Notice the qualities of this place. Is it serene, vibrant, comforting, or powerful? Take time to be with whatever feelings are arising for you, however subtle or strong.

Now allow this environment to express itself to you. If right now your full experience had a voice, or some way of communicating, what does it want you to know? Take time to be receptive to the message, knowing it may come in any form—an impression, symbol, physical sensation, flash of insight. Let this message include recognizing the gift of your own being, gratitude for life, and the ways you can help cultivate this for yourself and others. Ask clarifying questions back to the environment that is speaking to you, if needed. Take as much time as you'd like, and allow the qualities of this watershed moment to be fully experienced.

When your experience feels complete for now, know that you can return to this time and place again in a similar way. Register once more anything that feels valuable from today's imagery practice so that it is easy to access, easy to remember. Thank your innate inner wisdom for coming forth, and recognize your enduring relationship with this faithful inner ally.

> Allow the shift back into your current place and time to be a seamless transition, keeping with you any feelings and insights you wish to integrate into your life. Take a few full breaths, feel again the natural weight and shape of your body. Notice the temperature of the air on your skin. Sense the light through your eyelids. As you are ready, gently open your eyes again.

It is valuable to take a few moments to write or even draw your experience before returning to your other plans for the day.

INTENTION: SET YOUR INNER COMPASS

It's easy to find great advocacy opportunities and tools, given all the resources on the Internet. There is a wealth of wonderful books to read, and organizations, leaders, and communities doing valuable work. The challenge for most of us is keeping what we most deeply value front and center in the midst of addressing life's daily details and challenges. It can be helpful to cultivate a strong intention.

Imagery can shape our intention into an inner compass, a tool that helps us stay pointed in the direction we want to go. You can think of the previous imagery practice of Remembering as "finding your North Star," a bright and constant reference point by which to navigate through the many moving parts of your life. The practice of Intention creates and links your "inner compass" to your most meaningful vision.

VISION AND INTENTION

Begin with the imagery preparation described above. Now recall the images that evoked your true nature and feelings of awe from your Remembering imagery session. Once they are fully present, allow them to move from the past into the future, arcing above you like a bright star until they land before you in a possible future. Now imagine the same imagery experience of your own vital presence that you experienced in the past, coming alive within that vision of the future. Notice where you are, what you are doing and who is with you. The forms of your gifts and participation will likely evolve and change in surprising ways. Take time to imagine stepping into one of those future possibilities, taking in the sights, sounds, qualities, and activities and fully experiencing them now. Linger for a few moments, becoming familiar with this new way of bringing your gifts into the world.

Staying in the imagery practice, come back to the present and see the path before you to that future vision. Feel what it is like to clearly orient toward your goal, to have your inner compass set to your own North Star. Where and how do you experience it in your body, heart, mind? What do you need in order to move forward? If there are obstacles, begin to explore how to clear the path using your creative imagination. Feel what it would be like to have what you need right now, and step toward the future you are already in the process of creating.

When you feel that the experience is complete for now, gradually transition back to the present time and place, and take time to write about your experience.

Imagery Action Practices

While the inner imagery practices connect us to a numinous center within ourselves, after the sessions we face the challenge of engaging the world around us guided by our deep vision. The outer imagery exercises help us take practical steps to *promote* change.

BALANCE: FIND "ENOUGH"

Recent research on "compassion fatigue" is packed with statistics that reveal high stress levels and burnout among both paid and voluntary workers in advocacy and service fields. Those who work with trauma victims—whether hospital patients, veterans, or physical or sexual abuse survivors—are at increased risk for experiencing vicarious traumatization (Figley 1995). Setting healthy limits and working actively on self-care are the essential but often overlooked components to surviving and thriving in this important work.

One of the biggest challenges we face in advocacy work is coming to terms with our limitations as we recognize the scale and urgency of suffering and need. It can feel counterintuitive to our passion and commitment to step away, even for a while. We wouldn't be called to this work if we weren't already empathetic to the pain around us, and that pain can be a useful initiation that catalyzes our gifts and abilities into action. But like the mother in an aircraft who receives emergency instructions to place the oxygen mask over her own face before attending to her child, we must ensure our own well-being in order to effectively be of service to others.

Our bodies are programmed to send us signals when we are hungry or tired. Many of us have found clever ways to override those natural cues by pushing through fatigue and postponing the replenishment of good nutrition. Not only does this contribute to burnout, over time it creates adverse health impacts. Overriding our bodies' essential needs is a lot like ignoring the "check engine" light on the car dashboard: it can create a dangerous situation.

The imagery practice of finding balance helps us reconnect to the natural cues arising in our bodies and respond to them, as well as to mindfully take stock of our time and energy commitments and then follow through with effective action while also maintaining self-care.

SUSTAINING BALANCE

Begin with the imagery preparation described above. In your relaxed state of heightened awareness, let your focus now extend from the breath to sensing, on a more subtle level, your vitality. Note your level of physical fatigue in this moment on a scale of 1–10. Now note your degree of mental fatigue on the same numeric scale. And then rate your emotional ease or distress. In this state of receptive awareness, ask the simple question, "What do I need right now to support my full health and well-being?" Take a few moments to respond to the answer using imagery and your deepest intuitive awareness. This may require you to drop even more deeply into relaxation, or enjoy some full, vitalizing in-breaths.

Now bring your attention to the part of your mind that helps you organize and stay on track, a kind of personal inner advocate. Allow that part of you to reveal itself symbolically, as an image. It could appear in any form. It may be an inner organizer, taskmaster, cheerleader, or tyrant. Once it takes shape, really explore it. How does it look? Does it carry a clipboard, a whip? Notice in particular its qualities: is it kind, wise, confused, critical, lethargic, panicked, rigid? Then ask the question, "What does this part of me need, my inner advocate, right now to support my health and well-being?" Once the answer arrives, if it feels right to do so, go ahead and imagine that change: transform your inner advocate to a healthier, more effective version. Take time to register the new, evolved inner advocate, and notice how the change feels.

When the imagery experience feels complete for now, gradually transition back to the present time and place, and take time to write about your experience.

If your inner advocate shifted into a healthier version of itself during the Balance practice, be sure to write down what needed to change and how that modification occurred. Staying present in this balanced perspective, take out your calendar right now and look at the activities and commitments for the day, the week, and the month. Does your schedule reflect the balance needed for the health of your body, heart, and mind? Is there room for the advocacy work you so value? Experiment with reducing or increasing your commitments, guided once again by your inner compass and keeping "North Star," your deepest values, in view.

Connection: Find your Colleagues

Wherever you are with advocacy work, whether you're a seasoned veteran or newly curious about ways to get involved, know that you are already part of the world's wisdom circles. There are others all over the globe who feel a similar imperative for change. The more we can join forces, the more potent the outcome.

The outer strategies of creative imagery include what I call, "eyes-open imagery."[6] This is a process where we use the same elements of imagery practice—being relaxed with active receptive awareness, seeing with fewer preconceived notions, adopting an attitude of curiosity while grounded in the present moment—but we apply them to the living images in the environment around us. For example, we could close our eyes and imagine a magnificent tree and feel inspired by its grandeur and aliveness. With eyes-open imagery, we bring conscious attention to the trees that we walk past on a daily basis, recognizing their vibrancy and splendor in the moment. We see our environment with new, awakened eyes.

Have you had the experience of hearing about a book that piques your interest, and you suddenly notice that the topic pops up in conversations, and you keep seeing it referenced in articles, news stories, and store windows? Perhaps it has been there all along, but you are now attuned to recognizing it. You've developed a kind of radar—your antennae are up and dialed into that particular channel.

Raising your antennae in order to recognize like-minded individuals and organizations that resonate with your vision is a wonderful way to discover your colleagues and connect with community.

Connection and Support

After doing the Remembering imagery exercise, slowly open your eyes while remaining strongly connected to the energy, qualities, and feelings that the practice engenders. Intentionally take

20 minutes now to practice eyes-open imagery, recognizing the energy you are feeling internally reflected in the world around you. You can do this as you take a walk, sit in a park, or even browse the Internet. Intentionally close the practice by noting and planning specific times for action steps that may include contacting a person, writing a blog piece, attending a meeting, or other creative options that arose out of your eyes-open imagery practice.

From Advocacy to Stewardship

We can think of stewardship as bringing the spirit of advocacy into all aspects of daily life. Embracing a life of stewardship is not easy, and it can be confusing. The good news *and* the bad news is that this is lifelong learning. It is a complex and meaningful path requiring that we dynamically come to know and use all of who we are as we grow—while seeing more clearly the opportunities and timing for effective change. There are three components of stewardship:

- The science, gaining and refining tools, methods, and knowledge

- The art, sensing how and when to skillfully apply what we know

- The mystery, the grace and grit of dancing with the surprises that life introduces to the process.

Deepening stewardship requires discernment that is refined though inner inquiry, life experience, and learning from the communities and leaders engaged in this work. You may wonder when self-care becomes indulgence or when acceptance slides into resignation. Where is the line between fearlessness and recklessness? Can we choose a lifestyle of service without becoming codependent? The answers to these kinds of questions are waiting to be explored inside your own heart, and the faithful path of imagery stands before you now with a welcome invitation.

ENDNOTES

1. Susan Murphy, from the essay, "The Koan of the Earth" in Llewellyn Vaughan-Lee (ed.) (2013) *Spiritual Ecology: The Cry of the Earth*. Point Reyes, CA: The Golden Sufi Center Publishing, p.125.
2. While this quote is widely attributed to Einstein, there is no confirmation of the source.
3. Widely attributed to Pierre Teilhard de Chardin, but the source is unknown.
4. The quote is commonly attributed to the poet Jalāl ad-Dīn Rumi, although there is no confirmation of the source.

5. Free downloadable mp3s for relaxation can be found on my website, www. lesliedavenport.com. They are another good way to relax prior to entering your imagery exploration.
6. "Eyes-open imagery" practices were first introduced in my book *Healing and Transformation Through Self Guided Imagery*. Berkeley, CA: Celestial Arts/ Random House (2009). This is a good source for additional eyes-open imagery practices.

References

Alexander, R. (2013) "Does a child die of hunger every 10 seconds?" *BBC News Magazine*. Available at www.bbc.com/news/magazine-22935692, accessed on May 28 2015.

Barnosky, A.D. (2014) *Dodging Extinction: Power, Food, Money and the Future of Life on Earth*. Berkeley, CA: University of California Press.

Davenport, L. (2009) *Healing and Transformation through Self Guided Imagery*. Berkeley, CA: Celestial Arts.

Federal Bureau of Investigation (2011) "Crime in the United States." *Federal Bureau of Investigation: Uniform Crime Reports*. Available at www.fbi.gov/about-us/ cjis/ucr/crime-in-the-u.s/2011/crime-in-the-u.s.-2011/offenses-known-to-law-enforcement/standard-links/national-data, accessed on February 28 2015.

Figley, C.R. (ed.) (1995) *Compassion Fatigue: Coping with Secondary Traumatic Stress Disorder in Those Who Treat the Traumatized*. London: Routledge.

Finneran, M. (2013) *More Extreme Weather Events Forecast*. NASA Langley Research Center. Available at www.nasa.gov/centers/langley/science/climate_ assessment_2012.html, accessed on February 5 2015.

Pollan, M. (2008) *In Defense of Food: An Eater's Manifesto*. New York, NY: Penguin Press.

Samples, B. (1976) *The Metaphoric Mind: A Celebration of Creative Consciousness*. Reading: Addison-Wesley Publishing Company.

Sterner, R.W., Esler, J.J., and Vitousek, P. (2002) *Ecological Stoichiometry: The Biology of Elements to the Biosphere*. Princeton, NJ: Princeton University Press.

United Nations Office on Drug and Crime (2010) *Fact Sheet on Human Trafficking*. Available at www.unodc.org/documents/human-trafficking/UNVTF_fs_HT_ EN.pdf, accessed on February 1 2015.

Vaughan-Lee, L. (ed.) (2013) *Spiritual Ecology: The Cry of the Earth*. Point Reyes, CA: The Golden Sufi Center.

Chapter 19

Enhancing Imagery with Focusing-Oriented Expressive Arts

Laury Rappaport

Guided imagery can be enhanced with Focusing-Oriented Expressive Arts (FOAT®), a mind-body method that integrates Eugene Gendlin's Focusing with the expressive arts (Rappaport 2009, 2014b; Gendlin 1981, 1996). Focusing provides a method for accessing the body's authentic imagery and guides one to access the bodily *felt sense* of an imagery experience. The expressive arts serve to concretize this inner experience, externalizing and carrying forward the healing benefits from the more inward experience of imagery.

Naperstek (1994) confirms the importance of experiencing imagery within the body's felt sense, as well as it being multi sensory: "We now know that it needs to be a multi-sensory experience, accessed in the altered state, and probably most effective when felt as a sensation in the body" (p.41). Focusing-oriented expressive arts provides a multi-sensory experience by incorporating Focusing as a mindful, inner-directed approach for accessing imagery, in conjunction with sensory-based expressive arts processes.

This chapter includes an overview of Focusing-Oriented Expressive Arts; three FOAT imagery methods with case vignettes—Theme Directed FOAT, Clearing a Space with Art, and Nondirective FOAT; examples of how to integrate Gestalt and Dialogue methods; and a summary of the benefits of a FOAT Imagery approach.

Focusing-Oriented Expressive Arts: A Guided Imagery Approach

I developed Focusing-Oriented Expressive Arts (FOAT) after 30 years of applying Focusing and the expressive arts with a wide variety of clinical populations, including adults, adolescents and children with chronic and terminal illnesses, trauma, severe mental health issues, as well as depression and anxiety. FOAT has also been used to enhance wellness and optimal performance (Rappaport 2009).

FOCUSING

Focusing begins with the Focusing Attitude of bringing mindful awareness into the body with an attitude of "friendly curiosity" and listening to the body's *felt sense*.

Accessing a felt sense can begin with an open-ended invitation in the moment: "Take a few deep breaths into your body…just noticing how you are on the inside right now. See if you can be 'friendly' toward whatever you find." Or a felt sense can be experienced in relation to a specific guided imagery experience, such as a peaceful place. After guiding a client to a peaceful place, Focusing can be used to access the felt sense of the peaceful place: "As you feel yourself in this peaceful place, take a moment to notice how it feels inside your body…see if you can be friendly toward that. Just notice and receive what comes."

Focusing includes finding a symbol for a felt sense. The therapist asks the client to check within the body: "Is there a word, phrase, image, gesture, or sound that matches the felt sense?" There is a pause, allowing time for the felt sense of the body to offer the answer.

In the application of FOAT with guided imagery, I typically ask, "Is there a color, shape, or image that matches the felt sense? The symbol may also come as a word, phrase, image, gesture, or sound. Receive whatever comes." It is important to trust the authentic language of the symbol that arises from the felt sense. Although Davenport (2009) does not use the language of the "felt sense," she describes a similar occurrence: "Through guided imagery we encounter shapes, colors, textures, movements, and sounds in liminal space, arising out of our own heart" (p.20). In FOAT, the symbol is then expressed using the arts.

EXPRESSIVE ARTS

The expressive arts therapies include art therapy, dance-movement therapy, drama therapy, psychodrama, poetry therapy, writing, and integrated expressive arts (Knill, Barba, and Fuch 2004; Levine and Levine 1999; Malchiodi 2005; McNiff 2009; Rogers 1993, 2011). This chapter highlights the application of FOAT using visual art and writing, as they most easily combine with imagery.

FOAT Guided Imagery Methods

FOAT includes three main imagery methods:

- Theme-Directed FOAT

- Clearing a Space with Art

- Nondirective FOAT.

A Theme-Directed FOAT approach is similar to a scripted approach to guided imagery in that a theme is chosen, such as an inner advisor. Clearing a Space with Art is useful as a wellness practice for stress reduction and accessing an intrinsic place of well-being. A Nondirective FOAT method is useful in psychotherapy, where imagery arises out of a moment-to-moment unfolding of the client's experiential process. Each of the three FOAT guided imagery methods incorporate the following: attending to how the image feels in the body (felt sense); symbolizing the felt sense as an image (or word, phrase, gesture, or sound); and expressing the symbol through the arts.

Clinical Application

FOAT is comprised of foundational principles that are important to attend to prior to facilitating the imagery experience:

- the client's safety

- the therapeutic relationship

- the client's ability to ground themselves and access their inner resources

- empathic listening.

I always give clients a choice about whether they would like to close their eyes or to keep them open during the guided Focusing and imagery exercises. These considerations are especially significant when working with people with trauma and severe mental illness (Rappaport 2009, 2010, 2014a, 2015).

THEME-DIRECTED FOAT

A Theme-Directed FOAT approach is used primarily to get in touch with a desired experience or goal.

Theme-directed FOAT imagery steps

1. Mindful awareness and grounding

2. Choose a theme

3. Felt sense

4. Symbol: image (word, phrase, gesture or sound)

5. Receive what comes with friendly curiosity

6. Expressive arts.

Additional expressive arts processes can be integrated into the experience to further the process, derive healing benefits, and gain insight. (See Inner Advisor example.)

THEME: PEACEFUL PLACE

Katelyn, 43, was in the midst of chemotherapy treatment for cancer. She wanted to feel less anxious and more relaxed. I guided her to find a peaceful place that would arise from within herself (rather than providing a script directing her how and what to visualize).

PEACEFUL PLACE

Take a few breaths into your body…breathing in…breathing out. Feel free to keep your eyes open or allow them to close, whichever is more comfortable to you. Become aware of your body where it meets the chair…the support of the floor and earth.

I'd like to invite you to become aware of a peaceful place. It may be a place that you already know or a place you make up in your imagination…(pause). Take some time to notice the details...the colors, sights, smells...the temperature of the air as you sense it on your body.

Turn your attention to inside your body and notice how it feels inside as you focus on this peaceful place (felt sense). See if there is an image, colors, or shapes (symbol) that match the inner felt sense. Check it against your body for a sense of rightness. If it's not right, let it go and invite a new image. If a word, phrase, gesture, or sound comes, welcome that...(pause). Receive what comes.

When you're ready, bring your attention to being in this room and stretch. Using the art materials, create the felt-sense image from your peaceful place.

After the guided Focusing, Katelyn chose to use crayons and glitter pens. Katelyn first began with an outline of a heart in pink and then began coloring it in yellow. She then drew water, symbolizing the ocean. She returned to the heart and added radiant petals, followed by expanding rays depicted with gold and red glitter (Figure 19.1).

Figure 19.1: Peaceful Place Felt Sense: Katelyn

After creating the art Katelyn shared, "I imagined myself at a favorite beach spot. I was lying down at the beach, with the gentle sounds of the waves and warm sun soothing me. It felt very peaceful. When you asked me to notice how it felt in the body to be in this place, I noticed warmth in my heart and chest. I noticed my breathing slow. The image that came to me was of my heart, radiating and being supported by the water. I felt so light."

I invited Katelyn to take a moment to reflect on the art and the experience. I guided her through Focusing to go back inside her body and ask, "Do you have a message for me?" She waited, and after a moment she told me, "It said, 'You have a strong, radiant heart...and support to rest in. I am here. Just take the time to listen within.'" She then added words to the art: "resting, vibrant heart radiating all healed."

As we've seen, the guided Focusing began with helping Katelyn access a peaceful place. Instead of drawing the scene of her peaceful place, FOAT emphasizes how the body is carrying it. Focusing helped Katelyn access the body's wisdom and the art helped the inner experience of the image become tangible. I often suggest to clients that they hang their drawing in a place where they'll see it often, or take a picture of it and use it as a screen saver. Looking at the image helps bring back the healing benefits from the experience.

Clearing a Space with Art

Clearing a Space with Art is based on the first step of Gendlin's original Focusing method. In Clearing a Space the client identifies issues that are in the way of feeling "All Fine" and imagines placing them at a distance outside the body (Gendlin 1981, 1996). Imagery is incorporated to help clear the space. For example, the client might imagine wrapping each issue up in a package and placing it at a comfortable distance, or putting their concerns on a boat and letting it float out onto a lake. After setting the issues aside, the client gets a felt sense of the "All Fine Place"—an inherent sense of well-being. In Clearing a Space with Art, instead of just imagining setting issues aside and getting a felt sense of the "All Fine Place," art is incorporated in order to concretize and symbolize the experience (Rappaport 2009).

Clearing a Space and Clearing a Space with Art have been found to be complete processes unto themselves and effective for stress reduction. Research on both approaches has shown benefits for people with cancer (Grindler Katonah 1999; Grindler Katonah and Flaxman 1999; Klagsbrun, Lennox, and Summers 2010; Klagsbrun et al. 2005), chronic pain (Ferraro 2008; Freeza 2008; McGrath 2013), weight issues (Antrobos 2008), stress (Castalia 2010; Weiland 2012), and for enhancing resiliency (Lee 2011).

Example: Clearing a Space with Art[1]

Mary, a 41-year-old woman, was feeling overwhelmed and stressed about her marriage and her career. I guided her through the following exercise.

CLEARING A SPACE WITH ART

Take a few deep breaths, inviting your body to relax... Feel free to close your eyes or keep them open, whichever is more comfortable for you. When you're ready, ask, "How am I on the inside right now?" Turn your attention like a searchlight inside your body, just noticing whatever you find... See if you can be accepting of whatever you find there, without judgment.

Now imagine yourself in some peaceful place... It may be a place you know already, or it may be one you create in your imagination... When you're ready, ask, "What's between me and feeling 'All Fine' right now?" Let whatever comes up, come up... Don't go inside any particular thing right now... As each issue comes up, imagine placing it at some distance from you... perhaps out on a park bench...or in a box...or use imagery like relaxing on the beach and putting all of the things between you and feeling "All Fine" on a boat...or wrap each issue or concern up in a package.

As each issue arises, place it at a comfortable distance from you while you stay in your peaceful place (pause). When the list stops, gently ask inside, "Except for all that, I'm 'All Fine,' right?" ... If more comes up, imagine placing it at a comfortable distance.

All Fine Place: Keeping everything at a distance, now I'd like to invite you to bring your attention to the "All Fine Place." See if there is an image that matches the "All Fine Place." Check it against your body for a sense of rightness.

Artistic Expression: When you're ready, use the art materials to create something that expresses your felt sense of the "All Fine Place."

After Focusing, Mary began to express her experience through art. She chose different pieces of colored construction paper to represent the different issues she was carrying: blue for sadness about her relationship, orange for confusion about her work situation, green for money issues, and brown for depression. Mary wrapped the papers up in a package of tissue paper tied with a bow. Next to the package, Mary created a circular shape with pink, yellow, and purple feathers and a golden center of glitter (Figure 19.2).

Figure 19.2: Clearing a Space with Art: Mary

Package of Mary's issues: (right)/"All Fine Place" with feathers and glitter (left).

Mary shared, "I took my sadness about my relationship, the confusion about my work, my issues with money, and my depression and put them in this package. It felt so good to imagine taking them outside of me and placing them in a package. What really amazed me was that as I wrote each issue on the construction paper, I felt my body let go of so much tension—like it just moved on out. I felt myself getting quieter and more peaceful. It was incredible to find this gold center inside this lighter place inside of me. I realized that I have this inner gold center that exists separate from what is happening in my relationship or career" (p.113). In Clearing a Space with Art, Mary was able to use her imagination and somatically feel the relief of moving the stressors outside of her body, followed by accessing an inner sense of well-being and radiance. She also saw the challenges as a gift.

Nondirective FOAT Imagery

Nondirective FOAT Imagery is most often applied to psychotherapy where there is a moment-to-moment unfolding of an issue being explored rather than a directed theme. A FOAT check-in can be interspersed throughout the therapeutic process (see FOAT Check-in Box below). Additional questions can be integrated into the FOAT process such as:

- "Imagine what it would look and feel like all healed."

- "What's needed?"

- "What's a good step in the right direction?"

After Focusing, clients are invited to express their felt sense imagery through an art form.

EXAMPLE: NONDIRECTIVE FOAT IMAGERY

Heather was in her late 20s when was diagnosed with a rare illness that caused chronic pain, weakness, and a myriad of other symptoms. Her treatments included various medications and chemotherapy infusions, which both helped and also caused unpleasant side effects.

Our work began with a FOAT Check-in.

FOAT CHECK-IN

Take a few deep breaths down inside your body. Notice the breath as it comes into your body and moves out of your body, feeling the support of whatever you're sitting on. When you're ready, gently bring your awareness to the inside of your body, just noticing how you are right now: sensations, energies, or feeling…being friendly toward whatever you find… See if there's an image that matches the inner felt sense. Check it for a sense of rightness. When you have it, express the felt sense using art materials.

Heather drew a red outline of a body with a smaller black figure clawing it (Figure 19.3).

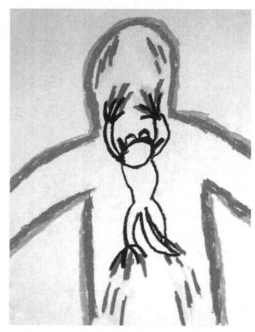

Figure 19.3: FOAT Check-in: Heather

She shared: "The illness is symbolized as a creature with black claws inside of the human figure in red. The creature was clawing and scratching inside the body, leaving bloody, red scratch marks" (Rappaport 2013, p.229).

A core aspect of Focusing is bringing a "friendly attitude" to what is there, even painful or scary feelings. I asked Heather if she could be friendly toward the creature. She said that she could sometimes, but usually she feels anger and hatred toward it. We discussed trying to bring greater friendliness toward it. Oftentimes *imagining* how something could be helps the client gain the experience of it. I guided Heather in another Focusing experience:

> Take a moment to go back inside...noticing your breath as it comes in your body and moves out of your body... Imagine what it would look like and feel like to bring more acceptance to the illness. What would it be like and feel like to be more accepting of the illness? Sense it in your body...and see if there's an image that matches the felt sense.

Heather drew a blue figure surrounded by yellow light (Figure 19.4):

Figure 19.4: Imagining Greater Acceptance Toward Illness

Heather shared, "When I brought the attitude of being friendly to the illness, I began to see the creature as trapped inside my body, and that it was scared and confused. It wasn't evil and it meant no harm. It was innocent and was trying to get free. The image that came was of a blue human figure surrounded by yellow light. Now it was cradling the same creature, now buried and sleeping softly in its arms... In cradling the creature, I was actually cradling the vulnerable part of me that was frightened and hurting. Seeing my pain as innocent and frightened led me to feel more compassion for myself. The claw marks are still visible inside the figure...but now they are black rather than red...symbolizing healing scars rather than fresh wounds" (Excerpt from Rappaport 2013, p.230).

After Heather shared her art and Focusing, I reflected her experience. I then invited Heather to Focus again, and inwardly ask, "*How can I carry this experience forward. What's needed?*" After a few moments Heather opened her eyes and drew an image of a figure with angel wings receiving a chemotherapy infusion (Figure 19.5).

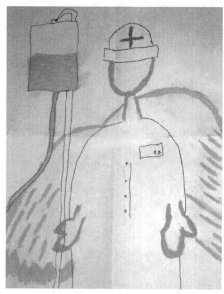

Figure 19.5: Asking What's Needed?

She shared, "Even though the more aggressive treatments cause more severe side effects, I know it will heal the hurting creature inside of me. My felt sense led me to this decision. I feel empowered."

FOAT enabled Heather to become more self-compassionate, access her inner knowing and to trust her body's wisdom. The changes reflected in the imagery (Figures 19.3–5) and the felt experience described by Heather is referred to as a "felt shift"—which is an actual change in the body-mind (Gendlin 1981, 1996). In FOAT, the felt shift is experienced in the body and reflected in the art.

Integrating Dialogue and Writing with FOAT

Combining more than one artistic modality is known as intermodal expressive arts (Knill, Barba, and Fuch 2004) or the "creative connection®" (Rogers 1993, 2011). Integrating other expressive arts modalities can serve to deepen the imagery experience and lead to a greater embodied knowing. The two most common methods I use with FOAT Imagery are "Gestalt the Art" and Dialogue (Rappaport 2009).

GESTALT THE ART

In Gestalt Art Therapy (Rhyne 1973), the client looks at specific images within the art, or the art as a whole and gives it a voice by saying, "I am _____." For example, in the Theme-Directed Peaceful Place (Figure 19.1), Katelyn can speak as the voice of the heart, "I am a luminous radiant heart spreading light and healing." Or she can become the voice of the water, "I am the blue water and I am gentle and calm; I can hold you." Katelyn can dance the movement of the water or play the strings on a harp to express the peacefulness of the heart.

DIALOGUE WITH ART

Dialogue can also be used with FOAT to deepen the imagery experience and harness our implicit knowing. Clients look at the art and ask a question to an image that they feel drawn to. They listen and receive the answer through their felt sense. The dialogue can be verbally expressed or written.

Example: Inner Advisor with dialogue
Nancy, 61 years old, came to see me for psychotherapy after her husband suffered a stroke. Two months prior to the stroke, Nancy had made the decision to quit her job and start her own business focused on women and creativity. As the eldest of eight children, Nancy had always taken care of others and put her own needs on the back burner. Just as she gave herself permission to follow her own heart and prioritize her own needs, Nancy's husband's illness triggered symptoms of anxiety, grief, and depression.

I led Nancy in a Focusing exercise to access her Inner Advisor.

INNER ADVISOR

Take a few deep breaths down into your body...breathing in... breathing out. Feel free to keep your eyes open or allow them to close, whichever is more comfortable to you.

Imagine you are taking a beautiful walk on an easy path up a mountain. As you walk, you can feel the soft earth beneath your feet...the quiet sounds with each step. You notice the clear, blue sky, warm sun with a soothing breeze. With each step, you feel yourself feeling more and more relaxed and peaceful.

As you climb toward the top of the mountain, you notice a spot that looks like it has been carved out just for you to sit and take in the beauty. You sense yourself sitting comfortably on a big flat stone, as you take in the vastness of sky and the stillness of the earth. As you look into the sky, you begin to sense the presence of a wise being—it may be in the form of a person, animal, nature element or spirit. It may be someone or something you know…or it may be new. You sense the safety, comfort and wisdom of this being or energy.

As you continue sitting, you sense this wise being or energy sitting with you. This wise being lets you know that it has a gift for you. You sense yourself opening your hands in a gesture of receiving. The wise being places the gift in your hands. Your heart feels soft and open as you receive this gift. The wise being lets you know that it is for you to take back on your journey back down the mountain. The wise being also lets you know that you can revisit each other at any moment. All you need to do is to bring your awareness back to it.

You take the gift with you and begin to descend the mountain. It is an easy and safe walk. As you reach the bottom of the mountain where you began, you take a few moments to take in the whole of the experience.

As you breathe, follow your breath into your body. Notice how it feels inside after taking this walk up the mountain, meeting your inner advisor, and receiving the gift. See if you can be friendly to whatever is there…(pause). See if there are colors, shapes, or images that match the inner felt sense. Check it against your body for a sense of rightness. When you're ready, be aware of sitting here, in the room, and stretch if you'd like to. Express your felt sense image from the experience through art.

Afterwards, Nancy created a line drawing of a small figure meditating on a mat, a sunflower in the distance, mountains, a tree, and pond with five fish (Figure 19.6).

Figure 19.6: Nancy's Inner Advisor

Nancy dialogues with the meditation figure:

Nancy: How can I bring more balance into my life?

Meditation figure: You need to sit still, like me. You need more stillness.

Nancy: I don't really know how to sit so still. What will help me stay focused?

Meditation figure: Just take a moment and look inside. You'll find me… and I am already still and calm. You will then get the energy and it will help you.

Nancy dialogues with the fish in the pond:

Nancy: What do you want to tell me?

Fish: We flow with the current. You need to move with it more. We feel a little stuck here, too. It's cramped.

Nancy: What do you need?

Fish: We'll feel better when you color us in.

Nancy: Okay… I get it. I need to do more art, and you're helping me see how much more vitality is evoked when I'm living with my creativity.

Fish: Yeah...when you feel stuck, create. You can't always change the situation, like your husband's stroke, but you can bring your creativity to it.

Nancy: Yes, creativity is one of my keys to balance. Through it I touch my deep knowing and calm. Through it I feel in balance and sense that stillness you talk about. Through it I am one with you, inner Buddha. Thank you!

Nancy shared that she was surprised that a meditation figure came to her, as she was not a regular meditator. Through the image and writing, Nancy was guided to a place of stillness inside. The dialogue helped her become more aware of her own need for creative practice as a resource for finding balance and a more peaceful center.

FOAT Guided Imagery Benefits

As can be seen throughout this chapter, there are numerous benefits to using FOAT as a guided imagery method. Focusing provides a method for calming the body and mind and accessing one's felt sense and embodied imagery. The expressive arts serve to externalize and concretize the internal imagery process. The expressive arts also help the therapist and client to see the same imagery, which deepens empathy and attunement. In addition, visual art and writing provide a tangible reference that can remind the client of the healing qualities they've discovered. As a guided imagery method, FOAT offers a multisensory approach to imagery, a wide variety of tools for processing it, and a method for carrying forward healing energies, insight, and wisdom.

ENDNOTES

1.   Excerpt from Rappaport 2009, pp.112–113.

References

Antrobos, J. (2008) *Focusing and you: Effects on body weight*. Unpublished dissertation. The American School of Professional Psychology, Chicago, IL.

Castalia, A. (2010) *The effects of clearing a space with art on stress reduction in sign language interpreters*. Unpublished Master's thesis, Notre Dame de Namur University, Belmont, CA.

Davenport, L. (2009) *Healing and Transformation through Self Guided Imagery*. Berkeley, CA: Celestial Arts.

Ferraro, E. (2008) "Focusing and chronic pain." *The Folio: A Journal for Focusing and the Experiential Therapy 21*, 1, 328–337.

Freeza, E. (2008) "Focusing and chronic pain." *The Folio: A Journal for Focusing and Experiential Therapy 21*, 1, 328-337.

Gendlin, E.T. (1980) "Imagery is More Powerful with Focusing: Theory and Practice." In J.T. Hart and T.M. Tomlinson (eds) *New Directions in Client-Centered Therapy*. Boston, MA: Houghton Mifflin, 544–562.

Gendlin, E.T. (1981) *Focusing,* 2nd edition New York, NY: Bantam Books.

Gendlin, E.T. (1996) *Focusing-Oriented Psychotherapy: A Manual of the Experiential Method*. New York, NY: Guilford Press.

Grindler Katonah, D. (1999) "Clearing a space with someone who has cancer." *The Folio: A Journal for Focusing and the Experiential Therapy 18*, 1, 19–26.

Grindler Katonah, D. and Flaxman, J. (1999) "Focusing: An adjunct treatment for adaptive recovery from cancer." *The Folio: A Journal for Focusing and the Experiential Therapy 18*, 1, 19.

Klagsbrun, J., Lennox, and Summers, L. (2010) "Effects of 'clearing a space' on quality of life in women with breast cancer." *United States Association for Body Oriented Psychotherapy Journal 9*, 10, 48–53.

Klagsbrun, J., Rappaport, L., Marcow-Speiser, V., Post, P., Stepakoff, S., and Byers, J. (2005) "Focusing and expressive arts therapy as a complementary treatment for women with breast cancer." *Journal of Creativity and Mental Health 1*, 1, 101–137.

Knill, P., Barba, H., and Fuch, F. (2004) *Minstrels of Soul: Intermodal Expressive Therapy*. Toronto: EGS Press.

Lee, H. (2011) *Focusing-oriented art therapy and bookmaking to promote protective resiliency of children living in a homeless shelter*. Unpublished Master's thesis, Notre Dame de Namur University, Belmont, CA.

Levine, S. and Levine, E. (eds) (1999) *Foundations of Expressive Arts Therapy: Theoretical and Clinical Foundations*. London: Jessica Kingsley Publishers.

Malchiodi, C. (ed.) (2005) *Expressive Therapies*. New York, NY: Guilford Press.

McGrath, J. (2013) *The effects of Clearing a Space with Art on women with chronic pain*. Unpublished Master's thesis, Notre Dame de Namur University, Belmont, CA.

McNiff, S. (2009) *Integrating the Arts in Therapy: History, Theory and Practice*. Springfield, IL: Charles C. Thomas.

Naperstek, B. (1994) *Staying Well with Guided Imagery*. New York, NY: Warner Books.

Rappaport, L. (2009) *Focusing-Oriented Art Therapy: Accessing the Body's Wisdom and Creative Intelligence*. London: Jessica Kingsley Publishers.

Rappaport, L. (2010) "Focusing-oriented art therapy and trauma." *Journal of Person-Centered and Experiential Psychotherapy 9*, 2, 128–142.

Rappaport, L. (2013) "Focusing-Oriented Art Therapy and Chronic Illnesses." In C. Malchiodi (ed.) *Art Therapy and Healthcare*. New York, NY: Guilford Press.

Rappaport, L. (2014a) "Focusing-Oriented Expressive Arts Therapy: Working on the Avenues." In G. Madison (ed.) *Theory and Practice of Focusing-Oriented Psychotherapy*. London: Jessica Kingsley Publishers.

Rappaport, L. (ed.) (2014b) *Mindfulness and the Art Therapies: Theory and Practice*. London: Jessica Kingsley Publishers.

Rappaport, L. (2015) "Focusing-Oriented Expressive Arts Therapy and Mindfulness with Children and Adolescents with Experiencing Trauma." In C. Malchiodi (ed.) *Creative Interventions with Traumatized Children,* 2nd edition. New York, NY: Guilford Press.

Rhyne, J. (1973) *The Gestalt Art Experience.* Florence, KY: Wordsworth.

Rogers, N. (1993) *The Creative Connection: Expressive Arts as Healing.* Palo Alto, CA: Science and Behavior Books.

Rogers, N. (2011) *The Creative Connection for Groups: Person-Centered Expressive Arts for Healing and Social Change.* Palo Alto, CA: Science and Behavior Books.

Weiland, L. (2012) *Focusing-oriented art therapy as a means of stress reduction with graduate students.* Unpublished Master's thesis, Notre Dame de Namur University, Belmont, CA.

Chapter 20

Music as a Catalyst for Enhancing and Transforming Imagery Experiences

Denise Grocke

From the time of the great Greek philosophers, music has been recognized for its therapeutic properties. Plato wrote that, "rhythm and harmony find their way to the inmost soul and take strongest hold upon it…imparting grace…to foster its growth" (*The Republic*, III, 399e; 402, in Hamilton and Cairns 1961), and that music "gives a soul to the universe, wings to the mind, flight to the imagination, a charm to sadness, and life to everything" (Watson 1991, p.45).

Music itself is transformative. In music of the classical genre, a melody transforms over time as it is passed from one instrument to another and is heard in a different tone. The harmonic sequence within a classical piece may change from major to minor, for example, and with the change comes emotion. In instrumental concertos, the solo instrument (oboe, violin, harp, classical guitar) can be heard unfolding a musical narrative in the form of the melody supported by the orchestra—which depicts life's solo journey supported by faithful friends and allies. Music therapy has been practiced internationally since the 1970s, and largely involves active participation in creating music through singing songs, creating songs, and various models of improvisation (Wheeler 2015). One of the receptive forms of music therapy is the Bonny Method of Guided Imagery and Music described in this chapter.

Imagery and the imagination also have a rich history, particularly in psychotherapeutic treatment. Jung's technique of active imagination is seminal to the enhanced meaning and interpretation of dreams, and imagery has played a significant role in the management of pain and living with cancer (Achterberg 1985; Simonton, Matthews-Simonton, and Creighton 1980).

The combination of music and imagery therefore provides a creative multi-modal therapeutic method with the potential to access the unconscious mind and encourage creativity in problem-solving strategies.

The Development of the Bonny Method of Guided Imagery and Music

The Bonny Method of Guided Imagery and Music (GIM) was developed during the 1970s when Dr. Helen Bonny served as a music therapist at the Maryland Psychiatric Research Center. The Center investigated the use of medically sanctioned lysergic acid diethylamide (LSD) to activate the unconscious mind and provide a transformative experience of a peak or spiritual nature that would ideally enable patients to see beyond themselves and their symptoms. Bonny's role was to select music to support the patients during the LSD sessions (Bonny 1978; 2002).

The LSD sessions lasted 12–16 hours, and Bonny began to study the most appropriate music chosen for each stage of the session. She identified characteristics of music that supported patients in the initial stages, matched the unfolding of the experience, and provided a safe, final grounding at the end of the session.

Phase 1 *Pre-onset* (of the effect of the drug): 0–1.5 hours
Music: Light-popular or patient's preferred music

Phase 2 *Onset*: 0.5–1.5 hours
Music: Quiet and positive in mood (e.g. slow movement of concerti)

Phase 3 *Building toward peak intensity*: 1.5–3.5 hours
Music: Instrumental and vocal music used alternatively (e.g. Beethoven: *Symphony no 5*; Brahms: *German Requiem*; Schubert: *Ave Maria*)

Phase 4 *Peak intensity*: 3–4.5 hours

Music that evoked powerful emotions to aid in facilitating peak experiences (e.g. Gounod: *St. Cecilia Mass;* Richard Strauss: *Transfiguration* from Death and Transfiguration; Fauré: *Requiem* (parts III and VII); Barber: *Adagio for Strings*)

Phase 5 *Re-entry*: 4.5–7 hours
Music: Depended on the emotional tone of the patient's peak experience (e.g. Wagner: *Lohengrin*, Prelude to Act 1, "Liebstod" from Tristan and Isolde)

Phase 6 *Return to normal consciousness*: 7–12 hours. The effect of the drug wanes and normal consciousness returns.
Music of the patient's choice is played (Bonny and Pahnke 1972, pp.82–83).

Over a period of 16 years (1973–1989) Helen Bonny developed 18 music programs to be used in GIM (Grocke 2002). The music in Bonny's GIM programs is drawn from the Western classical tradition, although contemporary programs are being developed by GIM practitioners that use other genres (jazz, world music), and culturally-sensitive programs (music in the Chinese tradition, Estonian composers, and music based on Norwegian folk tunes).

Bonny developed her first music program in 1973 to match the six phases of the LSD session. The program was titled "Positive Affect," reflecting her intention to evoke a spiritually uplifting experience for the patients. The program comprises six music selections:

1. Pre-onset: Elgar, *Enigma variations* #8 and #9

2. Onset: Mozart, *Vesperae Solemnes* (Laudate Dominum)

3. Plateau: Barber, *Adagio for Strings*

4. Build to peak: Gounod, *St. Cecilia Mass*, Offertoire

5. Plateau: Gounod, *St. Cecilia Mass*, Sanctus

6. Return: R. Strauss, *Death and Transfiguration*, Part 6 (excerpt).

Eventually the LSD research was no longer supported, but Bonny believed that music alone could evoke experiences of higher consciousness, and she evolved the method known today as the Bonny Method of Guided Imagery and Music (GIM). The Bonny Method of GIM "is a music-assisted transformational therapy that offers persons the opportunity to integrate mental, emotional, physical, and spiritual aspects of themselves" (Association for Music and Imagery 2008).

The practice of the Bonny Method today is based on the original principles and music programs developed by Helen Bonny. GIM is practiced over a series of sessions: a minimum of six sessions is required for the client to develop trust in the therapist, in the music, and the altered state of consciousness. However, longer series enable deep transformations to occur, and clients often extend their therapy series to 30+ sessions.

The Bonny Method GIM Session Outline

At the initial session, the therapist gathers a history of the client's physical, emotional, and spiritual health and their needs in these areas. Loosely defined goals or aims are set for the therapy series. The Bonny Method GIM session involves four components:

1. A pre-music discussion in which the client discusses the issues of the moment, and together with the therapist formulates a focus image for the music and imagery component.

2. A relaxation induction of some ten minutes is provided for the client, and is individually tailored to the person's preferred modality (for example, autogenic, Progressive Muscle Relaxation, breath, or mindfulness), and the client enters an altered state of consciousness (ASC) with eyes closed.

3. The music program of 35–45 minutes is chosen by the therapist to match the client's issue, energy level, and affect. As the music begins, the client is encouraged to recount any imagery, feelings, emotions, and memories that are stimulated by the music. The therapist makes occasional verbal interventions to encourage the client to stay close to the experience ("What is happening for you?" "Can you describe it?" "How does that feel for you?"). The therapist does not direct the imagery nor introduce any new images, but rather remains attentive as a witness to the client's experience.

4. At the end of the music program, the client is returned to a more normal level of consciousness (although still altered by the music program to some degree), and there is a phase of integrating the experience. This is usually facilitated by drawing a mandala (Kellogg 1984) where the client's inner experience is captured in shape, form, and color. The therapist observes the drawing of the mandala and notes the energy and emotion expressed by

the client. Finally there is a verbal processing of the mandala drawing that encapsulates the imagery experience of the session (Grocke 2005).

Multi-modal Imagery

The imagery in the Bonny Method is not only visual; all sensory modalities are utilized, as can be seen in the following table.

Table 20.1: Multi-modal Experiences in
Bonny Method of GIM (Grocke 1999)

Visual experiences	For example: colors, shapes, fragments of scenes, complete scenes, figures, people, animals, birds, and water (lakes, streams, oceans, pools).
Memories	Memories of childhood and significant events, people, and feelings in the client's life may be explored through reminiscences.
Emotions and feelings	From sadness, happiness, joy, sorrow, fear, anger, and surprise to the ineffable.
Body sensations	Parts of the body may feel lighter or heavier, become numb or feel split off from the body; there may be feelings of floating or falling, sensations of spinning, or a feeling that the body is changing in some way.
Body movements	The client may make expressive movements of the body in relation to the imagery being experienced (e.g. hands may create a shape, arms may reach up in response to an image, and fists or legs may pound on the chair/mat in expression of anger or frustration).
Somatic imagery	Changes within the internal organs of the body may be experienced, such as pain felt in the chest or heart, or an internal organ may be felt to change its shape or color, or a surge of energy may be felt through the entire body.
Altered auditory experiences	There may be an altered auditory perception of the music, including the music seeming to come from far away, the music seeming very close, or one particular instrument standing out (which can also be a transference to the music).

Associations with and transference to the music	The music may be associated with a person, place, or event; there may be memories of when the music was heard last, memories of playing the music, a sense that the music is being played especially for the person, or that the person is imagining playing the music being heard.
Abstract imagery	For example: mists, fog, geometrical shapes, and clouds that may signal a shift in consciousness or a moment of resistance before re-engaging.
Spiritual experiences	For example: being drawn toward a light; a sense of oneness with the world; a spiritual person appearing in the form of a monk, priest, or woman in flowing robes; being in a cathedral; feeling a presence very close.
Transpersonal/ transformative experiences	The body may become smaller or larger, or a change felt deep in the body (cells changing, or parts of body changing shape). The client may imagine flying on the back of an albatross and then become the bird in flight.
Archetypal figures	Figures from legendary stories may appear, such as King Arthur, Robin Hood, the Vikings, Aboriginal man/woman, the witch, Merlin, and more recently Harry Potter (and his Invisibility Cloak) and Dumbledore.
Dialogue with significant others	Significant figures from the client's life may appear in the imagery and often have a message, so that dialogue may occur (e.g. with parental or spiritual figures). Aspects of self may be symbolized in human form (a baby or small child) or significant companions (e.g. an albatross bird or an eagle), and dialogue may occur.
Aspects of the shadow or anima/animus	Aspects of the shadow frequently appear in the image of a person of the same gender, or aspects of the anima/animus in images of a person of the opposite gender.
Symbolic shapes and images that hold significant meaning	For example, a long tunnel or seeds opening can be symbolic of moments of change or transition. Symbolic images like an ancient book or writings often have specific meaning to the client and invite exploration by the therapist, as in "What do you think the writings say?"

Session Transcripts

During the music and imagery segment of the session, the therapist writes a transcript of the imagery as described by the client. At the end of the session the client is given a copy of the transcript as a permanent reminder of the imagery they experienced. The transcript also serves an important function for the therapist, who reviews it prior to the client's next session. In addition, the transcripts become valuable research tools, allowing changes in imagery to be tracked across a series of sessions.

Dynamics of Change over a Series of Sessions

As with all therapies, the Bonny Method of GIM is best practiced in a series of sessions. In the early sessions (1–3) the client becomes accustomed to what GIM therapy can offer, and learns to use the imagery and the music in service of his or her own needs. Trust needs to be established in three aspects: 1) the therapist (as with any therapy); 2) the music (in the Bonny Method of GIM, classical music of the Western tradition is used predominantly); and 3) the altered state of consciousness, through which the client may access memories and emotions locked in long-term memory, particularly those from childhood.

When clients enter long-term therapy, they implicitly make a commitment to uncover the underlying causes of whatever ails them, and the choice of music is critical in supporting them where they need to go. Bonny categorized her 18 music programs accordingly; impressionistic music of Debussy and Ravel is used in the early stages, as this music is evocative of visual imagery, the most easily accessed form of imagery for most people. In the working stage of the therapy series, there are stronger music programs that include well-structured music forms to support the client as he or she confronts the underlying issue. Music of the Germanic masters is best suited for this deep work (Grocke 1999), including the symphonic and choral music of Bach, Brahms, Richard Strauss, Mahler, and Wagner.

In the Bonny Method of GIM therapists typically track images and their transformations over a series of sessions, watching for changes that may indicate deep healing (Carlyle and Saunders 1981). In addition, the image may be represented in visual form in the mandala. As the underlying memory or feeling is worked through, the same image can take on different elements, and these too are reflected in the mandala.

Case Study: Peter

Peter was a participant in a research study that explored pivotal moments in Guided Imagery and Music (Grocke 1999). Interviewees were asked to reflect on a GIM session that stood out as distinctive and unique, in which there was a change in perspective that impacted their life in some way. They were asked to describe the imagery, and to expand on the experience by identifying any emotion attached to the imagery.

At the time of the interview, Peter had received 38 GIM sessions, and he described a set of images in which there was a dead baby being carried on a barge in the underworld. In the imagery Peter was pushing the boat with a long pole. He disclosed that the dead baby in the barge related to a foetus that had been aborted, prior to his marriage with his wife. Peter felt the image was connected to resolving the baby's death.

When asked about the session that was pivotal in his therapy, Peter identified two sessions: session 21 and session 32 that impacted his life. The written transcripts of those sessions indicate the transformation of the image of the dead baby and the change in Peter's emotional experience.

Session 21

At this point in his therapy, Peter and his wife were expecting their first child, who was due in a few weeks. It was a pivotal session in which Peter confronted challenging emotions. The music for this session was drawn from several GIM programs: 1) Siegfried's funeral march from Wagner's *Götterdämmerung*, and 2) Rachmaninoff's *The Isle of the Dead* (both from Bonny's "Death-Rebirth" program), 3) Holst's *Planets Suite* (Mars) (from Bonny's "Affect Release" program), 4) Marcello's Oboe Concerto in C minor (*Adagio*), and 5) Rodrigo's *Concierto de Aranjuez* for guitar (*Adagio*) (from a program developed by Linda Keiser Mardis entitled "Grieving").

During Wagner's funeral march, Peter reported feeling black and blue (an image of bruising), as if he had been pummelled. He felt that his throat was black and his heart red and black: these two colors together may suggest heat/anger and the blackness of sadness/depression (Fincher 1991). During Rachmaninoff's *The Isle of the Dead*, Peter felt lost in a void. The therapist's intervention was, "What do you want to do?" He replied, "Scream." At this point the music was changed to Holst's "Mars," from *Planets Suite* (a loud piece in which brass instruments predominate) that enabled Peter to let out the frustration from within his body. As often happens after the release of anger, tears emerged, and Peter said he felt "lost." The music chosen next was Marcello's Oboe Concerto, the slow movement, which gave voice to his sadness. Peter had images of the aborted baby. He saw himself in a death barge with the baby in a casket covered with blue cloth. Peter pushed the barge with a long pole, reminiscent of a ferryman. The therapist encouraged dialogue with the image of the aborted baby, and Peter asked the baby if he was angry that he had been aborted. The baby said he was. Peter said that he was sorry, and later on in the session named him. This is a Gestalt technique used in the Bonny Method to internalize a significant figure.

Some weeks after this session, Peter's wife gave birth to a baby boy. Session 32 became a pivotal session in the sequence of imagery around the aborted child and the new baby.

Session 32
In this session the music program titled "Nurturing" was chosen. This program comprises seven selections of music, including pieces sung by female and male singers and a beautiful chorus, "The Shepherd's Farewell," from Berlioz's *Childhood of Christ*. During this music selection Peter had imagery of a barge that was encrusted with precious jewels "red, green, and yellow." The dead baby was in the barge, "his soul long gone." Alongside him was the newborn son with pink cheeks. After the music and imagery segment had concluded, Peter commented that the imagery was, "somehow resolving a baby's death, and bringing that baby to some place where it is free, or where it is able to rest, or where I'm able to leave it." He further remarked that, "there was a shift in emotional tone, a lighter feeling," and that the image "stands the test of time."

Discussion
During the interview Peter recalled that the image of the dead baby had first appeared early in his therapy sessions, and that it was a recurring image. He commented that, "As it comes back it reminds me that the issue is not resolved…it seems to be something deep inside." The recurring image was always accompanied by sadness, and Peter's grief was finally expressed

in session 21, where he could dialogue with the image of the dead baby (foetus) and say he was sorry for the death.

In session 21, Peter was pushing the barge with a long wooden pole through the water in a series of caves, "like a Venetian Gondola." The image is reminiscent of the myth of the ferryman Charon who transports dead souls along the river Styx (Graves 1981). In the myth story the ferryman must be paid. Peter had taken on the responsibility of the baby's death, which required him to take an active part by guiding the barge through the caves.

In session 32, the transformation took place: the baby was in the death-barge, "his soul long gone" alongside the healthy newborn baby. The barge was now encrusted with precious jewels, and Peter's "emotional tone" was lighter.

Not all clients experience transformation of imagery as dynamically as Peter; many images are symbolic in themselves and can portend meaning for clients that transform aspects of their lives. But for Peter the transformation enabled him to resolve a recurring image from the past by expressing his grief, which, and in turn lightened his emotional burden.

The Bonny Method of Guided Imagery and Music evolved from Bonny's experiences with altered states of consciousness, where clients could experience spiritual or peak experiences. In the process of working through challenging imagery to reach peak experience, clients' imagery transforms in a multitude of ways—through the changing shape and form of the imagery, through emotion activated by the imagery, and most importantly, the impact of the music on the imagery.

References

Achterberg, J. (1985) *Imagery in Healing*. Boston, MA: New Science Library.

Association for Music and Imagery (2008) *The Bonny Method*. Available at www.ami-bonnymethod.org/the-bonny-method-2, accessed on March 26 2015.

Bonny, H. (1978) *The Role of Taped Music Programs in the GIM Process*. GIM Monograph #2. Baltimore, MD: ICM Books.

Bonny, H. (2002) *Music and Consciousness*. Gilsum, NH: Barcelona Publishers.

Bonny, H. and Pahnke, W. (1972) "The use of music in psychedelic (LSD) psychotherapy." *Journal of Music Therapy 9*, 2, 64–87.

Carlyle, C. and Saunders, M. (1981) "The Transformation of Key Images as Indicators of Change." In J.E. Shorr, G. Sobel-Whittington, P. Robin, and J.A. Connella (eds) *Imagery: Theoretical and Clinical Applications*, vol. 3. New York, NY: Plenum Press.

Fincher, S. (1991) *Creating Mandalas*. Boston, MA: Shambala.

Graves, R. (1981) *Greek Myths*. London: Penguin.

Grocke, D. (1999) *A phenomenological study of pivotal moments in guided imagery and music (GIM) therapy*. Unpublished PhD dissertation, The University of Melbourne. Available at www.repository.unimelb.edu.au/10187/461, accessed on October 7 2015.

Grocke, D. (2002) "The Bonny Music Programs." In K. Bruscia and D. Grocke (eds) *Guided Imagery and Music: The Bonny Method and Beyond*. Gilsum, NH: Barcelona Publishers.

Grocke, D. (2005) "The role of the therapist in the Bonny Method of Guided Imagery and Music." *Music Therapy Perspectives 23*, 1, 45–52.

Hamilton, E. and Cairns, H. (eds) (1961) *The Collected Dialogues of Plato Including Letters*. Bollingen Series LXXI. New York, NY: Pantheon Books.

Kellogg, J. (1984) *Mandala: Path of Beauty*. Clearwater, FL: MARI.

Simonton, O., Matthews-Simonton, S., and Creighton, J. (1980) *Getting Well Again*. New York, NY: Bantam.

Watson, D. (1991) *Wordsworth Dictionary of Musical Quotations*. Ware, Hertsfordshire: Wordsworth Editions Ltd.

Wheeler, B. (ed.) (2015) *Music Therapy Handbook*. New York, NY: Guilford Press.

Chapter 21

The Writer as Shaman

How Imagery Creates Worlds

Ruth L. Schwartz

Creating Worlds with Words

Writers use words to pay homage to worlds. We use words—strange shapes of ink on paper, sounds our brains have magically learned to link with actual things—to *create* worlds. As we imagine a world, we automatically begin to bring it into being. In fact, the shamanic teacher Sandra Ingerman (2011) tells us that *Abracadabra,* the word we know from children's stories as a magical utterance, comes from the Aramaic *abraq ad habra,* which means "I will create as I speak" (p.1).

We create as we speak because words make worlds within us. If you doubt this, try saying the word "waterfall." What do you see, hear, smell, taste, experience? How do you feel? Now try on the word "supermarket," or worse, "traffic." What do you see, hear, and feel now? A single word is powerful enough to create an entire sensory experience in someone who hears, reads, or thinks it. If you were in a laboratory with electrodes attached to your head, a neuroscientist could track your brain's response. If a single word can do that much, think of the possibilities of a line, a sentence, a paragraph, a page—or a sequence of pages!

To be a writer is to embrace the power of words to create worlds. We draw words in from around us, outside of us, and pass them through the filters of our bodies, our minds, our experience, and then we birth them in the form of imagery. Our imagination—the mechanism by which we bring images into being—creates something new, something ours and not-ours, where before there was nothing.

When we allow ourselves to imagine, and then commit what we have imagined—the images which have come to us or come through us—to the page, we create worlds not only for ourselves but for others, too. Words make bridges between our own imaginations, our inner landscapes, and the separate universes of our readers.

The Work of the Writer as Shaman

There are many similarities between the work of the writer and the work of the shaman. Both frequently feel that our calling has chosen *us,* rather than vice versa. Both often undergo lengthy passages through darkness and confusion in order to access our difficult bodies of wisdom. In the process, both writers and shamans become what anthropologist Joan Halifax calls "specialists in the human soul" (Halifax 1991, p.12).

Many well-known writers describe their work in language that might also be used to describe a shamanic journey. Novelist Isabel Allende says, "I feel that there's a dark space, and I go into that dark space where the story is…it's like going into another world" (Moyers 2003, p.1). Suspense writer James W. Hall speaks of "going down into the dark or mysterious or uncharted places in my memories and my consciousness" (Jepson 2008, p.127).

The mystic, a person who feels profoundly connected to all that exists, is a figure closely related to the shaman. Many and perhaps even most of the greatest writers have been mystics. Nobel Award-winning poet Pablo Neruda wrote, "You learn poetry moving step by step among things and beings, not isolating, but rather containing them all within a blind expansion of love" (Neruda 1994, cover quote by Yglisias).

Although some writers have explicitly studied esoteric or "occult" paths, most have arrived at their understandings through the most time-honored shamanic path of all: the path of direct revelation. Although it is possible to study shamanism—or writing—with living human teachers, most shamans receive the bulk of their instruction from inner, non-physical teachers, and most writers cultivate relationships with that inner guide often called "the Muse." Many fiction writers report that their characters take over and surprise them, that their stories develop "lives of their own." For instance, novelist William Styron explains, "The whole concept of my novel *Sophie's Choice* was the result of a kind of waking vision…a merging from the dream to a conscious vision and memory of this girl called Sophie" (Nolan 2013, p.1).

This phenomenon isn't limited exclusively to the writing of fiction. Memoirist Susan Tiberghien says, "Once the book and most of its characters came to me in a dream, I never doubted that I should write it" (Tiberghien 2007, p.32). From a shamanic perspective, we might even say that Tiberghien's dream showed her that her book *already existed* in a different, non-physical dimension of reality. Rather than needing to create it, then, she had only to midwife it from that level of reality into this one.

This begs the question: when we imagine, when we allow images to come to us and come through us, from whence do they come? Do we truly "make them up," or do we provide a conduit for what already exists to make its way onto our pages and into the world in some new form?

A Personal Story: My Path to Becoming a Writer as Shaman

In hindsight I see that my own path was always that of a mystic and shaman, although it took more than 40 years for me to name it as such. I have been a writer for as long as I could write. My first poem, "Ode to a Raccoon," was published in a children's magazine when I was five. As its title suggests, my earliest impulse as a writer was to praise the world.

As time went on and my experience of life grew more complex, my praise became more complicated as well. It was difficult to praise life-threatening illness, urban shootings, and romantic heartbreak, but I did my best. Most of my poems came about as a result of an internal process something like that of the oyster which, irritated by a grain of sand, produces a pearl in response. I wrote about what I found most difficult in life in order to bear, encompass, and illuminate it—and to find out, as poet Audre Lorde said, "what I didn't know I knew" (Lorde 1983). By writing poems, I accessed wisdom which was not then available to me via other means. I often said that my poems "knew more than I did." I had to keep writing them to find out whatever it was they knew.

When I was in my 20s, my mother commented that reading my poems showed her an entirely different side of me, one that she otherwise would not have known existed. Although she meant it as a compliment to my poetry, I was struck by the distance she observed between my outer persona and my poems. I decided then that I wanted my persona, the self with which I walked in the world, to know more of what my poems knew, and to reflect that knowing.

I followed a variety of paths on my journey of healing and self-inquiry: psychotherapy, energy healing, consultations with astrologers and psychics, a plethora of self-help books, and a mind-body practice called Focusing. At nearly 40, having already published three books of poems, I discovered shamanism in a way that seemed quite accidental—or perhaps came about through workings beyond my conscious awareness.

I spent the next four years studying intensively with a remarkable teacher of shamanic practice, while also developing strong relationships with inner teachers. Over time, these practices healed many of my emotional wounds, resolved much of my argument with the world, and returned me to the deep sense of magic, mystery, purpose, and joy that had infused my life as a child.

At first, the healing I realized through shamanic practice appeared to disrupt, even to render unnecessary, my life as a writer. Quite simply, I had reached the goal I had set for myself nearly 20 years before; I no longer needed to write poems in order to find out *what I didn't know I knew*. I could access that knowing through other means, including the shamanic journey, and as I did so, it became more and more a part of my everyday consciousness. After two decades of work, I was finally starting to catch up to what my poems had known all along.

I left my tenure-track job teaching writing at a state university, started a private practice as a shamanic healer, and for a time distanced myself from the world of writers and writing. There was much that troubled me in that world: its inevitable currents of grandiosity, self-aggrandizement, envy, and competition felt at odds with the deepest impulses behind my writing. Yet the impulse to write turned out to be deeply woven into my soul. Although the poems had largely stopped coming, I still turned to writing as a way to access and communicate deeper wisdom. Meanwhile, alongside my private healing practice, I continued to teach writing part-time.

Inevitably, the lines between these two avenues of work began to blur: some of my shamanic clients were writers, and some of my writing students were using writing as a way to grow, heal, and access awareness. Although my official role as their teacher was to critique their poems, I couldn't help responding to the impulse I sensed beneath the surface of their work.

Eventually I realized that as someone who was now writer and shaman, teacher and healer, I had a new gift to offer: an understanding of the deep threads connecting these two callings. Out of this realization, the work I called *The Writer as Shaman* was born.

I think of *The Writer as Shaman* work as a path of transformation that leads to stronger, deeper writing. It can also be thought of as an approach to writing that also brings about transformation. Whether you enter through the gate marked "Writer" or arrive via the seeker's trail, the terrain is challenging but well-marked, and the rewards are rich.

The Link Between "Imagining," Perceiving, and Knowing

When I teach writing, a major part of my work is to help my writing students perceive the world the way a shaman does: as a web of shimmering aliveness, a place where everything is inextricably connected to every other thing, and we ourselves are connected to the all. For inspiration, we need only enter this pulsating non-physical landscape through any of the myriad portals that surround us in physical reality.

For instance, I am writing these words on my laptop computer that sits on a wooden table in a café. When I first sat down, I related to this table simply as a convenient surface. My experience of it was narrow, functional, and confined to the physical world. I noticed that it was faintly sticky, that there were a few crumbs marring its sheen. Apart from those observations, the table barely existed for me.

This is the level of perception most of us live within, most of the time. It's considered "normal" in our complex, demanding, over stimulating world. Yet what we can create from this level of perception is extremely limited. It's only when I consciously invite myself to look at the table through the eyes of a mystic—to look at it with gratitude, reverence, awe and wonder—that I can truly see it.

Now, as I look at the table through new eyes, I see the scuff marks, smudges, and scratches left on its surface by the many hundreds of people who have eaten, drunk, read, written, talked, and thought while seated here. I can allow the table to connect me to every one of them. I realize that someone, perhaps the café's owner, bought the table and placed it here, and I feel grateful for how that person's action has served me; that way I connect to him or her, too. I see the train and whorls in the table's surface, which remind me that the tabletop was once a part of a living tree—and I know that hundreds of people, machines, materials, and processes were involved in making that tree into this table. Someone, or a whole team of someones, cut down the tree, using a saw made by other people, invented by others, created from materials extracted from the earth by others; someone drove the felled trunk to a mill, using a truck created by others, and so on.

This table, then, connects me to hundreds of other people and places on the earth—even though all I have done until now is acknowledge the physical-world history lived by the table! As that acknowledgement helps me connect to the table's *beingness*, the miracle of its existence, then we might say that the physical table has opened a non-physical portal through which I can connect with the vast mystery and wonder of life itself.

Once we travel through such a non-physical portal, there can be no such thing as writer's block. As I open more fully to the stories this table holds—which include the stories of a tree in a forest, and all of the living creatures who lived in and on that tree, as well as the people who felled the tree, made the table, transported it, purchased it, placed it here in this café, and have sat at it since then—I see that I could easily write for a lifetime about this single object.

Now the words of the poet Mary Oliver, "I don't ask for the sights in front of me to change, only the depth of my seeing"[1] make real sense. As our seeing deepens, even a humble scratched café table can create an opening to vast realms of experience and connection.

Am I actually "seeing" all this—or am I "imagining" it? On a literal, physical level, I can see only a fraction of what I've just described with my physical eyes. What I am actually using could be better described as "inner sight." I know what I've described is true, yet the act of simply knowing it doesn't allow me to experience it as alive. In order to step into what I know as reality—a reality that can feed me and from which, in turn, I can feed the readers of my work—I must "imagine" what I know, and thus see and know it far more deeply.

Accessing—or Preventing Access to —the Imaginal Realm

Obviously, this liminal shoreline, this place where physical and non-physical realities come together, is a tremendously rich place for a writer. Yet because our culture teaches us to privilege the physical world over the non-physical, and then overwhelms us with physical stimuli, most of us learn to shut down to all but the most dramatic phenomena around us: the cell phone, the computer, the television, the crying child, the yelling spouse. For many of us, this external overstimulation has become such a constant that it has actually grown difficult or uncomfortable for us to tolerate *less* stimulation. As a result, if and when we do finally find time for writing, we may find it difficult to open the rusty gates of our more mystical or shamanic perceptions. That's when the table in front of us remains just a table, and we find ourselves unable to think of anything to write.

I believe that most prolific writers have somehow stumbled on their own ways of opening portals between the socially functional—yet imaginatively drab state of ordinary consciousness—and the more open, dreamy, associative, multidimensional state that mystics and shamans inhabit. We may not be aware that this is what we're doing; we also may not consciously know how it is that we do it. There are many ways to pass through such portals. Writing teacher Jill Jepson suggests actually visualizing a door, gate, or threshold, then imagining ourselves passing through it to reach the mythic realm (Jepson 2008). But for many people meditating, praying, spending time in nature, walking, driving, exercising, drumming, dancing, listening to music, people watching, or simply *intending* work just as well.

In my experience, what actually matters most is our emotional posture, our attitude. Certain attitudes predispose us to entering that realm of expanded perception and creativity; others keep us locked outside.

As we've already seen, the postures of love, awe, reverence, and praise help us open portals. Those postures expand us internally, making us more able to perceive beyond the limits of the mundane. Therefore, it's not surprising that the opposite states—hatred, disgust, contempt, revulsion—would close off those portals to us.

For instance, what if, instead of inviting myself to experience the café table in the way that I did, I had invited myself to view the table through the lens of disgust? I might have railed against the people who had scuffed or smudged the table, criticized the café owner for having purchased such an ugly table, judged the logger who cut down the tree, and berated myself for being the kind of loser who would even sit at such a table. Of course, if I were hell-bent, I could even have criticized the asymmetrical tree the table had been made from, and the squawking, insignificant birds who had lived in its limbs.

"Hell-bent" is an interesting expression, since this attitude would certainly confine me to a kind of inner hell! Although this line of thought makes for a humorous parody, who would actually want to spend much time writing or reading it? Just writing those few sentences made me want to go take a nap! A shaman might say that that's because the postures of hatred, judgment, and criticism actually drain us and close down our energetic fields. Whether you believe that or not, it's easy to observe firsthand how it feels when you are harshly critical of anyone or anything, versus how you feel when you are loving, grateful, and reverent.

Negativity induces inner states that feel hellish; praise, on the other hand, helps us enter states that feel beautiful, alive, and, well, heavenly. Judgment closes us down; reverence opens us up. As writers and human beings, the choice is ours. Which states will we choose to cultivate?

The Larger Significance of Our Imaginal Choices

Many of us who would never dream of lashing out cruelly at anything else in the world still speak and relate to ourselves in brutal, punishing ways. Not surprisingly, that has a withering effect on our creativity and on our ability to access the subtle portals that lead to inspired writing. If we wish to access the keys to the kingdom of creativity, we must turn the same enriching gaze toward both our outer *and inner* worlds.

I recently had a writing student who wrote wonderfully lively, creative pieces in response to the exercises I assigned. Unfortunately, the "finished," formal poems she handed in were much less alive and interesting than her quickly-jotted exercises. When we talked about her process, it became clear to both of us that when she felt the stakes were low, she wrote with playful, light energy. Yet when it came time to write a capital-p Poem, she forced herself to sit down at her desk and do capital-w Work—a posture that constricted her access to creativity and squeezed the life out of what she produced.

Forcing ourselves to Write with a capital W—forcing ourselves to do anything, in fact—cannot open portals into deeper states of being or deeper ways of perceiving the world. In contrast, *allowing* or *inviting* ourselves to create, offering ourselves expanded *opportunities* to perceive, can work wonders.

Right now, you can try a simple experiment that will let you experience that for yourself. Read the following words aloud:

> *Forcing*
>
> *Requiring*
>
> *Demanding.*

Notice how they feel in your mouth and in your body. What images arise? What happens?

Now read this next set of words:

> *Allowing*
>
> *Inviting*
>
> *Offering.*

Again, observe what happens inside you. If you are able to tune in to your own set of responses on a subtle level, you may actually feel an inner gate closing—or opening—with each word.

Which set of words is more conducive to writing or to creating? Which set of feelings do you find it more enjoyable to experience? And which not only help you bring forth your own creative expression, but also help you (and all of us) to birth the world in which you most want to live?

The student I mentioned earlier, the one who forced herself to Work Hard on her poems, was a deeply thoughtful, caring mother and teacher. She would never have tried to force her young daughter or her own students to approach a creative act in the way she was attempting to force herself. And yet by taking that attitude toward herself, she was, from the shamanic perspective, putting a "forcing" energy into the world—where it not only impacted her own creative process, but also contributed to a harshness in the larger world.

The noted shamanic teacher Sandra Ingerman advises her students and readers to "notice what you send out and how it is affecting the energy field of the planet, and the web of life" (Ingerman 2011, p.1). She also compares human beings to fingers that believe they exist on their own, and have forgotten their connection to a hand and to a larger body (Ingerman 2011). This is the state in which many of us live. Yet it's easy to see that if we were to cut, burn, smash, or otherwise injure our own fingers, our entire hand would be affected; in fact, our whole body would feel the impact. On the purely physical level, an infection that begins in any part of the body can turn septic, becoming a systemic infection that affects the whole.

Therefore, from the shamanic perspective, it makes no difference whether our harshness is directed externally or internally, whether we are choosing to stream poison into the world at large, or "only" to bathe in it ourselves. Either way, it causes harm to the larger web of which each of us is part.

Seen through this lens, the act of nurturing our own creative unfolding becomes even more significant. A shaman—or a writer who is operating as a shaman—might say that the world actually *needs* both our creativity and the energy from which that creativity can come. The world needs not only what we may produce through our creative efforts, but *also*, and perhaps even more significantly, it needs the energy of the love and reverence that fuels them.

And how do we direct love and reverence toward the world instead of poison? By *choosing* to do so. By *allowing* and *inviting* ourselves to do so. By *imagining* that we are doing so. In the final analysis, these inner transactions are so closely connected to one another that it is fruitless even to attempt to tease them apart. What we choose, what we allow, what we invite, what we imagine: this is what we create.

Practices to Help You Go Deeper

Many cultures have honored the directions in some way. Some describe four, some six, some seven or ten, but no matter how many directions are explicitly acknowledged, the point of "calling in the directions" is essentially the same: by acknowledging and celebrating seemingly "opposing" currents, we honor all that is.

The following Six Directions Invocation was given to me by my inner teachers. I find that it both grounds and expands me, so I often use it before I write, and always before I meditate, teach or work with clients.

As I understand them, the six directions are real forces, energetic presences that truly give to us and teach us. Since they are vast, each one of us perceives them differently. I've named the qualities I experience most strongly, but you may find yourself in contact with other qualities in addition to, or instead of, the ones I've named here. In my experience, invocation and prayer are most powerful when they are dynamic, specific and particular—when we are truly engaging with our practices anew, each time we use them, rather than performing a ritual by rote. Therefore, I offer you this invocation for your use, but also encourage you to modify it according to your own experience and perceptions.

This practice can be done anywhere. I've used it sitting on a crowded airplane, for instance, thinking the words rather than saying them audibly. I've also used a very abbreviated version internally when I'm confronted with a tough emotional situation. For me, it works wonders!

However, if circumstances allow, I recommend standing up, turning to face each direction as you call it in, and speaking the invocation aloud. If you are so inclined, you can also rattle, drum, or ring a bell as you welcome each direction. Then pause for a few seconds and take the time to actually sense or imagine the feeling of each direction as it arrives.

SIX DIRECTIONS INVOCATION

I honor and call in the spirit of the North, which I perceive as the direction that teaches me and gives to me through the experience of Winter, through cold and darkness and night, through suffering, difficulty and hardship. I honor and accept what you give me, North, and I also honor and accept what you take away.

I honor and call in the spirit of the East, which I perceive as the direction that teaches me and gives to me through the experience of Spring, through sunrise, through new beginnings, hope, potential and possibility, the direction of new tender green shoots unfurling. I honor and accept what you give me, East, and I also honor and accept what you take away.

I honor and call in the spirit of the South, which I perceive as the direction that teaches me and gives to me through the experience of Summer, through ease and plenty, abundance, warm midday sunshine, the direction of fullness and blossoming, and everything happening so much more smoothly and easily than I could even have imagined. I honor and accept what you give me, South, and I also honor and accept what you take away.

I honor and call in the spirit of the West, which I perceive as the direction that teaches me and gives to me through the experience of Autumn, through late afternoon, through sunset, through times of completion and closure, the natural termination of cycles, through maturation and decay. I honor and accept what you give me, West, and I also honor and accept what you take away.

I honor and call in the spirit of Below, which I perceive as the direction that teaches me and gives to me through earthly experience, through living in a physical body on the physical plane: the gifts of hunger and fullness, discomfort and comfort, pain and pleasure, sickness and well-being, vitality and mortality, and all of the limitations inherent in being human. I honor and accept what you give me, direction of Below, and I also honor and accept what you take away.

I honor and call in the spirit of Above, which I perceive as the direction that teaches and gives to me through the vastness of the sky: the gifts of wonder and mystery, the timeless, eternal aspect of my own being, my connection to all that has ever been, and all that will ever be. I honor and accept what you bring me, direction of Above, and I also honor and accept what you take away.

And lastly, I honor myself as the perceiver of the six directions, and I remember and affirm that wherever I go, no matter what is happening inside me or outside of me, I am always at the center of the six directions, always being held and supported by North, East, South, West, Below and Above.

I've found that calling in the Six Directions helps me write, speak and feel more deeply. By welcoming and acknowledging all of the forces and currents that work with us and within us, and resisting none of them, we can access real strength and joy.

ENDNOTE

1. While this quote is widely attributed to Mary Oliver on the Internet, there is no verifiable source: www.azquotes.com/author/11081-Mary_Oliver?p=7.

References

Halifax, J. (1991) *Shamanic Voices: A Survey of Visionary Narratives,* London: Penguin Arkana.

Hall, J. quoted by Jepson, J. (2008) *Writing as a Sacred Path: A Practical Guide to Writing with Passion and Purpose.* Berkeley, CA: Celestial Arts Press.

Ingerman, S. (2011) *How to Heal Toxic Thoughts.* Available at www.sandraingerman. com/healingtoxicthoughts.html, accessed on April 6 2015.

Jepson, J. (2008) *Writing as a Sacred Path: A Practical Guide to Writing with Passion and Purpose.* Berkeley, CA: Celestial Arts Press.

Lorde, A. (1983) From a speech given at Wesleyan University (accessed from notes taken by Ruth Schwartz).

Moyers, B. (2003) *Transcript: Bill Moyers Interview of Isabel Allende.* Available at www. pbs.org/now/transcript/transcript_allende.html, accessed on April 6 2015.

Neruda, P. (1994) *Pablo Neruda, Late and Posthumous Poems, 1968–1974: Bilingual Edition.* New York, NY: Grove Press.

Nolan, A. (2013) quoting William Styron in *Ten Great Stories Inspired by Dreams and Visions.* Available at www.pastemagazine.com/blogs/lists/2013/10/10-great-stories-inspired-by-dreams-and-visions.html, accessed on April 6 2015.

Tiberghien, S. (2007) *One Year to a Writing Life.* Boston, MA: Da Capo Press.

Chapter 22

The Power of Imagination

Optimizing Sport Performance Through Imagery

Phillip Post

Since the beginning of competitive physical activity, athletes have spent time thinking about their sport. Some athletes, like the much decorated former Olympic U.S. distance swimmer Janet Evans, have moved beyond "just thinking" about their sport to purposefully creating vivid images in their mind that enable them to prepare for competition. Janet was known for spending days and weeks ahead of her competitions creating mental images of herself winning her races (Ungerleider 2005). Other athletes have also discovered that they can prepare for the physical and psychological demands of their sport by simply creating or recreating an experience in their mind.

You might already be familiar with imagery. If not, all you need to do is sit back, close your eyes, and think about a loved one or a close friend. In your mind's eye, have that person sit in a chair in front of you and see if you can get a sharp, vivid image of them. Visualize the person's facial features, mannerisms, and clothing. Hear this person speak, smell his/ her cologne, and feel the emotions that you have toward that person. The images and sensations that you experience when picturing this individual

...ut sport psychologists consider imagery. Often we use this skill without consciously thinking about it. For example, you are using imagery when you mentally rehearse an important presentation, when you think about having a difficult conversation with a coworker, and/or when you think about your future goals and dreams. Athletes use this skill as well, but instead of focusing on everyday experiences they create images that focus on their sport performance. For instance, athletes might imagine how they want to perform a specific motor skill in competition, to practice the proper feel of a certain movement, or to reinforce a desired attitude or an ideal psychological state.

Over the last few decades, several elite athletes have reported that imagery has benefited their sport performance and mental preparation. One notable example is former professional golfer Jack Nicklaus, who expounded on how a detailed imagery plan enhanced his golf performance; prior to hitting each shot on the course, Nicklaus would picture the desired flight of his golf ball. Such anecdotal accounts by elite athletes have fascinated sport psychologists and have led to numerous research investigations on this mental skill. These investigations have produced a wealth of knowledge about how imagery impacts sport performance and how athletes employ the mental skill. This essay will explore some of the major research findings on sport imagery and review best practices for implementing imagery in athletic settings.

What is Sport Imagery?

Imagery has been defined as the creation or re-creation of an experience in the mind (Vealey and Forlenza 2015). This means that athletes are re-creating an experience that they have already had or creating a new experience in their mind's eye. Athletes spend a lot of time thinking about their sport and sometimes without even knowing it engage in imagery in an effort to improve their current and future performance. If you are or were an athlete, you might recall rehearsing your sport performance over and over again the night before a competition. When engaging in this activity, you were essentially accessing previous experiences that were stored in long-term memory, and in doing so you were able to recall specific features about your sport performance, such as the sights and sounds of the competition, the kinesthetic sensations you experienced when executing a specific skill, and whether or not you met your expectations in that situation.

As athletes become more comfortable with their imagery skill, they begin to create new experiences in their mind's eye (MacIntyre and Moran 2007; Porter 2003; Post and Wrisberg 2012). This may include creating new movements, various competition scenarios, and/or future successes (for instance, winning a race, improving time, or increasing accuracy). When athletes create or recreate an experience, they do so by incorporating multiple sensations. For example, when sprinters image an upcoming race, they may see the track (vision), feel their muscles firing as they run (kinesthetic), hear the crowd roar after the starting gun fires (auditory), smell their surroundings (olfaction), and taste the saltiness of their sweat after warming up (taste). Incorporating and utilizing multiple senses enhances an athlete's overall imagery experience by making it more vivid and authentic (MacIntyre and Moran 2007; Porter 2003; Post *et al*. 2014; Post and Wrisberg 2012). As athletes continue to develop their imagery skill, they may also include emotional and/or psychological states associated with their desired performance (Munroe *et al*. 2000; Post and Wrisberg 2012). For instance, in addition to rehearsing the physical components of a floor routine, a gymnast might also experience the excitement of competition, feel confident, and/or to have a positive affect. On the whole, research with skilled athletes suggests that sport imagery is an active process that entails recreating or creating a poly-sensory experience.

How Do Athletes Use Imagery?

Since the 1980s researchers have conducted numerous investigations on how athletes use imagery. The results of this research have provided a wealth of information regarding the *where, when, why,* and *what* of athletes' imagery (see Hall *et al*. 1998; Munroe *et al*. 2000; Munroe *et al*. 1998; Post *et al*. 2014; Post and Wrisberg 2012). With respect to *where* and *when,* athletes typically report engaging in imagery at several points during and outside of a competition (Cumming and Hall 2002; Post and Wrisberg 2012; Weinberg *et al*. 2003). For instance, skilled divers reported using imagery the night before a competition, in practice, during the day, during warm-ups, between dives, and just prior to stepping on the diving board (Post *et al*. 2014). These reports reflect the flexibility of this mental skill, showing that it can be used anywhere and at any time for a variety of purposes.

There are several components that comprise the *what* of athletes' imagery. For example, when using imagery athletes typically incorporate two distinct perspectives—internal: seeing their performance from behind their own eyes; and external: seeing their performance from a third-person perspective (Callow and Roberts 2010; Hall, Rodgers, and Barr 1990; Munroe *et al*. 2000; Post and Wrisberg 2012; Weinberg *et al*. 2003). An internal perspective allows an athlete to replicate the perceptual/

kinesthetic elements associated with a particular skill. For example, when they adopt an internal perspective, springboard divers would see the pool as they stepped up onto the diving board, feel the board under their feet, see the environment move as they twisted and turned throughout the dive, and feel the water as they entered the pool. An external perspective enables athletes to evaluate their movement form as though they are a spectator watching themselves perform (Post *et al.* 2014). For example, a diver would see himself performing the dive from a judge's perspective to determine if his body was aligned correctly throughout the dive. The decision to use either perspective depends on the desired outcome of the imagery practice. If the athlete wants to invoke the feel or perceptual elements of one of their skills, then an internal perspective may be more beneficial. However, if they want to evaluate or fix their form, they would most likely make use of an external perspective. Athletes also report manipulating the speed of their imagery depending on the objective (O and Hall 2009; Post *et al.* 2014; Post and Wrisberg 2012). For example, if a gymnast wants to practice the correct rhythm of her beam routine, she would employ real time imagery, an image speed consistent with the speed of her actual performance. If that gymnast had difficulty executing a particular skill, then she might slow down the speed of her imagery in order to experience the correct movement form. It appears that athletes use real time imagery to experience the correct timing, tempo, and rhythm of their skills, while slow motion imagery is used to focus on important parts of the skill or to correct mistakes (Post *et al.* 2014; Post and Wrisberg 2012). Finally, athletes' imagery is multisensory and contains nuances (i.e. weather conditions, time of day, different competition scenarios, etc.) associated with their practice or competition environment (Munroe *et al.* 2000; White and Hardy 1998).

A primary focus of researchers who are describing athletes' use of imagery has been identifying *why* they use this mental skill. Paivio (1985) first suggested that imagery could be used to meet cognitive and motivational purposes, each of which can be directed toward a specific or general goal. Based on this early hypothesis, Hall and colleagues (Hall *et al.* 1998; Martin, Moritz, and Hall 1999) identified five possible functions of athletes' imagery:

1. *Motivational-Specific (MS):* imagery that represents specific goals and goal-oriented behaviors, such as winning a competition.

2. *Motivational General-Mastery (MG-M):* imagery that represents effective coping with and mastery of challenging situations, such as imaging confidence, focus, and mental toughness.

3. *Motivational General-Arousal (MG-A)*: imagery that represents feelings of relaxation, stress, arousal, and anxiety regulation, such as imaging yourself being relaxed before an event.

4. *Cognitive-Specific (CS)*: imagery of specific sport skills such as imaging the correct execution of a basketball free throw or a high jump.

5. *Cognitive-General (CG)*: imagery of strategies associated with a specific sport, such as imaging a race plan or a defensive scheme in football.

These five functions are considered to be independent. An athlete can image game strategies (CG) without imaging themselves being confident (MG-M). However, athletes can combine different imagery functions in order to meet a desired cognitive, behavioral, or affective outcome (Martin, Moritz, and Hall 1999; Post *et al.* 2014). For instance, a baseball pitcher who wants to practice the proper execution of his curveball while feeling relaxed could combine MG-A imagery (experiencing himself being calm) and CS imagery (seeing and feeling the correct execution of his pitch) to meet his desired behavioral and affective outcomes. While imagery serves a number of functions and can be used in various circumstances, the skill takes time to develop. Just like any physical skill, athletes have to dedicate practice time in order to develop vivid and controllable images (Post *et al.* 2014, Post and Wrisberg 2012). When starting out, athletes often report experiencing a disjointed image or a blank screen, or they can't experience the kinesthetic sensations associated with a desired image. However, with deliberate practice they can harness this skill to create vivid and controllable images that enable them to create realistic performance scenarios (Munroe *et al.* 2000; Post *et al.* 2014).

Collectively, the results of sport-psychology research suggest that athletes' imagery is a dynamic and multifaceted process that involves different perspectives (internal and external), speeds (slow and real time), and functions (cognitive and motivational). The results of this research also suggest that imagery is a flexible skill that athletes can use in a variety of locations (e.g. practice and competition), and times (e.g. just prior to executing a skill, during warm-up). The complex nature of imagery suggests that athletes need to practice this skill in order to realize its benefits, however, once it's mastered, they can use the skill to supplement their physical practice.

Does Imagery Benefit Athletic Performance?

The biggest question among athletes and coaches has been, "Does imagery work?" Sport-psychology researchers have spent several decades trying to answer this question. The findings from this extensive body of research indicate that imagery interventions enhance both sport performance and motor learning (Driskell, Copper, and Moran 1994; Feltz and Landers 1983; Rushall and Lippman 1998; Weinberg 2008). Imagery improves sport performance across a variety of motor tasks varying in cognitive and motor demands: in other words, tasks that primarily involve either decision-making or correct skill execution (Driskell et al. 1994; Feltz and Landers 1983; Weinberg 2008). For example, imagery has improved athletes' free throw shooting (Post, Wrisberg, and Mullins 2010), field hockey penalty flicks (Smith et al. 2007, study 1), gymnastics routines (Smith et al. 2007, study 2), bunker golf shots (Smith, Wright, and Cantwell 2008), skiing (Callow, Roberts, and Fawkes 2006), and swimming performance (Post, Muncie, and Simpson 2012).

Imagery interventions have also been shown to assist athletes and learners in acquiring novel motor skills. For instance, imagery rehearsal has benefited athletes' and learners' skill acquisition of a springboard dive (Grouis 1992), computer racing task (Wright and Smith 2007), typing skills (Wohldman, Healy, and Bourne 2007), balance (Waskiewicz and Zajac 2001), bicep curls (Wright and Smith 2009), and field hockey penalty flicks (Smith et al. 2001). While researchers have demonstrated that imagery can enhance learning and performance to a greater extent than no practice at all, it is not as beneficial as overt practice (Driskell et al. 1994; Feltz and Landers 1983; Hird et al. 1991; Weinberg 2008). However, there are many situations in which physical practice cannot be performed or is not possible. When the necessary equipment, environment, or practice time is not available or when an athlete is injured, imagery appears to be a useful substitute (Weinberg 2008). Given these findings, researchers recommend integrating the mental skill with physical practice in order to obtain the optimal results (Post, Muncie, and Simpson 2012; Waskiewicz and Zajac 2001). Like any mental skill, imagery has its greatest impact when practitioners integrate it into the athlete's physical practice.

In addition to examining the influence that the mental skill has on motor performance, researchers have also evaluated how imagery influences psychological variables associated with successful athletic performance. These include variables like self-efficacy (Feltz and Riessinger 1990; Garza and Feltz 1998), motivation (Martin and Hall 1995), attention (Calmels, Berthoumieux, and Arripe-Longueville 2004), confidence (Callow and Waters 2005; Mamassis and Doganis 2004), and competitive anxiety (Page, Sime, and Nordell 1999). The results of this research demonstrate that imagery also has a positive mediating effect on these psychological variables. For example, imagery interventions have enhanced confidence levels in high-level badminton players (Callow, Hardy, and Hall 2001), improved athletes' self-efficacy (Garza and Feltz 1998), enhanced motivation (Martin and Hall 1995), increased selective attention (Calmels *et al.* 2004), and decreased performance anxiety (Monsma and Overby 2004; Page, Sime, and Nordell 1999). As a whole, the research on imagery and sport performance suggests that this mental skill can benefit both the physical and mental aspects of an athlete's sport performance. For example, a soccer coach may use imagery to improve her players' motor performance (e.g. passing and set plays), tactical play (e.g. learning game strategies), and psychological states (e.g. to enhance confidence).

How Does Imagery Work?

Several theories have been proposed to explain the influence that imagery has on athletes' sport performance, cognitions, and affect. These include Jacobson's (1932) psychoneuromuscular theory, Sackett's (1934) symbolic learning theory, Paivio's dual code theory (1975), Lang's (1977, 1979) bio-informational theory, and Jeannerod's (1994) functional equivalence theory. Of these five theories, Jeannerod's (1994) functional equivalence theory and Lang's bio-informational theory (Lang 1977, 1979) have attracted the most attention, primarily because imagery interventions based on these theoretical frameworks have been shown to contribute to improved sport performance (Callow *et al.* 2006; Post *et al.* 2010; Smith *et al.* 2008). Using emerging neuroimaging research findings, Jeannerod (1994) argued that imagery and physical practice are functionally equivalent, in that imagery and overt practice access common neural mechanisms (Jeannerod 1994). Essentially, when you create or recreate a physical movement in your mind's eye, it activates the same neural mechanisms associated with the actual perception, motor control, and emotions of an overt movement (Holmes and Collins 2001; Jeannerod 1994). It is believed that athletes can strengthen the correct neural mechanisms, connections, and pathways associated with an ideal performance by utilizing repeated imagery rehearsal and make it more likely that the desired motor skill will actually be performed.

Alternatively, Lang (1977, 1979) proposed that individuals store an organized set of stimulus and response propositions in long-term memory. Stimulus propositions elicit the context of a particular event (e.g. the environment) and response propositions elicit potential responses (e.g. psychological and physiological responses) for that particular event.

Through imagery, individuals can become more adept at matching the most effective response propositions to a particular set of stimulus propositions. For example, when a downhill slalom skier images a specific run, they can recall from long-term memory the contextual aspects of what that specific run is like (the slope, gate placement, snow conditions, competition context, and other factors). Once they have created this environmental context in their mind's eye, the skier can then practice how they want to perform within that context (their approach to the run, getting through each gate seamlessly, feeling confident, having ideal movement, and other actions). As a result, when the athlete actually encounters the specific situation in the future, they have in effect already been there several times and can now simply recall the correct response to the situation.

How Can I Use Imagery Effectively?

When athletes and coaches are provided with the overwhelming evidence that imagery works, a common question they often ask is, "How can I utilize this skill effectively?" The answer varies depending on what the coach or athlete wants to get out of the imagery practice. One of the most important answers is that they develop their imagery consistent with well-founded theory. To assist athletes and coaches in creating effective theory-based imagery interventions, Holmes and Collins (2001) created the PETTLEP imagery model, which combines both Lang's (1977, 1979) bio-informational theory and Jeannerod's (1994) functional equivalence theory. The PETTLEP imagery model suggests that effective imagery should include stimulus and response propositions and should approximate physical practice along seven factors:

1. *Physical*

2. *Environment*

3. *Task*

4. *Timing*

5. *Learning*

6. *Emotion*

7. *Perspective.*

The *physical* factor refers to accurately imaging the perceived physical sensations experienced by the athlete during actual skill execution. To acquire a more precise set of sensations, athletes should image while in their performance stance or when holding an implement associated with their sport (e.g. a tennis player would hold their racquet). *Environment* involves completing the imagery while in the performance environment. If unable to image in the performance environment athletes should supplement their imagery sessions with video or photographs of the performance setting to assist them in creating an authentic image of the competition environment. *Task* refers to making the content of the skill being imaged appropriate for the skill level of the individual athlete. Skilled athletes should be encouraged to create complex images associated with their desired skill (i.e. platform divers would image all of the physical movements necessary to perform a specific dive from starting on the platform until they enter the water), while novices should focus on creating images of the basic movement elements needed to produce the skill. *Timing* refers to the timing of the imagery, which in most cases should be similar to the timing of the actual skill. *Learning* refers to the need for athletes to continually update their imagery scripts so that it matches their current skill level. *Perspective* involves imaging from an internal (first-person) or external (third-person) perspective. The PETTLEP model suggests that the imager should adopt a first-person perspective, because this is more congruent with what the athlete experiences during skill execution. However, if an athlete wants to work on form, adopting an external perspective may be helpful.

In addition to the seven-function PETTLEP model, practitioners also need to incorporate stimulus and response propositions. Essentially, athletes should choose specific situations that they want to practice (stimulus responses), and then think about how they want to perform in those situations (response propositions). For example, a basketball player who struggles with shooting free throws at the end of a game can begin his imagery session by creating this specific scenario in his mind's eye (for example, the pressure he feels) and then practice how he would like to respond to that specific situation (calmly executing the free throw). By considering the seven factors of the PETTLEP model and including stimulus and response propositions, athletes and coaches can maximize their imagery practice (Smith *et al.* 2007, 2008; Wakefield and Smith 2009).

In addition to using theory to develop effective imagery interventions, it is important that athletes practice this skill regularly (Porter 2003). Several skilled athletes reported that they initially had difficulty controlling their imagery or developing a clear picture (Post *et al.* 2014). Athletes who experience this issue should not give up: they should continue to practice the skill until it has been mastered. Athletes can make imagery a part of their daily routine by setting aside at least three to five minutes a day to practice their skill. If they continue to struggle, they can first practice using some basic images (a family member or familiar object). Once they master these simple images, they can progress to more complex images associated with their sport performance. Second, they can try to make the imagery experience as vivid as possible by using as many senses as possible (kinesthetic, vision, auditory, taste, and olfaction; Porter 2003). If an athlete has difficulty experiencing the kinesthetic sensations associated with a particular skill, they can combine their imagery training with overt body movements. This might include "walking through" the skill physically while imaging it, or alternating between imagery and actual movement. Finally, athletes can incorporate emotion into their imagery. When they rehearse a specific skill, they should invoke the emotions they would normally feel while in competition (e.g. anxiety, confidence, and/or ideal energy levels). Incorporating emotion will help athletes translate their ideal mental state to their physical execution of the skill.

Sport Imagery Summary

Research in sport psychology over the last several decades has shown that athletes use imagery to create or recreate athletic experiences in their mind's eye. This research has shown that athletes' imagery involves incorporating multiple sensations, it has two distinct perspectives, it includes various speeds, it takes deliberate effort to develop, it is used in various locations, and it serves multiple functions (Sordoni, Hall, and Forwell 2000). This research has also indicated that imagery has a positive impact on athletes' skill acquisition and motor performance as well as the psychological variables associated with successful sport performance (Garza and Feltz 1998; Post et al. 2012; Smith et al. 2008; Weinberg 2008). Imagery is a mental skill that when combined with physical practice is a powerful technique for changing athletic behavior and success. Overall, research in sport psychology strongly indicates that imagery works, and that it should be introduced to athletes to assist them in achieving their athletic goals.

References

Callow, N., Hardy, L., and Hall, C. (2001) "The effects of a motivational general-mastery imagery intervention on the sport confidence of high-level badminton players." *Research Quarterly for Exercise and Sport 72*, 389–400.

Callow, N. and Roberts, R. (2010) "Imagery research: An investigation of three issues." *Psychology of Sport and Exercise 11*, 325–329.

Callow, N., Roberts, R., and Fawkes, J.Z. (2006) "Effects of dynamic and static imagery on vividness of imagery, skiing performance, and confidence." *Journal of Imagery Research in Sport and Physical Activity 1*, 1.

Callow, N. and Waters, A. (2005) "The effect of kinesthetic imagery on the sport confidence of flat-race horse jockeys." *Psychology of Sport and Exercise 6*, 443–459.

Calmels, C., Berthoumieux, C., and Arripe-Longueville, F. (2004) "Effects of an imagery training program on selective attention of national softball players." *The Sport Psychologist 18*, 272–296.

Cumming, J. and Hall, C. (2002) "Athletes' use of imagery in the off-season." *The Sport Psychologist 16*, 160–172.

Driskell, J.E., Copper, C., and Moran, A. (1994) "Does mental practice enhance performance?" *Journal of Applied Psychology 79*, 481–492.

Feltz, D.L. and Landers, D.M. (1983) "The effects of mental practice on motor skill learning and performance: A meta-analysis." *Journal of Sport Psychology 5*, 25–57.

Feltz, D.L. and Riessinger, C.A. (1990) "Effects of in vivo emotive imagery and performance feedback on self-efficacy and muscular endurance." *Journal of Sport and Exercise Psychology 12*, 132–143.

Garza, D.L. and Feltz, D.L. (1998) "Effects of selected mental practice on performance, self-efficacy, and competition confidence of figure skaters. *The Sport Psychologist 12*, 1–15.

Grouios, G. (1992) "The effect of mental practice on diving performance." *International Journal of Sport Psychology 23*, 1, 60–69.

Hall, C.R., Mack, D.E., Paivio, A., and Hausenblas, H.A. (1998) "Imagery use by athletes: Development of the sport imagery questionnaire." *International Journal of Sport Psychology 29*, 1, 73–89.

Hall, C.R., Rodgers, W.M., and Barr, K.A. (1990) "The use of imagery by athletes in selected sports." *The Sport Psychologist 4*, 1–10.

Hird, J.S., Landers, D.M., Thomas, J.R., and Horan, J.J. (1991) "Physical practice is superior to mental practice in enhancing cognitive and motor task performance." *Journal of Sport and Exercise Psychology 13*, 281–293.

Holmes, P.S. and Collins, D.J. (2001) "The PETTLEP approach to motor imagery: A functional equivalence model for sport psychologists." *Journal of Applied Sport Psychology 13*, 60–83.

Jacobson, E. (1932) "Electrophysiology of mental activities." *American Journal of Psychology 44*, 677–694.

Jeannerod, M. (1994) "The representing brain: Neural correlates of motor intention and imagery." *Behavioral and Brain Sciences 17*, 187–245.

Lang, P.J. (1977) "Imagery in therapy: An informational processing analysis of fear." *Behavior Therapy 8*, 862–886.

Lang, P.J. (1979) "A bio-informational theory of emotional imagery." *Psychophysiology 16*, 495–512.

MacIntyre, T.E. and Moran, A.P. (2007) "A qualitative investigation of meta-imagery processes and imagery direction among elite athletes." *Journal of Imagery Research in Sport and Physical Activity 2*, 1.

Mamassis, G. and Doganis, G. (2004) "The effects of a mental training program on juniors pre-competitive anxiety, self-confidence, and tennis performance." *Journal of Applied Sport Psychology 16*, 118–137.

Martin, K.A. and Hall, C.R. (1995) "Using mental imagery to enhance intrinsic motivation." *Journal of Sport and Exercise Psychology 17*, 54–69.

Martin, K.A., Moritz, S.E., and Hall, C.R. (1999) "Imagery use in sport: A literature review and applied model." *The Sport Psychologist 13*, 245–268.

Monsma, E.V. and Overby, L.Y. (2004) "The relationship between imagery and competitive anxiety in ballet auditions." *Journal of Dance Medicine and Science 8*, 11-18.

Munroe, K., Giacobbi, P.R., Hall, C., and Weinberg, R. (2000) "The four Ws of imagery use: Where, when, why, and what." *The Sport Psychologist 14*, 119–137.

Munroe, K., Hall, C., Simms, S., and Weinberg, R. (1998) "The influence of type of sport and time of season on athletes' use of imagery." *The Sport Psychologist 12*, 440–449.

O, J. and Hall, C. (2009) "A quantitative analysis of athletes' voluntary use of slow motion, real time, and fast motion images." *Journal of Applied Sport Psychology 21*, 15–30.

Page, S.J., Sime, W., and Nordell, K. (1999) "The effects of imagery on female college swimmers' perceptions of anxiety. *The Sport Psychologist 13*, 458–469.

Paivio, A. (1985) "Cognitive and motivational functions of imagery in human performance." *Canadian Journal of Applied Sport Sciences 10*, 4, 22S–28S.

Paivio, A. (1975) "Coding Distinctions and Repetition Effects in Memory." In G.H. Bower (ed.) *Psychology of learning and motivation*, vol. 9. Orlando, FL: Academic Press.

Porter, K. (2003) *The Mental Athlete: Inner Training for Peak Performance in All Sports*. Champaign, IL: Human Kinetics.

Post, P.G., Muncie, S., and Simpson, D. (2012) "The effects of imagery training on swimming performance: An applied investigation." *Journal of Applied Sport Psychology 24*, 323–337.

Post, P.G., Simpson, D., Young, G., and Parker, J.F. (2014) "A phenomenological investigation of divers' lived experience of imagery." *Journal of Imagery Research in Sport and Physical Activity 8*, 1.

Post, P.G. and Wrisberg, C.A. (2012) "A phenomenological investigation of gymnasts' lived experience of imagery." *The Sport Psychologist 26*, 98–121.

Post, P.G., Wrisberg, C.A., and Mullins, S. (2010) "A field test of the influence of pre-game imagery on basketball free-throw shooting." *Journal of Imagery Research in Sport and Physical Activity 5*, 1.

Rushall, B.S. and Lippman, L.G. (1998) "The role of imagery in physical performance." *International Journal of Sport Psychology 29*, 57–72.

Sackett, R.S. (1934) "Influence of symbolic rehearsal upon retention of maze habit." *Journal of General Psychology 10*, 376–398.

Smith, D., Holmes, P., Whitemore, L., Collins, D., and Devonport, T. (2001) "The effect of theoretically-based imagery scripts on field hockey performance." *Journal of Sport Behavior 24*, 408–419.

Smith, D., Wright, C., Allsopp, A., and Westhead, H. (2007) "It's all in the mind: PETTLEP-based imagery and sports performance." *Journal of Applied Sport Psychology 19*, 80–92.

Smith, D., Wright, C.J., and Cantwell, C. (2008) "Beating the bunker: The effect of PETLLEP imagery on golf bunker shot performance." *Research Quarterly for Exercise and Sport 79*, 385–391.

Sordoni, C., Hall, C., and Forwell, L. (2000) "The use of imagery by athletes during injury rehabilitation." *Journal of Sport Rehabilitation 9*, 329–338.

Ungerleider, S. (2005) *Mental Training for Peak Performance*. Emmaus, PA: Rodale Inc.

Vealey, R.S. and Forlenza, S.T. (2015) "Understanding and Using Imagery in Sport." In J. Williams (ed.) *Applied Sport Psychology: Personal Growth to Peak Performance*, 7th edition. New York, NY: McGraw-Hill.

Wakefield, C.J. and Smith, D. (2009) "Impact of differing frequencies of PETTLEP imagery on netball shooting performance." *Journal of Imagery Research in Sport and Physical Activity 4*, 1.

Waskiewicz, Z. and Zajac, A. (2001) "The imagery and motor skills acquisition." *Biology of Sport 18*, 1, 71–83.

Weinberg, R. (2008) "Does imagery work? Effects on performance and mental skills." *Journal of Imagery Research in Sport and Physical Activity 3*, 1.

Weinberg, R., Butt, J., Knight, B., Burke, K. L., and Jackson, A. (2003) "The relationship between the use and effectiveness of imagery: An exploratory investigation." *Journal of Applied Sport Psychology 15*, 26–40.

White, A. and Hardy, L. (1998) "An in-depth analysis of the uses of imagery by high-level slalom canoeists and artistic gymnasts." *The Sport Psychologist 12*, 387–403.

Wohldmann, E.L., Healy, A.F., and Bourne, L.E. (2007) "Pushing the limits of imagination: Mental practice for learning sequences." *Journal of Experimental Psychology 33*, 254–361.

Wright, C. and Smith, D.K. (2007) "The effect of a short-term PETTLEP imagery intervention on a cognitive task." *Journal of Imagery Research in Sport and Physical Activity 2*, 1.

Wright, C. and Smith, D. (2007) "The effect of PETTLEP imagery on strength performance." *International Journal of Sport and Exercise Psychology 7*, 18.

Chapter 23

Imagery in the Assessment and Treatment of Trauma in Military Veterans

Judith A. Lyons

Imagery plays a key role in posttraumatic stress disorder's (PTSD) symptom presentation in the form of intrusive memories, nightmares, and dissociative flashbacks. Trauma-related imagery can be used in the assessment of clients' physiological and emotional reactivity for diagnostic purposes. Imagery is also a core component of some of the therapies used to treat PTSD, particularly exposure therapy and nightmare rescripting.

The Role of Imagery in Assessing PTSD

The APA's current diagnostic criteria for PTSD include the occurrence of a traumatic stressor plus persistent distressing/functionally-impairing symptoms in the following categories: intrusion symptoms, avoidance, changes in mood/cognition, and changes in arousal/reactivity (American Psychiatric Association 2013). Several of the symptoms within these criterion categories involve or are elicited by trauma-related imagery.

Intrusion symptoms in adults who have PTSD commonly include recurrent, involuntary, intrusive memories and nightmares of the traumatic event. Intrusive thoughts that typify PTSD are usually like a video clip that replays, not just recurrent rumination. The extent to which the client's intrusive memories involve specific imagery of the trauma is often diagnostic. More abstract ruminations such as a sense of loss or regret associated with the event often occur, but without specific imagery they would not typify PTSD.

Nightmares, particularly in adults, also tend to clearly be replays of the actual event with minimal, if any, symbolic distortion. In many cases, the individual awakens at or just prior to a peak point of terror/distress in the trauma experience. The person often cannot return to sleep and may even avoid sleep the next night. Determining what was occurring in the event sequence at the point of awakening, or what would have occurred just after the point at which the nightmare was interrupted, is often important in identifying the most crucial part of the trauma.

Dissociative reactions that involve reliving and even behaviorally reenacting the event (i.e. flashbacks) are less common but may also occur. In a flashback, the trauma imagery becomes substituted for most or all of the person's current surroundings (a veteran standing in their own driveway might suddenly see a Humvee or tank in place of their pickup truck, and their landscaping may suddenly appear as desert or jungle flora). The images tend to take on a narrow focus that can ignore or distort any surrounding context that does not conform to the traumatic memory.

Each of these types of intrusive re-experiencing, as well as any other reminders of the traumatic event, can elicit high levels of physiological arousal accompanied by significant distress that can persist for hours. During the 1980s and 1990s, numerous studies sought to tap these phenomena as diagnostic tools by measuring physiological reactivity to trauma-related cues (Orr 1994). These protocols proved to be too cumbersome and expensive, and their results did not concur consistently with diagnoses from clinical interviews, and so they have not been adopted for routine diagnostic use. The psychophysiological assessment paradigm most commonly used today (primarily in research programs) assesses reactivity to script-driven imagery: it measures the person's physical and emotional reactions to hearing a description of their individual trauma story (Bauer *et al.* 2013).

Using Imagery to Treat PTSD

Evidence-based therapies for PTSD include cognitive behavioral therapies such as cognitive processing therapy, exposure therapy, and eye-movement desensitization and reprocessing (EMDR) (Watts *et al.* 2013). Imagery plays a key role in both exposure therapies and EMDR, but its mechanism of action in EMDR remains subject to debate. Therefore, the focus in this chapter will be on exposure-based therapies, especially the implosive therapy model espoused by Keane (Keane *et al.* 1989; Lyons and Keane 1989) and Foa's prolonged exposure therapy (Foa, Hembree, and Rothbaum 2007).

EXPOSURE THERAPIES

Mowrer's (1960) two-factor model of learning provides a succinct framework for understanding exposure therapies and making clinical decisions during therapy. Mowrer focused on fear-based learning, but the model is also useful for understanding the persistence and spread of other negative reactions following trauma. Mowrer built on the idea that we learn to fear stimuli that have been associated with an aversive event, particularly those preceding and thus predictive of the aversive experience. He explained that this occurs via standard classical conditioning (the first factor), in which a naturally innocuous conditioned stimulus comes to elicit much the same fear that the original threat elicited. PTSD diagnostic Criterion B in DSM-5 (APA 2013)—intrusion symptoms like intense/ prolonged distress or physiologic reactivity after exposure to stimuli related to the trauma—coincide with this component of Mowrer's model.

Because fear is so unpleasant, Mowrer theorized that we are motivated to try to escape it. Our avoidance behavior is reinforced via instrumental conditioning (the second factor) as we not only learn to attempt to avoid the original traumatic event but also to avoid any reminders of that traumatic experience. Applied to PTSD, this establishes a self-perpetuating feedback loop that maintains the fear of a growing number of stimuli, as the traumatized person avoids not only reminders but also reminders of reminders. As the conditioned stimuli generalize, more things or events are avoided, the fear and other negative associations remain unchallenged, and the person's life becomes more and more constricted. We see this component of Mowrer's model in the deliberate avoidance of reminders, thoughts, feelings, or cues related to the traumatic event that comprises DSM-5's PTSD diagnostic Criterion C.

To illustrate Mowrer's model, consider the hypothetical case of a soldier who was in a crowded market on a very hot day when a suicide bomber detonated a massive explosion that killed several people. The classical conditioning component of Mowrer's model explains why the soldier might later feel anxious in any crowded venue, like a theater. It would also account for a pattern of increased distress on days when the weather was particularly warm. The instrumental conditioning (conditioned avoidance) component of the model explains why the soldier might avoid going to his son's ball games that are played in a crowded stadium. It would also explain why he becomes so anxious in a checkout line at the grocery store that he has to abandon his cart full of purchases and flee the store if the line moves too slowly.

Viewing trauma treatment through the lens of Mowrer's model, re-exposure to the actual traumatic event (e.g. another bombing, being shot at again, being raped again) is not therapeutic because the same aversive response will be repeated, and this will serve as yet another conditioning trial to consolidate the fear associated with surrounding situational cues. To create a therapeutic extinction trial that can reduce this paired association, the naturally occurring non-threatening cues from the original scenario will need to be experienced in the absence of the aversive components of the trauma (without pain or other aversive components like shaming). Using imagery to reconstruct the traumatic experience in a safe and supportive environment allows the client to practice repeated extinction trials.

In the hypothetical example of the veteran in the market bombing, the therapist would guide their client to repeatedly imagine the event from start to finish. As the client's distress level gradually reduced across repetitions, the focus would shift to segments of the incident that remained the most troubling. The goal would be to attain reductions in distress levels within and across sessions as the client increased his or her sense of safety even when presented with reminders of the trauma.

The key in exposure therapies, therefore, is the presentation of reminders/triggers/cues in a safe context. Early implosive therapy procedures incorporated several rapport-building progressive muscle-relaxation training and imagery-skills training sessions prior to the core intervention of walking the trauma survivor repeatedly through imagery of their trauma in the safety of the therapy office (Lyons and Keane 1989). Multisensory imagery skills were developed by conducting progressive muscle-relaxation training with guided imagery based on a scene the client has identified as a soothing place for them (like the beach or mountains). Once the client had sequentially relaxed each group of muscles, they were asked to visualize the soothing scene. The therapist helped the client tune in to each sensory modality by interjecting cues like, "See how blue the sky looks," "Feel the soft breeze on your face," and by querying, "What are you feeling?" and, "What is your focus on right now?" Once the client was skilled at fully engaging in a soothing scene (including kinesthetic sensations, thoughts, and feelings), the training would move to engaging in a variant of the soothing scene never previously experienced (such as flying over the scene with bird-like wings).

As previously described, the therapist would coach the client to ensure active engagement in all levels of this hypothetical scene, with all sensory modalities included. The purpose of allocating significant session time to development of a peaceful scenario was for the client and therapist to learn to build a scene together, for the client to be able to fully engage, to learn to follow prompts to shift or intensify their focus, and to learn a coping skill that the client could use to reduce their anxiety. The vast majority of clients found this approach very relaxing, and it helped build rapport and trust before tackling the more difficult trauma imagery. Several of these preparatory sessions would be followed by several sessions 2–2.5 hours in duration that included relaxation, then a period of trauma imagery, followed by relaxation. The recommended session frequency was at least once or twice per week to gain the benefit of massed practice.

The exposure therapy that the Department of Veterans Affairs in the United States has most recently adopted is the protocol developed by Foa and colleagues called prolonged exposure therapy. Imagery still plays a central role in building exposure to the actual traumatic memory, but less of a role in relaxation training compared with the protocol of Keane and colleagues. In this protocol (Foa *et al.* 2007), breathing retraining rather than progressive muscle relaxation and guided imagery is used during the initial sessions to develop coping skills.

The Foa protocol includes audio recording the exposure segment of each session for the client to listen to privately at home each day between sessions. Unlike the Keane model of implosive therapy—in which a reduction of avoidance behaviors in daily life was expected to occur spontaneously once the conditioned distress to trauma-related cues had been extinguished—the Foa model built *in vivo* practice sessions into their protocol. A hierarchical list is developed of situations the client avoids because of associations to the original trauma: for example, a person who was sexually assaulted may avoid casual and intimate touch and dating; a person whose Humvee was blown up by an explosive device buried in the road may avoid all driving, dangerously swerve around debris or potholes on the road, and be unable to walk near anomalous objects on a sidewalk. The client then systematically practices doing one of these activities daily, without distractions, until the associated distress recedes. The recommended session frequency is the same as for the Keane protocol, once or twice weekly, and the total number of sessions is similar (10–15); but each session is briefer, 90 minutes rather than 120–150 minutes as in the Keane protocol.

Foa and colleagues explain the active mechanism in exposure therapy somewhat differently than Mowrer/Keane and colleagues. Foa's theory, like Mowrer's, includes the concept that escape responses are learned and reinforced by the reduction in fear that results. However, her emotional processing theory involves more components and places a greater emphasis on cognition. To summarize it in a very simplified way: Foa's theory sees the goals of therapy as the modification of cognitive fear structures and the reduction of the response to trauma-related stimuli due to repetition of those stimuli (habituation). While finding no objections to Foa's theoretical model, this author finds the Mowrer extinction model to be as effective and also more efficient for explaining exposure therapy to clients and trainees, as well as for planning how to individualize care for a given client. The Mowrer model is flexible enough to help therapists decide how to incorporate exposure to disgust or to various hypothetical permutations of the traumatic event that elicit feelings like shame, guilt, blame, or anger in addition to fear-related cues related to the factual event.

Mowrer's model provides a clear framework for determining whether a given client is likely to benefit from exposure therapy. For example, a client with psychotic delusions might benefit from exposure therapy in spite of active concurrent psychosis as long as their delusions do not impinge on their ability to experience safety during the therapy sessions. On the other hand, exposure therapy may be contraindicated if the client's delusions include a paranoid idea that the therapist is out to hurt them. This client might experience exposure therapy sessions as conditioning trials that would ultimately reinforce their conditioned fears and avoidance, rather than as therapeutic extinction trials. Similarly, a client who tends to dissociate every time they imagine the trauma, and who cannot remain sufficiently grounded to retain awareness that the trauma is not actually recurring, would be unlikely to benefit from exposure therapy. This is because the dissociation will take them directly back to the emotions and arousal of the actual trauma, and as a result extinction would not be achieved.

Mowrer's model also addresses the common question of how imagining a horrible trauma deliberately and repeatedly can be helpful when years of re-experiencing it in nightmares, intrusive thoughts, and flashbacks have not made things better. Exposure therapy works because the experience of the original trauma is titrated in a safe, controlled manner and escape behaviors are discouraged, which paves the way for the extinction of learned responses. The client's willingness to directly and voluntarily recount and reimagine the traumatic event repeatedly and systematically is a reversal of the usual avoidance of any and all reminders. In contrast, nightmares and other intrusive re-experiencing symptoms occur without voluntary control over the timing or content, and so they feel very unsafe. Therefore, the person tends to awaken, distract, act out, and otherwise escape their distress, and the self-perpetuating cycle continues and expands.

When exposure therapy for PTSD was first introduced in the 1980s, there was some opposition that exposure therapy was unethical and dangerous because it could reduce the reality-based fear that signals the need for adaptive safety behaviors. Their argument was that the world can be an unsafe place and we should not try to train people to think otherwise, because then they may not exercise due caution. I encountered this wariness most often when talking with colleagues who worked at rape crisis centers. However, Mower's model easily counters this concern because the goal is only to extinguish the link between fear and *inherently safe* stimuli, not to attenuate the natural fear response itself. It also explains why you would not expect exposure therapy to be effective if the client is undergoing a new situation that closely resembles the original trauma while they are undergoing the therapy.

For example, imagine a veteran whose primary trauma was the helpless horror of seeing a buddy slowly die from battle wounds during a protracted siege. If that veteran sought PTSD treatment while also visiting his beloved wife in a hospice facility each evening during the final weeks of her life, prolonged exposure might not be the best treatment at that particular time due to the similarity between the current real-life impending loss and the past trauma. A more cognitively-based approach like cognitive processing therapy might be preferable in this circumstance.

Contextual primers can be used to assist the client in accessing multisensory memories/imagery. Rubbing sand in their hands (to bring back a desert context), handling raw meat (to simulate the feel of mangled bodies), recordings of gunfire, video clips of storms, photos of distraught children: a variety of tangible objects can be used to help set the stage if the client has difficulty fully engaging in trauma imagery without assistance. Virtual reality presentations of combat and other trauma experiences are available commercially. These prerecorded media do not allow the therapist to individualize and redirect the image on the spot as fluidly as can be done with imaginal immersion in the scene, but they may be advantageous for clients who have trouble producing imagery spontaneously.

The more vivid and multisensory the imagery, the more effective the treatment is because it pulls in more of the vast network of cues that are associated with the traumatic event. Imagining the sounds of vehicles and weapons, visualizing shimmering waves of heat, imagining the heat of the desert sun, feeling the fatigue of long hours in the heat, and the weight of carrying a heavy pack and weapon help bring the totality of the experience into focus to ensure that no significant cues are overlooked.

Across sessions the client visualizes the actual trauma as it occurred, and they may be asked to zoom in and out temporally and spatially for context, and in the later stages of therapy to focus on certain hot spots within the memory that are especially troubling. In Keane's protocol, the later stages of therapy involve imagining hypothetical versions of the event in order to address issues that may be more cognitively-based rather than fear-based. For example, "What do you want to tell your dying buddy? Go ahead, say it to him now;" "Picture your spouse becoming aware of the fact that you were raped. What is his/her reaction?" In Foa's protocol, such issues can be discussed during the client-therapist discussion ("processing") that follows the imaginal component of each intervention session.

One caveat for therapists that applies to their own well-being during the imaginal segments of these sessions: treating PTSD exposes the therapist to the risk of secondary traumatization. In other words, they may begin to intrusively re-experience some of the client's imagery and angst. While it is more beneficial for the client to imagine the traumatic scene from a first-person, real-time perspective—which makes the experience most vivid—it is protective for the therapist to avoid trying to imagine the client's experience in the first person. If the therapist imagines the scene from a "helicopter perspective" or as though viewed on a movie screen, this will provide enough distancing that the risk of secondary traumatization is minimized. However, a therapist will occasionally need to risk taking a first-person perspective to hypothesize what may have occurred during gaps in the client's memory or during segments that the client is unwilling to describe aloud.

NIGHTMARE RESCRIPTING

Another imagery-based treatment for PTSD that many programs are adopting, generally as an adjunctive treatment, is nightmare rescripting. Studies of this technique have been fewer in number and are not as robust in design as studies of exposure therapies.

The risk of mixing theoretically inconsistent interventions warrants mention here. Krakow et al. (2001) reported symptom reduction in a majority of female sexual assault survivors following a three-session intervention (sessions of one to three hours in duration). The intervention is based on the premise that nightmares are partially a function of habit. The client is encouraged to change their dream in any way they wish and to practice visualizing the revised dream for five to 20 minutes daily. Contrary to the exposure therapies previously described, in nightmare rescripting clients are actively dissuaded from recounting or imagining the original trauma. From an exposure-therapy perspective, this would seem to be encouraging avoidance rather than applying response-prevention strategies to counter avoidance tendencies. Therefore, attempting to conduct rescripting and exposure therapy concurrently would seem inherently contradictory. However, rescripting may be worth considering as an alternative if a client is not a good candidate for exposure therapy, and if their PTSD symptom presentation is limited largely to nightmares.

A variant of the rescripting protocol that incorporates an exposure therapy component (albeit rather briefly) has been used with veterans (Long *et al.* 2011). Long and colleagues expanded the protocol from three to six sessions. The added sessions initially involve exposure to the original nightmare narrative, and later sessions shift to practicing the rescripted version of the dream.

Intrusive re-experiencing of trauma images is among the core diagnostic criteria of PTSD, as are the distress and psychophysiological reactivity that such re-experiencing elicits. The power of imagery can be harnessed clinically for both the assessment and the treatment of PTSD. Imagery plays a major role in the symptom pattern that defines PTSD, and it is also central in successful PTSD treatment protocols like exposure therapies and nightmare rescripting.

References

American Psychiatric Association (2013) *Diagnostic and Statistical Manual of Mental Disorders,* 5th edition. Washington, DC: American Psychiatric Association.

Bauer, M.R., Ruef, A.M., Pineles, S.L., Japuntich, S.J, *et al.* (2013) "Psychophysiological assessment of PTSD: A potential research domain criteria construct." *Psychological Assessment 25,* 3, 1037–1043.

Foa, E.B., Hembree, E.A., and Rothbaum, B.O. (2007) *Prolonged Exposure Therapy for PTSD: Emotional Processing of Traumatic Experienced, Therapist Guide.* New York, NY: Oxford University Press.

Keane, T.M., Fairbank, J.A., Caddell, J.M., and Zimmering, R.T. (1989) "Implosive (flooding) therapy reduces symptoms of PTSD in Vietnam combat veterans." *Behavior Therapy 20,* 245–260.

Krakow, B., Hollifield, M., Johnston, L., Koss, M., *et al.* (2001) "Imagery rehearsal therapy for chronic nightmares in sexual assault survivors with posttraumatic stress disorder: A randomized controlled trial." *Journal of the American Medical Association 286,* 5, 537–545.

Long, M.E., Hammons, M.E., Davis, J.L., Frueh, B.C., *et al.* (2011) "Imagery rescripting and exposure group treatment of posttraumatic nightmares in Veterans with PTSD." *Journal of Anxiety Disorders 25,* 4, 531–535.

Mowrer, O.H. (1960) *Learning Theory and Behavior.* New York, NY: Wiley.

Lyons, J.A. and Keane, T.M. (1989) "Implosive therapy for the treatment of combat-related PTSD." *Journal of Traumatic Stress 2,* 2, 137–152.

Orr, S.P. (1994) "An overview of psychophysiological studies of PTSD." *PTSD Research Quarterly 5*, 1, 1–6.

Watts, B.V., Schnurr, P.S., Mayo, L., Young-Xu, Y., Weeks, W.B., and Friedman, M.J. (2013) "Meta-analysis of the efficacy of treatments for posttraumatic stress disorder." *Journal of Clinical Psychiatry 74*, 6, e541–e550.

Chapter 24

When Imagination Leads

Cultural Leadership and the Power of Transformative Learning[1]

Aftab Omer

The Primacy of Imagination

Imagination is at the core of human experience and is the essence of human consciousness. We are in imagination even as we are reading about imagination. Imagination is primary in any inquiry into human knowledge, consciousness, experience, healing, and transformation. Imagination shapes, amplifies, and integrates the cognitive, affective, and sensory dimensions of our experience: thinking, feeling, and sensing are all constituted by imagination. It is the bedrock of the participatory reality we humans experience. This is not to be confused with what is "imaginary" in the sense of possibility and what is "real" in the sense of actuality. Rather, the capacity for imagination brings the ability to creatively perceive and handle complex situations with an immediacy of insight and clarity.

When we recognize someone as a leader, it is implied that others are following. However, we might ask: Who or what is the leader following?

When leadership is most creative—and sometimes most harmful— that leader is following their imagination. Our ability to follow where imagination leads in the service of the greater good is of profound significance to both our individual and collective development. This chapter explores how individuals and groups like families, organizations, communities, and societies can be transformed by following where the imagination leads. Through imagination a much larger story, the human journey, continuously unfolds into our individual and collective life.

The Imaginal Core of Experience

There is an imaginal core to our human experience that functions as a bridge between the interior and exterior dimensions of personal reality as well as the individual and collective levels of social reality. Imagination both integrates and transforms our experience. Traumatic experience is healed through the restoration and liberation of imagination. Imagination helps us to link actuality with possibility, past with future, and self with other. When our experience has been disrupted, dislocated, and damaged, returning to the deep flow of core imagery has a healing impact. Empathic imagination is the mode of imagination that is most relevant to relationships between humans as well as our human connection to the *more than human*. Empathic imagination is a great healer and reconciler of divisions among individuals and communities.

The Gating of Experience

Learning to follow imagination is a competency that is achieved through liberation from narrow, culturally enforced identity frames that constrain imagination. Imagination is deepest and most valuable when it is allowed to arise and flow spontaneously, without being subjected to policing by personal identity and/or representatives of culture. Like breathing, imagination has its own flow and rhythm that is reciprocally shaped by the ever-changing human and natural landscape.

The individual and social dynamic of gatekeeping inhibits and distorts the spontaneous flow of imagination, resisting and restricting experience, demanding perfection and conformity and thus hindering the individual from taking risks, seeking out new experience, and transforming a static and familiar identity. Gatekeeping is an adaptive dynamic that may arise as a protective measure: it can help living systems survive under specific circumstances, but it becomes maladaptive when those circumstances change. Because of its protective nature, when we are hurt or threatened by others one of its essential mechanisms is to defend us from the experience of dependence on others and protect us from failure—at the cost of denying us new experiences.

Considered more broadly: each culture has its own complex, historically derived belief systems and patterns and norms of behavior, all of which combine to restrict the experience of its citizens beginning at birth. As with individual gatekeeping, over time these systems become internalized. We think of these culturally sourced restrictive patterns as cultural gatekeepers. They function in individuals, families, organizations, communities, and societies to ensure conformity with a culture's current rules, norms, values, and taboos via cultural trance and coercion. Cultural gatekeepers are the personification of collective dynamics that, in a given culture, resist cultural transformation.

The lynchpin of a consumerist economic system is how effectively imagination can be captured and enslaved. When imagination becomes formulaic and is fed through the channels of mass advertising, we become consumers of predigested, suburbanized, and canned imagery. A vicious cycle begins of the slave-enslaving-others. Experience becomes colonized, dominated by the imagination of others. This canning and selling of experience blocks the wild, spontaneous, and unique imagery that can heal, transform, and lead individuals and collectives to create broader dimensions of value and meaning.

One of the greatest shadows of educational institutions is their service as colonizers of our experience: consider, for example, standardized testing. When institutions focus almost exclusively on the transmission of information, there is a fundamental derailment of the learning process. The acquisition of information is secondary, not primary, to learning and development. Self- and imagination-directed learning, on the other hand, is essential to our development. In this approach, the self learns to follow where imagination leads. When imagination leads, new domains of awareness are liberated to which new information can adhere. When the learner is free from constraint to joyously and creatively follow the flow of their imagination, information becomes part of the learner, rather than baggage the learner carries. When learning is rooted in this flow of imagination, it transforms our perceptions, enabling us to acquire information as needed for creative and functional endeavors.

Transformative Learning Catalyzes Development: The Journey to Complexity

Life on our planet is evolving into greater and greater complexity, and imagination is a primary vehicle for this journey. An essential feature in this evolution is the appearance of discreet and stable levels of human development. When we follow our imagination, we are challenged by the requirements of more complex developmental thresholds. These challenges require an approach that draws on the imagination, not one that is based in informational learning. *Transformative learning* works with imagination, not information.

Human culture has transformed in significant ways with each historical epoch. The historical and cross-cultural view of transformative learning suggests that this process has been ubiquitous in the human cultural journey. When we consider, for example, the initiatory practices of diverse cultures, we recognize the significance of socially integrated transformative learning in the life of human communities. Contemporary postmodern communities, without necessarily using the term transformative learning, take secular approaches to this process within multiple institutional domains and at various levels of human systems.

Transformative learning is learning that fosters the emergence of distinct human capacities in a unique and interconnected way. It takes us beyond acquiring information and technical skills to developing capacities, habits, integrated skills, and values. Such learning always entails a shift in our perceptual lenses, enabling more complex and emergent landscapes. Competencies like these enable individuals, communities, and organizations to become capable of wise and creative action. Transformative learning entails shifts that have been characterized as shifts in perspective, perceptual lenses, core beliefs, schemas, mental models, and mindsets. Transformative learning is messy, difficult, dangerous, and threatening. It is natural to turn away from what might be perceived as risky or dangerous—and so individuals in transformative learning settings must choose to forego the comfort of familiarity.

Overwhelming or intense experiences and the associated intrinsic threat/fear of "losing our mind," our normative identity, goes with the landscape of transformative learning. However, as Plato stated over 2000 years ago in his *Phaedrus* dialogue, "There are two types of madness, one arising from human disease, the other when heaven sets us free from established convention" (Plato 1973, pp.80–81). In a very real sense, profound shifts in perspectives, mindsets, and mental models are often experienced as losing one's familiar mind or identity. But a corresponding outcome is emotion being transmuted into capacities: for example, the emotion of fear transmuting into the capacity of courage, or the emotion of shame transformed into the capacity of conscience.

We have been acculturated to develop habits that resist and avoid the perils that we sense await us if we allow the full depth and measure of our experience to emerge. As such, it is a natural tendency—even for those who are drawn to learning environments that support transformative learning—to avoid fully being with one's experience. It is important to note that if there is no resistance to the learning experience from the individual or collective participants, then it is likely that a transformative threshold has not yet been reached. This implies that our felt resistance to our experience is a signal that a transformative learning threshold has been engaged. A comprehensive understanding of this type of learning therefore calls for an understanding of the dynamics of resistance and the barriers to transformative learning.

Types of Transformative Experiences

Four distinct dynamisms serve to contain the actual risk and the perceived threat of learning experiences that have the potential to transform identity:

- *Diversifying*: Working with multiple nodes of identity as well as states and structures of consciousness

- *Deepening*: Engaging the symbolic depths of experience through story and myth

- *Embodying*: Reconnecting the somatic dimension of experience with the cognitive and emotional dimensions

- *Personalizing*: Cohering diverse and new experiences of personal identity in the present moment.

In the course of individual development, an *experiencing I* emerges into consciousness. This *experiencing I* is embodied but has undergone enough significant cycles of integrative work that dissociative adaptations to trauma and stress do not impinge on our consciousness.

Transformative learning appears to be as old as culture itself. In fact, transformative learning is arguably the engine of cultural evolution. Excavating its mysterious history and even prehistory provides a window into both individual human development and our collective cultural evolution. The mythologies of both ancient and contemporary indigenous cultures provide numerous metaphors for the journey of transformative learning. One such example would be the journey of Odysseus, whose decades-long journey finding his way home after the Trojan War serves as a metaphor for the gift of deep insight and understanding that difficult journeys can offer us. Our long human journey, much of it shrouded in the mists of time, may be imagined as a passage toward wisdom that follows the aspirations embodied in the name of our species, *homo sapiens*.

The receptivity, openness, and curiosity of "beginner's mind" is essential to transformative learning, because every transformative leap forward in competency is preceded by a liminal period of disorientation and de-integration. An effective holding environment that is sustained by a supportive learning community along with a disciplined facilitator and/or team has always been essential for ensuring a safe passage across the threshold phase of this kind of learning. It is also clear that learners progress at the speed of their own practice, not at the predefined speed of the learning activity or the facilitator's wishes. Transformative learning is much more like a sea journey than a land journey, in that there are no landmarks at sea.

Transformative learning works through encountering failure: certain beliefs, belief systems, mental maps, and even our identities must "fail" in order for more complexity to emerge. However, this kind of failure can be risky. Just as the caterpillar who fails to emerge from the chrysalis as a butterfly is doomed, individuals can become stuck in the failed places and not emerge into more complex levels of perception. We can see that transformative learning necessitates bringing discipline to the experience of failure. Such discipline entails the understanding that without failure, there is no transformation—and so we need to relearn our relationship to failure. Transformative learning flourishes when learners act with developmental humility and facilitators act with developmental compassion.

Modes of Imagination

Imagination may be further differentiated into various modes of imagining that are sense-, capacity-, and context-specific. Attending to images enables both our recognition of differentiation and the integrative imperative of experiencing. This deepening and diversification of experience is an encounter with "otherness," those aspects of one's experience of self and other that can evoke barriers to recognition, empathy, engagement, and understanding. Otherness can be understood as difference experienced problematically. Differences perceived as other may be denied, disavowed, suppressed, repressed, tolerated, or trivialized instead of being recognized and engaged in order to enhance and diversify learning.

The Post-Cultural Possibilities of Development

As several strands of developmental theory have articulated, development proceeds from pre-conventional to conventional, and then to post-conventional levels. Furthermore, there are intimations and intuitions of developmental complexity that transcend even the post-conventional level. This next phase or level of development can be termed post-cultural, implying that the individual has deeply integrated the norms and habits of their local culture but they are not constrained by its conventions, assumptions, premises, and epistemic prejudices.

To be developmentally post-cultural is to be able to act on and shape culture, not just to be embedded in it. To be the piano player, not the piano keys. Great poets and other artists can be understood developmentally as post-cultural and hence able to make profound contributions to the creation of culture. For the cultural leader, culture is an object to be acted on, not just the prevailing subjectivity where they find themselves embedded. Cultural leadership can implement and facilitate transformative learning at the collective level, described in the next section.

Only when a person has evolved from self-absorption to self-possession does post-cultural consciousness become possible. Post-cultural consciousness does not take culture as its primary source of meaning, guidance, and understanding. In post-cultural development, there is essential immunity from cultural gatekeeping. The collective field of habits that constitute culture is no longer the primary shaper of consciousness and behavior for a post-cultural adult.

What can lead individuals into a post-cultural life? Following the imagination. Imagination both creates and transcends culture: it is pre-, trans-, and post-cultural. In order for imagination to lead an individual or a collective, wise discernment is needed to interpret the guidance condensed in the existing flow of images to productive and useful ends. The regulation of instinct is also an essential dimension of the evolution of culture. Post-cultural development requires a whole new relationship to instinctual reality that is bound neither to our animal nature nor by culture, but that is encouraged by a potent relationship to a rich imagination mediated by wise discernment. Shame-discerning awareness is one aspect of post-cultural consciousness. Ultimately, wisdom is a fruit of post-cultural development.

Cultural Leadership: Engaging Transformative Learning at Collective Levels of Complexity

On a balmy morning in the spring of 1930, on the anniversary of the Amritsar massacre, Mohandas Gandhi set out to lead a procession of 78 people to march the 240 miles to India's western coast.[2] As they walked, thousands joined the journey to the sea to gather salt. This simple act profoundly and creatively challenged the British law that limited the manufacture and sale of salt to only those who were licensed by British authorities. This licensing regulation had enabled the British to tax even the poorest of the poor for their personal use of salt—a daily requirement for human functioning, especially in India's brutal heat. Gandhi's leadership of the "Salt March" became the defining moment in the cultural transformation that was to culminate in India's sovereignty.

Just four years after the Salt March, on another continent Adolf Hitler would orchestrate the massive spectacle of the Nuremberg Rallies in which thousands of Nazi troops entranced many more thousands of German citizens. The Nazis went to great effort to design elaborate speeches, banners, marching bands, and stunning architecture to stage these rallies, which were skillfully filmed and broadcast to further disseminate their propaganda. The Nuremberg Rallies would take their place in history as significant events in the consolidation of Nazi domination.

Separated by only four years, Gandhi's march and Hitler's rallies were momentous historical events whose influence defined and determined the vast cultural transformations that were to take place in subsequent decades. In both these events, each leader envisioned major cultural transformations, and each chose to use large collective events as catalysts for their vision.

These two events, however, were fundamentally different in both their intention and their outcome. The Salt March is an example of transgression structured as a *creative ritual*, while the Nuremberg Rallies are an example of *repressive ritualism*. Through the Nuremberg Rallies, Hitler—who had once unsuccessfully sought admission to the most prominent art school in Vienna—abused the transformative power of art and ritual to intensify Germany's cultural trance, a collective state of complacency and passivity that limits imagination and transformative potential. Conversely, Gandhi inspired an experience of collective sovereignty as an *awakening* from cultural trance. Gandhi's intuitive transgression of the prevailing laws and cultural norms provides a stunning example of creative cultural transformation.

Our families, communities, organizations, and societies all function within distinct and overlapping cultural patterns. Human systems, including cultures, are configured as a web of habits with a normative center and a periphery. The interaction between center and periphery is organized differently during steady-state periods versus periods of change. During steady-state periods, the conventional center of a culture is dense with rules, norms, taboos, and consensual notions of "truth," while the creative periphery is marginalized and remains disenfranchised, disempowered, and at worst, scapegoated.

In contrast, during periods of instability, conflict, or chaos, the creative periphery comes into dynamic interaction with the culture's center.

During such times of transition, the cultural core can become spacious with receptivity for the new and unknown. By engaging and recognizing differences that were previously denied, suppressed, and/or trivialized, a culture's web of habits can then transform into greater complexity by incorporating the perspectives and practices found at the periphery. The dynamic flow between a spacious center and a creative periphery is central to the possibility of creative cultural transformation and keeps the culture vital and adaptive.

Cultural leaders catalyze conscious, difficult interactions between a culture's center and its periphery, and they may recognize this as the engine of creative cultural transformation. They take principled and imaginative actions that engender new and unexpected meanings. Cultural leadership is distinct from political and administrative leadership. While political leaders primarily make rules and administrative leaders typically enforce them, cultural leaders intuit ways to transgress those rules that inhibit a greater and more complex future.

We deepen our participation in our collective life, our life with others, through the engagement of differences: as has been noted, this means encountering "otherness." Much of human social life is organized to avoid dealing with differences, which may be denied, disavowed, suppressed, repressed, tolerated, or trivialized. Creative transgression is a way to break the cultural trance that denies difference and to catalyze the recognition and engagement of those differences between people that have been denied, suppressed, or trivialized. Creative transgressions are characterized by three distinct features: principled actions, imaginative actions, and conscious sacrifice.

PRINCIPLED ACTION

A creative transgression is principled when it is in alignment with the deeper truths. It is this alignment that gives principled action its potency. It was unjust and exploitative of the British colonizers to tax the making and selling of salt. Principled action requires the transgressor to have a deep relationship with passionate objectivity, which is comprised of a quality of emotional engagement as well as an objective perception of the necessities, meanings, and possibilities inherent in the present moment. Both Gandhi and Hitler employed ritual in their leadership: however, Gandhi's use of ritual was guided by principled action, while Hitler's was driven by unprincipled action.

IMAGINATIVE ACTION

A creative transgression is imaginative when it evokes a new, specific, and unexpected experience that "shakes up" its participants such that a subsequent labor of meaning-making becomes a necessity. In addition to its practical implications, the transgression then has symbolic impact. Symbols are images condensed with meanings. New or revitalized symbols disrupt the prevailing cultural fundamentalism that exists at the core of the culture. Gandhi focused on the salt laws as a symbol of British exploitation; his focus on making salt symbolized cultural sovereignty.

CONSCIOUS SACRIFICE

A creative transgression entails conscious sacrifice if it requires the willingness to experience loss of privilege, difficulty, and/or failure. Mohandas Gandhi was an attorney educated in London at the center of the British Empire. His understanding of British law was one source of the disciplined action he brought to his transgressive and provocative actions. His gradual transformation from a conventional barrister of means and status to a peasant leader clothed in simple white cotton garments also involved significant sacrifice. Paradoxically and sometimes ironically, coming into alignment with the objective truth of a personal or cultural situation entails a disciplined surrender in which we sacrifice what we wish were true for what is actually true.

In the Wake of Modernity

Modernity's cultural core has fallen apart. Its former appearance in terms of norms, values, and practices is no longer convincing. Most noteworthy, our planetary ecological crisis is also a cultural crisis: the ways we consume and share our planet's resources are ecologically unsustainable as well as profoundly oppressive to millions of people. Extreme economic injustice and other oppressive conditions are giving rise to chronic conflict at a global level.

After the traumatic cataclysms of the 20th century, there is a great need for personal and social healing. Like most personal healing, social healing also initially requires a series of difficult events that serve to wake a culture up from its entrenched trances. Creative cultural transformation can be an agonizing, dangerous, and sometimes ecstatic ordeal that promises personal and social healing in our time.

This kind of cultural transformation is facilitated by our capacity as cultural leaders to surrender through creative action to the meanings, possibilities, and necessities inherent in the present moment—which is required in order to recognize and engage the force of truth.

As individuals and groups find ways to engage in cultural leadership in a given moment, the culture's center strives to maintain the status quo and begins to push back—to resist the transformative potential of creative action. It is at this transformative threshold that cultural leaders are often scapegoated or even destroyed by the cultural gatekeepers who serve to maintain the culture trance. Through creative ritual utilizing improvisational methods, we can elicit these internalized gatekeepers in order to discern and give voice to these resistant forces. By literally giving voice to the destructive, culturally-installed voices that reside in us, their believability—and therefore their power—can be greatly reduced.

Given the magnitude and strength of these pervasive forces, in William Stafford's words, "It is important that awake people be awake" (Stafford 2007, para. 5). Even those of us who are committed to "waking up" can easily be drawn into a cultural trance that renders us passive, complacent, and collusive. For instance, it is common in workplaces for deeply thoughtful individuals to become bystanders when engagement with conflict, while risky, would be of service to the whole.

Cultural gatekeeping often manifests itself as scapegoating. Human collectives at all levels resort to scapegoating as a way of exiling and marginalizing certain differences, and cultures provide legitimacy for this excluding dynamic through their rigid adoption of rules, norms, taboos, and values. Leaders involved in transforming culture—those who consciously dare to question, challenge, or provoke the consensus at the cultural core—are very likely to be scapegoated. The cultural leader's capacity for imaginative action is also applied to creating actions that minimize the likelihood of scapegoating by the culture's fundamentalist center. Part of the creativity of a leader's transgression lies in the hermetic quality of their ability to blend and so mitigate the experience of being scapegoated. A dynamic relationship with Hermes, the trickster, will greatly serve our potential for effecting cultural transformation. Hermes' quick and shrewd moves can prove to be very powerful in what can seem like intractable David and Goliath situations in which "speaking truth to power" might only make the necessary changes even harder to effect.

Creative Transgression and Ritualization

Creative ritual allows us to turn *toward* the taboo aspects of experiences like greed, psychosis, grandiosity, hate, cruelty, victimization, and failure through an active unfolding of our living imagination. The lives and work of individuals like Shakespeare, Goethe, Blake, and Mother Theresa serve as examples. Creative ritual provides an occasion that encourages our surrender to the imagery emerging from the imagination and allows participants to be carried by the river of imagination. This act of surrender requires an entrance into the unknown and unfolding mystery of the present moment and the reception of images that can guide creative action in the moment. In this way, creative ritual creates a context and container for principled and imaginative transgression so that the exiled, rejected, devalued, and difficult parts of our experience can express themselves in ways that have new meanings and can carry us toward the future—even past our own resistance. Creative ritual is imagination in action that can tap into our *non-verbal* indigenous knowing, thereby releasing creative potentials into our collective life.

Cultural trauma entails a collective forgetting. In part, cultural trauma is healed by ritualizing cultural shame about the defeats, failures, and losses of the past; the imaginative art installation of the Holocaust memorial in postwar Germany is one example of such ritualization. Certainty and dogma, not failure, are our enemies. Again, failure is a trustworthy and loyal friend, in part because it illuminates both reality and necessity. Failure shows us where we actually are and helps define our learning edges. It brings our awareness in a decisive way to the present moment—which is where we must be in order to launch our next creative inquiry.

Through ritualizing the difficult experiences of shame and failure, we access our cultural memory necessary for the healing of cultural trauma, reversing the collective forgetting that cultural trauma induces. (Note that Gandhi chose the anniversary of the Amritsar massacre as the day his procession arrived at the beach to make salt.) Our recharged memory enables us paradoxically to "remember the future." The ancient Greeks understood this connection between memory and the future: they made their goddess of memory, Mnemosyne, the mother of the nine muses that invite and guide us into creative expression.

Working with cultural trauma is a delicate and perilous process. Creative ritual creates a climate of acceptance and curiosity that allows ritual trust to emerge which, when anchored within specific accountability processes and other cultural practices, can enable a temporary submerging of difference, ambivalence, conflict, and even hatred and revitalize the forces of *eros* between individuals or within a group. As we work through cultural trauma, renewed cultural practices of accountability, forgiveness, reconciliation, and conviviality emerge. A strong example is the Truth and Reconciliation work in post-apartheid South Africa, where perpetrator and victim took a leap of faith to face the other in ritualized dialogue.

The ritual trust that is built, however, is susceptible to being eroded by the densities and resistance of the cultural core. For example, Elizabeth Stanley writes of how the Truth and Reconciliation Commission partially failed, in that people implicated through the process nonetheless remained in positions of power, and individuals who were victims of atrocities and merited governmental support as victims of state crime have not received reparation (2001).

Cultural leaders employ creative ritual to heal cultural trauma and overcome resistance to cultural transformation. They do not advocate, prescribe, or even predict the specific goals and outcomes that the cultural transformation should manifest. Rather, like Gandhi, they ritualize the transgression, which offers opportunities to work with the wounds of cultural trauma. Attention to healing these wounds begins to loosen the packed densities of the conventional center, finally opening an empty space of *unknowing* through which the future is born.

When our actions emerge from a spacious center, we are creating the future: we open to our collective destiny through creative engagement and collaborative surrender. The spacious center is our gathering place: seated face to face around the fiery and perilous gifts of the unknown, without the density of certainty.

Integral Vision and Integral Praxis

An integral vision of transformation requires an integral praxis, the integration of theory and practice, reflection and action. Whether it's the transformation of individuals, groups, organizations, or societies, integral praxis means attending to all dimensions of reality: individual, collective, interior, and exterior. In assisting a couple caught in an entrenched conflict, for example, each person is asked to explore their individual interior experience as well as the ways that the culture the couple inhabits—the exterior of their lives—affects their perception of the conflict and the content of the conflict itself. We cannot wisely transform a part without sensing the whole.

When a culture's goal for education is to teach how to act creatively in the service of building and renewing our world, the integration of informational and transformative learning plays a pivotal role. Creative action, when it is pragmatically transgressive, transforms culture and enables new experience that shapes the next cycle of learning. In this way, cultural transformation supports the complex generational learning cycles that constitute the emergence of *collective wisdom*. While wisdom is not a fixed destination, it emerges during the journey of transformative learning within an archetypal pattern of eternal return. Wisdom may be understood as the ability to discern quality and to take creative action on behalf of quality. When cultural leaders wisely discern and follow where imagination leads, we create and transform our culture. May all our families, communities, organizations, and societies grow a spacious center where a true and imaginative future takes shape.

ENDNOTES

1. This article is a revised expansion of *The Spacious Center* and *Wisdom Journey* articles listed in the bibliography.
2. In 1919, the Amritsar Massacre took place when a crowd of nonviolent protesters gathered in Amritsar, Punjab to protest the arrest of two nationalist leaders, in spite of a recently decreed government curfew. The protesters were fired on by the British Indian Army, who directed their bullets largely toward the few open gates through which people were trying to escape. The British government reported 370 deaths and 1200 wounded, but non-governmental sources declared that over 1000 individuals died. This government-sanctioned violence resulted in widespread anger, fueling the Non-cooperation Movement of 1920–1922.

References

Plato (1973) *Phaedrus and the Seventh and Eighth Letters*. Translated by W. Hamilton. New York: Penguin.

Stafford, W. (2007) "A Ritual to Read to Each Other" in *Reflections*. Available at http://reflections.yale.edu/article/faith-and-citizenship-turbulent-times/ritual-read-each-other, accessed on February 7 2016.

Stanley, E. (2001) "Evaluating the Truth and Reconciliation Commission." *The Journal of Modern African Studies 39*, 3, 525–46.

Further Reading

Damasio, A. (1994) *Descarte's Error: Emotion, Reason, and the Human Brain*. New York, NY: Avon Books.

Dewey, J. (1933) *Democracy and Education*. New York, NY: Simon and Brown.

Freire, P. (1970) *Pedagogy of the Oppressed*. New York, NY: Continuum.

Habermas, J. (1984) *The Theory of Communicative Action*. Boston, MA: Beacon.

Homer (1965) *Odyssey of Homer*. Translated by. R. Lattimore. New York, NY: Harper.

Kuhn, T. (1970) *The Structure of Scientific Revolutions*. Chicago, IL: University of Chicago Press.

Omer, A. (2005) "The spacious center: Leadership and the creative transformation of culture." *Shift: At the Frontiers of Consciousness*, March–May.

Omer, A. (2003) "Between Columbine and the twin towers: Fundamentalist culture as a failure of imagination." *ReVision: A Journal of Consciousness and Transformation 26*, 2, 27–40.

Omer, A., Schwartz, M., Lubell, C., and Gall, R. (2012) "Wisdom Journey: The Role of Experience and Culture in Transformative Learning Praxis." Presented and published in proceedings of the *10th International Conference on Transformative Learning*, San Francisco, 2012.

Palmer, P.J. and Zajonc, A. (2010) *The Heart of Higher Education*. San Francisco, CA: Wiley.

Pink, D. (2005) *The Whole New Mind*. New York, NY: Penguin.

Varela, F.J., Thompson, E., and Rosch, E. (1991) *The Embodied Mind*. Cambridge, MA: MIT Press.

Appendix 1
ADDITIONAL GUIDED IMAGERY RESOURCES

The majority of the contributing authors have other books and recordings on guided imagery, and I encourage you to become familiar with their websites. I have listed a few below that offer a wide array of audios, as well as additional practitioners and organizations not mentioned in other parts of the book.

Guided Imagery Self-Care Audio Recordings
FREE GUIDED IMAGERY AUDIO RECORDINGS

- Leslie Davenport, MFT: www.lesliedavenport.com
  Free click-and-play or downloadable recordings for surgery preparation and recovery, stress management, and more.

- Kaiser Permanente: https://healthy.kaiserpermanente.org (Type "guided imagery podcasts" into the search button)
  Kaiser currently offers 21 guided imagery recording and podcasts developed in coordination with Health Journeys. Themes include fibromyalgia and fatigue, stopping smoking, weight loss, and many others.

- Ohio State University, Wexner Medical Center: www.wexnermedical. osu.edu/patient-care/healthcare-services/integrative-complementary-medicine/guided-imagery
Fourteen click-and-play audios with relaxation for children, sleeping deeply and others.

- University of Michigan, Comprehensive Cancer Center: www.mcancer. org/support/managing-emotions/complementary-therapies/guided-imagery/audio-library
This site currently offers 12 free audios, including A Healthy Cell Alliance for Treatment, and Daily Intention.

- CDs and Audio Programs for Sale Jerry Epstein, M.D.: www. drjerryepstein.org
A unique feature of Dr. Epstein's site is the availability of some of his imagery books in French, Spanish, Portuguese, and Hebrew, in addition to a broad audio selection.

- The Healing Mind: www.thehealingmind.org
Guided imagery audio programs are available from Martin Rossman, M.D., Jeanne Achterberg, Ph.D., Kenneth Pelletier, Ph.D., Rachel Remen, M.D., Emmett Miller, M.D., and more.

- Health Journeys: www.healthjourneys.com
Belleruth Naparstek has created an excellent collection of guided imagery audios, and also offers the work of Dean Shrock, Ph.D., and many other practitioners.

- Emmet Miller, M.D.: www.drmiller.com
Guided imagery and self-hypnosis audios are available from the eminent Dr. Miller.

- MindBody Sessions: www.mindbodysessions.com
This is a new subscription service streaming audio of hundreds of guided imagery, hypnosis, and mindfulness audios.

Professional Training and Certification in Guided Imagery and Mind-Body Programs

- Academy for Guided Imagery: www.acadgi.com
  The Academy provides professional training and Certification in Interactive Guided Imagerysm and referrals to certified practitioners.

- American Institute for Mental Imagery: www.drjerryepstein.org/american-institute-mental-imagery-aimi
  AIMI is chartered by the New York State Regents and is focused on the "phenomenology" of imagery and a holistic model of health, offering trainings and certification.

- American Society for Clinical Hypnosis: www.asch.net
  This Society has offered training and Certification in Clinical Hypnosis since 1957.

- California Institute of Integral Studies: Transformative Imagery Certification: www.ciis.edu/academics/graduate-programs/integrative p-health-studies/guided-imagery-certificate
  This three unit course is offered through the Master's Degree in Integrative Health Studies, but is open for non-credit community enrollment.

- The Center for Healing and Imagery: www.centerforhealingand imagery.com/trainings
  The Center offers certification in Somatic Imagery and Ego State Psychotherapy.

- Center for Mind-Body Medicine: www.cmbm.org
  This program offers certification in mind-body medicine, where guided imagery is included with meditation, biofeedback and creative self-expression.

- Deep Imagery: http://deepimagery.net/
  Deep Imagery/Personal Totem Pole Process (PTPP) is part of the International Institute for Visualization Research, and offers certification, seminars and conferences.

- Integrative Imagery: http://wisdomofthewhole.com/integrative-imagery
  This course is taught as a six week teleclass, and offers CE credit for nurses.

- John F. Kennedy University: Guided Imagery Certification: www.jfku.edu/Programs-and-Courses/Continuing-Extended-Education/Deep-Imagination.html
  This program is offered in weekend workshops in the San Francisco Bay Area and offers CE credits. Courses can also be taken independently, without enrolling in the Certification Series. Courses include Somatic Imagery, Resolving Complex Grief, Deepening Imagery with Expressive Arts.

- Milton Erickson Foundation: www.erickson-foundation.org
  The Foundation offers hypnosis trainings with CE credit, and conferences nationally and internationally.

Guided Imagery Associations and Communities

- Google+ Guided Imagery Community: www.google.com/+/learnmore
  The Google+ Guided Imagery Community is a newly launched and moderated social media site where all members can post and comment on guided imagery trainings, questions, articles and research. You do not need to use gmail to access, but you do need to register for a Google account.

- Imagery International: www.imageryinternational.org
  Imagery International is a professional association providing a forum for the exchange of ideas around the benefits and diverse applications of guided imagery. There are many features including podcasts, newsletter, annual conference, and a directory of trainings and practitioners.

Guided Imagery Research

- Google Scholar: www.scholar.google.com
  Google Scholar works as much like the standard Google search engine, but the search base is scholarly literature including medical journals, abstracts, academic publishers and professional societies.

- The Healing Mind: www.thehealingmind.org/research
  Dr. Rossman's site has a downloadable, 49 page PDF of relevant imagery research sorted by topics such as insomnia, hypertension, headache, etc.

- Health Journeys: blog.healthjourneys.com/hot-research/index.php
  Belleruth Naparstek's site does an excellent job of posting guided
  imagery research summaries as they hit the press. It also offers a
  search button to find topics of interest.

Appendix 2

CONTRIBUTOR LIST
AND BIOGRAPHIES

Editor and Contributor

Leslie Davenport, M.A., M.S., MFT has unique qualifications in the body–mind–spirit field. *San Francisco Chronicle*'s dance critic Allan Ulrich reviewed Leslie as a professional dancer endowed with "powers of communication that set her apart from the herd." As a psychotherapist she understands the health impact of thoughts and emotions. And a passion for the mystery of the human spirit drew her to become an ordained interfaith minister in 1984. She is a founding member of the Institute for Health and Healing at California Pacific Medical Center, and faculty at the California Institute of Integral Studies and John F. Kennedy University. Her first book, *Healing and Transformation Through Self Guided Imagery*, is a classic in the field. www.lesliedavenport.com

Contributors

Sondra Barrett, Ph.D., author of three books: *Secrets of Your Cells, Ultimate Immunity,* and *Wine's Hidden Beauty,* received her degree in biochemistry from the University of Illinois followed by postdoctoral training in immunology/hematology at the University of California Medical School (UCSF). Heading her own cancer research laboratory, while on the faculty there, she began working with children with cancer, which ultimately led her to develop programs bridging medical science, art, and healing. Her award-winning photomicroscopy has been key to enhancing her educational approach that marries science, indigenous wisdom, and expressive arts for both children and adults with life-threatening illnesses. www.SondraBarrett.com

Carolyn J. Stahl Bohler, Rel.D., Ph.D. recently retired in Dayton, OH where she was Professor of Pastoral Theology and Counseling at United Theological Seminary for two decades. The first editor of the *Journal of Pastoral Theology,* her books include *God the* What?: *What Our Metaphors for God Reveal About Our Beliefs in God* (SkyLight Paths); *God is Like a Mother Hen and Much Much More* (children's); *Opening to God: Guided Imagery Meditation on Scripture* (and Expanded, Revised edition). She was Senior Pastor of United Methodist Churches (San Diego, Tustin, Redlands) and is a mother of two and, recently, a grandmother.

Michael F. Cantwell, M.D., MPH is a board-certified pediatrician with postgraduate training including fellowships in pediatric infectious diseases and geographic medicine, a Master's in Public Health, and service with the Centers for Disease Control and Prevention (CDC) in Atlanta, GA. His holistic medicine credentials include Lead Physician at the Institute for Health and Healing Clinic in San Francisco, CA (1998–2013), current practice at Rising Phoenix Integrative Medicine Center in San Francisco, CA, and service on the first National Advisory Council for the National Center for Complementary and Alternative Medicine (NCCAM) of the NIH in Bethesda, MD (1999–2003). He is the author of the multi-award winning book, *Map of the Spirit: Diagnosis and Treatment of the Spirit.* www.mapofthespirit.com

Brian Dietrich, M.A., MFT is a licensed psychotherapist in private practice and certified guided imagery practitioner. Brian was a clinical faculty member and training supervisor for the California Pacific Medical Center's Integrative Medicine Education Program. He served as adjunct faculty for the California Institute of Integral Studies where he earned his Master's degree in counseling psychology. Brian received a second Master's degree in depth psychology from the Pacifica Graduate Institute where he is now a Ph.D. candidate. Brian is currently conducting research for his doctoral thesis which explores the intersection of Jungian and archetypal psychology and guided imagery.

Gerald Epstein, M.D. is a pioneer in the use of mental imagery to heal physical and emotional illness. He is Director of the *American Institute for Mental Imagery* and is Assistant Clinical Professor of Psychiatry at Mt. Sinai Medical Center in New York City. He has authored many books including *Healing Visualizations* and *Waking Dream Therapy*. Dr. Epstein has conducted successful research in the efficacy of mental imagery in the treatment of of asthma and heart strength. He apprenticed with Colette Aboulker-Muscat in imagination, healing, and western spirituality. Most recently, he edited the *Encyclopedia of Mental Imagery*. www. drjerryepstein.org

Judith Goleman, M.A., MFT, Rabbinic Chaplain has been a psychotherapist in private practice in Sebastopol, CA, for over 30 years. In the early years of Esalen Institute she learned to use Body Felt Imagery from John Heider, a gifted facilitator and teacher. He modeled basic elements of Body Felt Imagery, and taught how just being present with what is organically leads to healing. Judith gives workshops at her office in Sebastopol, in "Jewish Spirituality: Deep, Optimistic, Powerful, Lovely— and Often Unknown by American Jews," "Jewish Mysticism as a Basis for Psychotherapy," and "Finding Your Truest Self in the Later Time of Life."

Linda Graham, M.A., MFT is an experienced psychotherapist in full-time private practice in the San Francisco Bay Area. She integrates modern neuroscience, mindfulness practices, and relational psychology in her nationwide trainings. She is the author of *Bouncing Back: Rewiring Your Brain for Maximum Resilience and Well-Being*, winner of the 2013 Books for a Better Life award and the 2014 Better Books for a Better World award. She publishes a monthly e-newsletter, *Healing and Awakening into Aliveness and Wholeness*. www.lindagraham-mft.net

Denise Grocke Ph.D., RMT, RGIMT, FAMI founded the music therapy course at the University of Melbourne in 1978, and retired from that position in 2012. She continues to lead Guided Imagery and Music (GIM) training at the University of Melbourne, and is the Coordinator of the Consortium of Music Therapy Research Universities. She is coauthor of *Receptive Methods in Music Therapy* (2007), co-editor of *Guided Imagery and Music: The Bonny Method and Beyond* (2002), and co-editor of *Guided Imagery & Music and Music Imagery Methods for Individuals and Groups* (2015). She has numerous book chapters and articles in refereed journals on music therapy and Guided Imagery and Music.

Glenn Hartelius, Ph.D. is developing a new Ph.D. program in Integral and Transpersonal Psychology at the California Institute of Integral Studies (CIIS) in San Francisco, where he serves as Associate Professor and leads an initiative to develop a new laboratory for research in consciousness, phenomenology, and neuroscience. Glenn is main editor for the *International Journal of Transpersonal Studies*, a peer-reviewed academic journal. He is co-editor of *The Wiley-Blackwell Handbook of Transpersonal Psychology*, Secretary of the International Transpersonal Association, and a Director of ITA Professional. He has taught at the Institute of Transpersonal Psychology, Naropa University, Saybrook University, and Middlesex University in the UK. www.attentiondynamics. com

Judith A. Lyons, Ph.D. studied in Montreal, Quebec (McGill and Concordia universities) and interned in Jackson, MS. She served as the founding clinical director of the National Center for PTSD at the Boston VA Medical Center, then returned to Mississippi to establish the Trauma Recovery Program at the VA Medical Center in Jackson. She is an associate professor of Psychiatry and Human Behavior at the University of Mississippi Medical Center. Post-trauma resilience, moral conflict, and impact of trauma on relationships are major clinical and research interests. Enjoying nature, fostering shelter dogs, Rotary Club and faith-based activities balance her trauma interests.

Emmett Miller, M.D. is best known for his seminal work in the field of holistic mind–body medicine in the 1970s, introducing the medical and psychological professions to guided imagery by publishing the first guided imagery tapes. He earned his M.D. from The Albert Einstein College of Medicine and has served as lecturer and preceptor at Stanford, University of California, UC Davis Medical School, and other universities. In 1977, he cofounded and served as Medical Director of the Cancer Support and

Education Center in Menlo Park, the first such cancer group and training center in the world. His CDs continue to be the gold standard worldwide. www.drmiller.com

Alan Morinis, D.Phil. is Dean of The Mussar Institute, which he founded in 2004. Raised in a culturally Jewish but non-observant home, he earned his doctorate in anthropology at Oxford University on a Rhodes Scholarship. Alan has written books and produced films and taught at several universities. He is a leading interpreter of Mussar teachings about which he regularly gives lectures and workshops. His journey to discover Mussar is recorded in his book *Climbing Jacob's Ladder* (2002). His guide to Mussar practice, *Everyday Holiness*, was published in 2007. His book on Judaism as a practice of personal transformation is *With Heart in Mind* (2014). www.mussarinstitute.org

Aftab Omer, Ph.D. is a sociologist, psychologist, futurist and President of Meridian University, California. Raised in Pakistan, India, Hawaii, and Turkey, he was educated at the universities of MIT, Harvard and Brandeis. His publications have addressed the topics of transformative learning, cultural leadership, generative entrepreneurship, collective wisdom, and the power of imagination. His work includes assisting organizations in tapping the creative potentials of conflict, diversity, and complexity. He is a Fellow of the International Futures Forum and the World Academy of Arts and Sciences.

David Pincus, Ph.D. is Associate Professor of Psychology at Chapman University in Orange, CA, and also maintains private practice. He has published over 20 peer-reviewed journal articles and book chapters focused on understanding psychotherapy and human resilience using systems science. In addition, Dr. Pincus has authored a book (with A. Sheikh): *Imagery for Pain Relief: A Scientifically Grounded Guidebook for Clinicians*, and has served as a co-editor of the text: *Chaos and Complexity in Psychology: The Theory of Nonlinear Dynamical Systems*.

Phillip Post, Ph.D., CC-AASP is an associate professor in the Department of Kinesiology and Dance at New Mexico State University (NMSU). He teaches courses in sport/exercise psychology, motor learning, and motor development. His research interests include examining the essential mental skills and motor components associated with effective sport performance and motor learning. He has produced ten research publications examining the effects of imagery and self-regulation on motor learning and sport performance and has delivered over 20 research presentations at national and international conferences. Phillip has over 600 hundred hours of applied sport psychology experience and currently provides mental skills training to NMSU student athletes.

Laury Rappaport, Ph.D., MFT, ATR-BC, REAT is a pioneer in the expressive arts field and a certifying Focusing coordinator with The Focusing Institute. She has been on the faculties of Lesley University, Sonoma State University, Notre Dame de Namur University, and trains others internationally. She is the author of *Focusing-Oriented Art Therapy: Accessing the Body's Wisdom and Creative Intelligence* and editor/author of *Mindfulness and the Arts Therapies: Theory and Practice*. Laury is also the Founder and Director of the Focusing and Expressive Arts Institute, and is an Integrative Psychotherapist at the Institute for Health & Healing, Sutter Health in California. www.focusingarts.com

Rachel Naomi Remen, M.D., Founder and Director of the Institute for the Study of Health and Illness at Commonweal and Clinical Professor at UCSF Medical School, sees medicine as a spiritual path. A master therapist and educator, her work has enabled many thousand physicians to practice medicine from the heart and patients to remember their power to heal. Her Healer's Art curriculum is taught in 82 American medical schools and seven schools abroad, and her best-selling books, *Kitchen Table Wisdom* and *My Grandfather's Blessings*, are translated into 23 languages. Dr. Remen has had Crohn's disease for over 60 years. www. rachelremen.com

Charlotte Reznick, Ph.D. is a child educational psychologist, former UCLA Associate Clinical Professor of Psychology, and author of the *Los Angeles Times* best-selling book, *The Power of Your Child's Imagination: How to Transform Stress and Anxiety into Joy and Success* (Penguin Group). She is the creator of *Imagery For Kids: Breakthrough for Learning, Creativity, and Empowerment*, a mindful, positive coping skills program. In addition to her private practice in Los Angeles, CA, she creates therapeutic guided imagery/meditation CDs for children, teens, and parents, and teaches workshops internationally on the healing power of children's imagination. www.ImageryForKids.com

Bruce Roberts, M.D. is an Integrative Medicine physician in San Francisco, CA. He is the cofounder and Medical Director of LightHearted Medicine. He received his medical degree from Michigan State University College of Human Medicine and board-certification in family practice and psychiatry though the University of Arizona. Dr. Roberts is certified in Integrative Medicine through the American Board of Integrative Health and Medicine with additional certification through the Center for Mind Body Medicine. He is a certified shamanic breathwork facilitator and a non-denominational minister through the Venus Rising Institute for Shamanic Healing Arts. Dr. Roberts specializes in the treatment of the whole person—mind, body, and spirit. www.lightheartedmedicine.com

Martin L. Rossman, M.D., Dipl. Ac. (NCCAOM) is an integrative physician practicing in Greenbrae, CA. A graduate of the University of Michigan Medical School, he has had a long-standing interest in the practical importance of lifestyle, nutrition, and mind–body practices in medicine and health. Author of *The Worry Solution, Fighting Cancer from Within, Guided Imagery for Self-Healing* and numerous medical textbook chapters on imagery and mind–body medicine, Dr. Rossman has also recorded dozens of guided imagery audios to support self-healing. He is a clinical faculty member at the UCSF Medical School, an accomplished public speaker, and a consultant to numerous university-based integrative health centers and healthcare organizations. www.thehealingmind.org

Michael Samuels, M.D. is a physician who has used creativity, art, and guided imagery with patients with life crises for over 30 years in private practice and consultation. He is Founder and Director of Art as a Healing Force, a project devoted to healing yourself, others, the community and the earth and making art and healing one. He teaches Art and Healing at San Francisco State University, Institute of Holistic Studies. He is a bear dancer with the Chumash people. He is the author of 23 books including the bestselling *Well Body Book*, and the guided imagery classic *Seeing With the Mind's Eye*. Other books include *Creative Healing, Spirit Body Healing, The Path of the Feather, Shaman Wisdom- Shaman Healing*. www.michaelsamuels.com

Ruth L. Schwartz, Ph.D. is the author of *Soul on Earth: A Guide to Living & Loving Your Human Life,* a comprehensive resource guide to transformation and healing. She has also published five books of poems, including the National Poetry Series winner *Edgewater* (HarperCollins 2001) a memoir, *Death in Reverse.* A shamanic healer in private practice since 2003, Ruth is the creator of The Writer As Shaman, workshops and mentorship which combine powerful shamanic and creative practices to help people heal more deeply, write more deeply, or both. She teaches and mentors clients nationally and internationally. www.Evolutionary Support.com

Anees A. Sheikh, Ph.D. is a former chair of the Psychology Department at Marquette University and Clinical Professor of Psychiatry and Behavioral Medicine at the Medical College of Wisconsin. Now he is Professor Emeritus at Marquette University. He was the founding editor of the *Journal of Mental Imagery* and served as the President of the American Association for the Study of Mental Imagery. Dr. Sheikh has published numerous scholarly articles and 17 books on imagery and related topics. He currently edits the *Imagery and Human Development Series.*

Dean Shrock, Ph.D. is a psychologist and former Director of Mind-Body Medicine for a physician management group of cancer treatment centers. He is the author of *Doctor's Orders: Go Fishing, Why Love Heals,* and *Living and Thriving: A Mind-Body-Spirit Program for Wellness.* His doctoral dissertation is titled, *Relaxation, Guided Imagery, and Wellness.* For his postdoctoral internship he developed a research proposal for The Cleveland Clinic to test the effectiveness of guided imagery with breast cancer. He also co-authored the chapter on mind-body medicine in the 2014 textbook, *Integrative Oncology.* www.deanshrock.com

Llewellyn Vaughan-Lee Ph.D. is a Sufi teacher and author. Born in London in 1953, he has followed the Naqshbandi Sufi path since he was 19. In 1991 he moved to Northern California and founded The Golden Sufi Center (www.goldensufi.org). In recent years the focus of his writing and teaching has been on spiritual responsibility in our present time of global crisis, and an awakening global consciousness of oneness (www.workingwithoneness.org). More recently he has written about the feminine, and the emerging subject of spiritual ecology (www. spiritualecology.org). He has been interviewed by Oprah Winfrey on Super Soul Sunday, and featured on the Global Spirit Series shown on PBS.

Master Zhongxian Wu, a lifelong Daoist practitioner, is the lineage holder of four different schools of Qigong and martial arts. Since 1988, Master Wu has instructed thousands of students, both Eastern and Western, in his unique and professionally designed courses and training programs. He has authored 12 books (five in Chinese) on Chinese wisdom traditions. He and his wife, Dr. Karin Taylor Wu, founded Blue Willow World Healing Center and QinJian Akademin to preserve and promote the classical Chinese arts throughout Europe, North America and China. www.masterwu.net

Subject Index

AUTHOR INDEX